THE GOODNICK FAMILY EDITION

TORAH TAVLIN YAMIM NORAIM

Stories and Sayings, Wit and Wisdom from Our Torah Leaders

Rabbi Dovid Hoffman

THE GOODNICK FAMILY EDITION

YAMIM NORAIM

Stories and Sayings, Wit and Wisdom from Our Torah Leaders

Rabbi Dovid Hoffman

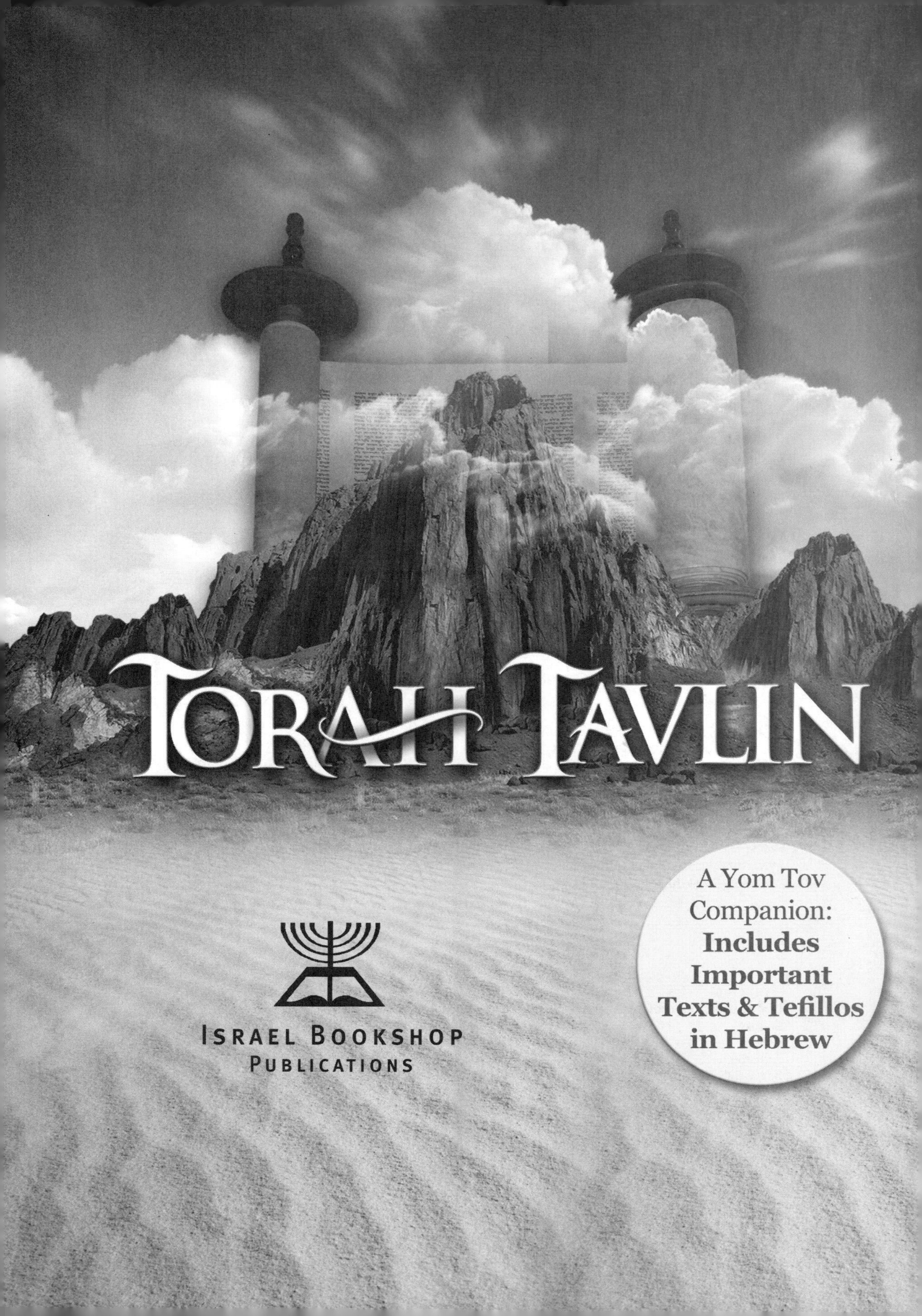
TORAH TAVLIN
A Yom Tov Companion:
Includes Important Texts & Tefillos in Hebrew
ISRAEL BOOKSHOP PUBLICATIONS

A Project of

HASEFER

The Jewish Literary Foundation

ISBN 978-1-60091-223-8

Book & Cover design by:

vividesign

SRULY PERL • 845.694.7186
mechelp@gmail.com

Distributed by:

Israel Bookshop Publications
501 Prospect Street
Lakewood, NJ 08701

Tel: (732) 901-3009
Fax: (732) 901-4012
www.israelbookshoppublications.com
info@israelbookshoppublications.com

The Torah Tavlin weekly newsletter is available free of charge. To receive copies by mail for your shul, or to have it emailed to you directly, please contact us at:
torahtavlin@yahoo.com

Printed in USA

Distributed in Israel by:
Shanky's
Petach Tikva 16
Jerusalem
972-2-538-6936

Distributed in Europe by:
Lehmanns
Unit E Viking Industrial Park
Rolling Mill Road,
Jarrow , Tyne & Wear NE32 3DP
44-191-430-0333

Distributed in Australia by:
Gold's Book and Gift Company
3- 13 William Street
Balaclava 3183
613-9527-8775

Distributed in South Africa by:
Kollel Bookshop
Ivy Common
107 William Road, Norwood
Johannesburg 2192
27-11-728-1822

As this sefer was going to print, the Jewish world was saddened to learn of the petirah of

Maran Hagaon Rav Yosef Shalom Elyashiv

Zecher Tzaddik VKadosh Lvracha.

As we all mourn the loss of the preeminent Gadol and Posek Hador, may this sefer be an aliya for his neshoma and may he serve as a meilitz yosher on behalf of all of Klal Yisroel.

מרן הגאון

הרב **יוסף שלום** בן הרב **אברהם אלישיב** זצוק״ל

נתבקש לישיבה של מעלה בכ״ח תמוז תשע״ב

זכותו יגן עלינו ועל כל ישראל אמן.

תהא נשמתו צרורה בצרור החיים

מצוה גדולה להיות בשמחה תמיד

This *sefer* is dedicated in memory of my parents:

Benjamin and Regina Goodnick *a"h*

ר׳ דוב ב״ר זכריה צבי ע״ה
רבקה פערל בת מרדכי ע״ה

A couple who found *simchah* daily, uniting in prayer and serving Hashem with their every breath.

How does Hashem remember them?

As a couple who...reveled in singing His praises every Shabbat, particularly *Yom Zeh Mechubad*, which reverberated throughout their house.

As a couple who...elevated the most mundane meal with words of Torah learning, of *Ein Yaakov*, and recalling the wondrous events of the past.

As a couple who...always walked together to shul, united in their love for Hashem.

As a couple who...loved their fellow Jew and Eretz Yisrael, who were dedicated to the Association of Orthodox Jewish Scientists, the Sisterhood, their synagogues, and their rabbi, Rabbi Abraham A. Levene of Lower Merion Synagogue, grandson of the *tzaddik* of Jerusalem, Rabbi Aryeh Levin *zt"l*.

As a couple who...gave to Hashem and His people בכל לבבך ובכל נפשך ובכל מאדך—with all their heart, their souls, their might.

As a couple who...gave *tzedakah* to all those in need, without hesitation—not only of their funds, but most of all, of their souls.

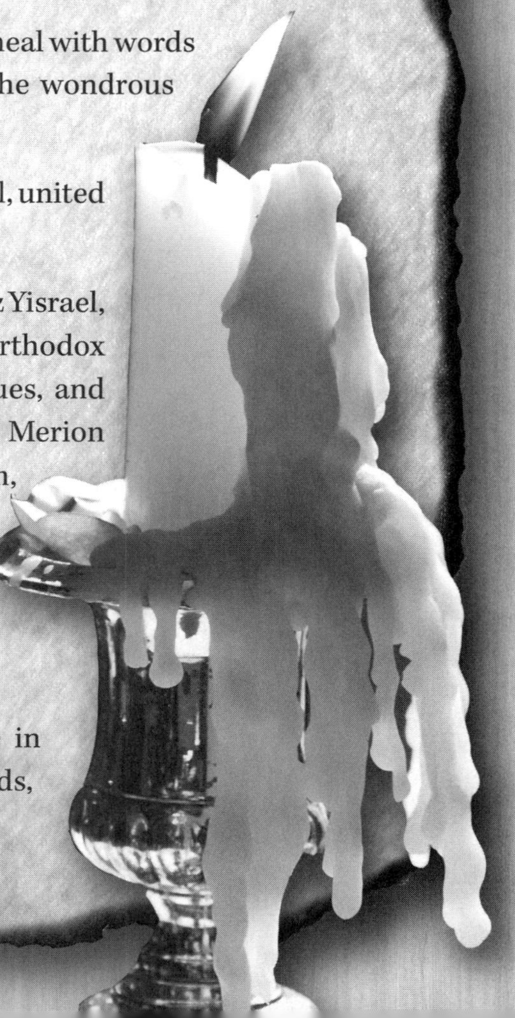

My dear mother *a"h* merited passing away on Erev Yom Kippur (5771) and my father on Erev Pesach (7 Nissan, 5771). They left an example of love, warmth, and closeness to Hashem for their children and for the world.

עִבְדוּ אֶת ה' בְּשִׂמְחָה בֹּאוּ לְפָנָיו בִּרְנָנָה.

Serve Hashem with joy, come before Him with jubilation.

This book is also dedicated in the *zechus* of my sister, Joan Westenholz and her family; my daughters, Sarah Devora and Chana Rochel; and my granddaughter, Zissel Leah. May they all merit health and happiness with Hashem's blessings, and to see Mashiach *bimheirah b'yameinu*, amen.

Pesach Yoel (Paul) Goodnick

פרי צדיק עץ חיים (משלי י:יא)

אמרו צדיק כי טוב כי פרי מעלליהם יאכלו (ישעי' ג:1)

The Malbim (*Bereishis* 12:3) utilizes the aforementioned *pesukim* to reinforce the principle that the descendants of goodness are, themselves, the greatest proof to the goodness of their progenitors. The truth and purity of emotion exhibited in Dr. Paul Goodnick's moving dedication of a work of Torah to the memory of his beloved parents, Dr. Ben and Regina Goodnick *a"h*, is in and of itself, the most moving tribute possible.

Dr. Benjamin and Regina Goodnick were two "good" people who walked together for many years with grace, dignity, and most of all, *yiras Shamayim*. They both departed from this world *b'seivah tovah* within the same year. The knowledge that they share eternity together serves as a great source of comfort to their loved ones.

The *maasim tovim* and exemplary Torah-true lives of Benjamin and Regina Goodnick, along with יב"ל their exceptional children and grandchildren, remain a bright and shining legacy of inspiration to myself and to all who knew them.

ת.נ.צ.ב.ה.

Rabbi Abraham A. Levene

Table of Contents

סוכות

שמיני עצרת/ שמחת תורה

440-943-5300
440-585-2350

הישיבה הגדולה והקדושה דטעלז . קליוולאַנד אָהייא

TELSHE YESHIVA
RABBINICAL COLLEGE OF TELSHE, INC.
28400 EUCLID AVENUE . WICKLIFFE, OHIO 44092

הרב חיים שטיין
ראש הישיבה
RABBI CHAIM STEIN
ROSH HAYESHIVA

לס' הנה [illegible] לקחתי תשס"ח

הנני ובאתי הרב דוד הופמן שליט"א בן ידידי הרב
פנחס שליט"א תלמיד ותיק של הישיבה והכולל כדי ויתמה
ה' חבורי דעניני [illegible] זצ"ל. התורה תבלין שמוציאו
לאור מידה שהוא דבקות שמאוסף בעניין יקרים דהלכה
ומעשה מגדולי תורה לדורות ומוסר מישראל
כי יחד הולמה נפשו להודיע לאור חדש שלו על פרשת
הקדוש דשם תורה תבלין
חפצי דבר יצליח זה מאליך דרכי דקדק שיהא עם עסקו
דעניני העולם עסוק בלימוד התורה. דהלכה ואגדה דבוחן עם [illegible]
ורצון להגדיל תורה ולהאדירה והיטיב רבים [illegible]
מיקרני דברכה דבודאות והוקרה
לכבוד התורה ולומדיה

חיים שטיין

440-943-5300
440-585-2350

הישיבה הגדולה והקדושה דטעלז . קליוולאַנד אָהייא
TELSHE YESHIVA
RABBINICAL COLLEGE OF TELSHE, INC.
28400 EUCLID AVENUE . WICKLIFFE, OHIO 44092

הרב חיים שטיין
ראש הישיבה
RABBI CHAIM STEIN
ROSH HAYESHIVA

The Sedrah of: "Behold, I have taken a blessing." - 5768

Behold, our good friend, **Horav Dovid Hoffman Shlit"a,** the son of our good friend, Horav Pinchos Hoffman Shlit"a, a longtime student of the Yeshiva and the Kollel, is already recognized through his writings on Aggadah topics, and through Torah Tavlin, published weekly, which incorporates valuable pearls of Halachah and Aggadah, from our *Gedolim* in Torah and *Yirah*, and he adds from his own.

Now, his soul yearns to publish a complete book on the weekly parshah by the name **Torah Tavlin.**

Hashem should make him successful in his endeavors to continue in his sacred work, and together with his worldly ventures, he should continue to occupy himself in Torah learning, in Halachah, Aggadah with his friends and acquaintances, to magnify the Torah and glorify it, and bring pleasure to the multitudes with his light.

With blessings of success, with friendship and esteem,
For the honor of the Torah and those who learn it,
(Rabbi) Chaim Stein

YESHIVAS MIR YERUSHALAYIM

בס"ד נוסדה במיר בשנת תקע"ז. בירושלים בשנת תש"ד
ע"ר 580037638
Founded in Mir 1817. In Jerusalem 1944

הרב נ.צ. פינקל
ראש הישיבה

RABBI N.Z. FINKEL
DEAN

י"ד אדר הראשון תשע"א

בואו ונחזיק טיבותא לאיש מהיר במלאכתו, מלאכת שמים, ה"ה האברך המצוין והנעלה הרב דוד יואל הופמן שליט"א אשר בעט סופר שבו ניחן השכיל להעלות עלי ספר פנינים יקרים מלאי תוכן בהשקפת התורה ובמידות מתוקנות מסודרים לפי פרשיות התורה וקרא שם הספר תורה תבלין. זכה הרב המחבר שליט"א ונתקבלו דבריו בתוך ציבור בני התורה ולואי שיזכה עוד ועוד שיתגלגל זכות על ידו ויתחזקו שלומי אמוני ישראל בתורה ובאמונה וכל מעלות ומדות טובות שמנו חכמים וברכותי שלוחות לו שיזכה לשבת על התורה ועל העבודה עד שנזכה לשמע קול מבשר טוב לעמו ישראל בביאת גוא"צ בב"א.

כ"ד במברך בכבוד ויקר,

נתן צבי פינקל

הרב נתן צבי פינקל
ראש הישיבה

רח. בית ישראל 3 ת.ד. 5022 ירושלים 91050 טל. 02-5410999 פקס. 02-5323446 ע"ר 580037638 ● 3 Beth Israel St. P.O.B. 5022 Jerusalem 91050 Tel. 02-5410999 Fax. 02-5323446

Yeshivas Mir Jerusalem

Founded in Mir 1817. In Jerusalem 1944
Rabbi N.Z. Finkel, DEAN

14 Adar 5771

Let us give credit to a man who is expedient in his work—the work of Heaven—the exceptional and exalted young man, Rav Dovid Yoel Hoffman *shlit"a*, who with a scribe's pen was wise to offer a book with pages of valuable insights, full of content with the viewpoint of the Torah and the instituted *middos*, organized according to the *parshiyos* of the Torah, called *Torah Tavlin*. The author was worthy and his words were accepted by the Torah public; he should continue more and more, so that merits should come about from his hand and the faith and well-being of Israel should be strengthened, with all the advantages and attributes that our sages counted. My blessings are that he may sit in the area of Torah and *avodah*, until we will all merit to hear the good tidings for all of the Jewish nation, with the coming of the righteous redeemer, speedily and in our days.

I bless him with honor and splendor,
Nosson Tzvi Finkel
Rosh Hayeshivah

יעקב מאיר שכטער
ר"מ ישיבת המקובלים "שער השמים"
נשיא מוסדות "קרן אור"
בעיה"ק ירושלים תובב"א
רח' שמעון רוקח 21 י-ם טל. 02-6264619

YAAKOV MEIR SHECHTER
Rav Yeshivas Hamekubolim
"Shaar Hashomayim"
President "**Keren Or**" Institutions
JERUSALEM
21 Shimon Rokach St. Tel. 972-2-6264619

בעזהי"ת סיון תשע"ב

תודה וברכה למע"כ הרה"ג ר' דוד יואל הופמן שליט"א מפיץ תורה בעיר גדולה לאלקים מאנסי יע"א, עבור ששיגר לי את ספרו (ב' חלקים) אשר בשמו יקבנו "ליקוטי תורה תבלין" שזכה זה עתה להוציא לאור עולם, דברי תורה ולקחי מוסר, לקט נפלא מתורת רבותינו אבות הדורות לכל שבטי ישראל, על פרשיות התורה ומועדי השנה.

אמנם אין עתותי בידי לעיין בספר רב כמות ורב איכות הלזה, וכמו כן גדרתי עצמי ב"נ מלתת הסכמות לספרים, עם כל זה לא אמנע עצמי מלברכו שישגא ה' חילו ויזכה להפיץ תורתו מתוך נחת והרחבה, רב ברכות ושובע שמחות וכט"ס. וזכאה חולקיה שזוכה להפיץ דברי תורה, תבלינים ערבים ומתוקים מנופת צופים, סלסלה ותרוממך.

והברכה אחת היא לאביו הדגול, אציל הנפש, בר לבב ורב תבונות, אשרי משכיל אל דל, ידיד נפשי היקר ואיש חסדי, מגדולי תמכי אורייתא כש"ת רבי פנחס הופמן שליט"א. והנני משתתף עמו בשמחת התורה לרגל הוצאת הספר היקר של בנו שליט"א. אברכהו שיזכה להרבות חיילים לתורה וחסד עוד רבות בשנים מתוך בריות גופא ונהורא מעליא, בכל אשר יפנה יצליח, וירוה רוב נחת ועונג דקדושה אמיתי מכל יו"ח שיחיו, אריכות ימים ושנים טובות עדי יזכה יחד עם ב"ב לשמחת עולם על ראשם בישועה כללית ופרטית במהרה בקרוב.

הכ"ד ידידו מוקירו דורש שלומו וטובתו כל הימים

יעקב מאיר שכטער

יעקב מאיר שכטער
ר"מ ישיבת שער השמים
נשיא מוסדות קרן אור
בעיה"ק ירושלים תובב"א

Yaakov Meir Shechter
Rav Yeshivas Hamekubalim
"Shaar Hashamayim"
President "Keren Or" Institutions
JERUSALEM
21 Shimon Rokach St. Tel. 972-2-6264619

B'ezras Hashem, Sivan 5772

Thanks and blessings to Rav Dovid Yoel Hoffman *shlit"a*—who spreads Torah from the great city of Torah, Monsey, NY—who has sent me his books (two volumes) known as *Likutei Torah Tavlin* that have recently been published and released to the public, words of Torah and ethics, a wonderful collection from the teachings of our masters, fathers of the generations for all the tribes of Klal Yisrael, on the weekly *parshiyos* and the Yamim Tovim.

Although I do not have enough time to deeply peruse the great volume and quality of the *sefer*, and I have already distanced myself from writing approbations for other books, nevertheless, I cannot withhold from blessing him that Hashem should infuse him with strength, and he should merit to spread Torah with ease and a broadened mind, bountiful blessings satiated with joyous occasions and all good things forever. His portion should be meritorious to enable him to spread uplifting words of Torah, pleasant spices sweetened with the dripping from honeycombs.

And a singular blessing to his outstanding father, one of noble spirit, full of heart and much understanding—"praised is the wise one to the indigent"—my dearest friend and kind individual, from the greatest supporters of Torah today, Reb Pinchos Hoffman *shlit"a*. I hereby join with him in the joy of the Torah on the occasion of the publication of his dear son's book. I bless him that he add many soldiers to the Torah and to kindness for many years, with good health and a Divine light. May all that he turns to be successful, and may he gain much pride and pleasure from the true holiness from all of his descendants *sheyichyu*, with length of days and good years, until he and his wife will merit an everlasting happiness, with a general and personal salvation, speedily and soon.

Signed and sealed by his friend who seeks his peace and well-being all his days,
Yaakov Meir Shechter
RA"M Yeshivas Shaar Hashamayim

ב"ה

ישראל הלוי בעלסקי

941 - 0112

Rabbi Y. Belsky
506 EAST 7th STREET
BROOKLYN, NEW YORK 11218

ידידי הר"ר ישראל בלנדר נ"י הראה לי טופס מהספר
"תורה תבלין" שהוא פרי מחשבתו של חתנו היקר
מוה"ר דוד יצחק הופמן נ"י, ליקוט יפה וענינים על פרשיות
התורה מסודר מדפים שבועיים שמוציאו ומפזר זה כמה
שנה לבתים שולחנות שבת בדברי תורה מתוקים מדבש
ונופת צופים. חיבור זה מושך את הלב במאמריו הקצרים
וקילורית הוא לעינים ומשמח אלקים ואנשים ומושך את
הלב להשתעשע במאמרים הכוללים דברי מוסר ורעיונות
חשובים ויסודיים. אמרתי עליו טוב להדפיסו ולהפיצו
בין אוהבי התורה וישמח לב מבקשי ה'. ויה"ר שיזכה
שיוציא חיבורים אחרים כמותו ויפוצו הרבה מעיינותיו.
יום רביעי לחדש סיון שנת תשס"ט לפ"ק
ישראל הלוי בעלסקי

Rabbi Y. Belsky
506 EAST 7th STREET
BROOKLYN, NEW YORK 11218

My dear friend, Rav Yisroel Blonder showed me a copy of the sefer "Torah Tavlin" which is the splendid work of his son-in-law, Harav Dovid Yoel Hoffman. It is a fine collection on the sedros of the Torah, organized from the weekly publication that he gives out that adorns many Shabbos tables, for many years, with Divrei Torah as sweet as honey and dripping honeycombs. This publication settles on one's heart with sharp words and a presence for the eyes; it gladdens thousands of people, pulls on their heartstrings and entertains them with excerpts that include words of ethics, and important and fundamental novellae. I say about him, it is good to print them and distribute them amongst those who love the holy Torah, and "the happy heart who beseeches Hashem." May it be His will, that he merit to give out other publications like this and may he be successful in all that he does.

Fifth day of the month of Sivan, 5770
Yisroel Halevi Belsky

הרב זונדל קרויזר
רחוב פרי חדש 70 בעיה"ק ירושלים
מח"ס **אור החמה** עה"ת, ש"ס, שו"ע,
אבות, הגדה של פסח, פי' הסידור, ועוד
וספר **תפארת יעקב** על הלכות עירובין

הנה לזכות הרבה הגאון ה"ה
הרה"ג ר' דוד יואל הופמן שליט"א
מתמיד ומפיץ גם דנן ילדים נ"י
דברי תורה ברבים
ולזכותם בלמוד תורה ע"י קרובים
ורחוקים ויה"ר שיתקיים בו יפוצו
מעינותיך חוצה

כב סיון תשע"ג
זונדל קרויזר

Rabbi Baruch M. Ezrachi
Rosh Yeshivah

ישיבת עטרת ישראל
ATERETH ISRAEL RABBINICAL COLLEGE

הרב ברוך מרדכי אזרחי
ראש הישיבה

בס"ד ר"ח סיון התשע"[illegible]

בשמחה וגיל אשיש לקראת ביכורי המחבר [illegible]. ברוך המעשים
ובחוץ [illegible] [illegible] בהפצת תורה במקומות [illegible]. הלא הוא הרה"ג
רבי דוד הי"ו נ"י [illegible]. בן [illegible] [illegible] [illegible] תורה [illegible] [illegible]
רבי פנחס שליט"א.

"כי ידעתיו" [illegible] [illegible], [illegible] [illegible] [illegible] [illegible] [illegible]
[illegible] [illegible] [illegible] [illegible]. [illegible] [illegible] [illegible] [illegible], [illegible] [illegible] [illegible]
[illegible] [illegible] [illegible] עטרת ישראל [illegible].

[illegible] [illegible] [illegible] [illegible] [illegible] [illegible] [illegible] [illegible] [illegible]
[illegible] [illegible] [illegible] [illegible] היא התורה [illegible] [illegible]. [illegible]
[illegible] הרה"ג רבי דוד הי"ו. [illegible] [illegible] [illegible] [illegible] [illegible]
[illegible] [illegible] [illegible] [illegible] [illegible] [illegible] [illegible] [illegible] [illegible]
[illegible] [illegible] [illegible] [illegible] [illegible] [illegible] [illegible] [illegible] [illegible].

[illegible] [illegible] [illegible] [illegible] [illegible] [illegible]
[illegible]. [illegible] [illegible] [illegible] [illegible] [illegible] [illegible] [illegible] [illegible]
[illegible] [illegible] [illegible] [illegible] [illegible] [illegible] [illegible] [illegible]
[illegible] [illegible] [illegible] [illegible] [illegible] [illegible] [illegible] [illegible] [illegible]
[illegible] [illegible] [illegible] [illegible] [illegible] [illegible] [illegible] [illegible] [illegible].
[illegible] [illegible] [illegible] [illegible] [illegible] [illegible] [illegible] בני ישראל.
[illegible] [illegible] [illegible] [illegible] [illegible] [illegible] [illegible] [illegible]
[illegible]. [illegible] [illegible] [illegible]. [illegible] [illegible] [illegible] [illegible] [illegible] [illegible]
[illegible]. רב [illegible] בן רב [illegible] [illegible] [illegible].

[illegible] [illegible] [illegible] [illegible] [illegible]
התורה והיראה. [illegible] [illegible] [illegible] [illegible] [illegible] [illegible]
[illegible] [illegible] הקב"ה [illegible] [illegible] [illegible] [illegible] [illegible] [illegible] [illegible]
[illegible] [illegible] [illegible] [illegible] [illegible] [illegible] [illegible] [illegible] [illegible] [illegible]
[illegible] [illegible] [illegible] [illegible] [illegible] [illegible] [illegible] [illegible] [illegible]
[illegible] [illegible] [illegible] [illegible] [illegible] [illegible] [illegible]

[illegible] [illegible]

22 Kassuto Jerusalem 96433, Tel. 02-6421337 .טל P.O.B. 16246 .רח' קסוטו 22, ירושלים 96433, ת.ד

Rabbi I. Scheiner
Dean of Kamenitzer Yeshiva
51 Zephania St., Jerusalem
Tel. (02) 532-2512

הרב יצחק שיינר
ראש ישיבת קמניץ
רחוב צפניה 51, ירושלים
טלפון 532-2512

בס"ד ב' תמוז תש"ע

Dear R' David שי',

When Heshie נ"י told me you are preparing an additional volume for publication, I felt obliged to write you a few words. I am greatly indebted to you. Your books have afforded me many moments of intense pleasure. Many times at the Shabbos table, I have told one of your heart-warming, soul-searching, poignant stories. Every single one of them is a gem – to be remembered and treasured. I eagerly anticipate seeing your next book. May you and your dear wife תח' have much nachas from your dear children, and both sets of parents שי' much nachas from every one of their offspring.

With sincere best wishes,

יצחק שיינר

Acknowledgments

In the solemn prayer known as *Hineni he'ani mi'maas*, the *chazzan* begins the *Mussaf tefillah* on Rosh Hashanah and Yom Kippur by beseeching the Al-mighty to accept him as the selected representative of the congregation and permit his tearful prayers to penetrate the Heavens in order to deliver kindness and good judgment on behalf of the people. In a voice full of trepidation he intones, "Grant me success upon the path which I tread, to stand and beg for mercy on myself and upon those who have sent me." It is this sincere plea which propels the entire day's *tefillos* into an other-worldly experience, and few can disregard the feelings of awe and inspiration as they are recited.

As I complete this next volume of *Torah Tavlin* on the holy days of Rosh Hashanah, Yom Kippur, Sukkos and Shemini Atzeres, I, too, offer up a sincere prayer that Hashem should "grant me success" and allow this path—the path of *harbatzas Torah* through the promulgation of the *Torah Tavlin sefarim* and weekly *parshah* sheets—to be the one that guides my life, as well as a beacon into the future for my family. However, as in all cases, I mustn't forget "those who have sent me," the wonderful people to whom I owe a debt of gratitude.

Over the past year, I felt the tragedy of loss with the *petirah* of my *roshei yeshivah*, **Harav Chaim Stein *zt"l*** and **Harav Aizik Ausband *zt"l***, two of my mentors in Telshe Yeshivah. I feel privileged to include words of Torah and *mussar* from both of them, and may it be a *zechus* for their *neshamos* to have their Torah printed in this volume.

Baruch Hashem, I feel blessed to maintain a Torah relationship with various *gedolim* and *rabbanim*, whom I wish to thank. First and foremost, **Harav Baruch Hirschfeld *shlit"a***, *rav* and *rosh kollel* of Kollel Ateres Baruch, Torah Life Institute, in Cleveland Heights, Ohio, who continues to write a weekly halachah article in the *Torah Tavlin* sheets, as well as the many halachah pieces that are sprinkled all throughout this book. His Halachic Overview on *Teshuvah* at the beginning of this book is a culmination of a series that he wrote for *Torah Tavlin* and is the perfect way for each and every one of us to embark on our own personal *teshuvah* journey. **Harav Gamliel Hakohen Rabinowitz *shlit"a***, a *rav* to whom I turn for inspiration and guidance, never lets me down; his *Tiv HaTavlin* column in the weekly *Torah Tavlin* sheets is supremely popular and adds a great deal of *chashivus* to the sheets. I owe

a specific debt of gratitude to **Harav Shmuel Kamenetsky *shlit"a***, *rosh yeshivah* of Philadelphia Yeshivah, through whom I was *zocheh* to a special dose of *hashgachah pratis*. **Rav Simcha Bunim Berger *shlit"a***, *rosh yeshivah* of Yeshivah Gedolah of Bridgeport, Connecticut, and my daily *chavrusa*, certainly keeps me on my toes, while at the same time sends my head spinning into the clouds with his deep and esoteric explanations. I asked—and he responded to my call, and so, as a result, we are all blessed with the exquisite Foreword on the purpose of *teshuvah* in the Aseres Yemei Teshuvah that he wrote to lend an air of respect and "Maharalism" to this *sefer*. **Rav Sholom Perl *shlit"a***, the *maggid* of Beit Shemesh, reliably writes his *chiddushei Torah* each week for the *Torah Tavlin*, as well as the wonderful *dvar Torah* he wrote in the back of this *sefer*. May Hashem bless you all with continued *his'chazkus* in Torah—*lilmod u'lilamed*—to be *mashpia* on the world of Torah as you've always done.

My parents, Rav Pinchos and Helen Hoffman, have always taken pride in my accomplishments and I am thrilled to be able to return a little bit of *nachas* to them with the publication of this *sefer* and the weekly sheets. They have always taught me to follow the path of Torah and *yashrus*, and my hope is to be able to emulate their fine examples as well as pass it along to my children. My in-laws, R' Yisroel and Leah Blonder, have likewise taken pride in the *Torah Tavlin* books and sheets, and I thank them for their constant support, their *dikduk* corrections and the great quotations (sometimes even my *shver* is the "Wise Man"!).

My sister and brother-in-law, the "*Dargah Yeseirah* Duo" continue to shine and inspire; and I, as well as the thousands of individuals who are elevated by the *Dargah Yeseirah* lessons and values on a weekly basis, thank you for your valuable efforts. My sister, brother, sisters-in-law, brothers-in-law, in-laws of brother and brothers-in-law, sister of sisters-in-law, mother of brother-in-law, brothers of sisters-in-law...whew! It's all a bit confusing, but suffice it to say...thanks to all of you for all of your support! Honorable mention to my nephew and niece, Yankel and Nechama Taub, for going the extra mile to get what I need for the *sefer*. And a special shout-out to UDK just... because!

My dear wife Estee deserves all the credit and believe me, Upstairs she will surely get it—and not just because she's punched her ticket with seven boys! Once again, I will defer to her wishes and just say a simple thank you. My kids, on the other hand, like it when I mention them and thank them by name, and therefore I will do just that! Yitzy, (President) Pepi, Tzvi, Alti, Naftali, Daniel, Yehudah Zev and Shlomo Yedidya (Fo) are the most wonderful and helpful children one can ever hope for, and if you don't believe me, just watch the assembly-line system they've put together every Thursday evening, as the *Torah Tavlin* weekly gets prepared and mailed out! Hashem should guide them, protect them, and give them wings to fly to the highest heights of their abilities—both in Torah and *derech eretz*—with blessings of health, happiness and *hatzlachah* for many years to come.

Without the many content contributions and contributors to *Torah Tavlin*, I don't think it would have seen the light of day, and they deserve a tremendous amount of credit. Of special mention is my dear friend Mendy Schonbrun, who sends me great stuff all the time. Thanks is also well-deserved by Rabbi Shimshon Sherer *shlit"a*; Shloime Pollak, who helps me in so many ways; Eli Gelb for being such a good friend and arranging the *Divrei Elazar* that is found in this *sefer*; Rabbi Bodenheimer and Rabbi Schechter for taking such good care of my boys; Reb Yosef Chaim Golding for his critical insight and (unusual) sense of humor; R' Eli Ausband and his sons who provided me with the beautiful Torah from his father; Reb Dovid Greenwald of Telshe Yeshivah for directing me to the *rosh yeshivah's kever*; R' Zecharyah Wallerstein (for all the plugs!); Yaakov Glatter for reserving two—just in case; my partner Chezkie Neeman; Shragie Lieber for his devotion, capabilities, the *ratzon* to "do it all," good cheer, friendship, and *chessed* (the list goes on and on); Chatzkel Bennet; and his father Dr. Leslie Bennet. I would be remiss not to take a bit of extra space to thank Dr. Bennet personally, for he truly goes above and beyond the call of duty to ensure that every person he comes in contact with on Shabbos reads the *Torah Tavlin*. Hey, Doc, if I could hire you as my PR man, I'd be doing alright!

Thank you to all of the sponsors who contributed to this book and to all those who sponsor and distribute the weekly *parshah* sheet, in your shuls, *yeshivos* and homes, thereby joining in the mitzvah of *harbatzas Torah* to Jews all over the world. Of notable mention are the people who print and distribute to their entire cities respectively: Tzvi Fleischman (Los Angeles, CA), Stan Perl (Montreal, Quebec), Gavin Schwartz (Sydney, Australia), Eli Grossbard (Miami, FL), W. Carless (Johannesburg, South Africa), Mo Koval and Shuie Davis (Chicago, IL), and Avi Kupfer (Cleveland, OH). I believe there are quite a few others in numerous cities around the world and I don't know them by name, but either way, thank you for all your efforts. May you all be *zocheh* to an influx of *zechuyos, hatzlachah* and *parnassah, ad b'li dai*!

Israel Bookshop—R' Moshe Kaufman and the entire staff—has again put out a wonderful product. I am deeply grateful to him as well as the entire Israel Bookshop staff that worked on this book. This includes the wonderful editing job done by Mrs. Malkie Gendelman, Mrs. Batsheva Morgenstern, and Mrs. Esther Malky Sonenblick, as well as the input of Mrs. Liron Delmar. Special thanks to Reb Sruly Perl of ViviDesign, for his expertise and marvelous job of graphic design, typesetting, and basically giving *Torah Tavlin* the "face lift" it deserves. As usual, working with all of you was a pleasure, and *b'ezras Hashem* I hope to do so again on future projects. May Hashem continue to bless Israel Bookshop, Judaica Plaza, and ViviDesign with continued success in all their many endeavors.

This book would not have been possible without the generous endowment of Reb Pesach Yoel (Paul) Goodnick of Kew Gardens Hills, NY. He has literally put his "heart and soul" into this project, as evidenced by the remarkably warm and emotional

dedication he wrote in memory of his parents, Benjamin and Regina Goodnick, and I am humbled by the manner in which he expresses his deepest feelings. Although we haven't actually met in person, I feel as if I can see directly into his real and expansive soul through our numerous e-mail correspondences, and after reading the moving testimonial about his parents, I wish I would have known them personally. Hashem should bless you with continued success in all that you do, and He should shower you with an abundance of happiness, *gezunt*, and *harchavas hadaas. Hashem yishmarcha mekol ra, yishmor es nafshecha*—"Hashem will protect you from all evil; He will guard your soul," as you make *aliyah* to Eretz Yisrael, and in all your future endeavors.

Hashem, in His infinite wisdom, knows what is right for me and what I need to fulfill and accomplish in my life. He sends the trials, but He also helps me overcome the tribulations that I face and sees to it that I have all that I need, for if there is something that I don't have, it is because I don't need it. My thanks and appreciation to the Al-mighty is paramount and constant, and I pray that He continue to grant me *harchavas hadaas* and *menuchas hanefesh* through every situation. My joy in life is to write *Torah Tavlin* and I hope that the *Ribono Shel Olam* will allow me to continue to bring enlightenment and enjoyment to the many readers all over the world. May all of Klal Yisrael merit a *kesivah v'chasimah tovah*, and may this book accomplish its *tafkid* of drawing people ever closer to the ultimate purpose of these days; a *teshuvah sheleimah* and a *piska tova*.

Dovid Hoffman

2 Tammuz 5772

Foreword

by Rabbi Simcha Bunim Berger *shlit"a*

Rosh Yeshivah of Yeshivah Gedolah of Bridgeport

Rosh Hashanah

The Rambam in *Hilchos Teshuvah* (chapter 3) writes: *Just as an individual's merits and sins are weighed at the time of his death, so too, the sins of every inhabitant of the world together with his merits are weighed on the festival of Rosh Hashanah. If one is found righteous, his [verdict] is sealed for life. If one is found wicked, his [verdict] is sealed for death. A* beinoni's *verdict remains tentative until Yom Kippur. If he repents, his [verdict] is sealed for life. If not, his [verdict] is sealed for death.*

The Gemara in Rosh Hashanah presents the concept of the Book of Life, in which righteous people are inscribed. The Gemara actually tells of three books—one of life, one of death (for the wicked), and one for those who are in the middle—between righteous and wicked. The Gemara states that the first two groups are inscribed and sealed immediately on Rosh Hashanah in their respective books, while those in the middle group are not inscribed until ten days later, on Yom Kippur. Now, it would seem obvious that the delay in inscribing those in the middle is due to the fact that they must decide to which group they belong. However, once that happens, they should be inscribed either in the book of life or in the book of death. Why are they inscribed in a separate book?

The Struggle of Man

From the moment that Adam listened to the serpent and ate of the *Eitz Hadaas*, the Tree of Knowledge, man has struggled in choosing between good and evil. In every decision, we find ourselves weighing different options of right and wrong. Sometimes, these choices are clear, and often, they are clouded by doubt and uncertainty. The repeated decisions that we make ultimately mold us into what we become. Those who make positive choices again and again will be positive and good people, while those who make the wrong decisions will find themselves in a negative spiral, until they become negative and bad people.

There is a third category, however—the middle group. These people make both good and bad decisions. This group is neither exclusively righteous nor definitively wicked. Rather, they have both the good and the bad inside. This group continuously struggles.

The Three Books

The Three Books represent the essence of people, which can be divided into three groups: righteous, wicked, and *beinoni.* We live in a world where no one is perfect. As the saying goes, "Everyone makes mistakes."

Yet for the righteous, their essence is pure and holy, their mistakes are their sins, and their sins are seen as "mistakes." On the other side are the wicked. Their core is rotten. Although they might perform random acts of goodness, that too, is considered a mistake. For the middle group—known as the "*beinoni*"—there are no mistakes! When they do good, they are good and fulfilling their true inner essence. However, when they choose to do the wrong thing, they are actually being evil. These are the three books that are opened every year on Rosh Hashanah. The righteous and the wicked are immediately inscribed in their books, for their previous choices in life have molded them into whom and what they've become. These two groups are clearly defined.

The middle group is really a category in itself. Even when they make the right choice and are inscribed, they are not like the righteous, and therefore don't enter into their group. Rather, they clarify who they really are and as such purify themselves. They have to stop their endless struggle and take a stand. It is a process that the righteous have no need to experience. This process begins on Rosh Hashanah, continues over the Aseres Yemei Teshuvah, and culminates on Yom Kippur. They are a group unto themselves, and they are inscribed as "*beinonim*" who have reached their clarity and ultimately achieved their essence. Their book opens on Rosh Hashanah, but they are not inscribed and sealed until Yom Kippur. The question is: How does this happen?

Shofar

The Rambam in *Hilchos Teshuvah* provides us with an explanation. He writes that the shofar contains a special message. *Even though the sounding of the shofar on Rosh Hashanah is a decree, it contains an allusion. It is as if [the shofar's call] is saying: Wake up, you sleepy ones from your sleep, and you who slumber, arise. Inspect your deeds, repent, remember your Creator. Those who forget the truth in the vanities of time and throughout the entire year, who devote their energies to vanity and emptiness which will not benefit or save them—look to your souls. Improve your ways and your deeds and let every one of you abandon your evil path and thoughts.*

The Rambam explains that for those who have forgotten what is real and what is truly important, the shofar has the power to awaken them. The shofar does that by

touching their core. It is, as *Chazal* refer to it: *Devarim hayotzim min halev nichnasim el halev*—"Things that emanate from the heart, pierce the heart." The shofar reminds us of *Akeidas Yitzchak*, when Avraham sacrificed his son Yitzchak. It was then that Avraham gave his entire heart to Hashem and Yitzchak gave his soul.

The "voice" of the shofar comes from the heart and soul of our *Avos* (forefathers). It is a call from their soul to our soul. It comes from the innermost part of a Jew, his *neshamah*, and as such can arouse his true essence. With this, the *beinoni* begins the separation process.

Aseres Yemei Teshuvah—The Ten Days of Repentance

Teshuvah literally means "return." For those people who *forget the truth and devote their energies to vanity and emptiness* (Rambam), in other words, they have gone astray from their own sense of righteousness, the awakening of the shofar on Rosh Hashanah will begin their *teshuvah* process. Their *neshamos* have been touched and are now "wide awake." Indeed, they are ready and primed to move on to the next step—when they are *modeh al ha'emes*, admitting the truth of their wayward actions. The Aseres Yemei Teshuvah is a period of introspection when the *beinoni* can take a "step back" and reexamine all that he has done in the past year. The Torah allows a person these days between Rosh Hashanah and Yom Kippur to reflect on who he really is and what is important in his life. This time of reflection and repentance is what allows the actual separation of the man from his misdeeds to take effect on Yom Kippur.

Yom Kippur: The Two Goats

The Torah portion that we read on Yom Kippur describes the *Avodah*—the service that was performed by the *kohen gadol* on Yom Kippur. An integral part of the *Avodah* involved the two identical goats brought to the Temple. One goat was designated to Hashem and brought as a *korban* (sacrifice). The other goat was sent to a barren wasteland called Azazel. Before sending away this second goat, the *kohen gadol* leaned his hands on the head of the goat, and confessed all the sins of Klal Yisrael.

Let us see how this *Avodah* is connected to the *beinoni*. The Torah requires that these goats must be identical. Why? The two goats represent the *beinoni*, who, as mentioned above, has both good and evil inside of him. He identifies equally to both parts of the internal struggle between good and evil. The animals look exactly the same, and so does the *beinoni*. Although one goat represents the good of the nation and its blood will be brought before Hashem, while the other carries the sins of the entire people to Azazel, the animals look exactly alike. This truly exemplifies the *beinoni*. However, Yom Kippur is the day that completes the process which began on Rosh Hashanah.

The *Baal Teshuvah*

Let us say that the *kohen gadol* who separates the two identical goats, bad from the good, represents the division that clarifies the status of the *beinoni*; thus, bringing the first goat to Hashem actually allows the second goat to go to Azazel, and separates the *beinoni* from his other self. The ultimate separation of self happens when the blood, or *nefesh*—which is considered to be the lower level of the soul—of the first goat is sprayed on the *Mizbe'ach* (Altar), and the second goat is sent away.

This teaches us a valuable lesson. **It is the soul that was awakened on Rosh Hashanah, and has spent the last week struggling to distance itself from all that it shouldn't have done, that is now offered upon the altar.** It is a process directly connected to the goat-separation process. The bringing of the first goat to Hashem actually allows the second goat to go to Azazel, and separates the *beinoni* from his other self. The closeness of our *nefesh* now completes the process. What is the end result?

This is the book of the *beinoni*—and in reality it is the book of the *baal teshuvah*, the one who repents his evil deeds. Our sages tell us: *The place where the* baal teshuvah *stands, even the complete righteous cannot stand.*

Now we can better understand why the *baalei teshuvah* have their own book. While this book is harder to write, and definitely takes a lot longer than the book of the righteous, it is written and sealed on the holiest day of the year—Yom Kippur. For this reason, no one—not even the completely righteous—can stand near them.

It is our *brachah* and *tefillah* that this *sefer*, *Torah Tavlin on Yamim Nora'im*, written by my dear friend and *chavrusa*, Reb Dovid Hoffman, will inspire many to reveal their *pintele Yid.* As the shofar has the *koach* (strength) to awaken because it comes from the heart, so should the words of this *sefer* arouse those Jews who thirst for the *dvar Hashem*—the word of G-d.

B'ezras Hashem, may we all be inscribed in the Book of Life.

Simcha Bunim Berger

Erev Shabbos

11 Sivan 5772

דברי ברכה מאת
הגאון רבי דוד סאלאוויציק שליט"א

הנה מע"כ הרב המפו' והנעלה מ' ר' דוד יואל הופמן שי', שהננו מכירו מזמן שלמד בישיבתנו הק' ליקר רוח, והי' עמל על הבנת דברי הגמ' והראשונים, וזכה עי"ז לקנות הרבה חכמה, והואיל שכעת חפצו להדפיס ד"ת ולהפיצם ברבים, ע"כ יבוא בזה דברי לברכו באה"ר שיזכה שיתקבלו דבריו בשערים המצויינים בהלכה, והשי"ת יהא בעזרו להיות דבוק בעץ החיים, ולהנצל מלהיות נמשך אחרי הדעות ועול החשבונות הרבים אשר בקשו בני אדם, ולעסוק בשקידת הלימוד מתוך מנוחת הנפש ביחד עם אהבתו ויראתו ית"ש, שזה תכלית הבריאה וחובת האדם בעולמו, ולהגדיל תורה ולהאדירה,

וע"ז באעה"ח יום ג' ו' אלול התשנ"ה לפ"ג ירושלם ת"ו

משולם דוד באאמו"ר הגה"ח רשכבה"ג

מרן יצחק זאב הלוי זצוקללה"ה סאלאוויציק

הנה מע"כ הרב המפו' והנעלה מ' ר' דוד יואל הופמן שי', שהננו מכירו מזמן שלמד בישיבתנו הק' ליקר רוח, והי' עמל על הבנת דברי הגמ' והראשונים, וזכה עי"ז לקנות הרבה חכמה, והואיל שכעת חפצו להדפיס ד"ת ולהפיצם ברבים, ע"כ יבוא בזה דברי לברכו באה"ר שיזכה שיתקבלו דבריו בשערים המצויינים בהלכה, והשי"ת יהא בעזרו להיות דבוק בעץ החיים, ולהנצל מלהיות נמשך אחרי הדעות ועול החשבונות הרבים אשר בקשו בני אדם, ולעסוק בשקידת הלימוד מתוך מנוחת הנפש ביחד עם אהבתו ויראתו ית"ש, שזה תכלית הבריאה וחובת האדם בעולמו, ולהגדיל תורה ולהאדירה,

וע"ז באעה"ח יום ג' ו' אלול התשנ"ה לפ"ג ירושלם ת"ו

משולם דוד באאמו"ר הגה"ח רשכבה"ג מרן יצחק זאב הלוי זצוקללה"ה סאלאווייציק

Birchas Av

My heart is overjoyed to see the new *sefer* on Yamim Nora'im by my son, Harav Dovid Yoel *shlit"a.* He has already put out many *sefarim* that have been accepted by the public *b'ayin yaffah.* He does this between his many endeavors and interests. We see from this that his mind is not idle in his free time but constantly thinking in Torah. His children see this and it sets a positive example for them to follow. This brings a great *nachas ruach* for the whole family, and especially to us, his parents, as well as a *nachas ruach* to Klal Yisrael, due to the mitzvah of spreading Torah. May he be *zocheh* to go *m'chayil el chayil*—from strength to strength—in good health and with *nachas* from his family for many, many years to come, until the coming of Mashiach soon and in our time.

Your loving father,
Pinchos ben Harav Yitzchok *zt"l* Hoffman

A Concise Halachic Overview: The Mitzvah Of *Teshuvah*

Harav Baruch Hirschfeld *shlit"a*
Rosh Kollel Ateres Baruch,
Rav D'Khal Ahavas Yisrael, Cleveland Heights, Ohio

Introduction

Beginning from the first day of the month of Elul, and continuing over the next forty days, is an awe-inspiring and spiritually uplifting period of time, which lasts until after Yom Kippur. These days are special in their own right, as we know that the Almighty's Thirteen Attributes of Mercy shine brighter during this time than throughout the rest of the year. As a result, a person is more capable of drawing himself closer to Hashem and eradicating undesirable thoughts and deeds than at other times.

This transformation is known as *teshuvah*, and contrary to what one may think, it is not an abstract and vague theory, but rather a well-defined halachic activity, which unleashes a tremendous force and power within an individual to erase both deliberate and unintentional sins from his record.

Now, a devoutly religious person who is careful to fulfill all the precepts of the Torah, as well as the commandments, might wonder to himself, "What has this mitzvah to do with me?" In fact, he may be strict in his observance of Shabbos and Yom Tov, eat only kosher food with the best *hechsher*, *daven* three times a day, put on *tallis* and *tefillin* every day, and he may be a generally good person. Indeed, what does he need *teshuvah* for?

Yet, if one is truly honest with himself, he can certainly find that many of his year-round actions leave much to be desired and, indeed, require the act of "erasing." A few simple and all-too-common examples are: forgetting something that is prohibited (or being ignorant of it), thereby causing a desecration of Shabbos; eating or drinking and forgetting to recite a *brachah acharonah*; not being entirely honest or truthful in business and personal matters at all times; *bitul zman* (wasting time) and *bitul Torah* (neglectful in Torah study).

Is there an individual out there who can honestly say that he never fell victim to the ploys of the *yetzer hara*?

Steps to *Teshuvah*

Rabbeinu Yonah in *Shaarei Teshuvah* lists twenty components of *teshuvah*, of which three are absolutely essential: *charatah al ha'avar*, remorse and regret over past misdeeds; *kabbalah al ha'asid*, accepting to give up sin in the future; and *vidui*, verbal confession.

Sin consists of two parts: thought and deed. First the sinner contemplates his transgression and then he commits it. By regretting his transgressions, he repudiates his plans and negates his impure thoughts. By giving up sin, he demonstrates the reality of his resolution. Thus he has rectified both his thoughts of the past and his deeds of the future.

In a basic sense, the act of *teshuvah* is a three-step process:

1. ***Charatah al ha'avar***: Initially, one must make an accounting of his actions and sort out the *aveiros* he has done. He must recognize and regret these sins, either in fear of the punishment he is likely to receive, or because he has distanced himself from Hashem and lost a close relationship with the One Above.
2. ***Azivas hachet***: One must accept upon himself the appropriate steps necessary to ensure that he does not repeat the sins and deeds that brought about his sad situation.
3. ***Vidui***: After the first two steps comes *vidui*, which is a verbal confession of one's misdeeds before Hashem. Although it is preferable to specify each and every sin, if one just said a general חטאתי—"I have sinned," he has fulfilled the requirement of *vidui*[1]. Thus, the confessions that are recited during *Selichos* and on Yom Kippur are, in actuality, the third all-important step of *teshuvah*, for those who have fulfilled the first two steps.

The **Rambam** in *Sefer Hamitzvos*[2] adds a fourth step: *bakashas mechilah*, requesting forgiveness. According to this, the *teshuvah* process is not complete until one actually asks Hashem for forgiveness.

An Additional Step

Although the *teshuvah* process of regret, resolution and confession deletes one's sin forever, regarding sins that are *bein adam lachaveiro*, interpersonal sins against another individual, there is one additional step that is necessary: asking and obtaining forgiveness from the person(s) he mistreated. *Chazal* tell us that Yom Kippur, and even death itself, cannot atone for a sin against another Jew until one appeases the wronged

1. או"ח תרז:ב
2. עשין ע"ג

party[3]. If the sin was a monetary one, such as theft or misusing funds belonging to another person, one must ask for forgiveness as well as return the money. Even if no money is involved, e.g. he offended, embarrassed, or slandered another person, he is still obligated to ask for forgiveness from the person he victimized.

This obligation is relevant all year-round and not just before Yom Kippur. Erev Yom Kippur is the absolute deadline for one to complete this process so as to effect a total *kapparah* for himself on Yom Kippur[4].

Asking for Forgiveness

Notwithstanding the Talmudic dictum[5], *The messenger of a person is like that person*, with regard to asking for forgiveness, one should go himself and not send a messenger to do it for him. If this is too hard for him, or the middleman will present his request better than he can do it himself, one may send another to ask for forgiveness on his behalf, or even write his request in a letter[6].

When asking for forgiveness, it is extremely important that one specify the sin that was committed. This is an integral part of the *teshuvah* process. However, if by doing so, he will embarrass the victim, then in that case he need not be too specific; rather, he may generalize and say, "I have done something wrong to you[7]." If even that will cause the victim anguish, one should ask forgiveness for whatever he **might** have done without saying that he mistreated him[8]. One cannot fulfill his *bakashas mechilah* by asking forgiveness from a whole group which includes the victim[9]. (Before Yom Kippur, one is required to ask forgiveness from his parents, his spouse and his *rabbeim*[10].)

Granting Forgiveness

One who has been victimized by another person should be quick to forgive the sinner[11]. Our Sages have taught us that in the merit of granting forgiveness to another, no matter how seriously he has been wronged, Hashem will grant him forgiveness as well[12]. He should verbalize his words and say, *machul lach*—"I forgive you." One should

3. גמ' יומא פה
4. משנה ברורה תרו:א
5. בבא מציעא צו
6. משנה ברורה תרו:ב
7. שם:ג
8. אז נדברו ז:סו
9. משנה ברורה תרו:ג
10. בן איש חי פרשת וילך ו'
11. רמ"א תרו:א
12. אליהו רבה תרו:א

not just imply his forgiveness nor leave it as a mutual understanding, but rather spell it out in clear words[13].

There are certain unique situations when one is not required to forgive:

- If the victim is concerned that granting forgiveness to the aggressor will cause that person to harm and persecute him again, he need not forgive him.
- If it is beneficial to the sinner that he humble himself.
- If one was slandered publicly and those who heard the slander might not hear about the *bakashas mechilah*, then one is not required to grant forgiveness.

The **Chafetz Chaim** ***zt"l*** explains that in the first two cases, although he need not forgive, one should still remove the hatred from his heart. In the third case (slander), it is the way of humble people to forgive[14].

Restitution

If a person stole money from another, he must return all the money to its owner. If one took money wrongly from a number of people or even caused others to lose money because of him (e.g. breaking or deliberately leaving a faulty vending machine where people will lose their money), he must attempt to return the money to as many people as he can remember. For those he cannot remember, he should contribute *tzedakah* to a community service which benefits many people, e.g. a *mikvah*[15], and by doing all that is within his power to make proper restitution, Hashem will cause the victims to forgive him[16].

If one is unable to contact a victim, he should accept upon himself to ask forgiveness at his earliest opportunity[17]. If the victim is not alive anymore, he should go to the person's grave with ten men and publicly ask for forgiveness from the dead person, or send a messenger with ten men to do it for him. If he is present, the people answer מחול לך—"You are forgiven," three times, and if he is not, they say מחול לו—"He is forgiven" three times on his behalf[18].

---

13. עיין רבינו בחיי פרשת ויחי נ:יז
14. משנה ברורה תרו:ט-יא
15. חושן משפט שסו:ב
16. חובות הלבבות
17. אלף המגן תרו:יא
18. או"ח תרו:ב

Unwilling to Grant Forgiveness

If one locates his victim and asks for *mechilah*, but the victim refuses to grant forgiveness the first time he is asked (which is often done without others being present), one should go back and ask three more times in front of three other people. If he still refuses, one is not required to ask anymore, but he should inform ten people that he tried to attain forgiveness for his sin and was turned down. If the victim was his *rebbi*, he must keep asking[19].

During the nightly *Krias Shema Al Hamittah*, some people recite a short prayer in which they forgive all those who sinned against them. The Gemara[20] attests that one who does this can merit long life. However, if one knows of a sin that he's done against another, he should not rely on that person's recitation of this prayer for his forgiveness (the same is true of *Tefillas Zakkah* before Yom Kippur); rather he must personally ask *mechilah* from the individual whom he wronged and caused hardship, as these *tefillos* work primarily for sins that have been forgotten.

Every *bein adam lachaveiro* sin is also a sin against Hashem, and after asking forgiveness, one still requires the three steps of *teshuvah*: Regret, Resolution and Confession.

The "Formula" for *Teshuvah*

The letters contained in the word *teshuvah* actually spell out the formula needed to complete honest repentance:

ת - תמים תהיה עם ה' אלקיך—*Be pure with Hashem your G-d.* (*Devarim* 18:13)

ש - שויתי ה' לנגדי תמיד—*I place Hashem before me constantly.* (*Tehillim* 16:8)

ו - ואהבת לרעך כמוך—*You shall love your neighbor like yourself.* (*Vayikra* 19:18)

ב - בכל דרכיך דעהו— *Know Him on all your pathways.* (*Mishlei* 3:6)

ה - הצנע לכת עם ה' אלקיך—*Be humble when with your G-d.* (*Michah* 6:8)

All these qualities are necessary to do real *teshuvah* and repent fully. May each and every one of us merit a complete and wholehearted repentance, so that we may all be inscribed for a year of good life and peace.

---

19. שם:א

20. מגילה כח

אלול

פרשת התשובה

לדוד ה' אורי

Dedicated

לעילוי נשמת האשה

חנה בת ר׳ **איסר בלונדר** ע״ה

רישא רחל בת ר׳ **אברהם שלמה קורץ** ע״ה

רחל לאה בת ר׳ **ארי׳ זאב הופמן** ע״ה

אלול

DRUSH
דרוש

Picture this: A crowd is waiting anxiously at a Jerusalem bus stop. A woman, holding a sleeping baby in her arms, is also standing among the crowd there. Finally, the bus arrives and she boards, sits down, and watches the scenery on the trip to Bnei Brak. After many twists and turns of the bus, she finally arrives at her destination and descends from the vehicle with her baby still sleeping in her arms. Did that baby travel the same distance that she did? Of course he did. Is that baby aware of the journey that transpired? Of course not. As far as the baby is concerned, he has not moved at all. He is still in the loving embrace of his mother. It makes no difference where he started or how long he traveled. He expended no worries or fears on the entire journey, for all he felt was the love and security of his mother.

This is how we must feel, says **Rav Chaim Shmulevitz *zt"l***: so closely connected to Hashem, that no matter what would transpire in our lives, we would feel safe and secure as a baby in his mother's arms. This, perhaps we can say, is the underlying feeling of אני לדודי ודודי לי—*I am to my Beloved and my Beloved is to me.* The closer we bring ourselves to Hashem, the closer He will come to us. Isn't that the true goal and yearning of a Jew? Isn't that the purpose of all our *tefillos*, no matter what it is that we are asking for? There is no greater joy than the sense of being close to Hashem—the feeling of security and love, of being carried in the arms of the *Kol Yachol.*

We know that in a few short days, we will stand before our Creator in judgment and everything that will happen to us in the coming year will be decided! There are three primary actions that we can do to effect a positive outcome, three actions that epitomize the very three foundations upon which the world stands: *teshuvah, tefillah*, and *tzedakah*. Each of these objectives symbolizes one of the three relationships in life that we all need to strengthen: בין אדם למקום, בין אדם לחבירו, בין אדם לעצמו (between man and G-d, man and man, man and himself). Likewise, each one of these three ideas is hinted at in the word א-ל-ו-ל, in order to keep us focused on our *avodah* at this time.

In *Shir Hashirim* we learn: אני לדודי ודודי לי, which reminds us of our special bond with Hashem; the need to maximize our Torah learning and "*chap arayn*" as many *mitzvos* as we can in order to feel His closeness. This will create the atmosphere we need for objective number one: *teshuvah.*

In *Megillas Esther* it says: איש לרעהו ומתנות לאביונים, which again spells out the acronym א-ל-ו-ל. This reminds us of our second great objective—that of loving and helping our fellow Jews, of doing *tzedakah* with our fellow man.

The Torah infers our third objective. We read: ומל ה' אלקיך את לבבך ואת לבב זרעך, which alludes to our great power of *tefillah*, known as *avodah shebalev*—"service of the heart."

Here is a practical suggestion. Try this and see if it helps: During Elul, write down each night how you've accomplished one small act in each of these areas. This way, when Rosh Hashanah arrives, you can come to Hashem with the many *mitzvos* of the 'Three Big T's' that you did—***Teshuvah, Tefillah and Tzedakah***—and you will thereby have the power to change any and all decrees to good.

And then, close your eyes and imagine yourself as a tiny baby being carried by Hashem, without worry or fear, the ultimate feeling of security and love of Hashem. This year, may we actually achieve אני לדודי so that we will merit the ultimate goal of ודודי לי.

STORIES
מעשה

The damaging winds of the Enlightenment and the Reform movement struck many cities throughout Eastern and Western Europe during the nineteenth century, but none more so than in the Romanian capital of Bucharest. Few *rabbanim* had the ability and the fortitude to stand up to this plague that threatened the values of Torah Judaism, and those brave rabbis that tried did not end up faring well in their respective communities.

One *rav* who would not bow to the pressures of the *maskilim* was the renowned *iluy* of Volhynia, **Rav Meir Leibush, the Malbim *zt"l*,** who became the chief rabbi of Bucharest in 1859. He spent the next five years in a constant battle that cut his tenure short in 1864, when he was forced to resign his position and leave Romania. During this time, the Malbim was a vocal opponent to the building of the Choral Temple, with its choir and organ, which would soon become the main neo-Orthodox synagogue in Romania. He also condemned the founding of the first two elementary schools with a general knowledge curriculum, which resulted in friction between the Malbim and the "enlightened" intellectuals in the Jewish community, who were actually wealthy, foreign nationals.

Although he was eventually forced out of his position, the Malbim did claim victory on one occasion. There was a group of unscrupulous Jews who had abandoned Torah and *mitzvos* and had caused much trouble for the Orthodox community. This group was headed by a number of influential and wealthy community leaders, *parnassim*

who robbed the poor in order to increase their own wealth. No act of extortion, no matter how heartless, was beneath these *parnassim.*

One day, shortly before Rosh Hashanah, these malicious men approached the authorities and drew their attention to a "worrisome" trend: the city's Jewish population was increasing rapidly, and the city would soon become unbearably crowded. They therefore suggested that the government banish from the city all Jews who had arrived after the year 1846. Only Jews who were born in the city or were long-time residents would be permitted to remain. The authorities agreed to the suggestion immediately, and issued the decree. The entire city was in an uproar.

Soon after the edict was issued, the *parnassim* employed various agents to publicize that as community leaders, they had drawn up a list of approximately one thousand Jews who were to be deported. However, out of the "goodness of their hearts," these unfortunate Jews had the option of purchasing documents attesting to their validity as long-standing members of the community. Of course, the sum the *parnassim* demanded for such documents was astronomical.

The wealthy citizens on the list, many who had amassed their wealth through robbery and trickery themselves, paid the ransom and received an official document from the community ledger stating that they were upright citizens who had been born in the city. The poor people, who could not afford to pay the ransom, were arrested to await deportation.

That year, on Rosh Hashanah, the Bucharest community gathered in the main shul to beseech the King of kings to grant them a blessed new year. Before shofar blowing, the Malbim ascended the *bimah* to address the community and deliver words of rebuke, as was the custom.

"Listen, my brothers," he began, "and I will tell you about a vision that I saw last year, on Rosh Hashanah. In the Heavenly Court, all the kingdoms and countries in the world passed before the Al-mighty to be judged like sheep before a shepherd. I saw our city, Bucharest, come before the Heavenly Throne. The record books were opened, and the deeds of the inhabitants were weighed on the Heavenly scale. Two angels—one for the defense and the other for the prosecution—stood before the King of kings. The defending angel placed a sack full of gold coins on the side of the scale marked 'merit' and said, 'Here is the astronomical sum of one thousand dinars which the people of Bucharest collected from the meat tax and set aside for acts of charity and kindness, Torah study, visiting the sick and various other good causes.'"

The Malbim said, "My friends, the sack of coins tipped the scale in our favor." The congregants smiled, pleased.

"But then, the prosecuting angel rose and brought forward a ragged seventeen-year-old boy with wild, unruly hair. The angel took two paltry coins from the youth's hand and placed them on the other side of the scale. Amazingly, the two coins

outweighed the thousand dinars. The Heavenly Court was in an uproar! How could it be?

"'This boy,' said the prosecution, 'is from a family of *maskilim* who live in Bucharest, and like the others, they have thrown off the yoke of Torah and *mitzvos*. One Erev Shabbos, this young boy was wandering the streets when he realized that he had no money in his pockets save for these two coins, and he knew he did not have enough to purchase both food and tobacco with so paltry a sum. He therefore decided to fast on Shabbos and bought only tobacco. On Shabbos he smoked publicly, and no one protested.' Here, the prosecuting angel turned to the Heavenly Court and declared, 'There are others like him, who profane Shabbos and trample upon all things holy. How can a city like that be judged favorably?'

"'Why should the entire city bear the sin of this boy or his family who are just like him?' countered the defending angel. 'They were neither born nor raised in this city. They have only settled there recently.'

"The Heavenly Court deliberated and then announced its decision: 'We cannot destroy the city because of these wicked people, since they are strangers to the city. However, in the coming year, all sinners from this city must be banished!'"

The townspeople listened earnestly to the Malbim's words. What an interesting tale—but what did it have to do with them?

"*Rabbosai*!" the Malbim suddenly shouted. "It is one year later and once again, I see the same vision I saw on Rosh Hashanah of last year. But oh, how I tremble! The prosecuting angel is once again presenting the same youth with the two coins in his hand, and these two coins are tipping the scales. The shocked defending angel shouts, 'But we already told you that this boy and his friends are not natives of the city!'

"At this point, the prosecuting angel quickly steps forward and presents a document signed by the important community leaders stating that the boy and his family have been residing in the city for generations. Apparently, they had enough money to buy such a coveted document and it is this very document that is about to sink the entire city of Bucharest!"

The Malbim concluded his speech, and a deadly fear fell upon the congregants. Even the community leaders were shaken and afraid. Apparently, the speech had the desired effect upon the congregants, because on the day after Rosh Hashanah, the instigators rushed to the governmental authorities and arranged for the decree to be rescinded. All the Jews of Bucharest who had been facing deportation were freed from prison.

Halachah: Elul—Listening to the Shofar

HALACHAH
הלכה

While listening to the shofar during the month of Elul, we are preparing our minds and hearts to properly listen, absorb, commit and apply the many messages of the shofar on Rosh Hashanah. It is well known that the main judgment of a person takes place as he stands committed to serving Hashem at the time of shofar blowing. The sound of the shofar is a proclamation with several messages which demand our action:

- **MESSAGE 1:** The Day of Judgment and inspection is imminent. The future of the coming year is at stake, just as this past year's happenings were decided last year at this same time. The preparatory days of *Selichos* are used to purify ourselves with *teshuvah,* i.e. regret, resolutions, practical steps so as not to stumble in the future, confession and asking Hashem to forgive us.
- **MESSAGE 2:** Rosh Hashanah is the anniversary of the creation the world [i.e. mankind] and the ceremonial blow of the shofar serves to once again coronate Hashem on each anniversary, so that we will accept His Kingship in order to serve Him.
- **MESSAGE 3:** The shofar reminds us of the *Akeidah,* when our forefathers, Avraham and Yitzchak, were willing to give up everything to fulfill the will of Hashem. This should inspire us to fully commit ourselves to fulfilling the *mitzvos* and overcoming all obstacles.
- **MESSAGE 4:** When the Torah was given at Har Sinai, it was accompanied by loud sounds of the shofar. Just as we accepted the Torah with the expression of נעשה ונשמע—*We will do and we will listen,* so too, now, as the new year begins, we once again accept the Torah.
- **MESSAGE 5:** Every fifty years is the *yovel*—Jubilee year. On Yom Kippur, the shofar was blown in the same order as we blow today on Rosh Hashanah. It was a blow of freedom and all servants went free. If one is a servant to undesirable habits or a mediocre lifestyle, he can now break free with this "blow of freedom."
- **MESSAGE 6:** The future Redemption will be signaled by a blast of the great shofar, as we say in *Shemoneh Esrei,* תקע בשופר גדול לחרותינו. The call of the shofar reminds us to focus on praying for the arrival of Mashiach and *techiyas hameisim.*
- **MESSAGE 7:** This reminds us of the terrifying blow of the destroyers of the Beis Hamikdash.
- **MESSAGE 8:** When Hashem created man, the *pasuk* states (*Bereishis* 2:7): *He blew into his nostrils a soul of life.* The *Zohar* explains the expression "blew" to mean that just as when a person blows, he is giving out from his deep inner self; so too, Hashem blew from His "inner Self" a spark of G-dliness into man. The blow of the

פרשת התשובה

א וְהָיָה כִי יָבֹאוּ עָלֶיךָ כָּל הַדְּבָרִים הָאֵלֶּה הַבְּרָכָה וְהַקְּלָלָה אֲשֶׁר נָתַתִּי לְפָנֶיךָ
וַהֲשֵׁבֹתָ אֶל לְבָבֶךָ בְּכָל הַגּוֹיִם אֲשֶׁר הִדִּיחֲךָ יְיָ אֱלֹהֶיךָ שָׁמָּה. ב וְשַׁבְתָּ עַד יְיָ
אֱלֹהֶיךָ וְשָׁמַעְתָּ בְקֹלוֹ כְּכֹל אֲשֶׁר אָנֹכִי מְצַוְּךָ הַיּוֹם אַתָּה וּבָנֶיךָ בְּכָל לְבָבְךָ וּבְכָל
נַפְשֶׁךָ. ג וְשָׁב יְיָ אֱלֹהֶיךָ אֶת שְׁבוּתְךָ וְרִחֲמֶךָ וְשָׁב וְקִבֶּצְךָ מִכָּל הָעַמִּים אֲשֶׁר

---

shofar reminds us of the holiness of our soul and of our mission to use both body and soul to serve Hashem.

פרשת התשובה

והיה כי יבאו עליך כל הדברים האלה הברכה והקללה
אשר נתתי לפניך והשבות אל לבבך (ל-א)

When it happens that there comes upon you all these statements, the blessing and the curse that I have set before you, and you will restore to your perception… (30:1)

MUSSAR/ HASHKAFAH
מוסר/השקפה

The *pasuk* instructs a person to do *teshuvah* no matter whether he experiences "blessings or curses." We know that trials and tribulations—"curses"—awaken a person's heart to repentance. But how is it possible that "blessings" can bring one to repentance? Wouldn't it be just the opposite—the more one is blessed, the more he feels he has done everything right and therefore has no need for repentance?

Rav Yisrael Baal Shem Tov *zt"l* explains by way of a parable: This can be likened to a simple person who rebels against the king. Instead of punishing the man, the king gives him an important position. He brings him into his palace and, little by little, raises him to an honored position until he is second only to the king himself. With all the good the king has shown him, one would think the rebel would be thrilled, and yet, all he does is agonize over how he could have possibly rebelled. Every day, his thoughts are on one question: How could he have conspired against such a good and merciful king? What can he do, now that he is in a position of authority, to make it up to his king?

The *nimshal*, explains the holy Baal Shem, is that we see that even blessings, kindness, and mercy can awaken great repentance in a human being; in fact, such repentance can be even greater than the repentance brought on by punishment.

Today, many Jews "have it good." They enjoy prosperity, good health, a happy family life, and fulfillment. They do not experience many tribulations, and thus do not

הֱפִיצְךָ יְיָ אֱלֹהֶיךָ שָׁמָּה. ד אִם יִהְיֶה נִדַּחֲךָ בִּקְצֵה הַשָּׁמָיִם מִשָּׁם יְקַבֶּצְךָ יְיָ אֱלֹהֶיךָ
וּמִשָּׁם יִקָּחֶךָ. ה וֶהֱבִיאֲךָ יְיָ אֱלֹהֶיךָ אֶל הָאָרֶץ אֲשֶׁר יָרְשׁוּ אֲבֹתֶיךָ וִירִשְׁתָּהּ וְהֵיטִבְךָ
וְהִרְבְּךָ מֵאֲבֹתֶיךָ. ו וּמָל יְיָ אֱלֹהֶיךָ אֶת לְבָבְךָ וְאֶת לְבַב זַרְעֶךָ לְאַהֲבָה אֶת יְיָ
אֱלֹהֶיךָ בְּכָל לְבָבְךָ וּבְכָל נַפְשְׁךָ לְמַעַן חַיֶּיךָ. ז וְנָתַן יְיָ אֱלֹהֶיךָ אֵת כָּל הָאָלוֹת

---

have the opportunities borne out of desperate situations to turn to the Al-mighty and pour out their hearts in repentance. Yet, such a person is certainly not exempt from the mitzvah of *teshuvah*. The way he must go about this mitzvah is by recognizing all the good he has been given, and allow this thought to humble him to the point where he feels guilty for ever having "rebelled" against Hashem.

הברכה והקללה אשר נתתי לפניך

...the blessing and the curse that I have set before you...

MIDDOS/ DERECH ERETZ
מידות/דרך ארץ

The obvious question is asked: How could it be that the Jewish people are given the opportunity to choose blessing over curse? Who could possibly be so foolish as to even think of choosing otherwise?

Rabbi Abraham J. Twerski ***shlit"a*** explains that indeed it is quite necessary to spell out the choices. While everyone prefers life and blessing, we are sometimes deluded to mistake evil for good, death for life, and curse for blessing. A prime example of this is the addict, whose cravings make him think that the substances that he abuses are what give him life. He looks forward to ingesting them without thinking of the consequences. He is unable to see and comprehend how truly lethal these substances can be for him.

Rav Shloime Hakohen Rabinowitz ***zt"l*** **of Radomsk (*Tiferes Shloime*)** would say:

"The *parshah* of *teshuvah* continually reiterates over and over again a person's need to 'return' (ושב, תשוב, והשבת), because before a person does *teshuvah* and really tries to improve himself, he is unaware of many things he does wrong. He is far away from the Al-mighty and is drowning in transgressions. However, after he returns to the Al-mighty, he becomes elevated, and suddenly he realizes that he has done many improper things without paying attention to them. Now, as a result of his present awareness, he realizes his need to repent once more. But this time he will do so on a deeper level, and he will repent for the many things he had previously overlooked."

הָאֵלֶּה עַל אֹיְבֶיךָ וְעַל שֹׂנְאֶיךָ אֲשֶׁר רְדָפוּךָ. ח וְאַתָּה תָשׁוּב וְשָׁמַעְתָּ בְּקוֹל יְיָ
וְעָשִׂיתָ אֶת כָּל מִצְוֹתָיו אֲשֶׁר אָנֹכִי מְצַוְּךָ הַיּוֹם. ט וְהוֹתִירְךָ יְיָ אֱלֹהֶיךָ בְּכֹל מַעֲשֵׂה
יָדֶךָ בִּפְרִי בִטְנְךָ וּבִפְרִי בְהֶמְתְּךָ וּבִפְרִי אַדְמָתְךָ לְטוֹבָה כִּי יָשׁוּב יְיָ לָשׂוּשׂ עָלֶיךָ

Although most people are not confronted with so gross a distortion, there are still times when a person can be misled to mistake bad for good. On occasion, a person cannot trust his feelings. One's emotions can overwhelm his reason, and, as a result, the desire for something may so affect his judgment that he may see what he wants as being advantageous, when in fact it may be harmful.

ושבת עד ה' אלקיך ושמעת בקולו ככל אשר אנכי מצוך היום וכו' (ל-ב)

You will return to Hashem, your G-d, and obey Him exactly as I am commanding you today… (30:2)

STORIES
מעשה

When **Rav Shlomo Zalman Hakohen of Vilna** *zt"l* was young, he was once unable to contain himself and uttered a remark which embarrassed someone. He soon realized that he had done a terrible wrong, and wished to apologize, but that person couldn't be found. R' Shlomo Zalman immediately began searching for the man. He sought him tirelessly, going to every shul and *beis medrash* in Vilna, and through the marketplace day after day, but to no avail. Apparently, that person was a visitor to Vilna and had left town. R' Shlomo Zalman was beside himself with anxiety and regret, and could not forgive himself for having embarrassed another Jew.

R' Shlomo Zalman's father-in-law could not tolerate his son-in-law's suffering. It was consuming him night and day. Assuming that R' Shlomo Zalman had not really looked closely at the stranger, he asked a man to impersonate that individual. The plan was for this man to appear before R' Shlomo Zalman and allow the latter to apologize once and for all, ridding himself of his terrible feelings of angst. Thus, a few days later, while walking in the street, the "hired" man made it his business to run into R' Shlomo Zalman.

"*Shalom aleichem*, R' Shlomo Zalman," he said.

Rav Avrohom Blumenkrantz ***zt"l*** used to say: "ושבת עד ה' אלקיך— Return *until* Hashem is your personal G-d! This means that when you feel you have formed a special bond with Hashem, that He is 'your G-d,' then you know you are on the proper road to *teshuvah*".

לְטוֹב כַּאֲשֶׁר שָׂשׂ עַל אֲבֹתֶיךָ. י כִּי תִשְׁמַע בְּקוֹל יְיָ אֱלֹהֶיךָ לִשְׁמֹר מִצְוֹתָיו וְחֻקֹּתָיו הַכְּתוּבָה בְּסֵפֶר הַתּוֹרָה הַזֶּה כִּי תָשׁוּב אֶל יְיָ אֱלֹהֶיךָ בְּכָל לְבָבְךָ וּבְכָל נַפְשֶׁךָ.

R' Shlomo Zalman looked closely at the man. "*Aleichem shalom*," he replied. Then he added quickly, "I'm sorry, but I don't recognize you. Who are you?"

"Don't you remember?" the man asked with a big smile. "I met you when I visited Vilna a few months ago. We were talking then, and I can even remind you of the wisecrack you made that day."

R' Shlomo Zalman was shocked—and delighted. Here was his opportunity to apologize! But he quickly suspected a ruse; it was all too convenient. After talking to the man for a bit, he convinced himself that this was not the person whom he had insulted. "I'm sorry," he said after a while. "I don't believe I've ever met you before." His distress was not relieved.

This went on for some time until finally R' Shlomo Zalman's father-in-law brought the matter before the great **Gaon of Vilna, Rav Eliyahu *zt"l***, and explained the situation. The Gaon asked that R' Shlomo Zalman come to speak with him. When he came in, the Gaon sat him down.

He said to R' Shlomo Zalman, "My child, when a person does wrong, he must do everything in his power to set things right. That is the mitzvah of *teshuvah*. You have left no stone unturned in your quest to accomplish this. You have done everything possible to find the person whom you've insulted and apologize to him. Hashem only asks that which is within our means to do. More than that is impossible. Inasmuch as you were sincere in your efforts to make amends to that person, you can be absolutely certain that Hashem has put it in the heart of that person to forgive you. As a result, you need not carry that burden around with you any longer." Only after hearing the words of the Gaon, did R' Shlomo Zalman finally feel relieved.

אם יהיה נדחך בקצה השמים משם יקבצך ה' אלקיך ומשם יקחך (ל-ד)

If your exiled one will be at the edge of the heavens, from there will Hashem, your G-d, gather you… (30:4)

STORIES
מעשה

One day, during the month of Elul, the two *gabba'im* of the **Rebbe Maharash, R' Shmuel Schneerson of Lubavitch *zt"l***, were summoned and told that they were to prepare for a journey to Paris. This was unusual on such short notice and they had no idea what the rebbe's intentions were. When they arrived in Paris,

the rebbe told them that they would be staying in the Alexander Hotel, the most prestigious and luxurious hotel in the city.

At the front desk, the rebbe asked for the most expensive room in the hotel, a suite that was located right near the gaming rooms. A few hours after they settled in their room, the rebbe, followed by his two stunned *gabba'im*, made his way to the betting parlor. There he found a seat right next to a young man who was playing cards, wasting a large amount of money and refreshing himself from time to time with glasses of wine.

As he was about to drink from his glass, the rebbe rested his hand on the card-player's shoulder and said, "Young man! I'm sure you know that it is forbidden to drink non-kosher wine!" The young man was a bit taken aback, and after a moment, put the glass down.

The rebbe fixed his penetrating gaze on the man and said, "Non-kosher wine dulls the spiritual sensitivity of the mind and the heart. Remember, you must always behave like a Jew!"

Then, bidding him a good day, the Maharash left the room in great agitation. His *gabbai* later reported that he had never seen the rebbe so upset.

Several hours later, the young man came around inquiring after the person who had spoken to him earlier. He was shown into the rebbe's room, where he remained for quite some time. When he emerged, he was a transformed individual. The next day R' Shmuel told his *gabba'im* that it was time to leave and they set out to return to Lubavitch.

Upon his return, the Maharash explained to his curious *gabba'im*, "A soul as pure as this young man's had not descended to this world for many generations. However, just as many unfortunate people with good intentions may find themselves in a bad situation, so too, this soul had fallen into the depths of impurity. I felt that I must take upon myself to revive this lofty soul and restore its owner to where he truly belongs."

In the course of time, that young man became a true *baal teshuvah*, a sincere and truly G-d-fearing Jew, the pride of his entire generation.

Rav Yisrael of Ruzhin *zt"l* (Ruzhiner Rebbe) would say:

"How must you do *teshuvah*? In the same way that you committed a sin. When you sinned, you did what you did and then found out that it was a sin. When doing *teshuvah*, you must stop doing what you did and then you will find out that you have done *teshuvah*!"

והביאך ה' אלקיך אל־הארץ אשר־ירשו אבתיך וירשתה והיטבך והרבך מאבתיך (ל-ה)

And Hashem, your G-d, will bring you to the land that your forefathers inherited, and you will inherit it; and He will benefit you and multiply you more than your forefathers. (30:5)

What does Eretz Yisrael mean to the Jewish people?

DRUSH
דרוש

The **Bohusher Rebbe, Rav Yisrael Friedman** ***zt"l***, was very active in helping the *yishuv* in Eretz Yisrael get on its feet. The rebbe was once approached by a group of secular Zionists who wanted to enlist him in their group. They explained to him that the Jewish people needed their own homeland where they would be safe from outside elements.

"But why have you selected Israel as your land?" the rebbe asked them.

The group was rather surprised by the rebbe's question. In unison, they answered him, "Eretz Yisrael is our land; it belongs to the Jewish people."

"Do you have any documents proving that it is your land?" the rebbe asked them. The group just stood there, not knowing what to answer. They didn't have any documents whatsoever.

"Let me show you the document," the rebbe told them, and opened up a *Chumash*. "This is our document," he said. "Here it is written that Hashem has given Eretz Yisrael to the *Yidden*. But, there were conditions under which the deal was made. It says here that the Jews must keep the Torah and *mitzvos*. If you keep these conditions, then you have a rightful claim to the land, and I will gladly help you to achieve your goal. If not, you have no claim!"

ואתה תשוב ושמעת בקול ה' ועשית את כל מצותיו אשר אנכי מצוך היום וגו' (ל-ח)

And you will turn back and obey Hashem, and you will perform all His commandments that I am commanding you today. (30:8)

MASHAL
משל

משל: The kaiser of Germany once came to visit the czar of Russia. A state dinner with all the trimmings was served. On the menu that night was *kishke*, otherwise known as stuffed derma, and the kaiser, tasting it for the first time, loved it. He asked the czar to send his cooks the recipe. The czar graciously agreed to do so.

The next day, the Russian cooks wrote down the recipe and sent it via diplomatic pouch to the kaiser's chefs.

The day finally came when the kaiser was informed that he would be served *kishke*. Out came a tray. The kaiser's mouth watered, and he took a bite. Immediately, however, he spat out the piece and ordered the *kishke* to be thrown away.

An official protest was immediately dispatched to the czar. How dare he send a recipe for such a vile concoction! The czar summoned one of his cooks and demanded an explanation.

After some thought, the cook exclaimed, "Of course! We told them how to stuff and spice the *kishke*, but we didn't tell them to clean it out before it is cooked and stuffed!"

נמשל: On Rosh Hashanah, we decide on ways to improve ourselves. Indeed, resolutions are important. However, before we can improve, we must "clean out" all negative aspects that require fixing. This must be done first; otherwise, even with all of the "spices" (good resolutions) in the world, a person will remain a foul-smelling *kishke*!

ושבת עד ה' אלקיך... בכל לבבך ובכל נפשך וגו' (ל-ב)

You will return to Hashem, your G-d...wholeheartedly and with your whole being. (30:2)

MUSSAR/ HASHKAFAH
מוסר/השקפה

How does one do *teshuvah*? Well, let's try this: sit down in a quiet room with a pen and paper and try to remember your activities over the past year. Of course, most people will say, "Remember what I did last year? I can't even remember what I ate for breakfast!" So, a person can easily give up: "*Teshuvah* is too hard—I'll just hope for the best!"

Don't give up! Stick with the program. You'll be surprised at how much you will remember when you take the time to recall: Where was I last Rosh Hashanah? With whom? Whom did I meet? What did we talk about?

Slowly, your memory gets jogged...and now, get ready to write, because the memories come fast and furious. Yom Kippur, Sukkos, Chanukah, Pesach... You remember how you felt; if you were lazy, angry, impatient, unkind, sensitive, satisfied with your lot. Do this for a while, and then continue the next day. You'll be astounded at how much you remember, all the thoughts that pop into your head.

CONGRATULATIONS! You have now begun the *teshuvah* process! The Torah repeats itself regarding the mitzvah of *teshuvah*—ואתה תשוב, והשבת, ושב—to teach us that once you start the process, you can do it over and over again!

Rav Chaim Shmulevitz *zt"l* explains that by verbally committing oneself to *teshuvah*—בפיך ובלבבך לעשותו—one has already put himself on the road to a *teshuvah sheleimah* and a כתיבה וחתימה טובה.

לְדָוִד, יְיָ אוֹרִי וְיִשְׁעִי מִמִּי אִירָא, יְיָ מָעוֹז חַיַּי מִמִּי אֶפְחָד. בִּקְרֹב
עָלַי מְרֵעִים לֶאֱכֹל אֶת בְּשָׂרִי, צָרַי וְאֹיְבַי לִי, הֵמָּה כָּשְׁלוּ
וְנָפָלוּ. אִם תַּחֲנֶה עָלַי מַחֲנֶה לֹא יִירָא לִבִּי, אִם תָּקוּם עָלַי מִלְחָמָה

כי תשמע בקול ה' אלקיך לשמר מצותיו וחקתיו הכתובה בספר התורה הזה כי תשוב אל ה' אלקיך בכל־לבבך ובכל־נפשך (ל־י)

When you obey Hashem, your G-d, to guard His commandments and His statutes, written in this Torah scroll; when you turn back to Hashem, your G-d… (30:10)

MUSSAR/ HASHKAFAH
מוסר/השקפה

Unlike in other religions, where transgressors are advised by their "holy men" to subject themselves to severe penance in order to expurgate their sins, the Torah is concerned with the welfare of the Jewish people. We are not demanded to scale impossible peaks or travel across the sea to distant lands. How can a Jew accomplish the most coveted goal of realizing a *teshuvah sheleimah*? The *pasuk* tells us (*Devarim* 30:14): כי קרוב אליך הדבר מאד בפיך ובלבבך לעשותו — *This thing is near to you in your mouth and heart to do it.* What is "*this thing*"? It is *teshuvah*.

The Sephardic *gaon*, **Chacham Yitzchak Abohav *zt"l* (*Menoras Hamaor*)**, explains: these last three words—בפיך ובלבבך לעשותו—represent the three stages of *teshuvah*. First, the mouth must acknowledge one's sins and declare that these sins are abandoned. Second, one must heartbrokenly lament his transgressions. Finally, the sincerity of one's *teshuvah* will be manifest in his deeds when he never reverts back to his earlier, misguided actions.

Dedicated by
Mr. and Mrs.
Pinchos
Hoffman
לעי"נ הג"ר
יצחק בן
ר' פינחס
הופמן זצ"ל
ת.נ.צ.ב.ה.

לדוד ה' אורי וישעי

לדוד ה' אורי וישעי

Of Dovid, Hashem is my Light and my Salvation…

DVAR TORAH
דבר תורה

The twenty-seventh *perek* of Tehillim—לדוד ה' אורי וישעי—is the chapter we say throughout the entire month of Elul, as it has many allusions to the upcoming Yamim Nora'im. We know that אורי refers to Rosh Hashanah, and ישעי refers to Yom Kippur. Later on, the words כי יצפנני בסכה are a reference to Sukkos. The question is: where do we find a hint to Elul in this chapter?

בְּזֹאת אֲנִי בוֹטֵחַ. אַחַת שָׁאַלְתִּי מֵאֵת יְיָ, אוֹתָהּ אֲבַקֵּשׁ, שִׁבְתִּי בְּבֵית יְיָ כָּל יְמֵי חַיַּי, לַחֲזוֹת בְּנֹעַם יְיָ וּלְבַקֵּר בְּהֵיכָלוֹ. כִּי יִצְפְּנֵנִי בְּסֻכֹּה בְּיוֹם

The answer is found toward the end of the *perek*: לולא האמנתי לראות בטוב ה'. If you turn the word לולא around, you have אלול!

The significance of the word לולא gives us tremendous insight into our *avodah* for this very special month of the year. לולא means, *if only*. There are so many things in life we would have accomplished "*if only*" we had the right circumstances! *If only* we had greater mental capabilities; *if only* we had a different upbringing; *if only* we had a better family situation or successful financial conditions; *if only* we had more talent or opportunities; *if only* we had a happier marriage or more intelligent children; *if only* we had a higher social standing or lived in a more insulated neighborhood... We think to ourselves: If only I were brighter, more articulate, more outgoing, had better *middos*; if only something in my life was different—then I would be able to do *teshuvah*! Then I would be able to do or be all the things I should do and be!

Part of our *avodah* now is to turn the לולא—the "*if only*"—around and read it as אלול LOUD and CLEAR! Now is the time to change and improve, exactly with the circumstances Hashem has given us! It is Elul—time to do *teshuvah*, NOW!

כי קרוב אליך הדבר מאד—The matter is very close to you. *Teshuvah* is within everyone's reach. Just leave out the לולא!

בקרב עלי מרעים לאכל את בשרי צרי ואיבי לי המה כשלו ונפלו

When evildoers come upon me to eat my flesh, my tormentors and my foes, they stumble and fall.

MUSSAR/HASHKAFAH
מוסר/השקפה

The Gemara (*Sukkah* 52a) states that in the future, Hashem will show the *yetzer hara* (evil inclination) to the evildoers, and it will appear like a strand of hair (כחוט השערה). They will cry and wonder, "How is it that we were unable to overcome so slight an obstacle?"

How are we to understand this? Certainly, the evil inclination is a formidable foe. Is this "strand of hair" just an optical illusion designed to torture the wicked? Surely, this would be a grotesque violation of truth in a world of pure, uncompromised truth.

Rav Eliyahu Eliezer Dessler ***zt"l*** **(*Michtav M'Eliyahu*)** explains what it is that the wicked people will be asked when they'll be shown the *yetzer hara's* appearance in this way: Why did you remain where you were? What kept you from working on yourself? How difficult would it have been for you to take those first steps to self-

רָעָה, יַסְתִּרֵנִי בְּסֵתֶר אָהֳלוֹ, בְּצוּר יְרוֹמְמֵנִי. וְעַתָּה יָרוּם רֹאשִׁי עַל אֹיְבַי סְבִיבוֹתַי, וְאֶזְבְּחָה בְאָהֳלוֹ זִבְחֵי תְרוּעָה, אָשִׁירָה וַאֲזַמְּרָה לַיְיָ.

---

improvement? Had you taken the first step, you would have certainly taken one more step, then another, then another. Who knows how far you might have traveled spiritually had you but taken that first simple step!

Indeed, how hard would it be for us to study Torah for five more minutes, to say a blessing with proper concentration, each and every day? Could we not restrain ourselves, at least once, from speaking *lashon hara*, from saying something we shouldn't? We can do it without much effort. Shall we allow a "*strand of hair*" to stand in our way?

And this is just the start. *Chazal* tell us: *"One mitzvah drags another mitzvah."* Instead of the discouragement of looking back on another year that began with such good intentions but concluded without measurable progress, we will have something concrete to show for our efforts. This sense of accomplishment, this taste of success, will likely motivate us to take another step, to meet another challenge.

אם תחנה עלי מחנה לא יירא לבי אם תקום עלי מלחמה בזאת אני בוטח

If an army should encamp against me, my heart would not fear; if war were to rise against me, in this I trust.

MUSSAR/ HASHKAFAH
מוסר/השקפה

The world is a fearful place. There is danger lurking behind every curve, real physical danger which can harm any individual at any time. If entire countries are fearful of one another, due to the threat of atomic and nuclear warfare, how much more so are individual people afraid of what harm can befall them.

We Jews, writes **Rav Dr. Joseph Breuer** ***zt"l***, have but one fear: *Hakadosh Baruch Hu*. The Jewish concept of world and life is fully prepared for physical fears and anxieties. We believe that the continued existence of the universe depends on the will of Hashem. It is not a bomb that threatens the world's existence; rather, it is the absence of human beings who appreciate the concept of an omnipotent and merciful G-d; it is those who scorn and ridicule Hashem that can ultimately bring down this world.

Thus, our special *tefillah* on our holy Day of Judgment is: ובכן תן פחדך ה׳ אלקינו על כל מעשיך—*Give Your fear, Hashem our G-d, on all Your works.* Let every creation serve and worship You, and thereby unite into one bond—אגודה אחת—to fulfill Your will with all their hearts. This prayer is one that the Jewish nation has continually beseeched

שְׁמַע יְיָ קוֹלִי אֶקְרָא, וְחָנֵּנִי וַעֲנֵנִי. לְךָ אָמַר לִבִּי, בַּקְּשׁוּ פָנָי, אֶת פָּנֶיךָ יְיָ אֲבַקֵּשׁ. אַל תַּסְתֵּר פָּנֶיךָ מִמֶּנִּי, אַל תַּט בְּאַף עַבְדֶּךָ, עֶזְרָתִי הָיִיתָ, אַל תִּטְּשֵׁנִי וְאַל תַּעַזְבֵנִי אֱלֹהֵי יִשְׁעִי. כִּי אָבִי וְאִמִּי עֲזָבוּנִי, וַייָ יַאַסְפֵנִי. הוֹרֵנִי יְיָ דַּרְכֶּךָ, וּנְחֵנִי בְּאֹרַח מִישׁוֹר, לְמַעַן שׁוֹרְרָי. אַל תִּתְּנֵנִי בְּנֶפֶשׁ צָרָי, כִּי קָמוּ בִי עֵדֵי שֶׁקֶר וִיפֵחַ חָמָס. לוּלֵא הֶאֱמַנְתִּי, לִרְאוֹת בְּטוּב יְיָ, בְּאֶרֶץ חַיִּים. קַוֵּה אֶל יְיָ, חֲזַק וְיַאֲמֵץ לִבֶּךָ, וְקַוֵּה אֶל יְיָ:

Hashem with since time immemorial. This is our fervent hope and belief, and we express it succinctly on Rosh Hashanah, a day when the world sees itself reborn (היום הרת עולם), for there is no more appropriate time. Nothing else can save and preserve mankind from total destruction, nuclear or otherwise. It is but this fear—*yiras Shamayim*—that will redeem mankind from every other fear facing it, and no political, diplomatic, or military efforts of individuals or nations can have any effect on the bombs that threaten them.

שמע ה' קולי אקרא וחנני וענני

Hashem, hear my voice when I call; be gracious and answer me.

MUSSAR/HASHKAFAH
מוסר/השקפה

Why do we pray? If Hashem will, in any case, do what is best for us and for the world, what does our prayer accomplish? This is a crucial question! And the answer, says **Rav Zalman Guttman *shlit"a***, is even more crucial.

The Torah tells us that Moshe Rabbeinu poured out his heart to Hashem to allow him to enter Eretz Yisrael, and yet Hashem said no. Moshe tried everything. He said 515 different prayers, the numerical value of ואתחנן, and still Hashem said no. Finally, Hashem told him, "Moshe, stop praying! You cannot enter the land."

This teaches us that the purpose of prayer is not always getting what we want or what we ask for. Of course, when we pray, we beg Hashem for what we want, and very often, Hashem answers those prayers and our requests are fulfilled. However, when we don't get what we asked for, what we think is best, we must realize that all of our prayers were surely not in vain. For the purpose of prayer is to become close to Hashem. The more we pray, plead, and pour out our hearts and innermost desires and feelings, the more we develop a genuine, strong, unbreakable bond with our Father in Heaven, which is greater than anything we could ever have possibly asked for.

לך אמר לבי בקשו פני את פניך ה' אבקש

Of You my heart has said, "Seek My Presence." Your Presence, Hashem, I will seek.

DRUSH
דרוש

Did you ever wonder why these days are called "High Holy Days"? Well, these high and holy days are high and holy because Hashem is so close to us at this time. The Torah tells us how we may succeed in seeking Hashem and finding Him: *And you shall seek out Hashem from there and you shall find Him, because you sought with all your heart and all your soul* (*Devarim* 4:29).

What do we need? We need sincerity in our *avodah*, since, as we know, רחמנא ליבא בעי—*Hashem wants our heart.* If one is sincere in his quest for *teshuvah*, then no matter where he is, he will surely find Hashem. The word משם—*from there*, says the holy **Baal Shem Tov *zt"l***, means from wherever you happen to be! One should never feel that he is too far removed from Hashem to have a real connection, a loving relationship with his beloved Father. In fact, Hashem is forever waiting and beckoning for every one of His children to come home. It's not where He is; it's where we are!

It is told that when the **Baal HaTanya, Rav Shneur Zalman of Liadi *zt"l***, was imprisoned by the czar of Russia for his religious activities, one of the guards asked him with a smirk, "If your G-d knows everything, why did He call out to Adam in Paradise, 'Where are you?' Did He not know where Adam was?"

The Baal HaTanya answered, "Torah is not just a storybook. It is filled with timeless lessons that apply to every generation. Hashem calls out to every person, 'Where are you?'" What He means to say is, why are you here in this world? What have you accomplished; what are your goals? Adam symbolizes mankind, and everyone must be prepared at all times to answer the Al-mighty G-d when He asks the question.

Let us answer Hashem's call with the sincere cry of, *Hineini*—Hashem, here I am! I am as close to You as I can possibly be.

הורני ה' דרכך ונחני בארח מישור למען שררי

Hashem, teach me Your way, and lead me in the path of uprightness because of my watchers.

DVAR TORAH
דבר תורה

Shemos Rabbah Ki Sisa states: *Hashem showed Moshe all the treasures in which the rewards of the righteous are stored away... Later he (Moshe) saw a huge treasure and asked, "Whose is this great treasure?" Hashem replied to him, "Unto him who does not have [good deeds to his credit], I supply freely and I help him from this pile."*

The renowned Kabbalist, **Rav Moshe Cordovero *zt"l* (*Tomer Devorah*)**, comments that there are people who are unworthy of receiving good or Heavenly rewards, and yet *Hakadosh Baruch Hu* has mercy upon them. This is because of this storehouse of grace (חן) from which Hashem graciously dispenses gifts to them, for He says, "Their fathers had merit and I have made an oath to the *Avos* that even when their children will be unworthy, they will be shown grace." As it says וחנותי את אשר אחון ורחמתי את אשר ארחם—*And I will be gracious to whom I will be gracious, and show mercy to whom I will show mercy.* This includes those who may not even deserve it (*Brachos* 7a).

"So too," the *Tomer Devorah* writes, "should man behave. Even when he meets with the wicked, he should not display cruelty, nor insult them. He should have mercy on them, by saying, 'Are they not, after all, children of Avraham, Yitzchak, and Yaakov? If they are not worthy, their fathers were worthy.' This way, he should conceal their shame and help them improve as much as is in his power."

The **Chiddushei Harim, Rav Yitzchak Meir Alter *zt"l***, adds that the most abundant of all of Hashem's treasures is the one called the אוצר מתנת חנם—*treasury of free gifts.* This treasury contains an endless supply of goodness. A person has the ability to tap into this incredible resource, but only if he feels sincerely that he has no complaints or claims against Hashem, and that the Al-mighty owes him nothing.

קוה אל ה' חזק ויאמץ לבך וקוה אל ה'

Hope to Hashem, be strong and He will give you courage, and hope to Hashem.

MIDDOS/ DERECH ERETZ
מידות/דרך ארץ

As we approach the holy day of Rosh Hashanah, the day when we strive for self-improvement so as to warrant a positive verdict in the Heavenly Court, we must accept upon ourselves resolutions that are attainable. Our ultimate goal should be to fulfill the Torah in its entirety. However, this cannot be accomplished overnight. Moreover, if we set our goals too high, we are likely to fail. The proper way to self-improvement is step by step. **Rav Yehudah Zev Segal *zt"l*, the Manchester Rosh Yeshivah (*Yirah Vadaas*)**, suggests that each one of us accept upon ourselves *bli neder* the following three *kabbalos* (resolutions) as a first step:

1) To strive to strengthen our Torah study both qualitatively and quantitatively. Let us begin by increasing our daily Torah study by five minutes. One cannot imagine the impact that is made in Heaven when one sits down to study for five additional minutes in order to fulfill a resolution that he undertook on Rosh Hashanah. This seemingly insignificant act is a demonstration that one is translating his thoughts of self-improvement into action. And of course this is only a beginning.

2) To fortify matters of *bein adam lachaveiro*, between man and his fellow. *Baruch Hashem*, our generation is one in which *chessed* abounds, but we cannot be

content with this alone. It is imperative that each of us strives to improve his *middos*, particularly that of being *maavir al middosav*—one who overlooks the hurt that is caused to him. *Chazal* (*Rosh Hashanah* 17a) have taught that one who acquires this trait will have all his sins forgiven. Rashi explains this term to mean that one refrains from "measuring out" a corresponding response to those who have caused him pain. For this, says Rashi, the Attribute of Justice responds in kind by not scrutinizing this person's deeds; rather, it lets him be. Regarding development of this attribute, Rabbeinu Yonah (*Shaarei Teshuvah* 128) comments: *This is an extremely noteworthy pathway of hope (for gaining atonement), as it is written, "Let him put his mouth to the dust, there may be hope. Let one offer his cheek to the one who smites him, let him be filled with disgrace"* (*Eichah* 3:29-30).

One should view every personal slight as an opportunity to acquire the precious attribute of *maavir al middosav* and its reward. Then he will grow spiritually through such occurrences, rather than becoming ensnared in a net of hatred and strife.

3) To increase our zealousness in *shemiras halashon*, guarding one's tongue: Let us all accept upon ourselves to follow the worldwide calendar schedule which calls for daily study of two *halachos* in *Sefer Chafetz Chaim* and one page in *Sefer Shemiras Halashon*. Such daily study will make us knowledgeable in this all-important area of halachah and will leave us with the necessary awareness to refrain from forbidden speech once *shemiras halashon* becomes a matter of habit. Thus the battle will be won.

Ask yourself this: How are we able to refrain from talking during the entire *Mussaf* on Rosh Hashanah, a period of some two hours or more? The answer is: training. We are taught from early youth that one is forbidden to talk during this period of time, and it is this training which makes refraining from speaking during *Mussaf* easy to perform. In the same way, if we train ourselves not to speak *lashon hara* and other forbidden speech, then the matter of *shemiras halashon* will be that much easier.

Rav Shneur Zalman of Liadi *zt"l* (Baal HaTanya) would say:

"In the future, when Mashiach comes, every creation in this world will understand and recognize that there is a G-dly power within which makes it exist and gives it life-force. This is the meaning of the words from the *Amidah* prayer which we say on Rosh Hashanah. We beseech Hashem to reveal His Kingship in this world—*May everything that has been made know that You made it*—because in truth nothing exists without this G-dliness."

ראש השנה

קידוש

סימנים

תקיעת שופר

ונתנה תוקף

תשובה תפילה צדקה

Dedicated by

Dr. and Mrs. Yakov Kiffel

לעילוי נשמת האשה

חיה בת ר׳ **אברהם** ע״ה

נפ׳ ג׳ תשרי תש״ע

(לליל שבת)

בלחש - וַיְהִי עֶרֶב וַיְהִי בֹקֶר

יוֹם הַשִּׁשִּׁי. וַיְכֻלּוּ הַשָּׁמַיִם וְהָאָרֶץ וְכָל צְבָאָם. וַיְכַל אֱלֹהִים בַּיּוֹם הַשְּׁבִיעִי מְלַאכְתּוֹ אֲשֶׁר עָשָׂה, וַיִּשְׁבֹּת בַּיּוֹם הַשְּׁבִיעִי מִכָּל

קידוש

ויכלו השמים והארץ וכל צבאם

The heavens and the earth were completed, and all their conglomerations.

DVAR TORAH
דבר תורה

The simple translation of the word ויכולו means "it was completed." However, **Chacham Rabbeinu Yosef Kanafo *zt"l*** writes that in this *pasuk* the word is written without the letter *vav* in the middle, and therefore relates to the word כליה, which means "destruction." This is a frightful lesson for every Jew to remember: The *pasuk* is telling us clearly that Shabbos has a dual capacity—it can wreak destruction in the case of one's desecration of it, but it also has the potential, through one's observance of it, to help one complete his work and see the fruits of his labor.

ויכל אלקים ביום השביעי מלאכתו אשר עשה וישבת ביום השביעי מכל מלאכתו אשר עשה וגו'

Hashem completed by the seventh day His work which He had made, and He abstained on the seventh day from all His work which He had made.

STORIES
מעשה

The Tanna Rabi Shimon says: *"A (man) of flesh and blood, who does not know to calculate (the precise) moment and time, must add from weekday (*chol*) to Shabbos (*kodesh*), but the Holy One Blessed be He, Who knows how to configure the exact minute and second of time, entered the seventh day (Shabbos) like a hairsbreadth, and it appeared [to the untrained eye] like He finished Creation on the day [of Shabbos] itself"* (Rashi, *Bereishis* 2:2). This is a lesson in faith in the Al-mighty—to never doubt His words or actions, for only *Hakadosh Baruch Hu* knows the exact procession of life: how, what, where, and when everything is supposed to and will eventually take place—past, present and future.

The story is told about two of the great early Chassidic masters, the **"Toldos," Rav Yaakov Yosef of Polonye *zt"l***, and **Rav Nachman of Horodenka *zt"l***, who decided

מְלַאכְתּוֹ אֲשֶׁר עָשָׂה. וַיְבָרֶךְ אֱלֹהִים אֶת יוֹם הַשְּׁבִיעִי וַיְקַדֵּשׁ אֹתוֹ, כִּי בוֹ שָׁבַת מִכָּל מְלַאכְתּוֹ, אֲשֶׁר בָּרָא אֱלֹהִים לַעֲשׂוֹת.

---

to travel together to visit their holy and saintly rebbe, **R' Yisrael Baal Shem Tov** ***zt"l***, in Mezhibuzh. As their decision was a last-minute one, they headed out in a horse and wagon coach early Friday morning, figuring that they had more than enough time to travel the few hours and arrive in Mezhibuzh by midday, with plenty of time to spare before Shabbos.

They hadn't even traveled half the distance when they saw ahead of them a broad, regal carriage, trimmed with gold and ivory, and drawn by four white horses. Obviously, it was the carriage of a wealthy and important individual, perhaps a duke or a local landowner, who didn't seem to be in any particular hurry to get where he was going. The elegant coach was making its leisurely way along the road, with undoubtedly no clue or care that the holy day of Shabbos was to be expected later in the day. Passing was impossible at this time of year due to the mountainous snowdrifts piled high along both sides of the road, and besides, to brazenly swing around the coach would be perceived as an insult to the wealthy man inside, and who knew what sort of retribution he might exact. The wagon with the two *tzaddikim* inside had no choice but to slow down and follow along behind.

At first, it was no big deal, as they had plenty of time. But before long, R' Yaakov Yosef became agitated, predicting that at this pace, they would surely have to profane the Shabbos if they wanted to make it to Mezhibuzh. R' Nachman was perturbed, but he remained calm. He reminded his companion that everything would be okay, that all that Hashem does is for the best. Hadn't they, as disciples of the great Baal Shem Tov, learned that Hashem guides everything that occurs in the world—especially time? Surely their situation was Hashem's hand at work.

Less than an hour passed before they had to come to a complete halt. Spread out on the road ahead as far as the eye could see was a battalion of Russian soldiers, who were marching practically in place in the center of the road, packing down the mud and drifts with their boots, to allow military and civilian traffic to get by.

Now the Toldos became doubly agitated. They were quite literally stuck and not moving at all. There was no way they'd be able to reach their destination in time. He insisted that they turn around and go back.

Suddenly, the commander of the brigade looked up. Seeing the regal-looking coach coming his way, and recognizing that a personage of great importance was inside, he immediately gave orders for his entire brigade to move aside and make passage for the dignitary and his "entourage." In moments, the soldiers moved off the road, and

סַבְרִי מָרָנָן וְרַבָּנָן וְרַבּוֹתַי

בָּרוּךְ אַתָּה יְיָ אֱלֹהֵינוּ מֶלֶךְ הָעוֹלָם, בּוֹרֵא פְּרִי הַגָּפֶן.

בָּרוּךְ אַתָּה יְיָ אֱלֹהֵינוּ מֶלֶךְ הָעוֹלָם, אֲשֶׁר בָּחַר בָּנוּ מִכָּל עָם וְרוֹמְמָנוּ מִכָּל לָשׁוֹן, וְקִדְּשָׁנוּ בְּמִצְוֹתָיו. וַתִּתֶּן לָנוּ יְיָ אֱלֹהֵינוּ בְּאַהֲבָה אֶת יוֹם (בשבת: הַשַּׁבָּת הַזֶּה וְאֶת יוֹם) הַזִּכָּרוֹן הַזֶּה יוֹם (זִכְרוֹן) תְּרוּעָה (בשבת:

---

the two *tzaddikim*, following close behind the carriage of the dignitary, were beyond the sea of soldiers, continuing on the road to Mezhibuzh.

Not more than a few minutes passed until they came to a fork in the road. The dignitary in his coach went one way, and the Toldos and R' Nachman went the other way. The *tzaddikim* regained speed, and arrived in Mezhibuzh with ample time to prepare for Shabbos.

כי בו שבת מכל מלאכתו אשר ברא אלקים לעשות

...for on it He abstained from all His work which Hashem had created to do...

MIDDOS/ DERECH ERETZ
מידות/דרך ארץ

Two things Hashem considered creating before Shabbos, but He left them undone until Shabbos was over. Then, He imbued Adam with a wisdom that was almost Heavenly. Adam brought two stones and ground them together until fire emerged; he brought two animals and bred them together, and the mule was born (*Pesachim* 54a).

Why was everything created during the six days of Creation except for fire and the mule? And why were they created by man instead of directly by Hashem?

Rav Zalman Sorotzkin *zt"l* (*Azna'im L'Torah*) explains that this was done in order to comfort and encourage Adam in his grief, after he was removed from Gan Eden, by showing him that his purpose in life was to "create" new things from what already existed—to extract fire from stones, and a third species of an animal from two other ones. Hashem left room for man to develop, improve, and make use of everything that He had created. The reason why the two examples mentioned, fire and the mule, were singled out to be delegated to Adam at this point, is because the former (light) was the first thing created, and the latter (an animal) was the last thing created before man himself. This made it clear that man could refine and perfect everything created during the six days of Creation.

(בְּאַהֲבָה) מִקְרָא קֹדֶשׁ, זֵכֶר לִיצִיאַת מִצְרָיִם. כִּי בָנוּ בָחַרְתָּ וְאוֹתָנוּ קִדַּשְׁתָּ מִכָּל הָעַמִּים, וּדְבָרְךָ אֱמֶת וְקַיָּם לָעַד. בָּרוּךְ אַתָּה יְיָ, מְקַדֵּשׁ (בשבת: הַשַּׁבָּת וְ) יִשְׂרָאֵל וְיוֹם הַזִּכָּרוֹן.

ברוך אתה ה' אלקינו מלך העולם, בורא פרי הגפן

Blessed are You Hashem, our G-d, King of the world, Who creates fruit of the vine.

MIDDOS/ DERECH ERETZ
מידות/דרך ארץ

Wine is a unique drink. It contains both positive and negative qualities. On the one hand, wine is used for Kiddush, for *bentching*, and at a *simchah* celebration; it was even poured on the Altar in the Beis Hamikdash. It can elevate a Jewish soul when drunk in moderation and joy. On the other hand, wine can bring out the worst attributes in a human being. It causes one to lose himself in lustful pleasure, to use foul language, and speak of sinful ideas. When a person becomes drunk from wine, he will say and do things that he would never even consider if he were sober. Wine is the ultimate "double-edged sword."

Rav Baruch Sorotzkin ***zt"l*** delivers a brilliant insight: We find this concept when Yaakov and Eisav each brought food to their father Yitzchak. Yaakov brought a full meal of delicacies and with it, he brought wine. He recognized that for an auspicious occasion like the blessing of the *bechorah*, wine would elevate the proceedings and add joy to his father as he delivered the blessing. Eisav, though, knew wine for what it represented to him: an addictive alcoholic beverage which causes people to swear, curse, and act in shameful ways. In his mind, this drink had no place at his father's table while Yitzchak would be in the midst of performing this most meaningful ceremony on his behalf. For this reason, the *pasuk* makes no mention of any wine that Eisav brought to his father.

Similarly, a *nazir* is warned to refrain from wine. Since he is vulnerable to sin, and wine is a drink that can turn him the wrong way, he must remove himself from wine at all costs!

ותתן לנו ה' אלקינו באהבה את יום הזכרון הזה

And Hashem our G-d has given us, with love, this Day of Remembrance...

DVAR TORAH
דבר תורה

Three times a year, for Pesach, Shavuos, and Sukkos, the Jewish people were required to be *oleh regel*—to go up and celebrate Yom Tov in the Beis Hamikdash. Why is there no mitzvah to be *oleh regel* on Rosh Hashanah as well?

במוצאי שבת

בָּרוּךְ אַתָּה יְיָ אֱלֹהֵינוּ מֶלֶךְ הָעוֹלָם, בּוֹרֵא מְאוֹרֵי הָאֵשׁ.

בָּרוּךְ אַתָּה יְיָ, אֱלֹהֵינוּ מֶלֶךְ הָעוֹלָם, הַמַּבְדִּיל בֵּין קֹדֶשׁ לְחוֹל, בֵּין אוֹר לְחֹשֶׁךְ, בֵּין יִשְׂרָאֵל לָעַמִּים, בֵּין יוֹם הַשְּׁבִיעִי לְשֵׁשֶׁת יְמֵי הַמַּעֲשֶׂה. בֵּין

The **Sfas Emes, Rav Yehudah Aryeh Leib Alter** ***zt"l***, gives an explanation based on the Gemara *Rosh Hashanah* (26a): There are two things that are not permitted in the Beis Hamikdash due to the principle of אין קטיגור נעשה סניגור—*A prosecuting attorney cannot become a defense attorney*, and they are: wearing the golden vestments when the *kohen gadol* performs the Yom Kippur *avodah*, and blowing the horn of a cow as a shofar on Rosh Hashanah. Although the *kohen gadol* enters inside the Holy of Holies for the *avodah*, while the shofar is blown outside, the Gemara still equates the two. This is because the sound of the shofar is so effectual that Hashem "remembers" Klal Yisrael because of it, and bestows mercy upon them; thus, it is considered as if it was performed "inside," as well.

For this reason, we do not need to actually go up to the Beis Hamikdash on Rosh Hashanah; by properly performing the mitzvah of *tekiyas shofar*, it is deemed as if we are already בפנים—inside the Beis Hamikdash.

יום הזכרון הזה יום תרועה מקרא קודש זכר ליציאת מצרים

...this day of remembrance, a day for sounding the shofar, a day of holy assembly, commemorating the Exodus from Egypt...

MIDDOS/ DERECH ERETZ מידות/דרך ארץ

On this יום תרועה—Day of Sounding, we blow the shofar based on the *pasuk*, תקעו בחודש שופר. *Chazal* interpret this to mean: חדשו ושפרו מעשיכם—*Renew and improve your actions*. How do we renew our actions?

The **Meshech Chachmah, Rav Meir Simchah Hakohen** ***zt"l***, explains that if we bequeath to our children the importance of observing the Torah and its inherent values, we are renewing *Yiddishkeit*. The next generation's commitment to Torah will be as strong as if they themselves had received it. This is what *Chazal* meant when they said, *If someone teaches Torah to his grandchildren, it is as if they received it at Mount Sinai*. By educating their children to adhere to the Torah, parents will also improve their observance. When children stray from the Torah path, parents also become lax in their observance, for fear of becoming estranged from their sons and daughters. They often rationalize that their intentions are for the sake of Heaven, so that their children will still listen

קְדֻשַּׁת שַׁבָּת לִקְדֻשַּׁת יוֹם טוֹב הִבְדַּלְתָּ, וְאֶת יוֹם הַשְּׁבִיעִי מִשֵּׁשֶׁת יְמֵי הַמַּעֲשֶׂה קִדַּשְׁתָּ, הִבְדַּלְתָּ וְקִדַּשְׁתָּ אֶת עַמְּךָ יִשְׂרָאֵל בִּקְדֻשָּׁתֶךָ. בָּרוּךְ אַתָּה יְיָ, הַמַּבְדִּיל בֵּין קֹדֶשׁ לְקֹדֶשׁ.

בָּרוּךְ אַתָּה יְיָ אֱלֹהֵינוּ מֶלֶךְ הָעוֹלָם, שֶׁהֶחֱיָנוּ וְקִיְּמָנוּ וְהִגִּיעָנוּ לַזְּמַן הַזֶּה.

---

to them. Thus, when we train our children properly, we, too, will improve our conduct. חדשו מעשיכם—the renewal itself will engender שפרו מעשיכם—the improvement of our deeds.

The midrash quotes Rav Berachiah who said the converse: שפרו וחדשו מעשיכם—first improve your actions, and then renew them. If parents improve their Torah and mitzvah observance, their children will obey the Torah and be faithful to Hashem. Similarly, when children observe their parents neglecting minor laws, they will come to disobey even major ones. Thus, by enhancing our adherence (שפרו) to even the minute details, we maintain the new (חדשו), with *Yiddishkeit* practiced properly by the next generation.

(בשבת) יום זכרון תרועה באהבה מקרא קדש זכר ליציאת מצרים

...a day for the day of remembrance of sounding the shofar, with love, a day of holy assembly, commemorating the Exodus from Egypt.

MUSSAR/ HASHKAFAH
מוסר/השקפה

Chazal teach that the blowing of the shofar helps to confuse the *satan* so that he is no longer able to hurl accusations at us, and we then have a better chance for a favorable judgment. There is a halachah that if the first day of Rosh Hashanah falls out on Shabbos, we do not blow the shofar on that day. Rather, we blow the shofar only on the second day. The Gemara (*Rosh Hashanah* 29b) explains that there was concern that someone may mistakenly carry the shofar in a public domain and inadvertently violate the Shabbos. Thus, *Chazal* decreed that we would not blow the shofar when Rosh Hashanah falls out on Shabbos.

But how are we to understand this? In order to avoid a possible unintentional error, we are putting the entire nation in great danger! Without the shofar to stop the *satan*, we are defenseless against his accusations!

The great *baal mussar*, **Rav Yitzchak (Blazer) Peterburger** ***zt"l***, answers that the earlier generations had a much better understanding of the severity of sins, even accidental sins. They understood that the possibility of even one person committing a sin was far too great a risk. In their complete comprehension of the benefits of the

shofar blowing versus the possible violation of Shabbos, they determined that the risk was not worth the gain.

The message is clear. If this is the effect of a sin performed by mistake, how much more severe is a sin done deliberately! Now is the time to return to Hashem with humility and beg forgiveness for our past misdeeds. If we do this, we will hopefully merit a good year filled with blessing.

סימנים

Halachos Pertaining to the Yom Tov Table

HALACHAH
הלכה

Simanim. On the first night of Rosh Hashanah, it is customary to perform a number of *simanim*, positive omens, to augment the coming new year. The most important *siman* of them all, though, is not the edible kind, but rather the *siman* that comes from within each and every one of us. It is, in fact, the most essential of all: being pleasant, optimistic and creating a friendly environment. There should be no sharp or hostile comments during this time period, but only a "sweet-as-the-honey-on-the-table" atmosphere[1]. In that spirit, family members and guests should all wish each other a good, sweet year as is done in shul.

Anger on Rosh Hashanah. It is timely to mention the words of the ***Mishnah Berurah***[2] regarding getting angry on Rosh Hashanah. He says that we go to great lengths to eat special foods as a sign for a sweet new year. If these external signs can herald a good year, certainly being in a happy mood can enable much of the same, while anger can *chas v'shalom* do the opposite. One should guard himself well and curb any feelings of anger or distress on Rosh Hashanah as a good *siman* for the whole year.

Eating the *simanim*. When one recites *Ha'etz* on the fruit, he should have in mind to exempt the dessert if that will be a fruit item. One should eat small amounts of the *simanim* so as not to ruin his appetite for the rest of the meal. In general, one should not eat too much[3], in order to reflect the gravity of the day and also not to hinder the next day's *davening*.

1. מ"ב תקפג:ה
2. תקפג:ה
3. או"ח תקצז:א

When eating dates, one says:

יְהִי רָצוֹן מִלְּפָנֶיךָ ה׳ אֱלֹקֵינוּ וֵאלֹקֵי אֲבוֹתֵינוּ שֶׁיִּתַּמּוּ שׂוֹנְאֵינוּ

When eating apple in honey, one says:

יְהִי רָצוֹן מִלְּפָנֶיךָ ה׳ אֱלֹקֵינוּ וֵאלֹקֵי אֲבוֹתֵינוּ שֶׁתְּחַדֵּשׁ עָלֵינוּ שָׁנָה טוֹבָה וּמְתוּקָה

When eating leaks, one says:

יְהִי רָצוֹן מִלְּפָנֶיךָ ה׳ אֱלֹקֵינוּ וֵאלֹקֵי אֲבוֹתֵינוּ שֶׁיִּכָּרְתוּ שׂוֹנְאֵינוּ

Torah at the table. It is important that Torah thoughts about Rosh Hashanah and its *mitzvos* are spoken at the table. Some have a custom to learn the four chapters of *Mishnayos Rosh Hashanah* during the four meals of Rosh Hashanah[4].

What not to eat. The *poskim* cite the custom of not eating sour foods, such as fish cooked in vinegar[5], even though it might be tasty. Similarly, one should refrain from eating a sour fruit, like grapefruit. It would seem that if one sweetens it with sugar or honey, or puts lemon juice into a tea (being careful not to do *sechitah*) with plenty of sugar, it is permitted, since he does not taste an actual sour taste.

This custom of not eating sour foodshas spread to include sharp items, such as horseradish, as well. Although mayonnaise has some vinegar in it, it is not a sour item and can be put into tuna salads and the like, as one does all year round.

יְהִי רָצוֹן מִלְּפָנֶיךָ ה׳ אֱלֹקֵינוּ וֵאלֹקֵי אֲבוֹתֵינוּ שֶׁיִּתַּמּוּ שׂוֹנְאֵינוּ

May it be Your will, Hashem, our G-d and the G-d of our forefathers, that our enemies be consumed.

MASHAL
משל

משל: A low-ranking member of the king's court was accused of committing a terrible crime. The viceroy had been found murdered, and all signs pointed to this man's complicity in the crime. He was arrested and convicted.

To his surprise, however, rather than finding himself imprisoned in a dungeon, this low-ranking member was suddenly promoted! Soon he found himself in an important ministerial position. After a few short weeks, he was again promoted, and was now a senior member of the cabinet.

The man couldn't believe his good fortune. Instead of being punished, he was being rewarded!

4. אלף המטה תקפג:כג
5. מג"א תקפ"א

When eating beats, one says:

יְהִי רָצוֹן מִלְּפָנֶיךָ ה' אֱלֹקֵינוּ וֵאלֹקֵי אֲבוֹתֵינוּ שֶׁיִּסְתַּלְּקוּ שׂוֹנְאֵינוּ

When eating black-eyed peas (or carrots), one says:

יְהִי רָצוֹן מִלְּפָנֶיךָ ה' אֱלֹקֵינוּ וֵאלֹקֵי אֲבוֹתֵינוּ שֶׁיִּרְבּוּ זְכֻיּוֹתֵינוּ

It was not long before he rose to the highest office in the land—the position of viceroy. He reveled in his good fortune, and he relaxed in the knowledge that he was now the second most powerful person in the government. His arrogance and glory knew no bounds.

And then, at the height of his fame, he was suddenly arrested! He protested loudly, but to no avail. The king then ordered his execution. It was precisely at the point of the man's highest glory, when he believed himself to be so "high and mighty," that the king took his retribution and exacted punishment.

נמשל: This, explains **Rav Baruch of Kosov** ***zt"l***, is the meaning of the Gemara (*Gittin* 56b) that says, *Whoever harasses the Jewish people will attain leadership.* When Klal Yisrael sins and is in need of punishment, the Al-mighty raises an inferior nation and makes it great in order to subjugate the Jews. When the enemies feel mighty, that's when Hashem exacts His revenge against them in its most severe form.

יְהִי רָצוֹן מִלְּפָנֶיךָ ה' אֱלֹקֵינוּ וֵאלֹקֵי אֲבוֹתֵינוּ שֶׁתְּחַדֵּשׁ עָלֵינוּ שָׁנָה טוֹבָה וּמְתוּקָה

May it be Your will, Hashem, our G-d and the G-d of our forefathers, that You renew for us a good and a sweet year.

DRUSH
דרוש

On the night of Rosh Hashanah, there is a well-known custom to dip a piece of apple into honey. The *brachah* of *Borei Pri Ha'etz* is recited, and we add a prayer for a *shanah tovah u'mesukah*—a good and sweet year. One might think that the entire exercise is performed in order to stress upon us the "sweetness" of the new year; however, we do not make a *brachah* on the honey at all. Instead, we make the *brachah* on the apple, and the honey is simply added. Why? Because the apple is a symbol of life itself, since it comes from a tree, and Torah—our lifeblood—is called *eitz chaim*, the tree of life. While we may wish for a life filled with sweetness and happiness, the main object of our prayer is life itself! The *brachah* of *Borei Pri Ha'etz* that is recited indicates the main ingredient, the main focus of our prayers.

A student once came to the great founder of the Volozhiner yeshivah, **Rav Chaim Volozhiner** ***zt"l***, to ask his advice about a *shidduch*. He told the *rosh yeshivah* that a certain man had become extremely wealthy almost overnight and now desired the

When eating gourd, one says:

יְהִי רָצוֹן מִלְּפָנֶיךָ ה׳ אֱלֹקֵינוּ וֵאלֹקֵי אֲבוֹתֵינוּ שֶׁיִּקָּרַע גְּזַר דִּינֵנוּ וְיִקָּרְאוּ לְפָנֶיךָ זְכֻיּוֹתֵינוּ

When eating pomegranate, one says:

יְהִי רָצוֹן מִלְּפָנֶיךָ ה׳ אֱלֹקֵינוּ וֵאלֹקֵי אֲבוֹתֵינוּ שֶׁנִּרְבֶּה זְכֻיּוֹת כְּרִמּוֹן

---

best yeshivah student to marry his daughter. He promised the young man that he would support him and his bride in the very best lifestyle and would generously take care of all their needs. The only problem, explained the student, was that the man was extremely coarse and vulgar, despite his great wealth. What should he do?

R' Chaim replied with a story: "In Lithuania, there is a dish that is very popular: cucumbers fried in honey. And do you have any idea how this dish came about?" asked R' Chaim. The boy shook his head and R' Chaim smiled and said, "Well, I'll tell you. The cucumber very much desired to 'marry' the honey, so he sent a *shadchan* to propose the 'match.' The honey was very indignant and replied, 'How dare you even suggest such a match! The cucumber and I are complete opposites! I am so light, and he is so dark; I am so soft, and he is so hard; he is bitter, and I am sweet. How can there be any thought of a union between the two of us?'

"But the cucumber was very persistent. He promised to change his entire character to please the honey.

"'You say I am dark,' said the cucumber, 'so I will peel off my dark skin. You say I am hard; I will let myself be chopped up into small pieces. And to rid myself of my bitterness, I will let myself be fried in honey!'

"In the end, the honey consented, and they were joined together—in the frying pan. After the 'wedding,' the question arose as to which blessing should be made over the dish. Was it to be *Ha'adamah*, in which case the cucumber would be taking precedence? Or would it be *Shehakol*, for the honey? The majority opinion was that the cucumber was to be considered the main ingredient, and therefore, its blessing—*Ha'adamah*—would be the only one recited.

"And so you see," remarked R' Chaim to the yeshivah student, "even though the cucumber attempted to humble himself to please the honey, in the end he remained the dominant partner and his qualities are given precedence!"

From this, the young man drew his own conclusion, and he decided to refuse the rich man's proposal.

Thus, we see it is the *brachah* that reveals and determines that which is primary and that which is secondary. We first petition for life itself, reciting the *brachah* of

When eating fish, one says:

יְהִי רָצוֹן מִלְּפָנֶיךָ ה' אֱלֹקֵינוּ וֵאלֹקֵי אֲבוֹתֵינוּ שֶׁנִּפְרֶה וְנִרְבֶּה כַּדָּגִים

When eating head of a sheep (or fish), one says:

יְהִי רָצוֹן מִלְּפָנֶיךָ ה' אֱלֹקֵינוּ וֵאלֹקֵי אֲבוֹתֵינוּ שֶׁנִּהְיֶה לְרֹאשׁ וְלֹא לְזָנָב

Ha'etz on the apple, and only then do we beg for the "sugar coating," asking for a *shanah tovah u'mesukah* **(Rav Yitzchak Sender)**.

יְהִי רָצוֹן מִלְּפָנֶיךָ ה' אֱלֹקֵינוּ וֵאלֹקֵי אֲבוֹתֵינוּ שֶׁיִּכָּרְתוּ שׂוֹנְאֵינוּ

May it be Your will, Hashem, our G-d and the G-d of our forefathers, that our enemies be decimated.

The custom on the night of Rosh Hashanah is to eat leek, in the hopes that our enemies will be destroyed. The Hebrew word for leek is *karsi*, which retains the same source letters as *karas*, to be destroyed.

STORIES
מעשה

In the days immediately following the September 11, 2001 terror attacks in New York City, when Muslim fundamentalists made their intentions clear about unmercifully waging war and killing anyone whom they deemed to be a "non-believer," a grandson of the Mirrer Rosh Yeshivah, **Rav Shmuel Birnbaum** ***zt"l***, asked him the following question: What makes the Muslim concept of "Jihad" against their enemies so different from the Jewish concept of *mechiyas Amalek*, the Torah commandment to wipe out and eradicate any trace of the nation known as Amalek—men, women, and children included? Just as we must kill our eternal enemy, the nation of Amalek, unmercifully, the Muslim fundamentalists believe in their war with the same unrelenting zeal and passion.

R' Shmuel considered the question for only a short moment before answering, "How can one even consider comparing us to them? Why, to kill another human

Rav Meir Hurvitz ***zt"l*** **of Dzikov (*Imrei Noam*)** would say:

"On Rosh Hashanah, we dip a piece of apple in honey and say: *'May it be Your will to renew for us a good and sweet year.'* The *gematria* of the word תפוח (apple) amounts to 494, which equals the value of the words פרו רבו (be fruitful, multiply). Similarly, the word דבש (honey) is the same amount (306) as אשה (woman). We may derive from this that an apple dipped in honey on Rosh Hashanah is a *segulah* for a childless woman to conceive."

being in cold blood is the worst thing in the world, and no one has the right to take another human life on his own accord! The mitzvah of *mechiyas Amalek* is an obligation given to Klal Yisrael by *Hakadosh Baruch Hu* Himself, before hundreds of thousands of people who witnessed the great event of *Mattan Torah*. We did not make up this mitzvah, nor did we decide on our own to start killing people we do not like! There is no such thing in Klal Yisrael.

"The Muslims, however, kill people indiscriminately, because that's what they came up with as the best way to deal with those they do not like. And even if you'll say that it is written in their scriptures to kill and wage war, all that is based on the word of Mohammed, who 'claims' to have heard it from G-d. Who knows? Maybe he's lying! No one else was with him when he supposedly heard G-d's words, so there's no one who can attest to the truth of what he said. So his followers rely on his spoken word—and we rely on, *l'havdil*, the holy Torah!"

יְהִי רָצוֹן מִלְּפָנֶיךָ ה' אֱלֹקֵינוּ וֵאלֹקֵי אֲבוֹתֵינוּ שֶׁיִּסְתַּלְּקוּ שׂוֹנְאֵינוּ

May it be Your will, Hashem, our G-d and the G-d of our forefathers, that our adversaries be removed.

We eat *silka*, which is usually identified as beets. *Keter Shem Tov* says it refers to spinach. The word *siluk* means "to remove," and thus expresses our wish that this year our enemies should be removed.

REMEZ
רמז

יְהִי רָצוֹן מִלְּפָנֶיךָ ה' אֱלֹקֵינוּ וֵאלֹקֵי אֲבוֹתֵינוּ שֶׁיִּרְבּוּ זְכֻיּוֹתֵנוּ

May it be Your will, Hashem, our G-d and the G-d of our forefathers, that our merits increase.

We eat carrots or black-eyed peas. The Yiddish word for carrots is *mehren*, which means "more"; we are hoping for our merits to increase and become more and more in the eyes of Hashem. The custom to eat black-eyed peas is more Baghdadi. Peas are eaten as a symbol of abundance and fruitfulness, as in Aramaic, peas are known as *rubya*, which contains the root word *rov*, meaning "a lot."

REMEZ
רמז

Before eating *mehren* (carrots), we say, "May it be Your will that our merits increase." This gives rise to a question as to whether or not our merits increase depending on our own free will. If we do *mitzvos*, our merits increase automatically. Why then do we pray for increased merits?

A possible answer is based on the words of the **Rambam** (*Hilchos Teshuvah* 3-5), who says, *A person is not judged according to the number of merits and sins he has accrued, but rather according to the relative magnitude of his* mitzvos *and sins. He may have earned one merit that outweighs many sins, and he may have committed one sin that counterbalances numerous merits. Only G-d knows how to evaluate merits and transgressions.*

We therefore pray that the Holy One Blessed be He should attach greater weight to our good deeds. In light of the low moral climate of our generation, Hashem should rate our feeble merits as major virtues, for every good deed requires a great deal of effort and self-sacrifice on our part.

That is what we mean when we pray, "May it be Your will that our merits increase." We are asking that Hashem count our flimsy good deeds as great merits, in order to counterbalance our many sins.

יְהִי רָצוֹן מִלְּפָנֶיךָ ה' אֱלֹקֵינוּ וֵאלֹקֵי אֲבוֹתֵינוּ שֶׁיִּקָּרַע גְּזַר דִּינֵנוּ וְיִקָּרְאוּ לְפָנֶיךָ זְכוּיוֹתֵינוּ

May it be Your will, Hashem, our G-d and the G-d of our forefathers, that the decree of our sentence be torn asunder; and may our merits be proclaimed before You.

REMEZ
רמז

We eat gourds in the hopes that any evil decree against us be destroyed, and that our merits be proclaimed (rendering a favorable judgment). The Hebrew word for gourd is קרע (*k'ra*), which is also the word for 'tear/rip,' and which sounds like the word קרא (*kara*), meaning 'read/proclaim.'

שיקרע גזר דיננו ויקראו לפניך זכויותינו

MIDDOS/ DERECH ERETZ
מידות/דרך ארץ

Rav Eliyahu Dessler ***zt"l***, in ***Michtav M'Eliyahu*** (Chapter 5), makes a fascinating observation. He says that although a person spends the entire month of Elul involved in *teshuvah, tefillah* and *tzedakah*, and many other worthy endeavors, it is possible for one to fall on Rosh Hashanah—and have no clue why! He explains that there are specific negative traits that have the power to block *rachamei Shamayim* from reaching a person. One of those traits is not judging others favorably. We learn in *Pirkei Avos* (2:4) that one should not judge his friend until he has been in his place. Rav Dessler explains that "his place" means a combination of all of his circumstances, i.e. his family, personality, abilities, and so forth. Since nobody in the world has the exact same situation as another person, no one is allowed to judge the actions of someone else.

Judging favorably is not just a nice *middah*; it is one of the 613 commandments in the Torah. The *pasuk* states: *With righteousness shall you judge your friend*, and it is actually a halachic obligation which you can perform totally in your own mind. All you have to do is see people in a positive light. No other action is required! If someone's behavior is questionable, rather than castigate him, all you have to do is come up with an acceptable excuse and you have fulfilled the mitzvah! Not only that, but even if the excuse you came up with is not true, you still fulfill the mitzvah as long as you believe it and you have no negative feelings toward that person!

It is said in the name of the famous **Kotzker Rebbe *zt"l***, that everything in this world has a purpose, even distorted logic. It is meant to be used with a vivid imagination to figure out a way to get people off the hook and judge them favorably!

We must remember that Hashem works *middah k'negged middah*—measure for measure. Thus, if one will "sit in judgment" and look down at others, Hashem will sit on His Throne of Judgment looking carefully and even harshly at him. However, if one looks away from people's faults and focuses only on the positive, Hashem will do the exact same thing for him! So here's a bit of "legal" advice: Be smart and "hire" Hashem as your attorney for the Yom Hadin—by judging others favorably!

יְהִי רָצוֹן מִלְּפָנֶיךָ ה' אֱלֹקֵינוּ וֵאלֹקֵי אֲבוֹתֵינוּ שֶׁנִּרְבֶּה זְכֻיּוֹת כְּרִמּוֹן

May it be Your will, Hashem, our G-d and the G-d of our forefathers, that our merits increase as [the seeds of] a pomegranate.

REMEZ
רמז

We eat pomegranates on Rosh Hashanah in the hopes that our merits will be many and the Al-mighty Judge will see that we desire to fulfill His commandments. Pomegranates are known for their plentiful seeds, which are said to add up to 613. By eating the pomegranate, we are showing our desire to fulfill the 613 *mitzvos*.

In Mezhibuzh, the disciples of the **Baal Shem Tov *zt"l*** were *melamed zechus* and gave every Jew the benefit of the doubt. They ascribed holiness even to an ordinary Jew, citing the words of the Sages: *The transgressors in Israel are full of good deeds as a pomegranate with seeds* (*Eruvin* 19a).

In Kotzk, however, the interpretation was inverted. Here they translated this same dictum in the following manner: One can be as replete with *mitzvos* as a pomegranate is with seeds, and yet remain a transgressor in Israel.

The **Beis Avraham of Slonim *zt"l*** suggests yet another interpretation of the above maxim of our Sages. In commenting on the *pasuk*, *And my sin is always before me* (*Tehillim* 51:5), he explains that only those good deeds performed with thoroughly good intentions ascend to the Heavenly Tribunal to be recorded. Those done

halfheartedly remain here below. Good people perform *mitzvos* wholeheartedly, and their occasional misdeeds are done unintentionally; hence the good deeds ascend on High, and their transgressions remain below—before them. On the other hand, the wicked perform their occasional *mitzvos* without enthusiasm, and their sins with zest. Hence their good deeds remain below, and their transgressions ascend on High.

This is implied in the words: *The transgressors of Israel are full of good deeds.* In other words, the transgressors are full and left with their *mitzvos,* because having been performed without the proper spirit, these *mitzvos* do not ascend on High, but remain constantly with the transgressors on the earth below.

יְהִי רָצוֹן מִלְּפָנֶיךָ ה' אֱלֹקֵינוּ וֵאלֹקֵי אֲבוֹתֵינוּ שֶׁנִּהְיֶה לְרֹאשׁ וְלֹא לְזָנָב

May it be Your will, Hashem, our G-d and the G-d of our forefathers, that we be as the head and not as the tail.

REMEZ
רמז

It is customary to eat a sheep's head as a reminder of the ram that replaced Yitzchak at the *Akeidah.* We recite the prayer: "May it be Your will that we be as the head and not as the tail." (If a sheep's head is not available, the head of a chicken or fish may be substituted.)

A number of questions are raised on these words: Since we say, "that we be as the head," why is it necessary to mention the opposite, "and not as the tail," as well? If we are the head, we surely are not the tail! Moreover, why can't we simply say, "that we be the head," as opposed to "that we be *as* the head"? On top of that, why does each person say that he should "be as the head"? If everyone is a leader, whom would he lead?

The Apter Rav, Rav Avraham Yehoshua Heschel *zt"l* (Ohev Yisrael), would say:

"*And Hashem will place you to a head* (לראש) *and not to a tail* (לזנב). Why does the *pasuk* say לראש—'*to a head,*' and not ראש—'*as a head*'? Because being a head is not always advantageous. In *Avos* (4:20), Rav Masya ben Charash says that it is better for one to be a tail of a lion rather than a head of a fox. On a simple level, this means that it is better for one to be connected, even at the lowest level, to greatness, rather than to be at the highest level of mediocrity. Thus, the Torah says that Hashem will connect you 'to a head,' to greatness, rather than saying that Hashem will make you 'a head,' which could be construed as the 'head' of a fox (mediocrity), too—something we want to avoid."

The **Satmar Rebbe, Rav Yoel Teitelbaum** ***zt"l*** **(*Divrei Yoel*)**, provides an understanding of these words, based on a mishnah in *Avos D'Rabbi Nosson* (Ch. 30): *Rabbi Akiva says, "One who joins transgressors will be punished along with them, even if he himself does not join them in committing a sin."* It is safe to say that whoever joins people who do *mitzvos* will likewise be rewarded along with those people, even if he does not actually perform the particular mitzvah himself. One should, therefore, become a follower of the righteous *tzaddikim* and join together with them in all that they do.

Unfortunately, there are certain people who maintain a dual personality. When they are in the presence of a *tzaddik*, they try to demonstrate how devout they are, and become a part of the righteous man's camp. However, when they find themselves in the company of wicked evildoers, not only do they not object to the evil taking place, but they feel the need to befriend and emulate these wicked people in all that they do.

Now we may understand the seemingly redundant phrase. We ask Hashem to allow us to be a "head" and not a "tail," but not because we insist on being a leader. Rather, we are praying that Hashem assist us to commit our hearts to following His ways, and enable us to associate with *tzaddikim* who are the true "heads" of the people, so that we may also be righteous. At the same time, we also beg the Al-mighty that we should not be faced with the challenge of having to appease *resha'im*—the "tails"—by desiring to emulate them. As a result, this is truly a type of prayer that is appropriate for every individual to recite.

ונתנך ה' לראש ולא לזנב והיית רק למעלה ולא תהיה למטה (דברים כח-יג)

And Hashem will make you a head and not a tail; you will be on the top and not on the bottom.

What does this *pasuk* mean? Isn't it obvious that if you are on the top, you are not on the bottom?

DVAR TORAH
דבר תורה

Rav Tzadok Hakohen of Lublin ***zt"l*** cites *Divrei Hayamim I*, where there is a prayer by a man called Yaavetz. In this prayer, he says, *"If You (Hashem) will bless me and expand my borders..."* (4:10).

Rav Moshe Bick ***zt"l*** would say:

"The Torah tells us to be an ענו (a humble person), not a זנב (a tail)! We should be humble, but we should not debase ourselves to the point that we become like the tail of an animal."

Why does Yaavetz ask for both a blessing and then an expansion? Surely a blessing includes an expansion.

Many people receive great blessing, but they are ill-equipped to handle that blessing. This is a common occurrence among celebrities: someone of prominence can earn an astronomical amount of money at the peak of his career, yet by the time he retires, can often be broke, scorned and disgraced, because he did not deal wisely with the fame and fortune he was given. This, then, is the prayer of Yaavetz: May Hashem bless me, but also expand me as a person so that I am able to handle that blessing.

R' Tzadok says that this is seen in the famous statement of *Chazal*: עשר בשביל שתתעשר—*Tithe so that you become wealthy* (*Taanis* 9a). People think this means that as soon as one gives charity, the riches will come flying in through the door. But that is not so. Rather, it means that when one gives *maaser* (a tenth) to *tzedakah*, and consequently more people become dependent on him, then he will have to become a "bigger" person, so to speak, and Hashem will make sure he has enough to give to those people. The more one makes himself available to others, the more he is given in order to handle it.

This is the meaning of the *pasuk*: *You will be on the top*—Hashem will give you gifts. Then there is the second blessing, *and not on the bottom*. This means that Hashem will expand you, so that you'll be able to handle the blessings. You won't become stingy and head toward disaster because of them. The blessings will not cause you to fall.

יְהִי רָצוֹן מִלְּפָנֶיךָ ה' אֱלֹקֵינוּ וֵאלֹקֵי אֲבוֹתֵינוּ שֶׁנִּפְרֶה וְנִרְבֶּה כַּדָּגִים

May it be Your will, Hashem, our G-d and the G-d of our forefathers, that we be fruitful and multiply like fish.

Why do we eat fish on Rosh Hashanah? In the hopes that we will be fruitful and multiply like fish in the coming year. This should be in fulfillment of the *brachah* which Yaakov Avinu blessed his grandchildren, Menashe and Ephraim: וידגו לרב בקרב הארץ—*May they multiply abundantly like fish in the land.*

REMEZ
רמז

There is a question with this. Although fish are a symbol of abundance and fertility, fish do not roam the land! They must remain in the sea in order to exist. What, then, is the understanding of Yaakov's blessing?

The **Chasam Sofer, Rav Moshe Sofer** ***zt"l***, explains that the blessing of Yaakov Avinu—and, in fact, the blessing that each one of us hopes to merit in the coming year—is one of miraculous existence. Although our enemies are always looking to destroy us from without, while our enemy from within—the *yetzer hara*—works his

insidious schemes in order to bring us down, Hashem nevertheless maintains us and protects us from all harm. This protection is as miraculous as the preservation of fish on land!

It is this blessing that we hope to attain: Just as fish living in the land is extraordinary and unnatural, so too, may our existence continue miraculously through the hand of Hashem, with extraordinary kindness and prosperity.

תקיעת שופר

LISTENING TO THE CALL OF THE SHOFAR

HALACHAH
הלכה

The *mitzvah d'Oraisa* of *tekiyas shofar* on Rosh Hashanah is the obligation of every person to hear the first thirty blows of the shofar. There is also a Rabbinical commandment to hear the sound of the shofar during *chazaras hashatz* of the *Mussaf tefillah*[1]. In certain congregations, the shofar is blown during the silent *Shemoneh Esrei* as well.

The *zman* of *tekiyas shofar* is a critical time. The *sefarim* mention that the main judgment takes place right then, according to each person's spiritual level and commitment at that exact moment. Thus, it is quite appropriate for each and every person to prepare himself beforehand to make good use of this awesome time by:

1) Making appropriate resolutions for the coming year.

2) Understanding the shofar's message.

Relevant *Halachos* to Properly Observe the Mitzvah

1. One is required to hear the entire blow of the shofar, even if it stretches out for more than the minimal length[2]. One should be careful not to begin the *Yehi Ratzon* (said at the first set of *tekiyos*, although others say a *vidui*) and *Hayom Haras Olam* (said during *chazaras hashatz* after the blowing) until the final blast has ended. Some shuls announce this beforehand.
2. It is preferable for one to be aware which *tekiyah* (straight, unbroken blow) is being blown at all times, whether it is the one before the *teruah* or the one after[3].

1. או"ח תקצ:א
2. משנה ברורה תקצב:י
3. עיין שער הציון תקצ:כג

3. One should stand during the *tekiyos* without leaning[4].
4. One may not speak (besides the prescribed *tefillos*) until the last of the 100 *tekiyos* at the end of *Mussaf* have been sounded[5]. A common error that must be avoided is when people say "*yasher koach*" to the *kohanim* after *Birkas Kohanim.* Saying *Asher Yatzar* after using the restroom is permitted.
5. Eating before hearing the shofar is debatable. There is a way to permit it according to all opinions. If one appoints a *shomer* who has no intention of going out to eat, and tells him, "If I'm not back at such-and-such time, please come and get me," he is then permitted to go out and eat—since we are then not afraid that he will get "lost" in his eating and miss his mitzvah.

If the custom is to blow during the silent *Shemoneh Esrei*, one should stop at the set place and not continue until the blowing is done. If he is behind, he should stop wherever he is and listen when the shofar is blown.

STORIES
מעשה

The story is told about one of the foremost Torah scholars of his day, the **Rebbe Rav Heschel of Cracow *zt"l*,** who as a child was known as a prodigy, with wisdom and wit that were characteristic of one far beyond his years.

Once, on Rosh Hashanah, his father found him eating sweets and goodies in the morning, in violation of the accepted practice that a person should not put any food in his mouth before the sounding of the shofar. His father chastised him, "Heschel, don't you know that we are careful not to eat any food before the blowing of the shofar?"

The bright child was quick to defend himself. "We know that during the entire month of Elul, the shofar is blown each and every morning after we *daven* Shacharis. However, we do not blow the shofar on the day before Rosh Hashanah. Why not? In order to confuse the *satan*, so that he will not anticipate the shofar being sounded on Rosh Hashanah, and will therefore not be in a proper position to present his incriminations against Bnei Yisrael before the Heavenly Tribunal.

"I, too," continued the smooth-tongued public defender, "wish to do my best to confuse the *satan*. He knows that Jews are careful not to eat anything before hearing the blasts of the shofar. So when he observes me eating, he must then conclude that he had to have been mistaken in his calculations, and that today is not Rosh Hashanah, after all. In this way, I am helping to protect my people by preventing the

4. או"ח תקפה:א
5. חיי אדם קמא:ט

לַמְנַצֵּחַ ׀ לִבְנֵי־קֹרַח מִזְמוֹר: כָּל־הָעַמִּים תִּקְעוּ־כָף הָרִיעוּ לֵאלֹהִים בְּקוֹל רִנָּה: כִּי־יְיָ עֶלְיוֹן נוֹרָא מֶלֶךְ גָּדוֹל עַל־כָּל־הָאָרֶץ: יַדְבֵּר עַמִּים תַּחְתֵּינוּ וּלְאֻמִּים תַּחַת רַגְלֵינוּ: יִבְחַר־לָנוּ אֶת־נַחֲלָתֵנוּ

---

harsh accusations and incriminations of the *satan*, and they will be spared his evil schemes!"

R' Heschel, in his later years, conceded that indeed, this was superb reasoning for a child. However, he noted that we must be careful not to similarly justify all the myriad "goodies" life has to offer.

כל־העמים תקעו־כף הריעו לאלקים בקול רנה

All peoples clap hands, shout to Hashem with the voice of joyous song.

MUSSAR/HASHKAFAH
מוסר/השקפה

The Torah speaks about the תרועה, the loud shofar blast that was used to call people together for all kinds of holy purposes. The shofar was blown to call men to join the battle and fight the wars of Hashem. It was used as a form of prayer so that people should *daven* in times of trouble. The shofar was what announced the upcoming *shalosh regalim*, and of course, the shofar was blown on Rosh Hashanah, to incite the people to *teshuvah*.

The word *teruah* literally translates as a loud noise, a cheer or shout. The lesson of the *teruah* that is blown at auspicious times in Jewish life is that when it comes to service of Hashem, the proper way to serve our Creator is with a great tumult! This is akin to how the angels sing *shirah*. Every day in *davening* we recall how the angels sing in a *kol ra'ash gadol*—they make a lot of noise—for when it comes to expressing our love for Hashem, we are supposed to make a loud noise, to scream and shout and reverberate with excitement.

Look at the secular world and what they get excited about. A man takes a bat and hits a ball, and everyone stands and screams. **Rav Avigdor Miller *zt"l*** says that it is a gathering of *meshuga'im*! A horse runs around a track or a car drives in circles for hours and hours—and everyone starts screaming. Over what? Over nothing!

Let us not be swept up in the excitement of nonsense. Why should we scream and carry on for nothing? Let's remember the one thing that truly makes sense. The only thing worth shouting about is Hashem!

אֶת גְּאוֹן יַעֲקֹב אֲשֶׁר־אָהֵב סֶלָה: עָלָה אֱלֹהִים בִּתְרוּעָה יְיָ בְּקוֹל
שׁוֹפָר: זַמְּרוּ אֱלֹהִים זַמֵּרוּ זַמְּרוּ לְמַלְכֵּנוּ זַמֵּרוּ: כִּי מֶלֶךְ כָּל־הָאָרֶץ

ידבר עמים תחתינו ולאמים תחת רגלינו

He subdues people under us, and nations under our feet.

משל: In czarist Russia, a little more than two hundred years ago, the Russian crown was investigating the great **Baal HaTanya, Rav Shneur Zalman of Liadi *zt"l***, on trumped-up charges of treason. He was arrested and led through the courtyard of the Russian compound to a brutal interrogation. A few children of the royal family were playing there as well. Amongst them was young Nikolai, brother to the czar and a cruel child by nature, who later assumed the Russian throne himself.

Nikolai had a whip on him. As the rebbe was being led by, the boy boldly held up his whip as if to threaten the rebbe. The rebbe focused his gaze on the cruel child.

Suddenly, Nikolai felt himself becoming afraid of the prisoner. He dropped his whip and averted his gaze. Nikolai later commented to his tutor that he never before experienced such fear as when the prisoner looked at him.

Years later, the **Tzemach Tzedek** commented that if not for his grandfather's stern gaze at Nikolai when he was a child, which weakened Nikolai's boldness, the Jews of Russia would have simply buckled under the weight of his harsh decrees.

נמשל: The nations of the world are arrogant and assume that they can take advantage of the Jewish people, since the Jews are a nation of so few. But when *Hakadosh Baruch Hu* decides that the time has come to show His might and protect His most beloved, He does so by injecting a fear and dread into those who wish to do His nation harm. One stern warning from the Al-mighty is enough to weaken their power and allow Bnei Yisrael to survive.

עלה אלקים בתרועה ה' בקול שופר

Hashem has ascended with a blast, Hashem, with the sound of the shofar.

Bnei Yisrael are commanded to blow the shofar to rouse the people in the event that an enemy attacks them, as is stated in *Bamidbar* (10:9): *If war shall come into your land, against the oppressor who oppresses you, and you shall blow* teruahs *with the trumpets, and you will be remembered...* However, in *Parshas Ki Seitzei* (21:10), when it talks about the Jews waging war against their enemies (*When you will go*

אֱלֹהִים זַמְּרוּ מַשְׂכִּיל: מָלַךְ אֱלֹהִים עַל־גּוֹיִם אֱלֹהִים יָשַׁב | עַל־כִּסֵּא קָדְשׁוֹ: נְדִיבֵי עַמִּים | נֶאֱסָפוּ עַם אֱלֹהֵי אַבְרָהָם כִּי לֵאלֹהִים מָגִנֵּי־אֶרֶץ מְאֹד נַעֲלָה:

---

forth to war against your enemies, and Hashem, your G-d, puts them in your hand...), no mention is made of the blowing of the shofar. This is because seemingly there would be no need for it then, as the enemy would be routed easily and given over to Bnei Yisrael.

The holy **Kotzker, Rav Menachem Mendel of Kotzk** *zt"l*, explains that this is simple logic. If the people are going forth to wage war, assailing the enemy with an offensive-minded attack, they have this as an advantage, and it will help them attain victory in an easier manner. But if the enemy invades the Jews' land to attack *them*, the Jews are then at a disadvantage and need any and all means to rally the troops, build morale, and beat back the invaders. Thus, in the case *when you will go forth to war*, attacking the enemy in their lands, Hashem will make it easy and give the enemy over to your hands with minimal risk. If, however, the enemy becomes the aggressor and *war shall come into your land*, it is then that the shofar is needed to impress upon the people the urgency of the situation and rally them to victory.

In our everyday battle against the *yetzer hara*, the same formula holds true. If one can hold off his primal desires, and disallow them from consuming him, he'll win the battle easily. If, however, his urges have already overcome him, he then requires extra support and protection to rally and beat them back.

מן־המצר קראתי קה ענני במרחב קה

From the narrowness (of distress) I called to Hashem; He answered me with the breadth of Divine relief.

STORIES
מעשה

How does one go about fashioning a shofar and blowing it on Rosh Hashanah in a Nazi concentration camp? Where does one even find a shofar in the depths of gehinnom? To the holy rebbe of Radoshitz, **Rav Yitzchak'l Finkler** ***zt"l Hy"d***, the question was not how does one blow a shofar, but rather, how does one *not* blow a shofar on Rosh Hashanah!

The year was 1943. Rosh Hashanah was rapidly approaching, and R' Yitzchak'l of Radoshitz had decided that he would definitely fulfill the mitzvah of blowing the shofar on Rosh Hashanah, even under the horrible conditions in the Skarszysko concentration camp. When he told this to his fellow inmates, they looked at him

חו"ק

מִן־הַמֵּצַר קָרָאתִי יָּהּ עָנָנִי בַמֶּרְחָב יָהּ:
קוֹלִי שָׁמָעְתָּ אַל תַּעְלֵם אָזְנְךָ לְרַוְחָתִי לְשַׁוְעָתִי:
רֹאשׁ־דְּבָרְךָ אֱמֶת וּלְעוֹלָם כָּל־מִשְׁפַּט צִדְקֶךָ:
עֲרֹב עַבְדְּךָ לְטוֹב אַל־יַעַשְׁקֻנִי זֵדִים:

incredulously. "Blow the shofar? Here, in a concentration camp? It can't be done. Besides, Rebbe, we don't have a shofar!"

The rebbe replied calmly, "It can be done, and it will be done! I ask only for your help and cooperation."

The men who were close to R' Yitzchak'l and revered him as a *tzaddik* agreed to gather a small sum of money. With this, they bribed a Polish worker who lived outside the camp to bring them the head of a horned animal. To their great distress, however, he brought the head of an ox, whose horns may not be used for a shofar.

The inmates were crushed. They had used up most of their resources and had nothing to show for it. But the rebbe was undaunted. Disregarding the men's strong protests due to the dangers involved, he encouraged them to try again. This time, for a second fee, the Polish worker smuggled in the head of a ram. The rebbe was overjoyed.

But who would know how to make a shofar from the ram's horns? And who would undertake such a dangerous assignment? And where would he get the necessary tools? The task seemed impossible in the slave labor camp.

The rebbe remembered a former chassid of his, Moshe Naichatchitsky, who used to *daven* in his *shtiebel* and who now worked in the metal workshop of the camp. When the rebbe spoke to Moshe and outlined his plan, Moshe began to tremble, for every step of the way, he knew, would be filled with grave peril. Nor did he have the faintest idea of how to fashion a ram's horn into a shofar. But when he saw R' Yitzchak'l standing in front of him, with tears in his eyes, begging him to enable the poor Jews to fulfill this holy mitzvah, how could he possibly refuse? The rebbe promised him that if he accepted this perilous assignment, he would survive the war.

Somehow, Moshe was indeed successful. Shortly before Rosh Hashanah, he presented R' Yitzchak'l with a finished, completely kosher shofar. The rebbe's joy knew no bounds. On the morning of Rosh Hashanah, 5704, the rebbe's barracks was filled with Jews who wanted to join with him in his *minyan*, to *daven* with him, and to hear him blow shofar. The rebbe recited *Min Hameitzar* in a choked voice, and then sounded his precious shofar.

One of those present in the barracks at that time, R' Avraham Altman, later gave his impression of these events.

שָׂשׂ אָנֹכִי עַל־אִמְרָתֶךָ כְּמוֹצֵא שָׁלָל רָב׃
טוּב טַעַם וָדַעַת לַמְּדֵנִי כִּי בְמִצְוֺתֶיךָ הֶאֱמָנְתִּי׃
נִדְבוֹת פִּי רְצֵה־נָא יְיָ וּמִשְׁפָּטֶיךָ לַמְּדֵנִי׃

"What shall I say? For me, it was like the assembly at Har Sinai at the time of *Mattan Torah.* Don't laugh or ridicule me. This is how I felt then, and this is how many people who participated in that holy gathering felt."

Moshe Naichatchitsky did indeed survive the war. He moved to Israel, where he married the rebbe's youngest daughter, the only member of that great *tzaddik's* family to survive the Holocaust. After searching tirelessly, he located his precious shofar which had been lost for many years. The shofar today resides in the Yad Vashem Archives in Jerusalem.

ערב עבדך לטוב אל־יעשקני זדים

Be surety for Your servant for good; let me not be oppressed by insolent sinners.

REMEZ
רמז

The **Noam Elimelech, Rav Elimelech of Lizhensk** ***zt"l***, quotes the Gemara (*Kiddushin* 20a): *Whoever acquires a Jewish servant, acquires a master for himself.* What the Gemara means by this is that a master may not just benefit from the work of his servant; he must ensure his servant's welfare by providing for him fully—feeding, clothing, and housing him, and seeing to all of his needs, as the *pasuk* (*Devarim* 16:16) states: *For it is good for him with you.*

Thus, Hashem, Who has *acquired His servants in judgment,* must take pity on His people. As per the halachah, He is "required" to see to the provisions of the Jewish people and to their continued well-being throughout the coming year.

שש אנכי על אמרתך כמוצא שלל רב

I am happy with Your word like one who finds great gain.

MIDDOS/
DERECH ERETZ
מידות/דרך ארץ

The *navi* declares: *The enjoyment of Hashem is your strength* (*Nechemiah* 8:10). This pertains to us in the following way:

Any Rosh Hashanah, even the fifteenth of Shevat, the New Year of the trees, is a joyous Yom Tov. How much more so is the first day of Tishrei, which is the anniversary of the entire world, considered joyous!

On the other hand, writes the **Chasam Sofer, Rav Moshe Sofer** ***zt"l***, Rosh Hashanah also has the aura of fear, of judgment, of seriousness, and it is the first of the Aseres Yemei Teshuvah. If we do not do *teshuvah* now, when will we do it? It would seem to be appropriate for us to weep and pray for mercy and compassion on Rosh Hashanah. However, instead, we, Bnei Yisrael, announce, "Let us not be sad when Hashem, our holy King, rejoices on His royal anniversary. Let us rejoice with Him, no matter what will happen to us."

This attitude arouses Divine compassion even more than a string of fast days, for Hashem sees that the Jewish people are more concerned with honoring Him than with asking for mercy for themselves. He is overjoyed with our actions. This is what the Gemara in *Rosh Hashanah* (15a) means when it says: *The Holy One Blessed be He says, "Declare Me as your King, in order that your memory will rise up before Me for goodness."* It is because we rejoice with Hashem on this day that He "remembers" us for good. Indeed, *"the enjoyment of Hashem is your strength!"*

טוב טעם ודעת למדני כי במצותיך האמנתי

Good [Torah] reasoning and knowledge teach me, for in Your commandments I have believed.

MASHAL
משל

משל: During the period of British rule over Eretz Yisrael, many young people who dared to fight the British were arrested and sent to the infamous Latrun Prison. The only person who regularly visited these prisoners, who encouraged them and lifted their spirits during the most trying times of their lives, was **Rav Aryeh Levine** ***zt"l***, the "*tzaddik* of Yerushalayim." He would pray with the prisoners and learn Torah with them. His words of encouragement, coming straight from his heart, entered the hearts of his listeners. He treated the prison inmates like beloved children, and the prisoners treated him like a dear father. It is no wonder that R' Aryeh was commonly referred to as the "father of prisoners."

One morning, R' Aryeh arrived at the prison and presented his pass to the British soldier stationed there. To his surprise, though, the soldier refused him access. An on-duty Jewish guard was present and said, "Why do you not let the rabbi enter? All he wants to do is assist the prisoners and lift their spirits. Plus, he has an official pass."

The British soldier was mean and spiteful and barked at the guard, "His pass is worthless in my eyes! As for all of his 'help'—I have no doubt that he is getting paid by some organization somewhere for his 'selfless' actions. Otherwise, why would he keep coming back so often?" The soldier snorted dismissively. "Tell the rabbi to go home and find another way to earn some money! He's finished here!"

ויאמר התוקע קודם התקיעות:

עָלָה אֱלֹהִים בִּתְרוּעָה ה׳ בְּקוֹל שׁוֹפָר:

בָּרוּךְ אַתָּה ה׳ אֱלֹהֵינוּ מֶלֶךְ הָעוֹלָם אֲשֶׁר קִדְּשָׁנוּ בְּמִצְוֹתָיו
וְצִוָּנוּ לִשְׁמוֹעַ קוֹל שׁוֹפָר:

בָּרוּךְ אַתָּה ה׳ אֱלֹהֵינוּ מֶלֶךְ הָעוֹלָם שֶׁהֶחֱיָנוּ וְקִיְּמָנוּ וְהִגִּיעָנוּ לַזְּמַן הַזֶּה:

תקיעה שברים תרועה תקיעה:
תקיעה שברים תרועה תקיעה:
תקיעה שברים תרועה תקיעה:

יְהִי רָצוֹן מִלְּפָנֶיךָ שֶׁתְּקִיעַת קש״ק שֶׁאֲנַחְנוּ תּוֹקְעִים שֶׁתַּעֲשֶׂה עֲטָרָה מִמֶּנָּה לִהְיוֹת עוֹלֶה וְיוֹשֵׁב בְּרֹאשׁ אֱלֹהֵי הַצְּבָאוֹת וְיַעֲשֶׂה עִמָּנוּ אוֹת לְטוֹבָה וְתִמָּלֵא עָלֵינוּ בְּרַחֲמִים:
בָּרוּךְ אַתָּה בַּעַל הָרַחֲמִים:

R' Aryeh didn't say a word. He just turned around and walked away. But rather than head back home, he walked around the prison walls to another entrance, where he presented his pass to the guard stationed there and was immediately allowed entry. He then proceeded to the hall where the inmates were kept and began his usual rounds.

At one point during the day, R' Aryeh was walking from one building inside the compound to another, when he came across the same British soldier that had refused him entry in the morning. The soldier was surprised at first, but after a moment, he became philosophical.

"This rabbi is really something," he commented to his fellow soldier. "He truly gives of his time and does not expect a thing in return. For had he been receiving some sort of remuneration for his visit, he would surely not have exerted himself to get inside the prison walls after I refused to let him in earlier today. He would have gone home, happy not to have to do any work. The fact that he didn't leave proves that his intentions are pure!"

נמשל: Chacham Rabbeinu Yehudah Tzadka *zt"l* would use this story as an example to explain why we specifically blow the horn of a ram on Rosh Hashanah to show the greatness of *Akeidas Yitzchak*, as opposed to symbolizing the magnitude of the *Akeidah* with another object, like the knife that Avraham used to sacrifice the ram: The act of binding his son on the mountaintop, in and of itself, does not prove Avraham's faithfulness or self-sacrifice to Hashem, for perhaps he only did so out of fear that

תקיעה שברים תקיעה:

תקיעה שברים תקיעה:

תקיעה שברים תקיעה:

יְהִי רָצוֹן מִלְּפָנֶיךָ שֶׁתְּקִיעַת קר"ק שֶׁאֲנַחְנוּ תּוֹקְעִים הַיּוֹם תְּהֵא מְרֻקֶּמֶת בִּירִיעָה עַל יְדֵי הַמְּמֻנֶּה (טרטיא"ל) כְּשֵׁם שֶׁקִּבַּלְתָּ עַל יְדֵי אֵלִיָּהוּ זָכוּר לַטּוֹב וממט"ט שַׂר הַפָּנִים וְתִמָּלֵא עָלֵינוּ בְּרַחֲמִים: בָּרוּךְ אַתָּה בַּעַל הָרַחֲמִים:

תקיעה תרועה תקיעה:

תקיעה תרועה תקיעה:

תקיעה תרועה תקיעה גדולה:

ויתודה בלחש ואח"כ יאמר זה: יְהִי רָצוֹן מִלְּפָנֶיךָ ה' אֱלֹהֵינוּ וֵאלֹהֵי אֲבוֹתֵינוּ שֶׁיַּעֲלוּ אֵלּוּ הַמַּלְאָכִים הַיּוֹצְאִים מִן הַשּׁוֹפָר וּמִן הַתְּקִיעָה וּמִן הַשְּׁבָרִים וּמִן הַתְּרוּעָה וּמִן תשר"ת וּמִן תש"ת וּמִן תר"ת לִפְנֵי כִּסֵּא כְבוֹדֶךָ וְיַמְלִיצוּ טוֹב בַּעֲדֵנוּ וְתֵעָשֶׂה עִמָּנוּ אוֹת לְטוֹבָה: וּתְמַלֵּא עָלֵינוּ בְּרַחֲמִים בָּרוּךְ אַתָּה בַּעַל הָרַחֲמִים:

Hashem would punish him if he didn't. No, said the Chacham, the proof of Avraham's loyalty was in the fact that after the angel told him not to kill his son, Avraham did not immediately race home out of joy that his son was spared. Rather, he looked around and found a ram which he offered up as a *korban* to Hashem. He refused to leave until he brought a sacrifice—any sacrifice—to his Creator. This proved the extent of his *avodas Hashem*. For this reason, we use a shofar—the horn of a ram—to indicate that Avraham's pure intentions were even greater than his actions.

וימליצו טוב בעדנו ותעשה עמנו אות לטובה. ותמלא עלינו ברחמים

And may he advocate good on our behalf, and You will make with us a sign for good. And you will fill us up with mercy.

DVAR TORAH
דבר תורה

Rashi (*Rosh Hashanah* 16a) explains that the reason why the Torah commands us to blow the shofar (תוקעין) and also to sound the *shofar* (מריעין) is to confound the *satan*, who, upon seeing how the Jews perform the *mitzvos* with an intense love, will be unable to prosecute.

Rav Akiva Eiger *zt"l* adds the following: *Chazal* tell us that when a person sincerely repents out of love, rather than fear, of *Hakadosh Baruch Hu*, his repentance transforms his sins into merits. Thus, when the *satan* will see how the Jewish people are performing Hashem's commandments with

אַשְׁרֵי הָעָם יוֹדְעֵי תְרוּעָה יְיָ בְּאוֹר־פָּנֶיךָ יְהַלֵּכוּן:
בְּשִׁמְךָ יְגִילוּן כָּל־הַיּוֹם וּבְצִדְקָתְךָ יָרוּמוּ:
כִּי־תִפְאֶרֶת עֻזָּמוֹ אָתָּה וּבִרְצֹנְךָ תָּרִים [תָּרוּם] קַרְנֵנוּ:

---

such an intense love, he will not want to mention all of their iniquities in front of the Heavenly Court, since by doing so all of their sins will be converted into merits on their behalf!

אשרי העם יודעי תרועה ה׳ באור פניך יהלכון וגו׳

Fortunate is the nation who knows the sound of the teruah;
Hashem, in the light of Your presence they walk.

DRUSH
דרוש

There was once a man who was well-regarded as a most proficient *baal tokei'a*. He blew the shofar flawlessly in his synagogue for many years. Unfortunately, he began to develop doubts about his religion and, with the help of his non-Jewish friends and business associates, he eventually converted out of the faith of his forefathers, ר"ל.

As a musical individual, he would often get together with other musicians to play music and discuss new developments in that industry. Once, as he and some musician friends were sitting around discussing instruments, he mentioned that he could play an instrument that no one else had ever seen before: a ram's horn!

Rav Menachem Mendel Morgenstern *zt"l* (Kotzker Rebbe) would say:

"On this holy day, all of our deeds must be *l'shem Shamayim* (for Heaven's sake). Even our *l'shem Shamayim* must be *l'shem Shamayim*!"

Rav Simchah Bunim of Peshischah *zt"l* would say:

"If a person does not have *parnassah*, I understand how he lives—on *emunah* and *bitachon*. But I don't understand how a person who has all that he needs lives!"

The others asked how one went about playing a ram's horn, and by way of an answer, the man produced his old trusty shofar. Excitedly, he began blowing beautiful long blasts, and indeed, his cohorts were impressed.

First, the man blew one long blast—*tekiyah*, and then a series of three shorter sounds—a *shevarim*. But when he attempted to do a *teruah*—nine quick staccato-like blows, nothing came out! He tried and tried, but as well as he could produce the other sounds, he was totally incapable of sounding out the call of the *teruah*.

Something was amiss, and he knew it. He also knew who he could turn to with his problem. Eyes downcast, he made his way to the home of the old *chacham*, **Rabbeinu Avraham Yachini *zt"l*.** "Tell me, Chacham," he asked, "why am I unable to produce the sound of the *teruah*?"

Rabbeinu Avraham knew this man and how he had turned his back on his faith. He answered sharply, "Why, Dovid Hamelech clearly answers this in a *pasuk* in *Tehillim*: *Praiseworthy is the nation that knows [how to] sound the* teruah*; Hashem, in the light of Your presence they walk*. When you decided not to walk in the light of Hashem and His presence, you immediately lost the ability to '*know how to sound the* teruah.'"

The heretic was troubled by this. "But I am able to blow the *tekiyah* and *shevarim*. Why are they different from the *teruah*?"

The *chacham* replied, "Our great Sages have taught us that the three sounds of the shofar correspond to the three *Avos*—Avraham, Yitzchak, and Yaakov. The *tekiyah* alludes to Avraham Avinu; the *shevarim* to Yitzchak Avinu; and the *teruah* to Yaakov Avinu. Now, the nations of the world have the ability to harness the power of the *tekiyah*, since Avraham had two sons, one of which—Yishmael—created a large and indigenous nation of his own. The *shevarim*, too, is within the grasp of non-Jewish people, since Yitzchak Avinu fathered Eisav, the progenitor and predecessor of many nations. It is only Yaakov Avinu who is described as '*his bed is complete*'; in other words, all of his children followed in the ways of their holy father. Yaakov Avinu's twelve sons, the twelve tribes of Israel, brought forth our great nation. Thus, the *teruah* sound, which corresponds to Yaakov Avinu, is a sound that can only resonate within the realm of his children, the Bnei Yisrael!"

Tears welled up in the man's eyes. He now understood what he had not before: that the religion he had been born into was the true and authentic one, and that he had been sorely mistaken and misled.

He fled to a distant place, far away from all of his gentile friends and cronies, and repented for his sins. He became a *baal teshuvah*, and now, when he picked up his shofar to blow, he produced a *teruah* so perfect that he knew that he had come back to his people.

אשרי העם יודעי תרועה ה' באור פניך יהלכון וגו' (תהילים פט-טז)

Fortunate is the nation who knows the sound of the teruah;
Hashem, in the light of Your presence they walk.

DVAR TORAH
דבר תורה

The midrash writes: *"Fortunate is the nation who knows the sound of the* teruah.*" Does no other nation besides the Jews know how to blow [the shofar]? They have their own rams and their own horns. The difference is that the Jews know how to convince the Al-mighty with their blowing...and it fills Him with mercy so that He turns His attribute of judgment into an attribute of mercy.*

What is so special about our shofar-blowing that it will "convince" Hashem to judge us kindly?

Rav Shneur Kotler ***zt"l*** illuminates this midrash: When we blow the shofar, our innermost breath is utilized to create the sound of the blasts. This signifies that although our outer armor may have become chinked and we may have compromised our special relationship with the Al-mighty, deep down we have remained unscathed and faithful to Hashem. Our soul still yearns to bask in the spiritual light of Hashem's presence. When the Heavenly Court sees that our essence yearns to be close to Hashem, this "convinces" Him to overlook our tarnished exterior.

Rav Avraham Borenstein of Sochatchov ***zt"l***, the **Shem M'Shmuel**, answers in a different manner, based upon the symbolic meaning of the fragmental *teruah* note, which represents a broken heart: There are two causes for a broken heart. One is a state of depression, where one can look at the world through hopeless eyes and, as a result, become heartbroken. However, this is not the broken heart that "walks in the light of Hashem's presence," as the *pasuk* states. Fortunate is the person whose heart is broken through the intelligent realization of his worthlessness, in comparison to

Rav Yisrael Meir Kagan ***zt"l*** **(Chafetz Chaim)** would say:

"*Chazal* have taught us that one who overlooks any hurt that is caused to him will have all his sins forgiven. But no one ever causes me the slightest bit of hurt, and thus I can never have a chance to receive this reward!"

Rav Simchah Bunim of Peshischah ***zt"l*** would say:

"How can one ever know if he has achieved Divine forgiveness for his sins? If one never again repeats the sinful act, he can be certain that there has been total forgiveness."

הַיּוֹם הֲרַת עוֹלָם, הַיּוֹם יַעֲמִיד בַּמִּשְׁפָּט, כָּל יְצוּרֵי עוֹלָמִים, אִם כְּבָנִים אִם כַּעֲבָדִים. אִם כְּבָנִים רַחֲמֵנוּ כְּרַחֵם אָב עַל בָּנִים. וְאִם כַּעֲבָדִים עֵינֵינוּ לְךָ תְלוּיוֹת, עַד שֶׁתְּחָנֵּנוּ וְתוֹצִיא כָאוֹר מִשְׁפָּטֵנוּ, אָיוֹם קָדוֹשׁ:

---

his Creator. A broken, contrite heart, humbled by the knowledge of the greatness of the ways of Hashem, is what we are referring to by blowing the stuttered *teruah* blasts. Thus, the *pasuk* does not state, אשרי העם תוקעי תרועה—*Fortunate is the nation who blows the* teruah, but rather יודעי תרועה—*who knows the* teruah, who understands that the purpose of the shofar blasts is to effect a true broken heart.

אשרי העם יודעי תרועה ה' באור פניך יהלכון

Fortunate is the nation who knows the sound of the teruah;
Hashem, in the light of Your presence they walk.

MUSSAR/ HASHKAFAH
מוסר/השקפה

The *pasuk* praises Bnei Yisrael for knowing how to blow the shofar, thereby appeasing Hashem with the *teruah* sounds. However, we must understand: what exactly is this ability to arouse Hashem's mercy, and from where does it stem? Do the musical notes of the ram's horn contain a mystical quality that is capable of placating Hashem?

Rav Henoch Leibowitz *zt"l* gives a profound answer. The ability to appease Hashem derives from the same source as the ability to appease our fellow man—

Rav Menachem Mendel Schneerson *zt"l* (Lubavitcher Rebbe) would say:

"Rosh Hashanah recalls the creation of the world, as it says: *Today the world was born.* According to our Sages, however, the world was created on the 25th of Elul, so that Rosh Hashanah actually marks the sixth day of Creation, the day on which man was created. Why do our Rosh Hashanah prayers proclaim that the world was formed on that date? The answer is that the existence of the world prior to man's creation is to be considered unfinished. Through the creation of man, Hashem revealed a deeper purpose of Creation and a higher aspect of G-dliness; thus, the world did not previously exist. The anniversary of man's creation can therefore be considered the anniversary of Creation as a whole."

humbling and submitting ourselves to ask forgiveness. The ability of the Jewish people to placate Hashem and find mercy in judgment on Rosh Hashanah does not stem from some mystical quality of the shofar or the prayers—but rather, from the feelings of humility and submission to Hashem that accompany them. This is the secret of our people that no other nation possesses. Of course they can blow trumpets and they can even recite all kinds of prayers. But they cannot appease Hashem, because they lack the submission to Him that can only be achieved by Bnei Yisrael.

היום הרת עולם היום יעמיד במשפט כל יצורי עולמים וכו'

On this day the world was conceived. On this day He makes stand in judgment all the creatures of the worlds...

MIDDOS/ DERECH ERETZ מידות/דרך ארץ

The Gemara (*Rosh Hashanah* 10b) brings a disagreement regarding when exactly Creation took place. One view is that the six days of Creation began on the 25th of Elul and ended on the first of Tishrei; thus, Rosh Hashanah, on the first of Tishrei, is a commemoration of the completion of Creation—the first day of the world. The opposing view is that Creation occurred in the month of Nissan. Rabbeinu Tam reconciles and declares אלו ואלו דברי אלקים חיים—they are both correct! In Tishrei, Hashem created the world *in theory*, while in Nissan, Hashem put His thought into practice and created the world *in actuality*. But if the physical world was indeed created during the month of Nissan, why is the Day of Judgment for every living creature on the first of Tishrei?

The **Tchortkover Rebbe, Rav Yisrael Friedman** ***zt"l*** **(*Ginzei Yisrael*)**, gives a fascinating answer: It is human nature to want to be good, do the right thing, and fulfill the service of Hashem in the best and most optimal manner. Yet, obstacles pop up to block our way. The *yetzer hara* is always at hand to discourage us, and the strains of earning a livelihood, maintaining our health, and raising our families always seem to tug at us and lead us away from what we should be doing. However, Hashem's kindness to us is constantly present, and is shown even in judgment. On the first day of Tishrei, the day when, thousands of years ago, Hashem finished creating the world in thought, if not in action, He agrees to judge us *by our thoughts and good intentions*, as well as by our actions!

As we say, היום הרת עולם—*On this day the world was conceived.* The judgment on this day, the day when the creation of the world was originally intended, will include *our* good will and intentions.

וּנְתַנֶּה תֹּקֶף קְדֻשַּׁת הַיּוֹם כִּי הוּא נוֹרָא וְאָיֹם וּבוֹ תִנָּשֵׂא מַלְכוּתֶךָ וְיִכּוֹן בְּחֶסֶד כִּסְאֶךָ וְתֵשֵׁב עָלָיו בֶּאֱמֶת. אֱמֶת כִּי אַתָּה הוּא דַיָּן וּמוֹכִיחַ וְיוֹדֵעַ וָעֵד וְכוֹתֵב וְחוֹתֵם וְסוֹפֵר וּמוֹנֶה וְתִזְכֹּר כָּל הַנִּשְׁכָּחוֹת.

לז"נ הרב
אברהם רפאל
בן הרב **יצחק**
הופמן זצ"ל
נפ' כ"ח אלול
תשס"ו
ת.נ.צ.ב.ה.

ונתנה תוקף

וכותב וחותם וסופר ומונה ותזכר כל הנשכחות

And You inscribe, seal, record and count, and recall all forgotten things…

DVAR TORAH
דבר תורה

Three books are opened on Rosh Hashanah: one for the completely wicked, one for the completely righteous, and one for those in between. We learn this from the *pasuk, And if not, erase me please from Your book which You have written* (*Shemos* 32:32). How are we to understand these three books? And what is the relationship of the *pasuk* to the three books? We usually assume that Hashem writes in these books, whereas this *pasuk* speaks of erasing!

Rav Yosef Engel ***zt"l*** explains as follows: The Gemara (*Taanis* 11a) teaches that when a person sins in private, his soul will testify against him. All of the Torah is incorporated within the soul of a Jew. Each of the *mitzvos*, in all of its halachic detail, is engraved on a part of the soul. If a person observes a particular mitzvah properly, the corresponding part of the soul shines with holiness. But if a person neglects a particular mitzvah, the corresponding part of the soul is dulled. The writing on that part of the soul becomes erased. This is the "signature" of the soul and how the soul "testifies" against the sinner. When the Heavenly Court looks at the soul, the soul shows for all to see which *mitzvos* that person observed and which he neglected.

In a similar vein, the soul is itself the "book" which is opened on Rosh Hashanah. If a person has been a complete *tzaddik*, Hashem will be able to read the entire Torah from that person's soul. That soul will be "*Your book*"—the complete book of the

> **Rav Wolf of Zhitomir** ***zt"l*** **(*Ohr Hameir*)** would say:
>
> "Since the entire universe was created for the sake of Klal Yisrael, its entire existence hangs in the balance when Klal Yisrael is judged. Everything flourishes or withers according to the merit of Klal Yisrael."

וְתִפְתַּח אֶת סֵפֶר הַזִּכְרוֹנוֹת וּמֵאֵלָיו יִקָּרֵא. וְחוֹתָם יַד כָּל אָדָם בּוֹ
וּבְשׁוֹפָר גָּדוֹל יִתָּקַע וְקוֹל דְּמָמָה דַקָּה יִשָּׁמַע וּמַלְאָכִים יֵחָפֵזוּן, וְחִיל
וּרְעָדָה יֹאחֵזוּן, וְיֹאמְרוּ הִנֵּה יוֹם הַדִּין לִפְקֹד עַל צְבָא מָרוֹם בַּדִּין, כִּי

Torah. The soul of an "in-between" person will no longer contain the entire Torah, but will be a mix of writing and erasures. It will retain only some of that "*which You have written.*" But on the soul of the wicked person, the Torah which had been engraved will have been completely "*erased.*"

ותפתח את ספר הזכרונות ומאליו יקרא וחותם יד כל אדם בו

You open the book of records and it reads of itself;
and the signature of every man is in it…

MUSSAR/HASHKAFAH
מוסר/השקפה

Three books are opened on Rosh Hashanah [before the Al-mighty]: one is for the truly wicked; one is for the utterly righteous; and one is for those in between. The utterly righteous are signed and sealed immediately for life. The truly wicked are signed and sealed immediately for death. Those in between are standing and [their judgment] is suspended until Yom Kippur (*Rosh Hashanah* 16b).

Based on the words of *Chazal*, it seems so "black and white." A wicked person, who is clear to all as a person who does not embody the values of the Torah, one who causes others pain and wastes away his money in frivolous and unholy pursuits; such a person is slated for death and without question will meet his end in the coming year. And yet, our eyes see many such people who are alive and well and thriving in their environment, both socially and economically. So how can this be? Not only are they not dying in the coming year, but they are living happy lives, with good fortune, health, and *nachas* from their children!

The Sephardic *gaon*, **Chacham Yehudah Tzadka *zt"l***, gives a powerful and frightening answer. Suppose one sits in on a scene at the hospital, where two patients enter, both complaining of similar symptoms. The doctor comes in to check the sick men. He examines the first, orders tests, and prescribes special treatments. After some time to digest the medical data, the doctor announces, "This man must go into surgery right now!"

Then the doctor examines the second patient. He orders tests and prescribes the same treatment. Then, after a final review, the doctor says, "Sir, you may go home."

Why? What happened? Well, it is possible that the first patient is quite sick, whereas the second is healthy and can return home. It is also conceivable that the

לֹא יִזְכּוּ בְעֵינֶיךָ בַּדִּין וְכָל בָּאֵי עוֹלָם יַעַבְרוּן לְפָנֶיךָ כִּבְנֵי מָרוֹן. כְּבַקָּרַת רוֹעֶה עֶדְרוֹ מַעֲבִיר צאנו תַּחַת שִׁבְטוֹ. כֵּן תַּעֲבִיר וְתִסְפֹּר וְתִמְנֶה וְתִפְקֹד נֶפֶשׁ כָּל חָי וְתַחְתֹּךְ קִצְבָה לְכָל בְּרִיּוֹתֶיךָ וְתִכְתֹּב אֶת גְּזַר דִּינָם.

---

second man is so ill that there is nothing left to do for him. On the other hand, the first man is sick—but he is worth saving!

The trials and tribulations that a person undergoes in this world are for his own benefit. They allow him to clean his slate from his awful misdeeds. However, if a person is so wicked that he is "beyond saving," then Hashem allows him to go on living, with all his successes intact, so as to "pay him off" in this world. The person's soul is so lost that there truly is no hope for him. If we look at life in this prism, how can we not rush to repent before our awesome Day of Judgment?!

ובשופר גדול יתקע וקול דממה דקה ישמע ומלאכים יחפזון

A great shofar is sounded, and a silent, gentle voice is heard. And the angels are alarmed…

DRUSH
דרוש

In the *beis medrash* in Kotzk, the honor of blowing the shofar was given one year to the holy **Rav Yechiel Meir of Gustinin *zt"l*.** Despite all his strenuous efforts, however, he was unable to produce strong and vibrant blasts, and the sounds that came forth from his shofar were pale, indeed. Surprisingly, though, the **Kotzker Rebbe, Rav Menachem Mendel *zt"l*,** congratulated R' Yechiel Meir on his performance and said that in his opinion, R' Yechiel Meir had blown the shofar particularly well.

When asked how this was possible, since all had heard the weak sounds that had emanated from Rav Yechiel Meir's shofar, the Kotzker replied, "Why, we said in *davening*: ובשופר גדול יתקע—*the shofar is sounded by a great man,* וקול דממה דקה ישמע—*but all that is heard is a small, thin sound.* Nevertheless, ומלאכים יחפזון וחיל ורעדה יאחזון—*even the angels tremble in fear, and panic overtakes them ...*"

וחיל ורעדה יאחזון ויאמרו הנה יום הדין לפקוד על צבא מרום בדין

Pangs of fear and trembling seize them, and they declare, "Behold the Day of Judgment!" The Heavenly host is arraigned in judgment...

MASHAL
משל

משל: As the terrors of war crept into the tiny village, many people realized that it was time to escape. Inquiries were made and a seasoned guide who knew how to cross the heavily guarded border was located. He informed the escapees that he would meet them at a border village late the following night, and they were to be there with their money.

When all were assembled, the group headed out. Trembling with fear and uncertainty, the men, women, and children struggled to keep up with the guide, who, unlike them, appeared calm, cool and totally unconcerned about the danger. The more they traveled, the more frightened they became, while he remained totally unfazed, sitting tall atop his horse.

The moment they reached the actual border crossing, however, even the guide became serious. He took every precaution and nervously glanced back and forth until the entire group managed to cross. Only the horses remained unconcerned and unaware.

נמשל: Rav Chaim Brisker *zt"l* says that some people begin to feel the terror of the Yom Hadin from the onset of Elul. Others gradually come to feel the spirit of *teshuvah* during the next few weeks, and by the time Rosh Hashanah actually arrives, there is almost no one left who is not trembling with concern for himself and his family. Only the "horses" feel nothing...!

וכל באי עולם יעברון לפניך כבני מרון

All mankind pass before You like young sheep...

MUSSAR/
HASHKAFAH
מוסר/השקפה

We note that *all who come to this world pass before You like members of the flock.* Even the angels hurry past the Divine Tribunal on this fateful day. Why do they also pass by, and with such haste?

Our Sages have taught us that with each mitzvah a person performs, he creates an angel. One can perform a mitzvah with proper preparation and appropriate *kavanah,* fulfilling it in all its minute detail. The angel created from such a high-quality mitzvah observance is accordingly handsome and well-formed, and is certain to make a favorable impression on that most Supreme Court. When one performs *mitzvos* perfunctorily, however, as so often is the case when we rush through our prayers or *bentching,* the angels created are understandably defective. They may be deformed and/or lacking in parts of their

being, corresponding to the flaws in the performance of each mitzvah. Despite their lacking the uniquely human quality of vanity, these angels are ashamed of their less-than-flattering appearance, and when they appear for review by the Heavenly Tribunal that evaluates our deeds, they hurry by to avoid the embarrassment and inherent criminal implication that is their sorry state.

כן תעביר ותספר ותמנה ותפקד נפש כל חי

So do You cause to pass, count, number, and review the soul of every living being...

DRUSH
דרוש

Most of us grossly underestimate our personal potential. Based on our mistaken self-evaluation, we reason, "I am doing the best I can. I simply cannot accomplish more than this. This is the limit of my ability." What a tragic error. We do not recognize our potential!

On Rosh Hashanah, the Day of Judgment, a person is judged for his actions and also for his "mission." What is meant by "his mission"? How does a person's mission differ from his actions? A person's actions are the sum total of everything he did during the past year. If he performed a mitzvah, he is rewarded; if he did an *aveirah*, he is punished. "His mission," on the other hand, refers to his purpose, his potential; it is all that he could have accomplished. This is a completely different account. There are some people who had the ability to be among the *gedolei Yisrael*, but who fell far short of that goal, because they did not fulfill their potential.

A prime illustration of the distinction between actions and potential lies in a remarkable story about **Rav Naftali Tzvi Yehudah Berlin** ***zt"l***, better known as "the Netziv." When the Netziv wrote his first *sefer*, *Ha'emek She'eilah*, on the *She'iltos d'Rav Achai Gaon*, he made a big kiddush, and his ecstasy was evident on his glowing countenance. Someone asked him, "Why are you so unusually happy? Many people write *sefarim*!" The Netziv told him the following story:

"When I was about eleven years old, I was not doing well in my studies. One night, I lay awake in my bed, while my parents thought I was fast asleep. I overheard my father sighing and saying to my mother, 'I think I will have to bring our son to become an apprentice to a shoemaker or a tailor, so he can learn to be a tradesman. Apparently, he is not cut out to be a *talmid chacham*. There are some people who simply are not made for it. He will be an honest businessman, and he will *daven* every day, and between Minchah and Maariv he will learn *Chayei Adam*, or perhaps *Ein Yaakov*, maybe even a mishnah. I will wait another week or two, and then I will bring him.'

"My mother agreed. 'I think you are right.'

"Upon hearing all of this, I jumped out of my bed, ran to the kitchen, and cried out, 'Father! Mother! Please do not do this to me! Give me a chance, and I will learn. Just give me a chance.'

"My father was rather skeptical. 'But we do not see any evidence of you putting effort into your learning.'

"I pleaded, 'Just give me a chance until the end of the *zman*.' I began to learn in earnest. By the end of the *zman*, I had risen to the top of my class, and eventually, I got to where I am today."

The Netziv continued, "Imagine what would have happened had I not heard my parents speaking that night. I would have become a regular businessman, *davening* with a *minyan*, and setting times for learning. Then, after one hundred and twenty years, I would go up to the Heavenly Court, and they would ask me, 'What did you do with your life?'

"I would answer confidently, 'I *davened* and I engaged in honest labor. I set times for learning, and I supported a family.'

"Then they would ask me, 'But where is your commentary on the *She'iltos*?'

"I would say, 'What? A commentary on the *She'iltos*? I am a simple layman; what do I have to do with a commentary on the *She'iltos*?'

"And they would say, 'It says here that you were given a *neshamah* which could write a commentary on the *She'iltos*!'

"Now," concluded the Netziv, "after one hundred and twenty years, I will be able to say, 'Here is my commentary on the *She'iltos*. You asked for it; here it is!' Now do you understand why I am so happy?"

The *sefarim hakedoshim* teach us:

"In the *Mussaf* of Rosh Hashanah, we say: *You remember all that is forgotten.* Hashem remembers those things that man has forgotten, but ignores things that he remembers. How? A person commits a sin but later forgets about it. The sin doesn't truly bother him, and he is able to push it from his mind. Hashem, however, has not forgotten about the incident. On the other hand, if a person commits a sin but repents afterward, learning from his mistake and resolving not to repeat it, Hashem 'forgets' the matter completely."

בְּרֹאשׁ הַשָּׁנָה יִכָּתֵבוּן. וּבְיוֹם צוֹם כִּפּוּר יֵחָתֵמוּן. כַּמָּה יַעַבְרוּן. וְכַמָּה יִבָּרֵאוּן. מִי יִחְיֶה. וּמִי יָמוּת. מִי בְקִצּוֹ. וּמִי לֹא בְקִצּוֹ.

ותפקוד נפש כל חי ותחתוך קצבה לכל ברויתיך ותכתוב את גזר דינם

You review the soul of every living being, determining the life span of every creature, and You record the decree of their judgment.

MUSSAR/HASHKAFAH
מוסר/השקפה

The Gemara (*Rosh Hashanah* 16b) states: *There are three types of people who come for judgment on the Day of Judgment:* tzaddikim *(the righteous),* beinonim *(the average), and* resha'im *(the wicked). Tosafos* adds: *Every man is judged at the time of* techiyas hameisim *(resurrection of the dead).*

We can understand that a person is judged at the end of every year and at the end of his life. Yet it is difficult to comprehend why a person should be judged again at *techiyas hameisim*, if he was already judged at the end of his life. What good or evil could he have done after his death?

The Lakewood Rosh Yeshivah, **Rav Aharon Kotler** ***zt"l***, explains: Every year, each person cries on the Yom Hadin, hoping and praying that the merits borne of his good deeds of the previous year will keep him in good stead for the coming year's judgment. This continues until the end of one's life. However, in truth, it doesn't really end there. Rashi is still learning *Chumash* and Gemara with us and is still teaching us. His influence lives on, and his spiritual merits grow. A person's record does not end when he dies. It depends on the fruits of his labors, how much good he has accomplished and how much the world has benefited from those deeds. The influences, both good and evil, that remain after one's life are part of his judgment. Thus, before the eventual resurrection at the advent of the glorious time of Mashiach, each and every person will once again be judged for his everlasting achievements; the legacy that he has imparted to the world. One must prepare himself for this judgment as well.

בראש השנה יכתבון וביום צום כיפור יחתמון

On Rosh Hashanah their decree is inscribed, and on Yom Kippur it is sealed...

STORIES
מעשה

A few days before the Yamim Nora'im, one of the great Sephardic *rabbanim*, **Rav Yosef Sevi** ***zt"l***, came to visit the North African city of Garba. On the night of Rosh Hashanah, he prayed in the renowned *beit knesset* of Garba, and provided much inspiration to the congregants. When *davening* had ended and the great sage was making his way out of the synagogue, he suddenly stopped, lifted his eyes to the

מִי בַמַּיִם. וּמִי בָאֵשׁ. מִי בַחֶרֶב. וּמִי בַחַיָּה. מִי בָרָעָב. וּמִי בַצָּמָא. מִי בָרַעַשׁ. וּמִי בַמַּגֵּפָה. מִי בַחֲנִיקָה. וּמִי בַסְּקִילָה. מִי יָנוּחַ. וּמִי יָנוּעַ. מִי

heavens, and broke out crying, "Master of the world, please have compassion! How can Your children survive a drought without a single drop of rain?!" Those around him were startled, and the great rabbi repeated, "Without a single drop of rain!"

A sense of fear overtook the community as they recalled the last time they experienced a year of drought, when all the wells ran dry and the price of grain skyrocketed. Throngs of people suffered from starvation and many died after months of bitter suffering. Everything simply deteriorated from bad to worse. "Without a single drop!" cried the sage once again, in a voice filled with dread.

Everyone quickly proceeded to repent and plead for mercy, trying their utmost to annul the deadly decree. The prayers on that Rosh Hashanah took on an added sense of urgency, and the people of Garba truly felt the Yom Hadin. In this manner, Rosh Hashanah passed with a renewed sense of heartfelt prayer and contrition, and throughout the Aseres Yemei Teshuvah, the community strengthened their *teshuvah*, *tefillah* and *tzedakah* that are the traditional fortifications with which to annul harsh decrees.

On Yom Kippur night, after an entire day of emotional supplication, the people streamed out of the synagogue, led by their esteemed guest. Just as he did that first night, R' Yosef once again stopped short and raised his eyes to the heavens. Everyone simultaneously halted in their tracks and held their breaths in anticipation. The sage lifted his hands and cried in amazement, "What is this, Master of the world? Have You decided definitively to bring a flood to the world?"

Smiles broke out all around and everyone breathed a sigh of relief, thanking their Creator. Indeed, that season produced so much rain that the sea flooded the shore and people needed rafts and boats to get from Tripoli to the market in Garba!

This is what the Gemara (*Rosh Hashanah* 16b) means when it says, *Any year that is poor in the beginning is rich in the end!* When one humbles himself in prayer before

Rav Yehudah Zev Segal *zt"l* (Manchester Rosh Yeshivah) would say:

"When we stand before the *Ribono Shel Olam* on Rosh Hashanah, hopeful that our new resolutions will tip the scale of judgment in our favor, we must provide some sort of guarantee that we will follow through. That guarantee is the study of *mussar*! Only with the study of *mussar* can one truly refine himself and climb the ladder of spiritual improvement."

יִשָּׁקֵט. וּמִי יִטָּרֵף. מִי יִשָּׁלֵו. וּמִי יִתְיַסָּר. מִי יֵעָנִי וּמִי יֵעָשֵׁר מִי יִשָּׁפֵל. וּמִי יָרוּם.

the Al-mighty like a poor person, in the end he will reap the riches of a successful and prosperous year. We must remember that everything depends upon these holy days—our lives, our fortunes, the fortune of our nation at large, health and prosperity, peace and tranquility. We must pray and plead, for only then will we be blessed with goodness.

מי יחיה ומי ימות

...who will live and who will die...

In 5703 (1943), a thirteen-year-old boy traveled with his father from his tiny Hungarian village to the city of Satmar, to celebrate his bar mitzvah in the presence of the great **Satmar Rebbe, Rav Yoel Teitelbaum *zt"l*.** It was *Shabbos Parshas Va'eschanan*, and as per the custom in Satmar, the rebbe would *lein* from the Torah and also receive the sixth *aliyah*. The *gabba'im* would arrange the *aliyos* so that the *Aseres Hadibros* would be read by *shishi* (sixth *aliyah*) and the bar mitzvah boy was to be honored with *chamishi* (fifth *aliyah*).

STORIES
מעשה

The boy stood at the *bimah* and peered into the *sefer Torah* as the Satmar Rebbe *leined*. He felt a great charge of excitement and holiness. Suddenly, the rebbe's voice rose to a thunderous roar as he finished off the *aliyah* with the words: אנחנו אלה פה היום כולנו חיים—*All of us here today, we are all alive.* It was as if a bolt of lightning had pierced the hearts of all those standing around while the rebbe shouted these words. In those harrowing, terrifying days, these words proved to be a protective shield that surrounded all those who were blessed to be standing up at the *bimah* at that moment.

Indeed, the five men who were present, the Satmar Rebbe; his personal *gabbai*, Rav Yosef Ashkenazy *zt"l*; the *gabbai*; the bar-mitzvah boy; and his father all survived the war. The usual *gabbai*, R' Feivish, had not been present and missed the blessing. Tragically, he did not survive.

Rabbi Dr. Abraham J. Twerski *shlit"a* says, let us be careful to properly perform *mitzvos*, so that we create angels who proudly display themselves and eloquently plead our cause before the Heavenly bench.

מי בקצו ומי לא בקצו מי במים ומי באש

...who will come to his timely end, and who to an untimely end, who will perish by water and who by fire...

MIDDOS/ DERECH ERETZ
מידות/דרך ארץ

The Gemara (*Kesubos* 62b) relates a story about Rav Rechumi, who died as a result of causing his wife to cry when he failed to come home on time, right after *davening* on Yom Kippur. This poses a great difficulty. If Rav Rechumi's wife cried because he was late, certainly she would be shattered by his death! Why was he punished with death?

Rav Chaim Shmulevitz *zt"l* (*Sichos Mussar*) answers that the punishment for interpersonal sins has nothing to do with rectifying an injustice that took place. Causing others emotional pain is like playing with fire. If one places his hand in a fire, the burn he sustains is not a punishment; rather it is the result of the fact that fire burns. Thus, Rav Rechumi was not punished; he was "burned" by having caused his wife pain.

מי יעני ומי יעשר מי ישפל ומי ירום

...who will become poor, and who will become wealthy, who will be brought to a low state, and who will be uplifted.

STORIES
מעשה

On the eve of Yom Kippur, a poor man named Hershel hoped to eat a small bite before the fast, but with no money and no food, a meal was simply a dream. Instead, he received a tongue-lashing from his frustrated wife, and set out early for shul, hungry and depressed. Then a thought entered his head. Though he couldn't procure any food, maybe R' Baruch, the wealthy businessman who sat up front by the eastern wall, would give him a little smell of his snuff. That would, perhaps, revive his spirits enough to allow him to pray.

Hershel cautiously approached the front of the shul and tapped R' Baruch on the back. "R' Baruch? Maybe I could have a little sniff of your *tabak*?"

R' Baruch turned with an incredulous look on his face. With an unmistakable tone of disgust, he said only one word: "Now?!" Hershel turned stiffly and made his way back to his seat, totally humiliated. No one in the shul had witnessed the little episode, but on High, the ministering angels were in an uproar. How could the wealthy man have humiliated his poverty-stricken brother like that? It was decreed that in the upcoming year, things would be radically different.

וּתְשׁוּבָה וּתְפִלָּה וּצְדָקָה מַעֲבִירִין אֶת רֹעַ הַגְּזֵרָה.

כִּי כְּשִׁמְךָ כֵּן תְּהִלָּתֶךָ קָשֶׁה לִכְעֹס וְנוֹחַ לִרְצוֹת כִּי לֹא תַחְפֹּץ בְּמוֹת הַמֵּת כִּי אִם בְּשׁוּבוֹ מִדַּרְכּוֹ וְחָיָה וְעַד יוֹם מוֹתוֹ תְּחַכֶּה לוֹ אִם יָשׁוּב מִיַּד תְּקַבְּלוֹ. אֱמֶת כִּי אַתָּה הוּא יוֹצְרָם וְאַתָּה יוֹדֵעַ יִצְרָם כִּי הֵם בָּשָׂר וָדָם. אָדָם יְסוֹדוֹ מֵעָפָר וְסוֹפוֹ לֶעָפָר בְּנַפְשׁוֹ יָבִיא לַחְמוֹ מָשׁוּל

And so, right after Yom Kippur, Hershel received an unexpected inheritance and invested in some merchandise. He made an enormous profit and from that time on, whatever he touched turned to gold. At the same time, R' Baruch began losing money at every turn.

Many years passed and R' Baruch was unable to extricate himself from his crushing poverty. R' Hershel, however, continued to prosper. He was now a respected member of the community, and when his daughter became engaged to the son of the rabbi of Zhitomir, the whole town looked forward to celebrating this great event. R' Baruch's anticipation was perhaps greater than most, for he had a plan to recoup his wealth.

As the young couple stood under the wedding canopy surrounded by their happy parents, R' Baruch quietly came up to R' Hershel and said, "A *shmeck tabak*, R' Hershel?" Without a thought, R' Hershel removed his snuff box and handed it to R' Baruch. R' Baruch immediately fell to the ground in a dead faint.

When he regained consciousness, R' Hershel asked him, "Was it something I did that caused you to faint?" When the entire story was recounted, R' Hershel, under the advice of **Rav Levi Yitzchak of Berditchev *zt"l***, decided to divide his great wealth with R' Baruch and the two lived like brothers, in prosperity and health for the rest of their lives.

ותשובה ותפילה וצדקה מעבירין את רוע הגזירה...

But repentance and prayer and charity annul the evil decree.

DRUSH
דרוש

The words in the *Mussaf* prayer, *But repentance, and prayer, and charity annul the evil decree*, are shouted in unison by every member of the congregation. At this moment, each person believes that he is on the track of repentance, which will merit him a good year. In fact, the **Lev Simchah, R' Simchah Bunim Alter *zt"l* (Gerrer Rebbe)**, writes that the *Ribono Shel Olam* Himself does *teshuvah*, so to speak, as it says in the *pasuk*: *And Hashem your G-d will return.* What does Hashem do

כְּחֶרֶס הַנִּשְׁבָּר כְּחָצִיר יָבֵשׁ וּכְצִיץ נוֹבֵל כְּצֵל עוֹבֵר וּכְעָנָן כָּלָה וּכְרוּחַ נוֹשָׁבֶת וּכְאָבָק פּוֹרֵחַ וְכַחֲלוֹם יָעוּף.

וְאַתָּה הוּא מֶלֶךְ אֵל חַי וְקַיָּם.

---

teshuvah for? *Chazal* tell us (*Sukkah* 52b) that Hashem said to Michah, *On that day, I will gather in...that which was bad to Me* (*Michah* 4:6), a reference to the *yetzer hara* that Hashem, so to speak, regretted creating. So, if Hashem is doing *teshuvah*, surely we must follow in His ways. The Lev Simchah would teach his chassidim that overcoming one's natural desires is the way to emulate the Al-mighty, thereby causing a positive reaction in the Heavens which can ultimately change harsh decrees.

A man who was childless after many years of marriage came to the Lev Simchah for a *brachah*. He and his wife were heartbroken. They had tried many avenues—including myriad doctors and treatments—to enable them to have children, but to no avail. The Lev Simchah listened to the man's plight and advised him to stop smoking.

"I noticed that you have this habit and it is a bad thing. You must break this habit, for when you break things, i.e. change habits or tear yourself away from negative acts that you have grown used to," he explained, "it is possible to break things up in Heaven as well."

The chassid took these words to heart and with great effort, he succeeded in breaking his habit. He quit smoking permanently and *baruch Hashem*, his prayers for a child were soon answered.

ותשובה ותפילה וצדקה מעבירין את רוע הגזירה...

But repentance and prayer and charity annul the evil decree.

STORIES
מעשה

The **Yid Hakadosh, Rav Yaakov Yosef of Peshischah** ***zt"l***, and **Rav Yaakov of Lelov** ***zt"l*** both approached a wealthy individual to collect money for the poor. R' Yaakov Yosef was a large, well-built man while R' Yaakov was pale and slight. The rich man, not bothering to hear what the two were collecting for, told them, "I'll gladly give money to the small man, who is frail and cannot earn a living on his own. But as for you," he pointed to R' Yaakov Yosef, "you have two strong hands. If you want to eat, go find yourself a job."

Later, the man discovered that the person he had insulted was the great Yid Hakadosh. Rushing over to the two, the man cried and begged for forgiveness for insulting the *rav*.

"Me? You didn't insult me," R' Yaakov Yosef said. "You must have mistaken me for someone else."

"*Rebbi*, please forgive me," the man implored. "I regret every word I said."

"Well, that is impossible," explained the Yid Hakadosh. "Since you didn't insult me, I can't possibly forgive you."

"Then what should I do?" cried the man.

"Well, since you insulted the simple man you thought I was, you will have to ask and beg forgiveness from every simple man you meet for the rest of your life, and you will need to make amends to each and every one of them."

ותשובה...

But repentance...

MIDDOS/ DERECH ERETZ
מידות/דרך ארץ

Teshuvah means returning ourselves to our starting point—examining our actions, reassessing our goals. What unique attributes were we given when our *neshamos* were created, and are we fulfilling our purpose on this world? *Teshuvah* means returning to the awareness that Hashem is our King and we were placed on this world to serve Him and sanctify His Name.

When Hashem created Adam Harishon, all the angels looked down from Heaven and pleaded with Hashem not to create him. They were afraid. They saw that man's potential is greater than theirs. In fact, the very first words spoken by Adam when Hashem blew his soul into him were, *Hashem is the King.* Adam said it out of free choice, whereas angels have no *bechirah* (free will) at all—they only do what they were created to do. This is why we declare time and again on Rosh Hashanah, *Hashem is the King*—our King—to prove ourselves worthy of life, of being created, because only human beings, with our own free will, understand the true purpose of our existence.

Just as Hashem blew life into Adam Harishon on that first Rosh Hashanah of Creation, **Rav Moshe Chaim Luzzato *zt"l*** explains that each and every *neshamah* was created then and given its specific and unique purpose. Just as man immediately recognized and declared that Hashem is the King, we must also work and strive to

Rav Yehudah Zev Segal *zt"l* (Manchester Rosh Yeshivah) would say:

"Hashem does not expect us to become *tzaddikim* and *tzidkaniyos* overnight. What He does expect of us is that we seriously ponder our conduct and that we sincerely strive to better ourselves in the varied areas of mitzvah observance. This is *teshuvah*!"

subjugate ourselves to Him during this period of *teshuvah.* This is our goal. We must rededicate our lives to the service of Hashem, to return to Him with the single-minded decision to utilize every gift and aspect of our lives for His sake. May we all be worthy of this lofty achievement.

...ותפילה...

...and prayer...

MUSSAR/ HASHKAFAH מוסר/השקפה

The power of prayer is great indeed. Even when the wrath of *Hakadosh Baruch Hu* threatened to destroy the rebellious nation, it was the strength of *tefillah* that quelled the flames. It wasn't just the *tefillah* of Moshe Rabbeinu, a single individual amongst many, but a collective entreaty: *The people cried out.* When Jews pray together as a unified congregation, Hashem sees to it that their prayers do not go unanswered.

When the venerable *mashgiach* of the Kamenitz Yeshivah in Yerushalayim, **Rav Moshe Aharon Stern *zt"l*,** was only nine years old, he became very sick for a period of close to two years. His righteous father brought him to the best doctors; he received blessings from many *rabbanim*; he recited Tehillim, yet his son remained ill. Finally, after exhausting many avenues, his father said to him, "Moshe Aharon, everyone is working to heal you. It's time for you to help yourself!"

"But what can I do?" asked the young Moshe Aharon. His father answered, "Accept upon yourself a *middah tovah,* and in that merit, you will become well."

The boy agreed, and asked for a good suggestion. His father told him, "Accept upon yourself that if you get well, you will always *daven* with a *minyan.*" Moshe Aharon promised, and in a short time, he was cured!

He fulfilled his promise, and grew in Torah and *yiras Shamayim* until eventually he became the renowned *mashgiach* in the Kamenitz Yeshivah. *Baruch Hashem,* the yeshivah grew rapidly and a new building was necessary to house the students. The *mashgiach* was requested to fundraise in the United States since he was American and familiar with the locale. When he asked the travel agent if there was enough room on the plane for a *minyan,* he was informed, "Rabbi, this is a travel agency, and not a prayer agency. Usually there is room, but we cannot promise. If the weather is rough, the passengers may have to remain seated. Sometimes, there are not even enough people for a *minyan.*" Under those shaky terms and conditions, he felt he was unable to travel.

But then he was offered the option of an early morning stopover in Amsterdam, where he could catch a *minyan.* R' Moshe Aharon took the flight and landed in

Amsterdam right on time. He took his *tallis* and *tefillin*, and walked out of the terminal looking for someone who could properly direct him. For a while, cars just passed him by and he was beginning to think that maybe this wasn't such a good idea after all. Suddenly, a car stopped and the driver, who was Jewish, asked, "Where does the *rav* need to go?"

"I'm looking for a *minyan* for Shacharis," was his hopeful reply.

"Get in, rabbi," the driver offered. It turned out that the driver lived in the suburbs of Amsterdam, and drove into the city each day to pray and then go to work. After driving for a few minutes, they arrived at the synagogue, a nondescript building. There were eight men present, waiting for another two to arrive and complete the *minyan*. Now that they had ten, they began *davening* immediately. At the end of Shacharis, the driver completed his mitzvah, and drove his esteemed guest back to the airport.

When R' Moshe Aharon would recount this story, his eyes would shine. He would say, "Look and see. Eight people woke up early and went to shul to pray with a *minyan*. The ninth was driving in from a nearby town. Where will the tenth come from? Why, of course! Hashem arranged for a Jew from Eretz Yisrael, on his way to the United States, to be right there in order to complete the *minyan*! *On the path that a person wants to walk, he is directed.*"

...וצדקה...

and charity...

MASHAL
משל

משל: There was once a *meshulach* who would go around collecting money day after day. He would go to certain shuls on certain days of the week and walk around, hand outstretched. To one person, he would say that he was collecting for a certain institution that sorely needed the funds for their budget. To another, he would say that he was collecting for a sick child who couldn't afford the doctor's bills. To a third person, he told that a woman with twelve children needed financial assistance to marry off her daughter.

There was an individual in shul who complained to the rabbi that the collector had asked for money for three different needs.

The rabbi thought for a moment and asked, "Tell me, in your business you sell appliances, don't you?" The man nodded. "But you don't sell only one brand," the rabbi continued. "You have the same appliance made by five or more different companies. If you can be an agent for multiple firms, why can't a collector do the same for multiple *tzedakos*?"

נמשל: It may bother us to see a *meshulach* collecting for a few different needs. But why? Obviously he's not doing this because he "likes" to do it; there are unfortunately so many problems and issues that people face today. Countless people need help in numerous areas. If we can do even a small part to help as many as we can, then why not?

Rav Shimon Shkop ***zt"l*** writes that one of our main functions in this world is to help others. When a person is appointed to dispense a certain amount of money and he properly carries out his duties, he will subsequently be entrusted with larger amounts of money in the future. Similarly, if a person gives tithes from his income, distributing part of his wealth to the poor and to other worthy causes, he shows that he is a reliable treasurer and Hashem will entrust him with greater wealth.

The midrash relates the following story. Rav Elazar, Rav Yehoshua, and Rav Akiva were collecting money for needy Torah students and arrived in Antiochia, home of Abba Yudan, the famous magnate who contributed generously to charity.

When Abba Yudan saw the sages approaching, his face turned pale with shame and grief, for he had lost all his money and would not be able to give. His wife, who was even more generous than he was, advised, "Sell half of our remaining field and give them the money." When the sages received his gift, they blessed him, "May the Al-mighty replenish your loss!"

Some time later, while Abba Yudan was plowing his remaining portion, his cow fell into a ditch and broke her leg. As Abba Yudan descended to attend to her, he suddenly spotted a treasure that was buried there. Overjoyed, he exclaimed, "It was for my benefit that my cow was injured!"

The next time the sages visited, Abba Yudan came out to welcome them. "Your prayers for my success were immensely beneficial," he said. "Hashem not only replenished the money I gave you, but blessed me with more than I ever had!"

They replied, "Your success is due to your own charitable deeds. Since you donated so generously to *tzedakah*, Hashem considers you worthy of His blessing!"

Rav Yehoshua Leib Diskin ***zt"l*** would say:

"It is worth the effort to help improve someone's behavior even if the improvement will only last a short duration. Look, Yonah saved the city of Ninveh from impending disaster and that only lasted three months!"

כי לא תחפץ במות המת כי אם בשובו מדרכו וחיה ועד
יום מותו תחכה לו אם ישוב מיד תקבלו

For You do not desire death [for the sinner] but that he turn from his evil way and live. And even until his dying day, You wait for him—if he repents, You immediately accept him.

STORIES
מעשה

The years 589-1038 CE were the height of the Dark Ages in Europe. For the Jewish people it was the era of the Geonim, the period immediately following the closing of the Babylonian Talmud. In an epoch of Jewish greatness, **Rav Saadya Gaon of Sura** stood above the rest.

Once, R' Saadya Gaon traveled to a distant town on a communal matter. He arrived late at night, made his way to the local Jewish inn and requested lodging for a few nights. The innkeeper, not recognizing his guest, tossed a key at him and pointed to a room at the end of the corridor.

The next morning, as the innkeeper made his way through the local marketplace, he noticed that all the stores of the Jewish merchants were closed. He was baffled, for he knew there was no holiday that day. He made his way to the shul to find the entire community gathered to hear the famed R' Saadya Gaon deliver a lecture. When the innkeeper saw that the distinguished sage was none other than his guest of the previous night, he was disconsolate. "How could I have treated him so poorly?" he berated himself over and over. At the end of the lecture, the innkeeper raced to the podium from where R' Saadya was speaking, threw himself at his feet and began to wail, begging for forgiveness. "Had I only known who you were," he sobbed repentantly, "I would have served you differently."

Some years later, a disciple of R' Saadya Gaon discovered the great sage alone in his room weeping and pounding his chest with his fists. The disciple didn't reveal his presence, but looked on in wonderment and confusion. A short time later, he summoned the courage to ask the *gaon* for an explanation of his unusual behavior. "I am trying to do *teshuvah,*" admitted R' Saadya.

"Surely," protested the disciple, "the *gaon* is not in need of *teshuvah.* The *gaon* is engaged the entire day and night in Torah and *mitzvos.* How could it be that such *teshuvah* is required?"

R' Saadya Gaon sighed, and related the story of the innkeeper that had occurred years before. "You see," he haltingly revealed, "when I reflect on my Divine service, and what I have learned each day, I realize that yesterday I barely knew Hashem. If I had only known yesterday what I know now—how magnificent the Master of the world is and how great is His kindness—I would surely have served Him differently!"

כי לא תחפץ במות המת כי אם בשובו מדרכו וחיה ועד
יום מותו תחכה לו אם ישוב מיד תקבלו

For You do not desire death [for the sinner] but that he turn from his evil way and live. And even until his dying day, You wait for him—if he repents, You immediately accept him.

MUSSAR/
HASHKAFAH
מוסר/השקפה

In ***Mesillas Yesharim***, the **Ramchal** writes that once a person has committed a sin, theoretically it should be impossible for him to rectify it, for once an act is committed, it is done, and what would his regret accomplish anyway? However, Hashem, in His great kindness, has granted us an opportunity of *teshuvah* to undo—retroactively—the effects of an act committed previously.

Rav Elchanan Wasserman *zt"l H"yd* once asked his *rebbi*, the **Chafetz Chaim *zt"l***, the following question: The Gemara (*Kiddushin* 40b) tells us that one who is *toheh al harishonos* (regrets the *mitzvos* he has done in the past), loses the credit for their fulfillment. It would seem that the power to undo is universal, that this is just a simple function of regret. What, then, is the great phenomenon of *teshuvah*?

The Chafetz Chaim answered that although *charatah* (regret) can discredit good deeds, it is only referring to a deep and heartfelt regret. Indeed, one who does *teshuvah mei'ahavah* and repents with genuine remorse for distancing himself from Hashem, is no different than one who is *toheh al harishonos*, and his sins are automatically forgiven. However, when one returns to Hashem merely out of fear of punishment, *teshuvah mi'yirah*, but lacks the desired feelings of regret, it is only through this unique kindness of Hashem that his sins are erased.

The **Telshe Rosh Yeshivah, Rav Chaim Stein *zt"l***, offered a second approach. Perhaps the concept of *teshuvah* actually preceded this Gemara. Hashem, in His kindness and desire to give a sinner a second chance, created this function of regret, thus enabling a Jew to do *teshuvah*. In fact, only following this tremendous and novel concept of *teshuvah* can one also use this power in the reverse, and lose the credit for a mitzvah he has already performed **(Rav Yankel Cohen *shlit"a*)**.

The **Maggid of Mezeritch *zt"l*** would say:

"Even a peasant who has a message for the king from a long-lost beloved son, is promptly ushered into the throne room. The *tefillah* of a person who does *teshuvah* is precisely such a message and is warmly and promptly welcomed by Hashem."

ואתה הוא מלך א-ל חי וקים

But You are the King, the Al-mighty, the living and everlasting G-d.

DVAR TORAH
דבר תורה

Rosh Hashanah is known as the "head" or the "king" of the new Jewish year. It is therefore appropriate that on this day we declare *Hamelech*!—Hashem is our King. Yet there is no command in the Torah that requires Jews to ascend to Yerushalayim for the holiday of Rosh Hashanah (*oleh regel*), as we do on the other three Torah-ordained holidays. Wouldn't it be appropriate for every person to come and bask in the presence of Hashem, the King of all kings, on this solemn and awesome Yom Tov?

Rav Moshe Wolfson *shlit"a* explains that regarding the Aseres Yemei Teshuvah, the *navi* says: *Search out Hashem where He can be found; call Him when He is near.* It is a time when Hashem is easily accessible, more so than at any other time of the year. Thus, there is no need to make the pilgrimage to Yerushalayim for Rosh Hashanah; on Rosh Hashanah, Hashem comes to us!

This is why on Rosh Hashanah the *chazzan* shouts "*Hamelech*" from his place in shul and only then makes his way to the *amud*. This custom symbolizes that on this day, Rosh Hashanah, we need not travel far to be close to our Creator—wherever we are, we call out to Him—and He comes to us!

ROSH HASHANAH ON SHABBOS

HALACHAH
הלכה

Sometimes the first day of Rosh Hashanah (and the first day of Sukkos and Shemini Atzeres) falls out on Shabbos, while the second day of these Yamim Tovim, including Simchas Torah, are on Motza'ei Shabbos and Sunday. These days have special *halachos* which sometimes become forgotten because this situation doesn't occur every year.

In the *Shemoneh Esrei* of Shabbos/Yom Tov (twelve in all), there is special mention of Shabbos both in the middle and ending phrase of the long fourth *brachah*. If one completely omits Shabbos even one time in that fourth *brachah*, it invalidates the *brachah* and consequently, the *Shemoneh Esrei*. Therefore, if he remembers before he is ready to step back, he must go back and repeat from the fourth *brachah* until the end of *Shemoneh Esrei*. If he remembered after reaching the point of being ready to step back, he must repeat the entire *Shemoneh Esrei*[1].

1. או"ח תפז:א

Seudah Shlishis—Third Meal of Shabbos

On such a Shabbos/Yom Tov, one is obligated to eat a third meal in the afternoon as on every Shabbos, but not in a manner that would detract from his appetite for the nighttime Yom Tov meal. Thus, one should begin the third Shabbos meal before the last quarter of the day. Another opinion[1] maintains that the times are forty-two minutes later. *Bedi'eved*, one may start even later so long as he does not eat too much[2].

Havdalah—Leaving Shabbos

When night falls and Shabbos is over, it is prohibited to do any *melachah* for Yom Tov until one says *Vatodi'einu* in Maariv or ברוך המבדיל בין קודש לקודש.[3] Before the meal, יקנה"ז (Kiddush ushering in day two of Yom Tov combined with Havdalah ushering out Shabbos) is said, and Havdalah also concludes with המבדיל בין קודש לקודש.[4] If one mistakenly said the regular words of המבדיל בין קודש לחול and did not correct himself immediately, he is not *yotzei* and the *brachah* must be repeated[5]. (The *brachah* on *besamim* is omitted because the Yom Tov meal accomplishes the purpose of reviving the body when the *neshamah yeseirah* of Shabbos departs.)

There are different *minhagim* how to make the *brachah* on the fire in this Havdalah. Some bring two candles together like every Motza'ei Shabbos; others maintain that falling wax from the tilted candle will cause the candle to extinguish, which might be an *issur* on Yom Tov. They opine that one should say the *brachah* on the candles as they are, because a double flame is only a preference and does not invalidate the *brachah*. Others buy a double-wick Yom Tov candle for this Havdalah[6].

Halachah: Understanding the *Brachah* of *Shehecheyanu*

HALACHAH
הלכה

On the first night of Rosh Hashanah when one eats the *simanim* (fruit which symbolize good omens for a sweet year), and he has a *Shehecheyanu* fruit, it is not connected to the Kiddush. Therefore, one should make one *Shehecheyanu* during Kiddush and a second one on the fruit. In fact, it is better not to even have it on the table during Kiddush. If it was brought to the table, one should have in mind not to exempt it during Kiddush. This is in contrast to the second night of Yom Tov

---

1. מגן אברהם
2. רמ"א תקכט:א
3. משנה ברורה רצט:לו
4. שם תעג:א
5. שבט הלוי ח:קיח
6. עיין נטעי גבריאל ראש השנה פרק ע'

when one places the *Shehecheyanu* fruit on the table during Kiddush and does exempt it with the *brachah* by Kiddush[7]. When one makes the *brachah* of *Ha'etz* he should have in mind to exempt the dessert if it contains fruit which would also need the same *brachah*[8]. If a person is unable to eat any of the *simanim* fruit, he may just look at them and recite the prescribed *yehi ratzon* instead of eating it[9].

Second Night Meal

On the second night, there is a slight doubt whether we say (in candle-lighting and Kiddush) the *brachah* of *Shehecheyanu*. Therefore, we put a new fruit on the table to ensure that the *brachah* is not said needlessly, and eat it right after Kiddush[10]. The woman should light candles right before Kiddush with the appropriate *brachos*. Then, without delay or speaking out, Kiddush is recited, wine given out, and the fruit is eaten after the recital of *Ha'etz* (not *Shehecheyanu*). If one intends to eat more fruit during the meal or for dessert, he should exempt them with this *Ha'etz* and not recite a *brachah acharonah* on the fruit. If he doesn't plan to have any fruit during the meal or dessert, he does recite a *brachah acharonah* if he ate a sufficient amount.

קידושא רבא

תקעו בחודש שופר בכסה ליום חגנו כי חק לישראל הוא משפט לאלקי יעקב

Blow the shofar on Rosh Chodesh, at the appointed time for our festival day.
For it is a statute for Yisrael, a [day of] judgment of the G-d of Yaakov.

DVAR TORAH
דבר תורה

Hashem tells us what He wants us to do on this day, the holy day of Rosh Hashanah—say three blessings. One about His Kingship, one about memories, and one about *shofros*. Why do we do this? The Gemara states: *Malchiyos, k'dei shetamlichuni aleichem*—"Kingship—so that you should make Me King over you." *Zichronos, k'dei sheyaaleh zichroneichem l'tovah*—"Memories—so that your memories should come before Me for the good." *Ub'mah? B'shofar.* How can you evoke in Hashem this feeling of mercy toward us? By blowing the shofar.

7. הליכות שלמה ב:א:טז
8. עיין פסקי תשובות תקפג:ב
9. כף החיים תקפג:ו
10. או"ח תר:ב

אֵלֶּה מוֹעֲדֵי יְיָ מִקְרָאֵי קֹדֶשׁ אֲשֶׁר תִּקְרְאוּ אֹתָם בְּמוֹעֲדָם.

תִּקְעוּ בַחֹדֶשׁ שׁוֹפָר בַּכֶּסֶה לְיוֹם חַגֵּנוּ. כִּי חֹק לְיִשְׂרָאֵל הוּא מִשְׁפָּט לֵאלֹהֵי יַעֲקֹב.

סַבְרִי מָרָנָן וְרַבָּנָן וְרַבּוֹתַי:

בָּרוּךְ אַתָּה יְיָ אֱלֹהֵינוּ מֶלֶךְ הָעוֹלָם בּוֹרֵא פְּרִי הַגָּפֶן.

Chazal tell us what our *avodah* on Rosh Hashanah is—we do what Hashem wants us to do. And yet, we can ask the question: What does it mean to make Hashem our King? Don't we do this twice every day, when we say *Shema* and accept upon ourselves *ol malchus Shamayim*? What is so unique about Hashem's Kingship on Rosh Hashanah?

Rav Gedalya Rabinowitz *shlit"a* (Manistritzer Rebbe) gives us a powerful response. The *pasuk* tells us: ויהי בישרון מלך בהתאסף ראשי עם יחד שבטי ישראל (*Devarim* 33:5). Hashem is the King over His people when there is an *asifah* (gathering) of the heads of the nation and an *achdus* between the *shevatim*. This means that Hashem's rulership is contingent upon our unity! If Hashem is King over diverse people who do not live in harmony with one another, what kind of honor is that for the King? It is actually an embarrassment. The Jewish people were never meant to be exactly alike, as it says, יחד שבטי ישראל. There were always different tribes with different strengths, customs, and ideologies—and that is exactly the way Hashem wants it to be! If we would all be exactly the same, wouldn't it be a very boring world? We are, however, expected to value and appreciate each other. The more we do, the more honor we attach to our King; His majesty is magnified by the magnitude of our unity.

Next, we are told to say the blessings of *zichronos* so that Hashem will have pleasant recollections about us. How can Hashem evoke positive thoughts, so to speak, about us? Hashem knows everything! What does it mean to bring good memories before Him? Well, Hashem is our father. When a child wants a good judgment from his father (i.e. to let him do what he wants), he reminds his father of the times he helped his mother, watched his siblings, etc. And there is nothing that a father loves more than when his children are at peace with each other.

In *zichronos* we speak about our forefathers, Avraham, Yitzchak and Yaakov, and the *bris* that Hashem made with them. We talk about how together we all followed Hashem through the desert and how we all stood in unity, like one man with one heart, at Har Sinai. We say: *Haben yakir li Ephraim*—we refer to ourselves as Ephraim, for the blessing that he and his brother Menashe received from their grandfather

Yaakov became the example of brotherly love which we encourage our own sons to emulate! By talking about the times we were unified, we evoke good memories before Hashem.

And how do we accomplish this? How do we actually bring about great unity among the Jewish people? With the shofar! The shofar is the tool that bonds the nation. When the Jews assemble for various reasons, it is the shofar that is blown so that each and every individual gathered can join one another for one goal.

In the future, too, the shofar will be the catalyst for *kibbutz galuyos* and the final *Geulah*. By working to increase peace, love and harmony at this time, by improving our relationship with Hashem and all His children, may Hashem remember us all for the good, and may we merit a happy, healthy and wonderful year filled with *ahavah v'achvah v'shalom v'rei'us.*

Rav Yisrael M'Kazakov *zt"l* would say:

"This is a lesson that one should live by: Treat your friends as you do your artwork and your pictures, and always make sure to place them in their best light!"

Rav Mordechai of Densburg *zt"l* would say:

"Some people spend time reviewing the *machzor* before Rosh Hashanah. The *machzor* won't change! Better one should review his deeds and correct them!"

יום כיפור

Dedicated by

Mr. and Mrs. Eli Gelb

לעי״נ ר׳ **משה** ב״ר **יעקב גלב** ז״ל

יארצייט י״ג שבט

ת.נ.צ.ב.ה.

ב שׁוּבָה יִשְׂרָאֵל עַד יְיָ אֱלֹהֶיךָ כִּי כָשַׁלְתָּ בַּעֲוֺנֶךָ: ג קְחוּ עִמָּכֶם דְּבָרִים
וְשׁוּבוּ אֶל יְיָ אִמְרוּ אֵלָיו כָּל תִּשָּׂא עָוֺן וְקַח טוֹב וּנְשַׁלְּמָה פָרִים שְׂפָתֵינוּ:
ד אַשּׁוּר לֹא יוֹשִׁיעֵנוּ עַל סוּס לֹא נִרְכָּב וְלֹא נֹאמַר עוֹד אֱלֹהֵינוּ לְמַעֲשֵׂה
יָדֵינוּ אֲשֶׁר בְּךָ יְרֻחַם יָתוֹם: ה אֶרְפָּא מְשׁוּבָתָם אֹהֲבֵם נְדָבָה כִּי שָׁב

שבת שובה/עשרת ימי תשובה

MUSSAR/
HASHKAFAH
מוסר/השקפה

During the Aseres Yemei Teshuvah, the holy rebbe of Sanz, **Rav Chaim Halberstam** ***zt"l***, used to relate the following parable: There was once a poor woman who had many children. They would beg for some food, but she had none to offer. Once, to her great joy, she found an egg. She called her children over and told them, "My children, we no longer have anything to worry about. I have found an egg! And since I am a person with keen foresight, we will not eat this egg. I will ask our neighbor to allow me to place this egg under one of his hens, so that it will produce a small chicken. We will not eat the chicken, since she will be able to lay eggs in the future. Those eggs, too, we shall not eat but place them under her so that our eggs and chickens will increase. We shall not eat of them either, but we shall eventually sell them and I will buy a calf. And we shall allow the calf to grow and become a cow. The cow will bear calves, and we will allow them to grow as well, so that we shall have many cows and calves. Then I will sell them and buy a field; we shall then have fields, cows, calves, chickens, and eggs. We will not be lacking for anything." So animated was she with her grand speech that she didn't even realize that the egg had slipped from her hand and…shattered on the floor.

The holy Sanzer Rebbe explained, "This is the way people act. When the holy days arrive, every person makes plans in his mind and accepts upon himself to do *teshuvah*, thinking he has all the answers to transform himself. But when the days have passed and nothing has happened, all the grandiose plans fall to pieces and he is left with nothing. Therefore, people must consciously act upon their words."

אַפִּי מִמֶּנּוּ: ו אֶהְיֶה כַטַּל לְיִשְׂרָאֵל יִפְרַח כַּשּׁוֹשַׁנָּה וְיַךְ שָׁרָשָׁיו כַּלְּבָנוֹן:
ז יֵלְכוּ יֹנְקוֹתָיו וִיהִי כַזַּיִת הוֹדוֹ וְרֵיחַ לוֹ כַּלְּבָנוֹן: ח יָשֻׁבוּ יֹשְׁבֵי בְצִלּוֹ
יְחַיּוּ דָגָן וְיִפְרְחוּ כַגָּפֶן זִכְרוֹ כְּיֵין לְבָנוֹן: ט אֶפְרַיִם מַה לִּי עוֹד לָעֲצַבִּים

MASHAL
משל

משל: There was once a trail which wound around a dangerous road. It was on a very high, narrow mountain and one could easily trip and fall off the cliff. In addition, there were many wild animals stalking the area and the whole path had many pitfalls.

One person who was aware of the dangers involved in traveling on that path was naturally apprehensive. After thinking the matter over, he came up with an original solution. He would walk blindfolded! This way he would not be able to see the great dangers that surrounded him from all sides and he would then be able to remain calm. Obviously, anyone can easily see how this "solution" just adds to the problem without solving anything at all. He is now in even greater danger than before, since he is unaware of his true situation.

נמשל: During the Aseres Yemei Teshuvah, a Jew must open his eyes! He must look and see that reward and punishment are meted to each and every individual, and obviously he does not want to be stuck with a harsh punishment. The holy **Chafetz Chaim *zt"l*** would say that when we read the *Tochachah* (the harsh curses that will be brought upon the sinners of the Jewish people), there are people who close their eyes and ears to the warnings; they are afraid to listen to the *kriah*. In some shuls, some people even walk out during the *leining*. But merely avoiding the issue of improper behavior is not correct. By realizing the consequences of transgressions and the failure to do good, one will watch his behavior and will gain immensely.

Chacham Rabbeinu Ovadiah Yosef *shlit"a* would say:

"These days are particularly suited for *teshuvah*, as the prophet Yeshayahu declares, *Seek Hashem when He is found; call to Him when He is close*. One should not be spiteful and unwilling to forgive those who have wronged him; if one does not forgive another for his sin, he will not be forgiven for his own sins. No one can feel confident that he will earn a favorable judgment in the Heavens, but if one treats others kindly beyond the strict letter of the law, then he is similarly judged with compassion beyond the strict letter of the law."

אֲנִי עָנִיתִי וַאֲשׁוּרֶנּוּ אֲנִי כִּבְרוֹשׁ רַעֲנָן מִמֶּנִּי פֶּרְיְךָ נִמְצָא: י מִי חָכָם וְיָבֵן אֵלֶּה נָבוֹן וְיֵדָעֵם כִּי יְשָׁרִים דַּרְכֵי יְיָ וְצַדִּקִים יֵלְכוּ בָם וּפֹשְׁעִים יִכָּשְׁלוּ בָם:

שובה ישראל עד ה׳ אלקיך כי כשלת בעונך (שבת שובה)

Return, Yisrael, to Hashem, your G-d, for you have stumbled in your iniquity (Hoshea 14:2).

MIDDOS/ DERECH ERETZ
מידות/דרך ארץ

It is interesting to note that in previous generations, people died mainly from plagues or bacterial diseases. They may have been perfectly healthy, until they would succumb to a sudden attack of an outside force, such as germs and disease-bearing bacteria. Today, as the Mir/Ponovezher Mashgiach, **Rav Yechezkel Levenstein** ***zt"l***, pointed out, we find that it is not the "outside forces" that claim human lives; rather, man falls victim to the by-products of his own body. His system becomes overloaded with harmful deposits—cholesterol clogging the arteries, fat pockets constricting blood flow, or malignant cells overpowering the vital organs and interfering with their life-sustaining processes—which ultimately kill him.

How closely this reflects the shift in spiritual patterns, reflected R' Chatzkel. For many generations people were apparently "healthy" in a spiritual sense, yet a sudden assault by a Shabsai Tzvi or a wave of Haskalah (in its early stages) would claim hundreds of thousands of souls. Today, though, the problems arise from within us. While we are able to cope with external destructive forces to a certain degree, spiritual debilitation is a silent killer that occurs as a result of the inner "residue" which accumulates over the years, quietly starving the "heart" of its necessary "oxygen" and slowly disabling the vital "organs." Our spiritual beings become wastelands from the inside out until eventually the façade of holiness and divinity simply disintegrates.

When a person commits a sin, he inflicts a spiritual wound on himself, as the *pasuk* states: *For you have stumbled (injured) in your iniquity.* This wound is no less grievous than a physical bruise; in fact, it is even more so. The process of healing this injury is called *kapparah* (forgiveness). A person must want to repent in order to attain this necessary cure. Generally, though, people are unwilling to accept the thought that they suffer from defects, so instead of embarking on the time-consuming and laborious path of *teshuvah*, they apply a touch of cosmetic to disguise the wound, and continue with life as usual. But concealing a wound causes the infection to fester further, requiring even more touch-up, plus a generous dose of perfume to mask the foul odor emanating from the wound. Thus, they continue to delude themselves and

(ממשיכים וַיָי נָתַן קוֹלוֹ.... וְלֹא יֵבֹשׁוּ עַמִּי לְעוֹלָם:)

מִי אֵל כָּמוֹךָ נֹשֵׂא עָוֹן וְעֹבֵר עַל פֶּשַׁע, לִשְׁאֵרִית נַחֲלָתוֹ, לֹא הֶחֱזִיק לָעַד אַפּוֹ, כִּי חָפֵץ חֶסֶד הוּא: יָשׁוּב יְרַחֲמֵנוּ, יִכְבֹּשׁ עֲוֹנֹתֵינוּ, וְתַשְׁלִיךְ בִּמְצֻלוֹת יָם כָּל חַטֹּאתָם: תִּתֵּן אֱמֶת לְיַעֲקֹב, חֶסֶד לְאַבְרָהָם, אֲשֶׁר נִשְׁבַּעְתָּ לַאֲבֹתֵינוּ מִימֵי קֶדֶם:

---

others, not realizing that if they continue this way, they will eventually succumb to the progressive "rotting" of their souls **(A. Scheinman)**.

שובה ישראל עד ה' אלקיך כי כשלת בעוניך

Return, Yisrael, to Hashem, your G-d, for you have stumbled in your iniquity (Hoshea 14:2).

MUSSAR/ HASHKAFAH מוסר/השקפה

If a convicted person says that he will carry his trial as far as the king's own throne chamber, it means that he has no chance of acquittal in the lower courts. Since he really is guilty according to the law of the land, his only hope lies in the slim chance of obtaining a hearing from the king himself, who has the exclusive right to pardon even those whose guilt has been established beyond a reasonable doubt.

This, explains **Rav Yaakov Kranz *zt"l* (*Kochav Mi'Yaakov*)** is what Hoshea Hanavi is telling us here. *Return, Yisrael, unto Hashem your G-d*—You must attempt to come only to Hashem with your repentance, for He alone has the power to accept your *teshuvah* and forgive you; *For you have stumbled in your iniquity*—because your sins were too great for you to be worthy of acquittal in the earthly courts, only Hashem, in His infinite mercy, can forgive your sins now. Even though they are so numerous and grave, He will forgive you as long as you make the effort and approach Him.

קחו עמכם דברים ושובו אל ה'

Take words with yourselves and return to Hashem (Hoshea 14:3).

REMEZ רמז

There is an interesting phenomenon in Judaism. When a Jew wishes to forge a relationship with another human being, the "secret formula" is to give—not to take. The more you give to others, the more you will love them. This concept is demonstrated clearly in the relationship between parents and children. Logically, one might think that children would love their parents more; after all, they are the

constant recipients of their parents' kindness. However, we know this is not the reality. Parents love their children more—by virtue of the fact that they are constantly giving to them.

In our relationship with Hashem, however, the opposite is true. In order to become close to Hashem, it is unnecessary for us to give, because in essence there is nothing that we can give Him. Rather, we must take! *Take words with you!* By accepting all the good that Hashem gives us, we form a relationship with Him! But there is a disclaimer. If we simply take without acknowledging and appreciating all the goodness, our relationship will be a shallow one—not on Hashem's part, but on our own! The more we appreciate and thank Hashem, the more we will love Him and strive to become close to Him.

During this period of time when we are all searching for ways to do *teshuvah*—to return to Hashem, to become close to Him, one of the most effective methods to accomplish this is through *hakaras hatov*, appreciating and thanking Hashem for His every kindness that He bestows upon us. In this manner, we will be able to reach our goal of taking from Hashem, in order to draw ever closer to His awesome and enveloping Presence.

כי ישרים דרכי ה' וצדקים ילכו בם

For the ways of Hashem are straight, and the righteous shall walk in them, and the rebellious shall stumble on them (Hoshea 14:10).

DVAR TORAH
דבר תורה

The Gemara states: *If you see a Torah scholar who has committed a sin at night, do not harbor doubts about him by day for he may have repented* (*Brachos* 19a). On this statement, the Gemara asks a question: *Do you mean to say he may have repented? Say rather, he has certainly repented.* Now this is a remarkable statement. If *Chazal* deem this person a *talmid chacham*, a true Torah scholar, then he must certainly be a G-d-fearing man. How, then, is it conceivable that he should commit a sin—publicly, no less—so that we need to be given an assurance that he has since repented?

Rav Meir of Premishlan ***zt"l*** provides the following beautiful answer. A true *talmid chacham* does not commit a sin. His mind and body are properly trained in the service of Hashem and this prevents him from committing transgressions. What, then, could have happened? It is possible that one can find him at some point during the day or night not engaged in the study of Torah. Yet *Chazal* warn us, *Do not harbor doubts about him, for he was certainly repenting at that time.* Though he appeared to have been idling around, know that he must have been engaged in *teshuvah* at that exact moment.

לא־החזיק לעד אפו כי חפץ חסד הוא

He does not maintain His anger forever, for He desires kindness.

MASHAL
משל

משל: Two friends purchased a two-family house. After they moved into their respective residences, one of them ordered a phone line. The technician came to the home, drilled a tiny hole in the wall, pulled the telephone wire through it, and attached it to the telephone.

"Okay, I'm done," he announced. "Everything is ready. You can now call anywhere in the world. Your account will be charged for the installation service."

The neighbor thought to himself, "What a silly neighbor I have. He spent so much money for such minor work! I saw what the technician did; he drilled a small hole and pulled the wire through it. I can do the same thing on my own! I have a drill, so all I need is the telephone itself." He went to the store, purchased a phone and brought it home. He drilled a hole in his wall and pulled the wire through. Then he lifted the receiver and listened to the silence. Apparently, he thought, the hole was too small.

He took a hammer and nail to expand the hole, but he still heard nothing on the phone. He figured that maybe he had to move the hole. He tried drilling in several different places, each time with the same result. Eventually, his wall resembled a sieve. He grew so frustrated that he banged the hammer against the wall, and all the holes suddenly combined into one giant opening in the wall. Still, the telephone remained silent.

We know, of course, that all his work was futile. True, the hole is important, but it is only the wire connecting to the telephone network that can stimulate communication...

נמשל: Similarly, says the Novardhoker Rosh Yeshivah, **Rav Avraham Yaffen** ***zt"l***, the act of *teshuvah* begins with the directive, *"Open for Me a hole the size of a needle's eye."* We must drill a tiny hole in our hearts, so to speak. All the suffering of the exile—the financial difficulties, life's problems and pressures on both the individual and communal levels—may gradually expand this opening into a giant hole within our hearts of stone. But without creating a real connection to the One Above, all of these holes will remain huge and gaping—and our suffering will just persist. We must sincerely attach ourselves to our Creator through Torah and *mitzvos*. Then He will reach out to us and complete the circuit!

ישוב ירחמנו יכבש עונתינו ותשליך במצלות ים כל־חטאתם

He will return His mercy upon us, He will suppress our iniquities, and cast into the depths of the sea all of their transgressions.

MIDDOS/ DERECH ERETZ
מידות/דרך ארץ

It is related that when **Rav Simchah Bunim of Peshischah *zt"l*** was a young man, he once encountered his master, the **Chozeh of Lublin *zt"l*,** returning from the ritual of Tashlich (the symbolic casting of one's sins into the water). When the Chozeh asked the young man where he was headed, the latter responded, "I am going to retrieve all the 'sins' that the master has thrown away."

One need not be a complete *tzaddik* to do *teshuvah* on the inadequate performance of *mitzvos.* It is not unusual for a person who has made a profitable investment in a given stock to experience greater regret for not having invested more in that stock, than for losing money on another stock. Somehow, a loss is accepted as a part of the risk of investing, but to have underestimated a stock that surged is even more disappointing. Even our instinctive reaction to economics can be applied to our spirituality.

הנשמה לך והגוף פעלך חוסה על עמלך... (סליחות לימים נוראים)

The soul is Yours, and the body is Your doing, have mercy on Your handiwork.

TEFILLAH
תפילה

During this exalted period of Yamim Nora'im (the High Holy Days) the theme that encapsulates all our thoughts and prayers is the idea of elevating ourselves to return to the highest level a human being can reach in his relationship with Hashem. Each one of us is given a holy *neshamah* which, by virtue of its very essence, naturally gravitates toward Hashem. On the other hand, our bodies—the physical dimension of us—is forever pulling us away from our ultimate goal.

In *Selichos* we say: *The soul is Yours, and the body is Your doing, have mercy on Your handiwork.* This, explains the **Chasam Sofer *zt"l*,** is referring to all the people of the world. Just as an artist will protect his artwork devotedly because he produced it, likewise, we ask Hashem to have pity on us and protect all of His creations simply because He created them.

However, continues the Chasam Sofer, the next words: *do it (show pity) for the sake of Your Name*, refer to Klal Yisrael. The level that a Jew can attain is beyond the understanding of the rest of the world. The *neshamah* certainly belongs to Hashem, but a Yid has the ability to even elevate his physicality to the extent that his body is permeated with spirituality. The crowning glory of the Jew is when he uplifts his corporeal element in order to be *mekadesh shem Shamayim.* And so we ask Hashem to have mercy on us for the sake of His Great Name—the Name that the Jewish people have sanctified for thousands of years through their holy deeds.

אַךְ בֶּעָשׂוֹר לַחֹדֶשׁ הַשְּׁבִיעִי הַזֶּה יוֹם הַכִּפֻּרִים הוּא מִקְרָא קֹדֶשׁ יִהְיֶה לָכֶם וְעִנִּיתֶם אֶת־נַפְשֹׁתֵיכֶם...שַׁבַּת שַׁבָּתוֹן הוּא לָכֶם וְעִנִּיתֶם אֶת־נַפְשֹׁתֵיכֶם בְּתִשְׁעָה לַחֹדֶשׁ בָּעֶרֶב מֵעֶרֶב עַד־עֶרֶב תִּשְׁבְּתוּ שַׁבַּתְּכֶם: (ויקרא כג-כז, לב)

ערב יום כיפור

Yom Kippur is the Day of Atonement, when the sins of Klal Yisrael are wiped away.

MUSSAR/ HASHKAFAH מוסר/השקפה

Yet, more than atonement, Yom Kippur is about *taharah*, purification. The Torah itself emphasizes this. *Kapparah* is mentioned once, while *taharah* is mentioned twice.

The emphasis on purification can also be found at the conclusion of the central *brachah* of *Shemoneh Esrei*. Even on Shabbos, we recite the words, *Purify our hearts that we may truly serve you.* It is a request for *taharas halev*, a pure heart.

Rav Yisrael Belsky *shlit"a* explains that *taharah* is the removal of *tumah* (impurity). It is the process of removing foreign substances, contamination, and pollution. When everything extraneous and harmful is removed and only the pure essence remains, that is a state of *taharah*.

The concept of *taharah* is also applicable to the heart. There are deposits in the heart which do not belong there, and it is not within human power to completely remove this contamination. There is no way, given the circumstances in which we live today, that we can aspire to the *taharas halev* (purity of heart) that Bnei Yisrael achieved in the days of Moshe Rabbeinu, when they wandered in the desert. Nevertheless, we must do the best we can. There is much we can still do to remove the contaminating elements that exist in our hearts and minds.

Our generation's weakened state of *emunah* can easily lead one to attribute what are in fact Divine powers to mere mortals. Even the most devout person, upon witnessing a relative or close friend wither away in sickness, may turn to the doctor in desperation and cry, "Save him!" If he thinks that the doctor can actually bring about the healing, then he does not fully appreciate the concept of *ein od milvado*! He does not feel that Hashem alone fills the universe. If that is the case, he lends credence to some power aside from *Hakadosh Baruch Hu.*

The surest way to calm nerves and soothe the worries that plague mankind is the careful study of *Shaar Habitachon* in *Chovos Halevavos.* This will foster a growing sense of tranquility as one's *bitachon* will become deeper and more solidly rooted.

It is particularly important to work on *emunah* and *bitachon* during the Aseres Yemei Teshuvah. In doing so, one prepares himself for the *taharas hanefesh* that culminates with the experience of Yom Kippur: *Before Hashem you shall be purified.*

אך בעשור לחודש השביעי הזה יום כיפורים הוא

However, on the tenth day of this seventh month it is a day of atonement.

Rav Shloime Ephraim Luntzitz *zt"l* (*Kli Yakar*) would say:

REMEZ
רמז

"The *Sifri* tells us that the word אך indicates a limitation. What is the limitation? The Gemara (*Yuma* 81) states: *Whoever eats and drinks on the ninth (of Tishrei) is considered as if he fasted on the ninth and tenth.* Because eating on Erev Yom Kippur is considered like a fast on the holy day itself, one might think that this day, too, atones for his sins. Thus, the Torah writes אך to limit the time period when Hashem accepts *teshuvah* and forgives. This happens only on the actual day of Yom Kippur."

זה חליפתי זה כפרתי זה תמורתי זה (התרנגול) ילך למיתה ואני
אכנס ואלך לחיים טובים ארוכים ולשלום (סדר כפרות)

This is my exchange, this is my substitute, this is my atonement. This rooster shall go to its death, and I shall proceed to a good, long life and peace (Kapparos).

STORIES
מעשה

Once, on the evening before Yom Kippur, a chassid of **Rav Elimelech of Lizhensk *zt"l*** requested permission to observe how the rebbe performs the custom of *kapparos*.

"How I do *kapparos*?" asked R' Elimelech. "I take a rooster in one hand, a siddur in the other, and recite the text. There's nothing special about the way I do *kapparos*." But the chassid persisted, saying that surely the act of his rebbe's *kapparos* was no ordinary event. He had been coming to Lizhensk to *daven* at the rebbe's side every Yom Kippur for more than twenty years now, and had always wanted to observe his rebbe at this most solemn moment.

"You want to see extraordinary *kapparos*?" R' Elimelech finally asked. "Go observe how Moshe the tavern-keeper does *kapparos*. Now, there you'll see something far more inspiring than my ordinary *kapparos*."

The chassid was hesitant at first, but eventually he was convinced to follow his rebbe's words. He located Moshe's tavern at a crossroads several miles past Lizhensk

and asked to stay the night. The tavern was full and bustling, but Moshe agreed to find his guest lodging.

Later, after a full day tending to his unruly and mostly drunken patrons, it was time to close, and with much shouting, cajoling and threatening, Moshe succeeded in herding his boorish clientele out the door. Then, the chairs and tables were stacked in a corner, and the room, which also served as the family's living quarters, was readied for the night. The Chassid, wrapped in his blanket under a table, feigned sleep, but kept watch all night, determined not to miss a thing.

Before dawn, Moshe rose from his bed, washed his hands and recited the morning blessings. "Time for *kapparos*," he called softly to his wife, taking care not to wake his guest. "Please bring me the notebook sitting above the cupboard."

Moshe sat on a small stool, lit a candle, and began reading from the notebook, unaware that his "sleeping" guest was awake and straining to hear every word. The notebook was a diary of all the misdeeds and transgressions the tavern-keeper had committed in the course of the year; the date, time and circumstance of each scrupulously noted. His "sins" were quite benign—a word of gossip, oversleeping the time for prayer, neglecting to give his daily charity, and so forth. However, Moshe read each word slowly, and by the time he had read through the first few pages, his face was bathed in tears. For more than an hour Moshe read and wept, until the last page had been turned.

When he was done, he called his wife and asked her to bring him another notebook. This was a diary of all the troubles and misfortunes that had befallen him in the course of the year. On this day Moshe was beaten by a gang of peasants; on that day his child fell ill; once, in the dead of winter, the family had frozen for several nights for lack of firewood; another time their cow had died and there was no milk until they were able to afford another.

When he had finished reading the second notebook, the tavern-keeper lifted his eyes heavenward and sighed mightily, "My dear Father in Heaven, it is true that I have sinned against You. It is also true that last year I repented and promised to fulfill Your commandments, but I repeatedly succumbed to my evil inclination. But at the same time, I also prayed and begged You for a year of health and prosperity, and I trusted in You that it would indeed be this way.

"Dear Father, today is the eve of Yom Kippur, when everyone forgives and all is forgotten. Let us put the past behind us. I'll accept my troubles as atonement for my sins, and You, in Your great mercy, shall accept my repentance."

Moshe then raised the two notebooks aloft, circled them three times above his head, and recited, "This is my exchange, this is my atonement, this is in my stead."

He then threw the two notebooks into the fireplace, where the smoldering coals soon consumed the tearstained pages.

מקוה ישראל ה'

Hashem is the mikvah of Yisrael...

REMEZ
רמז

We find a parallel between the purification process of Yom Kippur and that of a *mikvah*. In his work, ***Binah L'itim*****, Rav Azaryah Pigo *zt"l*** explains that in a manner similar to a *mikvah*, Yom Kippur has the capacity to atone, but only if the individual makes the effort to immerse himself in the power of the day. Just as a person must be submerged in the *mikvah* in order for the purification waters to be effective, so too, on Yom Kippur, he must actually come through the doors of the shul and stand before his Creator with submission and genuine remorse.

This is also the explanation of the *pasuk*, *For on this day He will atone for you to purify you from all your sins* (*Vayikra* 16:30). Hashem is giving us excellent advice on how to prepare and eventually come to a complete repentance before Him. *On this day*—on the holy day of Yom Kippur, *He will atone for you to purify you from all your sins*—but only on one condition: *Before Hashem you will purified.* This means that before Hashem atones for you, you must come prepared to be purified. When Hashem will see your true intentions, He will grant you complete purification.

EATING MEALS ON EREV YOM KIPPUR

HALACHAH
הלכה

The Gemara[1] states: *One who eats and drinks on the ninth (of Tishrei) and fasts on the tenth, the* pasuk *considers it as if he fasted on the ninth and the tenth.* We learn from here that it is a mitzvah—**according to some commentators, an actual Torah obligation**[2] —to eat more than one usually does on Erev Yom Kippur. The reason for this is twofold: 1. To be physically sated and prepared, so as not to suffer any adverse effects from fasting on Yom Kippur[3]. (One is permitted to take pills on Erev Yom Kippur, in order to ensure an easier fast.[4]) 2. In order to celebrate the purity and

1. גמ' יומא פא:
2. משנה ברורה תר"ד:א
3. טור או"ח תר"ד
4. עיין בשו"ת ציץ אליעזר יז:לז

atonement that one will merit on Yom Kippur. Since one cannot partake of festive meals on Yom Kippur itself, it is to be celebrated joyously the day before.[5] Women are included in this mitzvah as well, according to most *poskim*.[6]

This mitzvah is applicable only during the day. Some *poskim*, however, maintain that the night before is included as well.[7] If one wishes to satisfy this opinion, he should eat something after *tzeis hakochavim* (nightfall) and have in mind to fulfill the mitzvah of eating on Erev Yom Kippur.

The custom is to eat two meals, one in the morning and the other after Minchah. The second meal should be finished early enough to allow one to make his final preparations before the fast, go to shul and put on his *tallis* (with a *brachah*) before *shkiah* (sunset).

Foods to be Eaten on Erev Yom Kippur

It is customary to eat fish at the first meal[8], since it is a light food that digests easily. We dip challah in honey at both meals to signify a sweet judgment, and most people eat chicken by both meals, as well. However, one should avoid eggs, warm milk products and beef by both meals, and he should definitely avoid spicy food and warm fish by the second meal (*seudas hamafsekes*[9]).

If a person feels that he might want to eat or drink after the second meal before sunset, he should preferably verbalize before *bentching* that he is not accepting upon himself the prohibitions of Yom Kippur with the commencement of *Birkas Hamazon*.[10]

It is quoted in certain *sefarim* that if a person is careful to eat the Erev Yom Kippur meals in a dignified and proper manner—all *brachos* and *bentching* are recited with concentration and proper *kavanah, divrei Torah* are discussed at the table, one eats for the sake of the mitzvah and does not overeat—one can rectify anything that may have been lacking during the course of his meals throughout the entire year. May we be *zocheh* to correct all of our shortcomings this Yom Kippur.

5. שערי תשובה
6. שדי חמד - יום הכיפורים א:ה
7. ערוך השלחן תר"ד:ה
8. טור או"ח תר"ד, עיין מש"כ הב"ח שם
9. שו"ע או"ח תר"ח:ד
10. משנה ברורה תר"ח:יב

הדליקו את הנר...

Light the candles...

MUSSAR/ HASHKAFAH מוסר/השקפה

The Gemara (*Shabbos* 34a) states as follows: *(There are) three things which a person must ask in his home, on the eve before Shabbos as it begins to get dark: "*עשרתם*—Did you take tithes?* ערבתם*—Did you make an* eruv*?* הדליקו את הנר*—Did you light the Shabbos lights?"*

The **Belzer Rebbe, Rav Shalom Rokeach** ***zt"l*** **(Sar Shalom),** makes a very interesting correlation between these words on Erev Shabbos to Yom Kippur. Just as we must ask these questions on every Erev Shabbos throughout the year, it is even more imperative that we ask on the eve of the שבת שבתון—the holy day of Yom Kippur—these three questions, albeit with a twist.

On Erev Yom Kippur, a Jew must look within himself and ponder: עשרתם—In the short amount of time, the ten (עשר) days of repentance since Rosh Hashanah, ערבתם—as the eve (ערב) of Yom Kippur is fast approaching, הדליקו את הנר—have we all kindled the lights of *teshuvah* in our hearts? Have we done all we can to ignite within ourselves the power to burn away our sins and draw close to Hashem? Are we ready to submit ourselves before the Heavenly Tribunal in our current state? These are the questions that a person must ask himself on "Erev Shabbos," the holiest of all days, the day of forgiveness. Let us hope that we can answer in the affirmative and that our repentance is truly accepted on High.

The chassidim would say that before *Kol Nidrei* in the big shul in Belz, R' Shalom would cry, "Oy, we have erred, we have wronged, we have sinned." When the people would hear this, they would all be struck with fear which would inspire a *teshuvah sheleimah.*

Rav Meir Leibush Malbim ***zt"l*** would say:

"*Chazal* tell us that a person who eats and drinks on the ninth of Tishrei in preparation for the fast is considered to have fasted on both the ninth and the tenth. And why is eating on the day before Yom Kippur deemed so important? Because eating for the sake of Heaven is far more difficult to accomplish than fasting for the sake of Heaven."

Rav Mordechai Yosef of Izhbitz ***zt"l*** would say:

"A rebbe can erect the ladder, but it is up to the chassid to climb the rungs of spirituality!"

ועיניתם את נפשתיכם בתשעה לחודש בערב

You shall afflict your souls on the ninth of the month.

DVAR TORAH
דבר תורה

There is a unique mitzvah that is applicable only to Yom Kippur. The *pasuk* declares, *You shall afflict your souls on the ninth of the month.* The Gemara asks, *Do we really fast on the ninth? But we know that it is on the tenth that we fast! Rather, it is to tell us that whoever eats and drinks on the ninth (Erev Yom Kippur), the* pasuk *considers it as if he truly fasted on the ninth and the tenth* (*Rosh Hashanah* 9a).

Furthermore, the Gemara describes how we are to eat on Erev Yom Kippur: *There is a requirement to confess one's sins on the eve of Yom Kippur. However, the wise men have said that one should confess before he eats and drinks the* seudas hamafsekes, *lest he lose his mind during the meal* (*Yuma* 87b). The **Rambam** adds, lest he choke (on his food). Accordingly, it seems that before a person sits down to a meal throughout the year, he should confess his sins. After all, maybe he will choke on his food while eating and die without repenting for his sins?

Rav Shimon Schwab *zt"l* explains: The reason a person is created with taste buds is in order for him to feel and taste the flavor of the food so that he won't ingest something spoiled and become sick. However, during the *seudas hamafsekes* on Erev Yom Kippur, which is a *mitzvah d'Oraisa*, one may become so engrossed in performing the mitzvah and completely overwhelmed by the thought of eating in order to satisfy the will of his Creator, that he won't be careful as he's eating and will choke on his food. Thus, it is especially regarding this meal that *Chazal* require us to confess our sins before eating.

STORIES
מעשה

One Yom Kippur eve, when everyone had gathered for the *Kol Nidrei* prayers and it was still before sunset, **Rav Levi Yitzchak of Berditchev *zt"l*** took a candle and began searching under all the benches in the shul. When asked what he was trying to find, he looked up incredulously and said, "What am I looking for? Why, an intoxicated Jew, of course!"

After completing his futile search, R' Levi Yitzchak approached the *aron kodesh*, opened it, and with the entire congregation looking on, he began to speak.

"Master of the world," he cried, "You commanded us to eat and drink on Erev Yom Kippur as if it were a festive holiday. Suppose You had given this mitzvah to the other nations of the world—what would have been the result? They would surely have eaten like gluttons, drank with abandon, and by now, have been thoroughly inebriated."

יְשִׂימְךָ אֱלֹהִים כְּאֶפְרַיִם וְכִמְנַשֶּׁה: יְבָרֶכְךָ יְיָ וְיִשְׁמְרֶךָ: יָאֵר יְיָ פָּנָיו
אֵלֶיךָ וִיחֻנֶּךָּ: יִשָּׂא יְיָ פָּנָיו אֵלֶיךָ וְיָשֵׂם לְךָ שָׁלוֹם:

וִיהִי רָצוֹן מִלִּפְנֵי אָבִינוּ שֶׁבַּשָּׁמַיִם שֶׁיִּתֵּן בְּלִבְּךָ אַהֲבָתוֹ וְיִרְאָתוֹ וְתִהְיֶה
יִרְאַת יְיָ עַל פָּנֶיךָ כָּל יְמֵי חַיֶּיךָ לְבִלְתִּי תֶחֱטָא, וִיהִי חִשְׁקְךָ

R' Levi Yitzchak gestured toward the people. "Merciful Father in Heaven," he continued, sobbing, "they have faithfully fulfilled Your commandment of eating and drinking in a festive manner. Now they have all gathered here in utter solemnity, ready to approach You in prayer. Yet is a single one of them drunk? Is even one of them sleepy or nodding off from the effects of their drink?"

With arms outstretched and a wail that pried open the hearts of all those assembled, he concluded, "You must appreciate Your people, Hashem. They are a spiritual people who devotedly adhere to Your commandments; indeed they are worthy of forgiveness for all of their sins and transgressions. The Jewish people truly deserve Your blessing for a year of life and prosperity!"

And with that, R' Levi Yitzchak began *Kol Nidrei.*

ברכת הבנים

Dedicated as a *zechus* for our parents and children, by **Susan and Meir Yoel Laub**

We find the following in the words of **Rav Avraham Danzig *zt"l*** (***Chayei Adam*** 144:19, *Hilchos Yom Hakippurim*): *It is the custom to bless one's children before one goes to shul [on the eve of Yom Kippur] because at that time the sanctity of the day is already established and the gates of mercy are open [as well].*

The blessing begins with the words: *May G-d make you like Ephraim and Menashe...* and then continues: *May it be our Father in Heaven's will that He place in your heart love of Him and fear of Him. May the fear of G-d be upon your face all the days of your life in order that you not sin, and may your desire be to fulfill Torah and* mitzvos*; may your eyes see what faces you [Hashem]; may your mouth utter wisdom; may your heart comprehend fear; may your hands be occupied with the commandments and your feet run to do the bidding of your Father in Heaven. May He give you sons and daughters who are righteous, who are occupied with Torah and* mitzvos *all the days of their lives; may your origins be a blessing; may He prepare for you your livelihood from permitted sources, in an easy and abundant manner from His munificent hand, without relying on the gifts of flesh and blood, a livelihood that leaves you free to serve Hashem; and may*

בְּתוֹרָה וּבְמִצְוֹת. עֵינֶיךָ לְנֹכַח יַבִּיטוּ, פִּיךָ יְדַבֵּר חָכְמוֹת, וְלִבְּךָ יֶהְגֶּה תְבוּנוֹת. יָדֶיךָ יִהְיוּ עוֹסְקִים בְּמִצְווֹת וְרַגְלֶיךָ יָרוּצוּ לַעֲשׂוֹת רְצוֹן אָבִיךָ שֶׁבַּשָּׁמַיִם. יִתֵּן לְךָ בָּנִים וּבָנוֹת צַדִּיקִים וְצִדְקָנִיּוֹת עוֹסְקִים כָּל יְמֵיהֶם בַּתּוֹרָה וּבְמִצְוֹת, וִיהִי מְקוֹרְךָ בָּרוּךְ. וְיַזְמִין לְךָ פַּרְנָסָתְךָ בְּהֶתֵּר וּבְנַחַת

you be inscribed and sealed for a good, long life in the midst of all the righteous of Israel, amen.

ישימך אלקים כאפרים וכמנשה...

May Hashem make you like Ephraim and Menashe.

MIDDOS/ DERECH ERETZ
מידות/דרך ארץ

Yaakov Avinu gave two separate blessings, one to Yosef and one to his grandchildren, Ephraim and Menashe. What is interesting to note is that the blessing to Yosef actually refers to Ephraim and Menashe, while the blessing to Ephraim and Menashe pertains to Yosef. The Torah states, *And he blessed Yosef,* and concludes, *the angel that spares me from all evil shall bless the lads.* The Torah tells us, *And he blessed them on that day*, referring in the plural to Yosef's two sons, but ends in the singular, *in you shall Yisrael be blessed*, addressing Yosef.

Rav Yisrael Belsky ***shlit"a*** explains that these blessings touch upon the core of the parent/child relationship. The greatest blessing one can give a father is that he may merit children of whom he can be proud; children who live up to his ideals and perpetuate his legacy. The greatest blessing one can give a child is that his parents are blessed because of him; that he is a source of pleasure and satisfaction in their eyes, and that others recognize his parents' efforts in raising him to be this way. *In you shall Yisrael be blessed*—Klal Yisrael should bless you, Yosef, because of your exemplary sons.

There is greater depth to these blessings, however. It is unfortunate that parents often act in a way that interferes with the proper transmission of *Yiddishkeit* to their children. They may lack the *emunah* and *bitachon* bequeathed to us by our forefathers, Avraham, Yitzchak, and Yaakov, and thus, the continuity of the blessing is severed. Instead of a blessing, their children inherit a curse.

This is Yaakov Avinu's implication in his unique blessings to Yosef and his children. He blessed Yosef specifically through his children, so that Yosef should merit to transmit the spiritual inheritance of the *Avos* in its entirety, and that no evil interfere with this process.

וּבְרֶוַח מִתַּחַת יָדוֹ הָרְחָבָה וְלֹא עַל יְדֵי מַתְּנַת בָּשָׂר וָדָם, פַּרְנָסָה שֶׁתְּהֵא פְּנוּי לַעֲבוֹדַת יְיָ וְתִכָּתֵב בְּסֵפֶר מְחִילָה וּסְלִיחָה וְכַפָּרָה לְחַיִּים טוֹבִים וַאֲרוּכִים בְּתוֹךְ כָּל צַדִּיקֵי יִשְׂרָאֵל, אָמֵן:

יברכך ה׳ וישמרך: יאר ה׳ פניו אליך ויחנך: ישא ה׳ פניו אליך וישם לך שלום

May Hashem bless you and guard you. May Hashem shine His countenance upon you and be gracious to you. May Hashem turn His countenance toward you and grant you peace.

DVAR TORAH
דבר תורה

The order of the *brachos* in *Birkas Kohanim* is a bit puzzling. First it says Hashem should bless you and watch over you—a reference to wealth. Then, He should shine His face upon you... This indicates fear of Heaven and *avodas Hashem*. It concludes with a blessing for peace. Yet shouldn't the *brachah* for *ruchniyus* precede that of *gashmiyus*? Furthermore, why is peace the last *brachah*, as opposed to the first?

Rav Simchah Hakohen Sheps *zt"l*, the *rosh yeshivah of Torah Vodaath*, explains that the true blessing of wealth does not mean having a lot of money. Far from it! In fact, sometimes excess wealth can be a person's greatest curse, due to jealousy, competition and lust for more and more money, which is the nature of man. This *brachah* for riches in *Birkas Kohanim* is therefore a blessing for contentment, satisfaction and joy with one's portion! For only when one is truly happy with his lot, can he grow in Torah and *avodas Hashem*!

Subsequently, this contentment brings an individual to the ultimate gift from *Hakadosh Baruch Hu*, the blessing of peace. But not just any peace; we refer here to inner peace, which is the definition of true physical and spiritual wealth. This is *shleimus*—a complete and wholesome perfection that is the goal of every Jew.

In Eretz Yisrael, the *kohanim* bless the people each and every day. But even in *chutz la'aretz*, where *Birkas Kohanim* is much less frequent, we can all aspire to a true *shleimus* as we answer amen to the beautiful *Birkas Kohanim*.

Rav Shlomo Zalman Auerbach ***zt"l*** would say:

"A father once asked me to give his son a blessing. Instead, I told him a very important lesson: 'Teach him to smile!'"

יברכך ה' וישמרך וגו' (ו-כד)

May Hashem bless you and guard you.

DRUSH
דרוש

If Hashem is already blessing you, why do you require His protection? Shouldn't the blessing include protection?

The **Ohr Hachaim Hakadosh, Rabbeinu Chaim ben Attar** ***zt"l***, answers this with a parable of a poor man who lived in a run-down shack, without any furniture or possessions. Since he owned nothing, he did not even lock his door, for there was nothing to safeguard. One night, he heard noises in the middle of the night; a thief had easily walked into his home. The poor man announced, "I'm so glad you came! Let us search together, and perhaps between the two of us we might find something!" The message is clear. The more wealth one amasses, the more he must protect his belongings, starting from a simple door lock, all the way to a complex alarm system. Thus we can understand the *brachah* of this *pasuk*: Hashem should bless you to the point where you need protection. And then, Hashem should protect you as well!

Moreover, this can be paralleled to our spiritual assets. *Chazal* teach us: *Whoever is greater than his friend, his evil inclination is greater.* The level of the *yetzer hara's* (evil inclination) success grows with the righteousness of an individual, and therefore *tzaddikim* face more threatening challenges than others.

Rav Pinchas Menachem Alter ***zt"l*** **(Pnei Menachem)** once told someone: "When a pebble is lodged in my shoe, I cannot walk, yet the Bedouins walk barefoot on rough turf exposed to the scorching sun. They feel neither the sharp rocks nor the searing heat. Would I consider removing my shoes and walking like a Bedouin? Of course not! Similarly, a person on a lower level of spirituality feels much less sensitivity to his loss than a great man on a higher level. He deserves more compassion for his loss."

יהא חשקך בתורה ובמצוות. עיניך לנוכח יביטו פיך ידבר חכמות

May your desire be for Torah and mitzvos; may your eyes look straightforward, may your mouth speak with wisdom...

MASHAL
משל

משל: The *beis medrash* was packed to the rafters. Old and young were waiting for *Kol Nidrei* to begin. But the *rav*, **Rav Binyamin Diskin** ***zt"l***, had not yet arrived. "What is keeping him?" people whispered to one another. The sun was setting, darkness was falling...and the rabbi was still missing. "Run to the rabbi's house," they urged the *shamash*, "and see what is detaining him."

The *shamash* hurried to the *rav's* house. When he entered, his eyebrows arched in surprise. R' Binyamin was calmly sitting and learning with his young son, Yehoshua Leib!

Immediately, R' Binyamin apologized. "I am terribly sorry for the delay. You see, the Holy Day was approaching and when I was reviewing my actions of the past year, I could not recall even one mitzvah that I had performed. How can a man usher in this awesome day in such a manner? I decided to fulfill at least one mitzvah before this time, *v'shinantem l'vanecha*—'And you shall teach to your children,' hoping that in the merit of this mitzvah, I might be judged favorably."

נמשל: Some people run far and wide to come up with *segulos* and other means in which they hope to merit a good year and forgiveness for their innumerable sins. But what they forget is the basics: If they would just learn Torah and study with their children, *daven* daily with a *minyan* and conduct themselves like Torah Jews—they would accrue the greatest *segulah* possible!

יתן לך בנים ובנות צדיקים וצדקניות עוסקים כל ימיהם בתורה ובמצות

May [Hashem] grant you children who will [grow up to] be righteous, occupying themselves with Torah and mitzvos all their days...

MIDDOS/ DERECH ERETZ
מידות/דרך ארץ

The work and effort that parents devote to the rearing of their child may be likened to the toil of a man who has found a pearl in a mud puddle and labors to clean and polish it. Just as this man cannot know until his task is complete whether he'd discovered a real pearl or just an ordinary piece of glass, so too, parents cannot know in advance how their child will develop. They may feel that their work will be in vain and the child will remain no better than a piece of glass, as it were.

However, while the man who polishes the pearl receives no reward for his work unless the end product is truly a pearl, the Torah specifies that regardless of how the child will turn out, the parents will be rewarded for the toil that they invested in the education of the child, because then they have performed their duty.

The ***Shaar Bas Rabbim*** explains this and concludes that we are taught from here that the effort spent in educating even a small child in the spirit of the Torah is a precious jewel in its own right for which one receives a reward, even if it does not yield perfect results.

יתן לך בנים ובנות צדיקים וצדקניות עוסקים כל ימיהם בתורה ובמצות ויהי מקורך ברוך

May [Hashem] grant you children who will [grow up to] be righteous, occupying themselves with Torah and mitzvos all their days; may your source be blessed…

STORIES
מעשה

During the early part of World War II, the **Belzer Rebbe, Rav Aharon Rokeach** ***zt"l*** along with his distinguished brother, **Rav Mordechai** ***zt"l,*** **the Bilgoray Rav**, found themselves in the Bochnia ghetto, before their dramatic escape to Hungary. Many of the ghetto inhabitants came to ask for a blessing and to seek the rebbe's advice. R' Aharon, who slept no more than two hours a night, and survived on mere sips of coffee and a glass of milk smuggled into the ghetto by his ardent followers, did not turn away a single soul. He offered comfort and solace to all who came to him, never mentioning his own great tragedy—the loss of his entire family.

Even the chief Nazi, a sadist by the name of Muller, went so far as to visit the "*Vunder Rabiner*," receive a blessing from him, and offer to double his rations! Such was the esteem that everyone—even the Nazis—held for the Belzer Rebbe, and they believed that keeping him contained within their midst was some kind of "good-luck charm."

Among those who came to the Belzer Rebbe's crowded apartment in the ghetto were Bronia Koczicki and her two little sons; Tzvi, age six, and Yitzchak, age three. At this stage in the war, they had all seen numerous miracles and salvation, especially little Tzvi, who was thrown from a speeding railcar on its way to Auschwitz, and lived to tell about it.

After the rebbe blessed her and her two children with a heartfelt, but general blessing—"*Di Eibishter vet helfen*" (G-d will help)—Bronia did not leave the rebbe's presence. The attendants attempted to move her along, but she refused to budge. Finally, she looked at the holy countenance of the rebbe and begged, "Please, rebbe, please bless my sons with fine generations in the future."

"Poor woman," someone whispered. "She probably lost her mind in these troubled times. Every day, *aktions* for children take place. Hundreds of children are constantly being murdered and this woman is asking not only that her children remain safe, but that they live to bear a future with fine generations, a future of living Jews!"

The Belzer Rebbe motioned to the young boys to come close to him. He placed his hands on their heads and blessed them with generations upon generations of fine Jews, his words practically shaking the very foundation of the world. When he concluded, he smiled brightly at the two young boys.

"We will live through this war, we will live through this war!" Bronia kept telling her bewildered children as she left the rebbe's presence. She was so convinced of

אֱלֹהֵינוּ וֵאלֹהֵי אֲבוֹתֵינוּ: (נ"א אָנָּא) תָּבֹא לְפָנֶיךָ תְּפִלָּתֵנוּ. וְאַל תִּתְעַלַּם מִתְּחִנָּתֵנוּ. שֶׁאֵין אָנוּ עַזֵּי פָנִים וּקְשֵׁי עֹרֶף לוֹמַר לְפָנֶיךָ יְיָ אֱלֹהֵינוּ וֵאלֹהֵי אֲבוֹתֵינוּ צַדִּיקִים אֲנַחְנוּ וְלֹא חָטָאנוּ אֲבָל אֲנַחְנוּ וַאֲבוֹתֵינוּ חָטָאנוּ:

the fulfillment of the holy Belzer Rebbe's blessing that she infused her children with tremendous hope and faith.

Many years later, when Bronia (who remarried the **Bluzhever Rebbe, Rav Yisrael Spira *zt"l***) would recount this story, surrounded by grandchildren and great-grandchildren, she would smile conspiratorially and say, "At times, one has to be aggressive when it comes to blessings." Then, she would add as if in an afterthought, in a manner of good-natured advice, "In times of war, one has to organize everything—even a blessing from a *tzaddik*!"

וידוי/אשמנו

For we are not so brazen-faced and stiff-necked to say to You, Hashem, our G-d, and the G-d of our fathers, "We are righteous and have not sinned."

DRUSH
דרוש

Every Jew experiences difficulties in life, challenges that attempt to disrupt his performance of *mitzvos*. However, Hashem instructs us not to reject the *mitzvos* when they are difficult to perform. We are to fulfill our duties despite the circumstances—because the greater the difficulty, the greater the reward.

Chacham Dovid Pinto *shlit"a* says that unfortunately, there are people who perform *mitzvos* only when it is convenient for them. For example, there are people who act like *tzaddikim* outside their homes. They are careful to accomplish both easy and difficult *mitzvos*, and people may even learn from them how to serve Hashem. However, in the privacy of their homes, these very people behave like non-Jews. They conduct themselves with absolutely no modesty, holiness, or purity; they do not even perform basic *mitzvos*.

When the *chacham* and Kabbalist Rabbeinu Chaim Pinto arrived in a certain town, he encountered a man who was involved in a dispute with the local *rav*. R' Chaim reprimanded the man for his behavior, yet the man was obstinate and leery.

R' Chaim then summoned him to an isolated room and said, "Is it true that you are suffering from terrible headaches?"

אָשַׁמְנוּ, בָּגַדְנוּ, גָּזַלְנוּ, דִּבַּרְנוּ דֹפִי: הֶעֱוִינוּ, וְהִרְשַׁעְנוּ, זַדְנוּ, חָמַסְנוּ, טָפַלְנוּ שֶׁקֶר: יָעַצְנוּ רָע, כִּזַּבְנוּ, לַצְנוּ, מָרַדְנוּ, נִאַצְנוּ, סָרַרְנוּ, עָוִינוּ, פָּשַׁעְנוּ, צָרַרְנוּ, קִשִּׁינוּ עֹרֶף: רָשַׁעְנוּ, שִׁחַתְנוּ, תִּעַבְנוּ, תָּעִינוּ, תִּעְתָּעְנוּ:

The man was quite frightened by this question, and he responded, "How does the *chacham* know this?"

R' Chaim replied, "I know, I know. On Taanis Esther, you became very hungry, and took some food with you into a side room. Since nobody could see you, you ate the food without reciting any blessings. You've been suffering from headaches ever since!"

If a Jew thinks that he can hide his transgressions from Hashem, he will yet realize how wrong he really is!

אשמנו, בגדנו, גזלנו...

We have become guilty, we have betrayed, we have stolen...

STORIES
מעשה

The dominant figure in the Feldafing D.P. camp immediately after the conclusion of WWII was the **Klausenberger Rebbe, Rav Yekusiel Yehudah Halberstam *zt"l.*** What he did for the broken survivors was immeasurable. Although he himself had lost a wife and eleven children, he was a constant source of strength and inspiration to his fellow survivors.

On the first Yom Kippur after the war, the rebbe held a *minyan* for the survivors and following *Kol Nidrei*, he delivered a tremendously powerful speech. When he had finished, more than two hours later, there was not a dry eye in the shul.

The rebbe stood by the *amud, tallis* over his head and looking for all the world like an angel. He held a *machzor* in his hand, flipping through its pages. Periodically, he would look up and ask, "*Vehr hut dos geshribben*—Who wrote this? Does this apply to us? Are we guilty of the sins enumerated here?" One by one, he went through each of the sins listed in the *Ashamnu* prayer and then the *Al Cheit.*

"*Ashamnu* (we have become guilty): Does this apply to us? Have we sinned against Hashem or man? How could we? Let's go on. *Bagadnu* (we have betrayed): Are we disloyal to Hashem? Have we betrayed our loved ones? No. *Bagadnu* does not apply to us. *Gazalnu* (we have stolen): From whom could we have stolen? There was nothing to steal in the camps. Definitely this does not apply to us. *Dibarnu dofi* (we have spoken slander): Impossible.

סַרְנוּ מִמִּצְוֹתֶיךָ וּמִמִּשְׁפָּטֶיךָ הַטּוֹבִים וְלֹא שָׁוָה לָנוּ, וְאַתָּה צַדִּיק עַל כָּל הַבָּא עָלֵינוּ כִּי אֱמֶת עָשִׂיתָ וַאֲנַחְנוּ הִרְשָׁעְנוּ:

מַה נֹּאמַר לְפָנֶיךָ יוֹשֵׁב מָרוֹם, וּמַה נְּסַפֵּר לְפָנֶיךָ שׁוֹכֵן שְׁחָקִים, הֲלֹא כָּל הַנִּסְתָּרוֹת וְהַנִּגְלוֹת אַתָּה יוֹדֵעַ:

"*He'evinu, v'hirshanu* (we have caused wickedness), *zadnu* (we have sinned willfully), *chamasnu* (we have extorted), *tafalnu sheker* (we have accused falsely): No, these don't apply to us. *Latznu* (we have scoffed): Who wrote this *machzor*? Who put it together? We were so serious in the camps. There was no such thing as smiling or making a joke."

When the Klausenberger Rebbe had finished the entire *Ashamnu* prayer in this fashion, he continued with *Al Cheit.*

"*Al cheit shechatanu l'fanecha b'ones uv'ratzon* (for the sin we have sinned before You under duress and willingly): In the camps, did we have a *ratzon* (will)? We were way beyond the category of *ones* (under duress).

"*B'maachal ub'mishteh* (with food and drink): Food and drink? What food and drink? We starved for years!

"*B'yetzer hara* (with the evil urge): To sin with the *yetzer hara* you must first have possession of your physical senses; a desire to touch, see, hear, or taste something forbidden. We had none of these, nor the ability to achieve them."

One by one, he eliminated every *Al Cheit.* The rebbe then closed his *machzor* and it seemed he had finally finished. But then he asked again, "Who wrote this *machzor*? These sins don't apply to us." He paused. "What I don't see anywhere is the sin that does apply to us. What is that sin? The sin of having lost our *emunah* and *bitachon* (faith and trust) in Hashem.

"What is the proof that we sinned in this fashion? How many times did we recite *Krias Shema* on our wooden slats at night and think to ourselves: '*Ribono Shel Olam,* let this be my last *Hamapil.* I'm so weak. I have no reason to carry on anymore. Is there no end to our suffering? *Ribono Shel Olam,* please take my *neshamah* so that I do not have to thank You once again for returning my soul to me in the morning. I don't need my soul. I don't want this wretched existence. You can keep it.'

"How many of us went to sleep thinking that we couldn't exist another day, with all our *bitachon* lost? And yet when the dawn broke, we once again recited *Modeh Ani* and thanked Hashem for having returned our souls.

"Yes, we did survive, but none of us expected to. Every morning, we saw this one didn't move and that one didn't move, and as we carried the dead away, we looked upon them with envy. Is that *emunah* in Hashem? Is that *bitachon* in Hashem?

"*Rabbosai*, we have sinned. We have sinned and now we must *klap Al Cheit.* We must pray to regain the *emunah* and *bitachon* we once had, the *emunah* and *bitachon* that went to sleep these last few years in the camps. Now that we are free, *Ribono Shel Olam*, we beg You to forgive us. Forgive every Jew in the world, *Ribono Shel Olam*!"

דברנו דפי...

We have slandered...

MIDDOS/ DERECH ERETZ
מידות/דרך ארץ

Rav Simchah Bunim of Peshischah *zt"l* explained that every single Jew has the capacity for doing *teshuvah.* Everyone, that is, except for a person who lies. A liar is someone who, after telling untruths for so long, comes to believe his own lies and does not even recognize his own wrongdoing. As a result, a person who tells lies is doing himself a terrible injustice, for he prevents himself from *teshuvah.* It is surely a sin to deceive others, but it is pure foolishness to deceive oneself.

טפלנו שקר...

We have added falsehood upon falsehood...

MASHAL
משל

משל: A student at Beis Medrash Govoha in Lakewood, N.J., had the special privilege of bringing the *rosh yeshivah*, **Rav Aharon Kotler *zt"l***, his daily cup of coffee.

One day, after placing the cup on the *rosh yeshivah's* desk, the student noticed that the cup went untouched. Assuming that R' Aharon had simply forgotten to drink his coffee because he was so engrossed in his learning, he replaced the cup with a fresh one. But this cup also went untouched. This time he asked the *rosh yeshivah* what was the matter.

R' Aharon sighed and replied, "A certain family that I'm well acquainted with is looking into a former student of the yeshivah regarding a marriage prospect. I am pretty sure they will call me to inquire about him. However, praising him with attributes he does not possess is a violation of the Torah precept of *midvar sheker tirchak*, and if unknown negative traits ultimately lead to divorce, it will be because honest information was withheld. On the other hand, I don't feel comfortable divulging my true feelings, since the couple may actually be happy with one another after marriage. My words might cause the end of the *shidduch.* Thus, I have decided

to designate this day for fasting and prayer so that Hashem may grant me a kindness and spare me the call!"

נמשל: *Sheker* extends beyond the common definition of "falsehood"; the law is not limited to one who tells a lie or deceives another. A person can be guilty even when he is trying to be helpful and useful. Withholding vital information or "bending" the truth just a bit in order to make others happy is not only a form of *sheker*—it can be destructive as well!

עוינו, פשענו, צררנו, קשינו ערף

We have sinned deliberately, we have been negligent in our performance of the commandments, we have caused our friends grief, we have been stiff-necked…

DVAR TORAH
דבר תורה

When the Jews committed the sin of the Golden Calf, Hashem threatened to transfer them to the custody of an angel. Moshe Rabbeinu pleaded on behalf of his people that they should not lose this exclusive personal protection of *Hakadosh Baruch Hu*: *"Please Hashem, You go among us Yourself, because they are a stubborn people, and You will forgive our sins"* (*Shemos* 34:9). What kind of a plea is that? Why should Hashem forgive us because we are a stubborn nation?

The **Maggid of Dubno, Rav Yaakov Krantz** ***zt"l***, explained this with a parable. Several peddlers were comparing notes after a long day of hawking their wares. One peddler complained that he'd had a very unsuccessful day. He had no customers at all for the cheap wooden forks and spoons which he had been trying to sell in the wealthiest section of town. "You fool!" the other peddlers chastised him. "Nobody in that section will buy wooden utensils. Those people use only gold and silver for their needs. You should peddle cheap utensils in the poor sections of town."

Similarly, the *maggid* observed, Hashem had just told Moshe that He was merciful and forgiving. Seizing the opportunity to effect total reconciliation, Moshe pointed out, "What will You do with Your mercy and forgiveness? The angels in heaven have no use for them. They are never disobedient or sinful, and You will never see actualization of these exalted qualities. It is more befitting that Your glory should accompany the Jewish people personally. It is because they are a stubborn and defiant people, and thus You will have many customers for Your mercy and forgiveness!"

Moshe Rabbeinu, in his inimitable wisdom, knew how to effect Divine forgiveness for Bnei Yisrael.

אַתָּה יוֹדֵעַ רָזֵי עוֹלָם, וְתַעֲלוּמוֹת סִתְרֵי כָּל חָי, אַתָּה חוֹפֵשׂ כָּל חַדְרֵי בָטֶן וּבוֹחֵן כְּלָיוֹת וָלֵב, אֵין דָּבָר נֶעְלָם מִמֶּךָּ וְאֵין נִסְתָּר מִנֶּגֶד עֵינֶיךָ: וּבְכֵן יְהִי רָצוֹן מִלְּפָנֶיךָ יְיָ אֱלֹהֵינוּ וֵאלֹהֵי אֲבוֹתֵינוּ שֶׁתְּכַפֵּר לָנוּ

סרנו ממצותיך וממשפטיך הטובים ולא שוה לנו...

We have turned away from Your commandments and from Your good laws, and we have gained nothing from it.

MASHAL
משל

משל: Several hundred years ago, an African tribesman traveled by ship in search of merchandise to trade, and by chance the ship docked in a European port. The African disembarked and began walking through the streets.

It didn't take long for him to realize that everyone he passed was staring at him. He was the only dark-skinned man they had ever seen and he stuck out quite drastically!

Panicking, he looked around to see if there was anybody he could associate himself with. Of course, there was no one like him; everyone was white as snow! He grew frightened that the white people would become hostile to him.

Suddenly, he saw a young boy walking his way. The boy was pitch-black—just like him! He ran over and said, "Oh, finally, I have found another who is like me!"

But the boy did not agree. "I am not like you," he said. "I have just come from the playground, where I was playing in the mud for the past hour. When I get home, I will wash off all the black mud that is on me and I will be white again. But you," said the boy, "will always remain black!"

נמשל: When the nations of the world see the Jewish people sinning, they finally feel vindicated. "You are no different than us. We sin as we please, and so do you. You are no different in the eyes of G-d than we are!"

But we have a ready answer: "Of course we are different. Sinning is part of your nature, it is who you are. But deep down, we are pure; we just became a bit soiled through our actions. When we cleanse ourselves and do *teshuvah*, we will once again be as pure and white as snow!" Thus, although we may have strayed from the *mitzvos*, in reality it bears no value—it is not who we intrinsically are! **(Chacham Avraham Cohen)**

אתה יודע רזי עולם ותעלומות סתרי כל חי אתה חופש כל חדרי בטן ובוחן כליות ולב

You know the mysteries of the universe, and the hidden secrets of every individual. You search all our innermost thoughts, and probe our mind and heart.

על חטא

עַל כָּל חַטֹּאתֵינוּ, וְתִסְלַח לָנוּ עַל כָּל עֲוֹנוֹתֵינוּ, וְתִמְחָל לָנוּ עַל כָּל פְּשָׁעֵינוּ:

DVAR TORAH
דבר תורה

The method of stern rigidity was always revered as proper Lithuanian pedagogy, where intellect was venerated and emotions barely acknowledged. Parents perpetually sought perfection from their children and love was not openly demonstrated. Even praise was withheld, due to a conviction that it might invest one with undue pride.

Rabbi Joseph B. Soloveitchik ***zt"l*** explained the rationale behind this approach at a memorial tribute to his father, **Rav Moshe Soloveitchik** ***zt"l***. "My beloved father used to say that our innermost thoughts are like the *Kodesh Kadashim* of the Beis Hamikdash, and the holier and more intimate the emotion, the less it can be verbalized or revealed. For an emotion that is truly deep and sanctified cannot be shared with another human being; it is preserved for the One Who knows all thoughts."

Similarly, we find that on Yom Kippur, the Torah strictly commands, *No man shall be permitted in the Mishkan (Tabernacle) from the time he (the* kohen gadol*) comes to atone in the sanctuary, until he departs.* Only one man was permitted to closet himself with his Maker and confess in the Holy of Holies, to the exclusion of all others. Our emotional holy of holies, that innermost chamber which contains our deepest sentiments—our love, our pain, our hidden emotions—requires a curtain to separate it from the outside world; otherwise its secrets might be revealed and its purity intruded upon, defiling its sanctity.

על חטא

על חטא שחטאנו לפניך בגלוי עריות

For the sin we committed before You in immorality...

MIDDOS/
DERECH ERETZ
מידות/דרך ארץ

The **Lubavitcher Rebbe, Rav Menachem Mendel Schneerson** ***zt"l***, in citing the Gemara, *A person does not commit a transgression unless a spirit of folly enters him. As it says, "If a man's wife goes astray and commits a sin against him"* (*Sotah* 3a), asks the following: Why is the sin of immorality, the breach between man and woman, the one that most conclusively declares—from among all other transgressions—that sin is always irrational?

עַל חֵטְא שֶׁחָטָאנוּ לְפָנֶיךָ בְּאֹנֶס וּבְרָצוֹן:
וְעַל חֵטְא שֶׁחָטָאנוּ לְפָנֶיךָ בְּאִמּוּץ הַלֵּב:
עַל חֵטְא שֶׁחָטָאנוּ לְפָנֶיךָ בִּבְלִי דָעַת:
וְעַל חֵטְא שֶׁחָטָאנוּ לְפָנֶיךָ בְּבִטּוּי שְׂפָתָיִם:
עַל חֵטְא שֶׁחָטָאנוּ לְפָנֶיךָ בְּגָלוּי וּבַסָּתֶר:
וְעַל חֵטְא שֶׁחָטָאנוּ לְפָנֶיךָ בְּגִלּוּי עֲרָיוֹת:
עַל חֵטְא שֶׁחָטָאנוּ לְפָנֶיךָ בְּדִבּוּר פֶּה:
וְעַל חֵטְא שֶׁחָטָאנוּ לְפָנֶיךָ בְּדַעַת וּבְמִרְמָה:
עַל חֵטְא שֶׁחָטָאנוּ לְפָנֶיךָ בְּהִרְהוּר הַלֵּב:
וְעַל חֵטְא שֶׁחָטָאנוּ לְפָנֶיךָ בְּהוֹנָאַת רֵעַ:
עַל חֵטְא שֶׁחָטָאנוּ לְפָנֶיךָ בְּוִדּוּי פֶּה:
וְעַל חֵטְא שֶׁחָטָאנוּ לְפָנֶיךָ בִּוְעִידַת זְנוּת:
עַל חֵטְא שֶׁחָטָאנוּ לְפָנֶיךָ בְּזָדוֹן וּבִשְׁגָגָה:
וְעַל חֵטְא שֶׁחָטָאנוּ לְפָנֶיךָ בְּזִלְזוּל הוֹרִים וּמוֹרִים:
עַל חֵטְא שֶׁחָטָאנוּ לְפָנֶיךָ בְּחֹזֶק יָד:
וְעַל חֵטְא שֶׁחָטָאנוּ לְפָנֶיךָ בְּחִלּוּל הַשֵּׁם:

The answer, says the Lubavitcher Rebbe, is that the sin of adultery is not just an isolated act of dishonor between a husband and a wife. Rather, it is the prototype of all sins. The Jewish people as a whole are regarded as the "wife" of the Al-mighty, and He is our "groom." The bond forged between us and *Hakadosh Baruch Hu* at Har Sinai was no less than a marriage. And so, every time a Jew commits a sin, however slight, he is betraying the covenant, the "marriage contract" between himself and Hashem. He is guilty of spiritual infidelity to his Divine partner. This is why even a trivial sin is considered a folly, for it causes a severing of the link between man and the Al-mighty. It is an act of infidelity, intervening in the marriage between Hashem and His beloved Jew. We must make sure not to betray our betrothed through unfaithfulness caused by sin.

ועל חטא שחטאנו לפניך בועידת זנות

For the sin we committed before You by joining in a lewd gathering...

STORIES
מעשה

A devastating epidemic once struck the city of Pinsk, and several young rabbinical students died suddenly, one after the other. This was a tremendous blow to the community and they were determined to learn the cause of this outbreak. After investigation, some of the influential members came to the belief that the immodest behavior of a certain individual in the community was to blame for the series of tragedies. After all, *Chazal* tell us (*Shabbos* 33a) that indiscriminate death and destruction often plague the world as a punishment for the immodest behavior of society. The people wanted to stage a demonstration at that man's house to register their protest against his manner of behavior, but they realized that the man had connections to the government, and that any steps taken against him were likely to result in trouble from the authorities. The community opted not to protest publicly yet, but resolved that should another calamity befall them, they would definitely do

עַל חֵטְא שֶׁחָטָאנוּ לְפָנֶיךָ בְּטִפְשׁוּת פֶּה:
וְעַל חֵטְא שֶׁחָטָאנוּ לְפָנֶיךָ בְּטֻמְאַת שְׂפָתָיִם:
עַל חֵטְא שֶׁחָטָאנוּ לְפָנֶיךָ בְּיֵצֶר הָרָע:
וְעַל חֵטְא שֶׁחָטָאנוּ לְפָנֶיךָ בְּיוֹדְעִים וּבְלֹא יוֹדְעִים:

וְעַל כֻּלָּם אֱלוֹהַּ סְלִיחוֹת, סְלַח לָנוּ, מְחַל לָנוּ, כַּפֶּר לָנוּ:

עַל חֵטְא שֶׁחָטָאנוּ לְפָנֶיךָ בְּכַפַּת שֹׁחַד:
וְעַל חֵטְא שֶׁחָטָאנוּ לְפָנֶיךָ בְּכַחַשׁ וּבְכָזָב:
עַל חֵטְא שֶׁחָטָאנוּ לְפָנֶיךָ בִּלְשׁוֹן הָרָע:
וְעַל חֵטְא שֶׁחָטָאנוּ לְפָנֶיךָ בְּלָצוֹן:
עַל חֵטְא שֶׁחָטָאנוּ לְפָנֶיךָ בְּמַשָּׂא וּבְמַתָּן:
וְעַל חֵטְא שֶׁחָטָאנוּ לְפָנֶיךָ בְּמַאֲכָל וּבְמִשְׁתֶּה:
עַל חֵטְא שֶׁחָטָאנוּ לְפָנֶיךָ בְּנֶשֶׁךְ וּבְמַרְבִּית:
וְעַל חֵטְא שֶׁחָטָאנוּ לְפָנֶיךָ בִּנְטִיַּת גָּרוֹן:
עַל חֵטְא שֶׁחָטָאנוּ לְפָנֶיךָ בְּשִׂקּוּר עָיִן:

---

something to show their displeasure. It was, literally, a matter of life and death. Thus, it was decided that should there be another funeral procession, it would pass demonstratively in front of this man's house.

And so it happened. Another young man passed away, and the funeral procession was routed to pass by the immodest man's house. As was feared, however, the man was incensed and pressed charges against the leaders of the Jewish community, summoning them to the local courthouse, known for its fierce anti-Jewish bias.

The defense on behalf of the Jewish community was none other than the *rav*, **Rav Elazar Moshe Horowitz** ***zt"l.*** At the appointed time, all assembled at the courthouse to witness this unusual event. The great scholar stood confidently before the judge, and when asked why the funeral procession was directed to pass by the plaintiff's house, he replied matter-of-factly, "Your honor, it is very clear that this man, who conducts himself in a manner which is wholly indecent, is responsible for several deaths in the Jewish community."

The judge was amused and replied incredulously, "Rabbi, surely you exaggerate. What possible connection could there be between immodest behavior and the life expectancy of the people in your community? You have no evidence to support such a wild claim."

At that point, R' Elazar Moshe opened up the volume of the Talmud that he had brought with him and translated the relevant passage, explaining that if matters remained status quo, more destruction could wreak havoc on the world. Amazingly, the non-Jewish judge understood the message of the Gemara and accepted the implication of the frightening citation. He immediately acquitted the community leaders of any wrongdoing.

וְעַל חֵטְא שֶׁחָטָאנוּ לְפָנֶיךָ בְּשִׂיחַ שִׂפְתוֹתֵינוּ:
עַל חֵטְא שֶׁחָטָאנוּ לְפָנֶיךָ בְּעֵינַיִם רָמוֹת:
וְעַל חֵטְא שֶׁחָטָאנוּ לְפָנֶיךָ בְּעַזּוּת מֵצַח:

וְעַל כֻּלָּם אֱלוֹהַּ סְלִיחוֹת, סְלַח לָנוּ, מְחַל לָנוּ, כַּפֶּר לָנוּ:
עַל חֵטְא שֶׁחָטָאנוּ לְפָנֶיךָ בִּפְרִיקַת עֹל:

על חטא שחטאנו לפניך בוידוי פה

For the sin we committed before You with [mere] verbal confession…

MUSSAR/ HASHKAFAH מוסר/השקפה

We encounter an interesting phenomenon each year during the Aseres Yemei Teshuvah and Yom Kippur that it is often the youngsters who become inspired with the awesomeness of these holy days, and inflamed with a true spirit of *teshuvah.* On the other hand, many older and more mature individuals, men with vast life experiences who should better understand the nature of the Yom Hadin, seem to view this time as "business as usual." Their *davening* is no different than the rest of the year; in fact, it seems to regress a bit. But why is this so? Wouldn't one think that the older a person, the more he would devote himself to the self-improvement of his soul?

Rav Gamliel Rabinowitz *shlit"a* uses a play on words to explain this point: *Chazal* tell us עולם הזה דומה לפרוזדור—*This world is compared to a vestibule.* The letters of פרוזדור can also spell פריזדור (refrigerator). The meaning is as follows: Our world is similar to a refrigerator, in that it cools off everything that is placed inside. If one does not make the effort to inflame his inner soul with Torah, *tefillah*, and *teshuvah*, his enthusiasm will steadily wear down and "cool off." A youngster is not in this world long enough to feel the effects of "global cooling." Unfortunately, the older one is, the greater the chance that he will feel this effect.

During these holy days, we must fire up our souls with the spirit of true repentance, and let our fiery prayers ignite the Divine mercy.

על חטא שחטאנו לפניך ביצר הרע

For the sin we committed before You with the evil inclination…

DVAR TORAH דבר תורה

Chazal enumerate ten miracles which were performed in the Beis Hamikdash. One of the miracles mentioned is: *No bodily impurity befell the* kohen gadol *on Yom Kippur*, rendering him unfit to perform the *avodah.*

Rav Yom Tov Lipman Heller *zt"l* (*Tosfos Yom Tov*) notes that for seven days before Yom Kippur, the *kohen gadol* would separate

וְעַל חֵטְא שֶׁחָטָאנוּ לְפָנֶיךָ בִּפְלִילוּת:
עַל חֵטְא שֶׁחָטָאנוּ לְפָנֶיךָ בִּצְדִיַּת רֵעַ:
וְעַל חֵטְא שֶׁחָטָאנוּ לְפָנֶיךָ בְּצָרוּת עָיִן:
עַל חֵטְא שֶׁחָטָאנוּ לְפָנֶיךָ בְּקַלּוּת רֹאשׁ:
וְעַל חֵטְא שֶׁחָטָאנוּ לְפָנֶיךָ בְּקַשְׁיוּת עֹרֶף:

עַל חֵטְא שֶׁחָטָאנוּ לְפָנֶיךָ בְּרִיצַת רַגְלַיִם לְהָרַע:
וְעַל חֵטְא שֶׁחָטָאנוּ לְפָנֶיךָ בִּרְכִילוּת:
עַל חֵטְא שֶׁחָטָאנוּ לְפָנֶיךָ בִּשְׁבוּעַת שָׁוְא:
וְעַל חֵטְא שֶׁחָטָאנוּ לְפָנֶיךָ בְּשִׂנְאַת חִנָּם:
עַל חֵטְא שֶׁחָטָאנוּ לְפָנֶיךָ בִּתְשׂוּמֶת יָד:

---

himself from the community, making it virtually impossible for him to become impure. What, then, is so miraculous about the fact that the *kohen gadol* did not become impure? We learn from here just how powerful the *yetzer hara* is. Were it not for Hashem's miraculous protection, the *yetzer hara* would still have been able to cause the *kohen gadol* to become impure, despite the interval of separation. Although the *yetzer hara* was steadily weakened during the *kohen gadol's* preparation for Yom Kippur, before he completely disappeared on Yom Kippur, he mustered up a final burst of energy to attempt one last thing: to render the *kohen gadol* impure so that he will not be able to perform the *avodah.*

Rav Moshe Aharon Stern *zt"l* adds that we are left with a difficult question: What was the *yetzer hara* seeking to accomplish? Even if it were to succeed in its efforts, the Mishnah already states (*Yuma* 2a) that each year, a back-up *kohen* was prepared in case the *kohen gadol* became unfit. Thus, the *avodah* would resume in any event. So what did the *yetzer hara* stand to gain? The answer is a fundamental principle: The *yetzer hara* wants to make a *hefsek* (interruption) in the *avodah.* He wants us to pause—even for a moment—in our mitzvah performance. This way, he can gain control over our minds. Thus, this miracle was of vital necessity.

על חטא שחטאנו לפניך בלשון הרע

For the sin we committed before You by evil talk…

MIDDOS/ DERECH ERETZ
מידות/דרך ארץ

When a person sins, prosecuting angels are created. If they come before Hashem's throne to prosecute, Hashem can remove them from His presence. However, **Rav Yisrael Meir Hakohen Kagan *zt"l* (Chafetz Chaim)** writes that there are accusing angels that cannot be removed—those emanating from improper speech. Since they were created through speech, these angels accuse verbally; even without any other presence or form in front of Hashem, their voices are heard. This is likened to a king who wishes to acquit someone in judgment, but since the accuser demands retribution in public, the king is forced to at least be seen meting justice.

וְעַל חֵטְא שֶׁחָטָאנוּ לְפָנֶיךָ בְּתִמְהוֹן לֵבָב:

וְעַל כֻּלָּם אֱלוֹהַּ סְלִיחוֹת, סְלַח לָנוּ, מְחַל לָנוּ, כַּפֶּר לָנוּ:

וְעַל חֲטָאִים שֶׁאָנוּ חַיָּבִים עֲלֵיהֶם עוֹלָה:

וְעַל חֲטָאִים שֶׁאָנוּ חַיָּבִים עֲלֵיהֶם חַטָּאת:

וְעַל חֲטָאִים שֶׁאָנוּ חַיָּבִים עֲלֵיהֶם קָרְבָּן עוֹלֶה וְיוֹרֵד:

וְעַל חֲטָאִים שֶׁאָנוּ חַיָּבִים עֲלֵיהֶם אָשָׁם וַדַּאי וְתָלוּי:

וְעַל חֲטָאִים שֶׁאָנוּ חַיָּבִים עֲלֵיהֶם מַכַּת מַרְדּוּת:

וְעַל חֲטָאִים שֶׁאָנוּ חַיָּבִים עֲלֵיהֶם מַלְקוּת אַרְבָּעִים:

וְעַל חֲטָאִים שֶׁאָנוּ חַיָּבִים עֲלֵיהֶם מִיתָה בִּידֵי שָׁמָיִם:

וְעַל חֲטָאִים שֶׁאָנוּ חַיָּבִים עֲלֵיהֶם כָּרֵת וַעֲרִירִי:

וְעַל חֲטָאִים שֶׁאָנוּ חַיָּבִים עֲלֵיהֶם אַרְבַּע מִיתוֹת בֵּית דִּין:
סְקִילָה, שְׂרֵפָה, הֶרֶג, וְחֶנֶק:

על חטא שחטאנו לפניך במשא ובמתן

For the sin we committed before You in business dealings...

DVAR TORAH
דבר תורה

The Gemara (*Bechoros* 13a) states: *When you make a sale to your fellow; to your fellow do not victimize (in business) but to an idol-worshipper you may victimize.* Many use these words of *Chazal* to justify unethical and even unlawful business practices with non-Jews. "One is permitted to steal from a non-Jew," is the refrain they say with misplaced self-righteousness. They are careful to be kind and "kosher" to fellow Jews, but have no qualms about ripping off non-Jews for their personal gain.

How wrong and misguided they are! **Rav Baruch Epstein *zt"l* (*Torah Temimah*)** denotes that the words, *Or if you bought from your fellow* (*Devarim* 25:14), does not refer to Jews; it means any person who is decent and obeys the law. Any person, whether Jew or gentile, who operates in the world of commerce and follows the guidelines established to ensure that people do not deceive or swindle each other is considered "your fellow." The Torah is very explicit in its warning: *Do not victimize anyone who is your fellow.*

It is appropriate to quote the words of the ***Sefer Chassidim***: *One may not commit an injustice to a gentile, just like a Jew, for such an act of impropriety will bring him down, with no success in his endeavors. And if it doesn't happen to him, it will happen to his children!*

The **Maharsha, Rav Shmuel Eidels *zt"l***, writes: *Many people in this generation amass great fortunes through trickery, cheating gentiles, and causing a terrible* chillul Hashem. *Then, they use that stolen money for respectable causes: to give themselves honor, to make a grand* Mi Shebeirach *in shul for self-aggrandizement and glorification! This is nothing less than a* mitzvah haba'ah b'aveirah *(benefit of a mitzvah obtained through a sin) and such "wealth" will have no lasting power.*

עַל מִצְוַת עֲשֵׂה וְעַל מִצְוַת לֹא תַעֲשֶׂה, בֵּין שֶׁיֵּשׁ בָּהּ קוּם עֲשֵׂה וּבֵין שֶׁאֵין בָּהּ קוּם עֲשֵׂה, אֶת הַגְּלוּיִים לָנוּ וְאֶת שֶׁאֵינָם גְּלוּיִים לָנוּ, אֶת הַגְּלוּיִים לָנוּ כְּבָר אֲמַרְנוּם לְפָנֶיךָ וְהוֹדִינוּ לְךָ עֲלֵיהֶם, וְאֶת שֶׁאֵינָם גְּלוּיִים לָנוּ לְפָנֶיךָ הֵם גְּלוּיִים וִידוּעִים, כַּדָּבָר שֶׁנֶּאֱמַר הַנִּסְתָּרֹת לַה׳ אֱלֹהֵינוּ וְהַנִּגְלֹת לָנוּ וּלְבָנֵינוּ עַד עוֹלָם לַעֲשׂוֹת אֶת כָּל דִּבְרֵי הַתּוֹרָה הַזֹּאת: כִּי אַתָּה סָלְחָן לְיִשְׂרָאֵל וּמָחֳלָן לְשִׁבְטֵי יְשֻׁרוּן בְּכָל דּוֹר וָדוֹר, וּמִבַּלְעָדֶיךָ אֵין לָנוּ מֶלֶךְ מוֹחֵל וְסוֹלֵחַ:

אֱלֹהַי, עַד שֶׁלֹּא נוֹצַרְתִּי אֵינִי כְדַאי, וְעַכְשָׁיו שֶׁנּוֹצַרְתִּי כְּאִלּוּ לֹא

על חטא שחטאנו לפניך במאכל ובמשתה

For the sin we committed before You in eating and drinking…

MASHAL
משל

משל: When the **Lev Simchah, Rav Simchah Bunim Alter** ***zt"l*****,** became the Gerrer Rebbe in 5737 (1977), unusually large crowds of chassidim streamed from all over to *daven* with the new rebbe on that first Yom Kippur of his leadership.

Though the rebbe began to receive visitors, *kvitlach* and *pidyonos* (spiritual redemptions) in the reception room before noon on Erev Yom Kippur, by the time the last people were seen it was too late for him to return home to eat the *seudas hamafsekes* (final meal) before the fast. Instead, he *davened* Minchah in his room with a private *minyan*, washed and ate a small meal before beginning the fast.

As he passed his *gabba'im* on his way into the large Gerrer Beis Medrash, he was heard murmuring the words *Al cheit shechatanu l'fanecha b'maachal ub'mishteh*—"(Forgive me) for the sin we have committed with food and drink." The Lev Simchah was alluding to the fact that he had not properly fulfilled the mitzvah of eating and drinking on Erev Yom Kippur, and for this "sin" he felt compelled to do *teshuvah*.

נמשל: There are certain sins that a person does without even realizing. Perhaps he is unaware that he is sinning, or that his action is, in fact, forbidden. Conversely, there are certain sins which are not really sins at all; one feels guilty when in truth it is not really forbidden. For all of these sins, whether performed unwittingly, or just perceived as sins, Hashem gives us a Yom Kippur, a time to reevaluate our position and do better in the future.

נוֹצַרְתִּי, עָפָר אֲנִי בְּחַיַּי קַל וָחֹמֶר בְּמִיתָתִי, הֲרֵי אֲנִי לְפָנֶיךָ כִּכְלִי מָלֵא בוּשָׁה וּכְלִמָּה:

על חטא שחטאנו לפניך בשבועת שוא

For the sin we committed before You by swearing in vain...

STORIES
מעשה

When the *kehillah* of Tzelem hired their new *rav*, **Rav Menachem Katz** ***zt"l***, he stipulated that the community support a group of ten to twelve *yungeleit* who would sit and learn all day. The arrangement was agreed upon, but after a few years, the cost to support these *yungeleit* and their families became too great for the *kehillah*, and they stubbornly refused to continue the support.

That year, R' Menachem got up to deliver his Shabbos Shuvah *drashah* and in the course of his words, he announced, "You should know, that when you agreed to sponsor these *yungeleit*, you forged a vow which is forbidden to break."

Afterwards, one community leader spoke up and said, "Our *rav* says that we made a vow when we hired him. If so, then on the night of *Kol Nidrei*, we will instruct the *chazzan* to have in mind to release us from this vow!" They all nodded in agreement.

That year, as the *chazzan* began to sing *Kol Nidrei*, he forgot the tune and couldn't articulate the words. On the night of Yom Kippur, we emphasize the extreme gravity the Torah attaches not only to formal vows, but also to the general concept that a Jew must keep his word. If a person (or a *kehillah*) is insincere in his vow, the *Kol Nidrei tefillah* will have no effect.

הנסתרת לה' אלקינו והנגלת לנו ולבנינו עד עולם לעשות את כל דברי התורה הזאת

The hidden things belong to Hashem, our G-d, but the revealed things are for us and for our children forever...

TEFILLAH
תפילה

There are two points in time that are propitious for Mashiach's arrival. One remains concealed; only Hashem knows of it. No prophet, not even Moshe Rabbeinu, knew when that time was. The second is clearly expressed; the ultimate Redemption can come on any given day, if *you will listen to His voice.* The **Ksav Sofer, Rav Avraham Shmuel Binyamin Sofer** ***zt"l***, derives an allusion from this *pasuk*. *The hidden things*, the Redemption which is concealed from man, *are for Hashem our G-d.*

יְהִי רָצוֹן מִלְּפָנֶיךָ יְיָ אֱלֹהַי וֵאלֹהֵי אֲבוֹתַי שֶׁלֹּא אֶחֱטָא עוֹד, וּמַה שֶּׁחָטָאתִי לְפָנֶיךָ מְחֹק בְּרַחֲמֶיךָ הָרַבִּים אֲבָל לֹא עַל יְדֵי יִסּוּרִים וָחֳלָיִים רָעִים:

But *the revealed things*, the scenario which man can engender, *are for us and our children*, since any generation can make themselves worthy *to carry out the words of this Torah*. Through Torah and *teshuvah*, the Redemption can occur instantly.

כי אתה סלחן לישראל ומחלן לשבטי ישרון בכל דור ודור

For You are the Pardoner of Yisrael, and the Forgiver of the tribes of Yeshurun in every generation…

Why do we refer to Hashem as a סלחן (Forgiver), instead of the more familiar term סולח, when both essentially mean the same thing?

DVAR TORAH
דבר תורה

The holy **Ruzhiner, Rav Yisrael of Ruzhin *zt"l***, gives the following explanation: In *Parshas Mishpatim* (23:5), the Torah commands us, כי תראה חמור שנאך רבץ תחת משאו...עזב תעזב עמו—*If you will see the donkey of your enemy crouching beneath its burden... you shall help it (unload).* The Gemara (*Bava Metzia* 33a) comments on this verse, רובץ ולא רבצן, one must only assist in unloading the donkey if the animal is presently collapsing beneath its burden. But if the animal is a רבצן—constantly and habitually overburdened—then there is no obligation to help unload it. The suffix ן at the end of the word signifies an act which is performed constantly or habitually.

Thus, when *Chazal* describe the Al-mighty as a סלחן as opposed to a סולח, the intention here is to underscore the point that Hashem is constantly forgiving of our sins, and always willing to accept our sincere *teshuvah*, no matter what we have done! Even a sinner who has tried numerous times to repent and for whatever reason has failed to truly return, must remember that Hashem is a סלחן—a consistent, constant G-d of Forgiveness. There is no limit as to how many times He will forgive our sins. One should never give up—it's never too late!

In his *sefer, Michtav M'Eliyahu,* **Rav Eliyahu Dessler *zt"l*** transcribes a remarkable adaptation of the *tefillah* of *Al Chet,* based not necessarily on the act of sin itself, but on the source and root from whence sin stems. When we pray and confess the long list of sins in this *tefillah,* says R' Dessler, we are baring our very souls before the Al-mighty and confessing our sins in a much deeper manner. However, now that we are aware of the foundational root of each sin, it makes it that much easier for us to reach a pure and true repentance based on a knowledge of how and why we may have sinned. The following is adapted from R' Dessler's monumental commentary.

עַל חֵטְא שֶׁחָטָאנוּ לְפָנֶיךָ...

For the sin that we have sinned before You...

בְּאֹנֶס וּבְרָצוֹן .... *by accident and by design.* By thinking that we are prone to sin accidentally (אונס), we relax our standards and sin more regularly. Our controlling will (רצון) is the root cause of most of our sins.

בְּאִמּוּץ הַלֵּב .... *with a stubborn heart.* Our stubbornness is a product of our arrogance, for we will never admit that we are wrong. Subjugating our arrogance will release our need to obstinately stick to our guns.

בִּבְלִי דָעַת .... *without knowledge.* Ignorance and lack of understanding (דעת)is a primary reason why we sin, for we do not know any better. By neglecting Torah study, we cause ourselves to sin even more.

בְּבִטּוּי שְׂפָתָיִם .... *with uttering lips.* By being quick to promise something that we cannot fulfill, we put ourselves in a position where we will be forced to break our word. We must watch what we say and not make unwarranted guarantees.

בְּגִלּוּי עֲרָיוֹת .... *with uncovering immorality.* Our Sages tell us: *The eyes see and the heart desires.* The root of almost every sin is when our desires become "uncovered" and easy for us to see and access. We must keep our eyes covered so that our heart doesn't even have a chance to desire.

בְּגָלוּי וּבַסָּתֶר .... *in public and in private.* We seek recognition and crave acclaim, so we put on a public display (גלוי) in order that people will see us. By doing this, we act improperly and quite often inappropriately. On the

other hand, when we assure ourselves that "no one is looking (סתר)," we tend to act more openly and consequently, more sinfully.

בְּדַעַת וּבְמִרְמָה .... *with knowledge and with deceit.* Sometimes too much knowledge (דעת) is not a good thing. A person must learn that which is within his abilities. Learning topics that he is not accustomed to or unable to comprehend properly will not help him grow in knowledge, but can cause him to turn astray with wild and uncontrolled thoughts. A prime example of this is a young, inexperienced person who studies Kabbalah. It is wrong and it is harmful, not only to his mind, but also to his level of *yiras Shamayim.* This, too, is classified as "deceit" (מרמה) for he is deceiving none other than himself.

בְּדִבּוּר פֶּה .... *with the words of our mouth.* We can control our anger by not losing our temper so quickly. However, when we talk harshly and spew words of anger and hatred, we cause ourselves to sin, as well as causing others to become embroiled in controversy.

בְּהוֹנָאַת רֵעַ ..... *with the influence of friends.* A friend is a person upon whom we rely for advice, criticism and friendship. A bad friend can severely influence how we think and act, for we do not believe that our friends are harmful to us at all. One must be careful to maintain only good friends who will steer him on the correct path.

בְּהַרְהוֹר הַלֵּב .... *with thoughts of the heart.* Thoughts are extremely powerful and when one thinks and plans to sin, it magnifies the sin. Thus, the Rambam says: *(The way for) a sinner to remove himself from sinning is by banishing the evil thoughts (from his mind).*

בִּוְעִידַת זְנוּת .... *with adulterous gatherings.* When we establish a ritual to do actions that our hearts are seduced to follow, as the *pasuk* states: *After our hearts—this is heresy—that you are seduced to follow*—we fall into the terrible pattern of sin. This includes reading newspapers, magazines and books that are atheistic in their approach to science, nature and the universe in general; we are causing our hearts to stray from Hashem. How much more so when we join in discussions that center around such heresy and denial, for we entrench our hearts and minds in falsehood that leads us to sin. We must break those established patterns so that we can break our mentality to sin.

בְּוִדּוּי פֶּה ..... *with false confessions.* Often, we really want to repent and we accept upon ourselves *kabbalos* to help us improve. But not all of those *kabbalos* are real—sometimes we conjure them up to make ourselves feel like

we're doing something practical. Our goal in *teshuvah* is to make sure it is real!

בְּזִלְזוּל הוֹרִים וּמוֹרִים ..... *by showing disrespect for parents and teachers.* What is disrespect? It is the polar opposite of the dictum of our Sages: *Fear of your teachers (who teach you Torah) is akin to fear of Heaven.* A *rebbi* who teaches us Torah, as well as a parent who teaches us life, is looked upon with the same regard as the Al-mighty Himself! One cannot be considered "learning" from these mentors, if he has no respect for his mentors—and by extension, for Hashem.

בְּזָדוֹן וּבִשְׁגָגָה .... *willfully and carelessly.* A sin borne out of anger against Hashem and a will to rebel against His word (זדון) is deplorable. But showing a lack of respect and regard to the important things in life and thereby forgetting to do what's right or act properly in the ways of the Torah, is inexcusable. A careless sin (שגגה) is a sin nonetheless.

בְּחֹזֶק יָד .... *by exercising power.* One is only capable of accomplishing in life if Hashem allows him to breathe, walk, move and thus accomplish. A person who thinks that he can "do it all" (כחי ועוצם ידי) is committing a grave sin, for he forgets that it is Hashem who provides him with the physical, intellectual, and emotional wherewithal to "do it all"!

בְּחִלּוּל הַשֵּׁם .... *through desecration of the Name.* It is one thing to desecrate Hashem's holy Name in front of others, but when we allow this desecration to seep into our own mindset, when we profane His Name because we do not keep it sanctified, we have committed the ultimate *chillul Hashem.*

בְּטֻמְאַת שְׂפָתָיִם .... *through impure lips.* The words that emerge from our mouths will set the tone for who we are. Defiled language, *nivul peh,* and promiscuous words are the worst form of arousal to sinful desires. In fact, there is no greater trigger for sin than filthy and disgraceful words.

בְּטִפְּשׁוּת פֶּה .... *through foolish speech.* A person who acts foolishly—a clown in public—both with words and with actions, is not only looked down upon with derision, but often leads to sin. Rav Yisrael Salanter zt"l summed it up succinctly: "The first commandment that every individual must abide by is *'Do not be a fool!'*"

בְּיֵצֶר הָרָע .... *with the evil inclination.* We have mentioned so many sins and most of them are instigated by the *yetzer hara,* the evil inclination. But there is another *yetzer hara* that we are referring to here: the evil inclination

that we arouse upon ourselves. This is not the *Satan*, whose entire existence is to cause us to sin. No! This is the evil inclination that we conjure up! Sometimes a person is not incited to desire. But he wants to sin! So what does he do? He incites his own desires so that he can sin gratuitously. How terrible is it when we do the *Satan's* job for him?

בְּיוֹדְעִים וּבְלֹא יוֹדְעִים .... *against those who know and against those who do not know.* It is embarrassing when someone learns about an indiscretion that we've done. But this is no reason to continue doing it—just because people already know (יודעים) about it and cajole us to continue doing it! And even if people do not know (לא יודעים), and there is no one to help him along in the act of sinning—stay away from it! Don't do it!

וְעַל כֻּלָּם אֱלוֹהַּ סְלִיחוֹת, סְלַח לָנוּ, מְחַל לָנוּ, כַּפֶּר לָנוּ:

For all these, O G-d of forgiveness, forgive us, pardon us, atone for us.

בְּכַחַשׁ וּבְכָזָב .... *through denial and false promises.* Denying the past, and worse, lying about it (כחש), is the road to sin. But denying the future, in other words, lying to yourself and to others, offering promises with absolutely no intention to fulfill them (כזב) is the new and continuing road to treachery. And worst of all, lying to Hashem with empty and baseless resolutions will get you nowhere since the Creator knows what's really in your heart.

בְּכַפַּת שֹׁחַד .... *for the sin that we have sinned before You by causing subservience through bribery.* When the *yetzer hara* takes hold of a person, it distorts his judgment. Now, any decision one makes in his life is influenced by the "bribery of sin." Is it any wonder that a person veers off the correct path since he has no idea that his judgment has been compromised? Stop for a moment and recognize that you are under the influence of a fraud—the *yetzer hara*—who has bribed you away from doing what you must.

בְּלָצוֹן .... *through scorning.* In bygone days, a warrior would slather his shield with oil so that any arrows or projectiles hurled at him would easily slide off his shield, without getting close to his body. So too, frivolity, jest, and banter act as a shield that blocks out any chance of constructive reproof (see *Mesillas Yesharim* chapter 5). How can one become a better person if he hides behind a veil of jokes aimed at discrediting any and all who wish to help him become a better man?

בְּלָשׁוֹן הָרָע .... *through evil talk.* The origins of *lashon hara* lie in the fateful words of the snake, the same snake that caused the first woman to sin: *And what benefit does the gossiper have?* In other words, a gossiper is like a snake that bites without receiving any real benefit and causes only harm. Similarly, *lashon hara* often hurts others for no reason whatsoever. If so, why do it?

בְּמַשָּׂא וּבְמַתָּן .... *in commercial dealings.* "Business is business," as the expression goes. But not every business is the right business for every individual. Some businesses, although lucrative monetarily, are "bad investments" in one's spirituality. Any enterprise that has the capability of pushing a person away from *emunah* is dangerous and definitely off-limits.

בְּמַאֲכָל וּבְמִשְׁתֶּה .... *with food and drink.* Food and drink represent desire. Of course, one must eat and drink to survive. But a person who utilizes these to whip up his *yetzer hara*, encouraging and exhorting him to pursue ever more pleasure and desire, has defeated the purpose of consumption that the Creator put into this world.

בְּנֶשֶׁךְ וּבְמַרְבִּית .... *through interest and extortion.* What is the underlying cause of extortion? What would cause someone to force another to pay interest? Because he is a money-grubbing, stubborn mule!

בִּנְטִיַּת גָּרוֹן .... *through haughtiness.* A haughty person is prone to sin. He cannot help it. Even if he just "puts on an act" and his arrogance is not real, by virtue of the fact that he displays his arrogance to the world, he will come to transgress many sins in numerous ways.

בְּשִׂיחַ שִׂפְתוֹתֵינוּ .... *with the idle chatter of our lips.* Idle chatter comes in many places and many forms; i.e. "shooting the breeze." *Bitul Torah* is wasting away one's precious moments of Torah study for unnecessary and unwarranted shmoozing. Either way, they all have one thing in common: they all lead one down the road to sin.

בְּשִׂקּוּר עָיִן .... *with prying eyes.* Sometimes, a person can "talk" with his eyes. A raised eyebrow, a sinister stare, or a rolled eyeball can often express a sentiment that is impossible or incapable of being expressed with one's mouth. Eyes can also be used to sin, for "eye contact" between two sinners goes a long way toward hinting, as well as fortifying, their mutual intention to indulge in a transgression.

בְּעֵינַיִם רָמוֹת .... *with haughty eyes.* A person can be pleasant on the outside and rotten on the inside. To the public, one displays a caring exterior,

a countenance portraying his good will and concern toward others. But deep down, he is so filled with arrogance and self-importance that he cannot look at another person without an air of superiority. No one is as good as him and no one comes close to his level of greatness. These are dangerous sentiments to harbor inside and it causes mistrust and iniquity.

בְּעַזּוּת מֵצַח .... *with brazenness.* When one is not afraid to do as he pleases, when one has so much chutzpah (brazenness) that he will say what he wants and do what he wants, to whomever he wants, there is no sin that he will not try. Since nothing is beyond him and he will stop at nothing to get what he wants, there is no sin that will not attach itself to him and drag him down to its depths.

וְעַל כֻּלָּם אֱלוֹהַּ סְלִיחוֹת, סְלַח לָנוּ, מְחַל לָנוּ, כַּפֶּר לָנוּ:

For all these, O G-d of forgiveness, forgive us, pardon us, atone for us.

בִּפְרִיקַת עֹל .... *in throwing off (Your) yoke.* Every Jew is born with a number of yokes—it is what defines us as a people. We have the "yoke of Torah" (עול התורה), the "yoke of *mitzvos*" (עול המצות), and the "yoke of the Heavenly Kingdom" (עול מלכות שמים). But we become lazy—or worse, we become cynical—and cast off the "yokes" that we were created for. If we don't strive to reach the levels of *avodah* (service) that Hashem has put into this world for us, then we must ask ourselves: What exactly are we doing here altogether?

בִּפְלִילוּת .... *in judgment.* The opposite of ישרות (straightforwardness) is פלילות (crookedness). In Yiddish, this is called *krumkeit*—a person who thinks and acts in a crooked, perverse, distorted, and deceitful manner. It is not just one thing that he does; it is his entire way of life. A person like this is practically incapable of walking down the "straight and narrow path," because he has no idea what the meaning of *yashar* (straight) is. A regimen of *teshuvah* "reprogramming" can jumpstart a new outlook on life.

בִּצְדִיַּת רֵעַ .... *through entrapping a neighbor.* Being persuasive and attracting followers is good if it is done for a good purpose. But using such a talent in order to "brainwash" the hearts and minds of impressionable devotees is dangerous for it leads to deceit, lies, theft and other sins. Too much control over others is what makes tyrants out of otherwise respectable leaders.

בְּצָרוּת עָיִן .... *through a begrudging eye.* Jealousy is the first item on the list mentioned in *Avos*: *Jealousy, desire, and honor will remove one from the world.* Jealousy begets desire, for if one cannot seem to get past the fact that his friend has more than he has, it only increases his desire. To begrudge another person what Hashem has given to him—and only to him—is nothing more than an exercise in futility.

בְּקַלּוּת רֹאשׁ .... *through light-headedness.* Life is serious. The Torah is serious. Belief in Hashem is serious. Frivolity is not just the antithesis of all that is important; it will not allow one to strengthen himself in order to pursue the word of Hashem—the most important thing of all.

בְּקַשְׁיוּת עֹרֶף .... *with obstinacy.* A person is not obstinate arbitrarily. Obviously, he feels strongly about something and that is why he will not change his mind. The worst kind of obstinacy, however, is when one has a desire to sin so badly that no matter how much he is shown the error of his ways, he refuses to change. His mind may be rational, but his heart is so ensconced in desire, that it will not allow him to act as he should. One should be an *akshan* (stubborn) for the right things; not a slave to passion.

בְּרִיצַת רַגְלַיִם לְהָרַע .... *with legs that run to do evil.* Being excited and hurrying to do something is an admirable trait—if it is done for the right purposes. Running to do something for less than honorable reasons, to aid and assist in a negative act or to cause harm to another person, is not just misplaced *zerizus* (alacrity), but is thoroughly evil. A prime example of one who ran to do evil is Lavan, the brother of Rivkah, who appeared to be filled with the attribute of *zerizus* but in reality was looking out for himself.

בִּרְכִילוּת .... *by gossip-mongering.* One who spreads gossip about others is not to be trusted. He is not a faithful person and has no inner confidence. If he has no compunctions to reveal what he knows about others, why would anyone want to entrust a secret with him?

בִּשְׁבוּעַת שָׁוְא .... *through swearing in vain.* An oath involves invoking the Name of Hashem to display the seriousness of one's intent. Swearing in vain, on the other hand, shows that one lacks any regard for the honor and dignity that is due to the Al-mighty. It's not just a lie to swear falsely; it is no less than a blatant disrespect for the stature and sanctification of the Master of the world.

בְּשִׂנְאַת חִנָּם .... *through baseless hatred.* Baseless hatred is the root cause to most of the serious transgressions (see *Kuntres Hachessed* in *Michtav M'Eliyahu* vol. 1).

בִּתְשׂוּמֶת יָד .... *in the matter of extending a hand.* Being an accessory to a crime is a crime in itself. Refraining from protesting evil is one thing, but helping and assisting the wicked in his evil act is much worse. One literally becomes a "partner in crime" and is thus punished as a criminal himself.

בְּתִמְהוֹן לֵבָב .... *through confusion of the heart.* A "confused heart" is a "blocked heart" (see Rashi, *Devarim* 28:28). The sin itself causes the blockage. The will to sin will not allow a person to do *mitzvos* or become interested in anything that might deflect his mind from the sin. This is true *timtum halev* (blockage of the heart).

וְעַל כֻּלָּם אֱלוֹהַ סְלִיחוֹת, סְלַח לָנוּ, מְחַל לָנוּ, כַּפֶּר לָנוּ:

For all these, O G-d of forgiveness, forgive us, pardon us, atone for us.

Rav Eliyahu Eliezer Dessler (Michtav M'Eliyahu) would say:

"*Chazal* teach: *Sin blocks (dulls) a man's heart.* In fact, the sin itself is the blockage. The will to sin will not allow a person to do *mitzvos* or become interested in anything that might deflect his mind from the sin. One must beware for this is real, true blockage of the heart."

Rav Mordechai of Lechovitz *zt"l* would say:

"*Chazal* tell us that one of the questions a person is asked when he comes before the Heavenly Tribunal is *nasasa v'nasata b'emunah*—'Did you deal in business with honesty and truth?' But another question is being asked at the very same time: Did you deal with your *emunah* (faith) in Hashem honestly and truthfully? Or did you just pretend to believe in Him?"

אבינו מלכנו

אָבִינוּ מַלְכֵּנוּ חָטָאנוּ לְפָנֶיךָ:
אָבִינוּ מַלְכֵּנוּ אֵין לָנוּ מֶלֶךְ אֶלָּא אָתָּה:
אָבִינוּ מַלְכֵּנוּ עֲשֵׂה עִמָּנוּ לְמַעַן שְׁמֶךָ:

אבינו מלכנו

Dedicated by **the Pollak family**

לעי"נ ר'
צבי אריה בן ר'
איתמר אפרים
הלוי פאללאק ז"ל
נפטר כ' טבת
תשס"ד
ת.נ.צ.ב.ה.

אבינו מלכנו אין לנו מלך אלא אתה

Our Father, our King, we have no king except You.

TEFILLAH
תפילה

Rav Meir Shapiro *zt"l* asks, how can we say the special *tefillah* of *Avinu Malkeinu* with real conviction and proper intent? Who do we think we are? The entire year, we turn our backs on the *Ribono Shel Olam*, on His Torah and *mitzvos*. But now that we are to be judged by Him, we turn to Him suddenly with tear-filled eyes and cry, "Our Father, our King!" How hypocritical are we? By every right, Hashem can turn us away: "Now I am your father? Now you call Me your king?" How terribly traumatized and embarrassed we should feel as we recite this awesome *tefillah*!

אבינו מלכנו חדש עלינו שנה טובה

Our Father, our King, renew for us a good year.

MUSSAR/
HASHKAFAH
מוסר/השקפה

There are many gates to Heaven, though all remain closed. All, that is, except one. The gate of tears. When one prays to Hashem with genuine tears, those prayers sail straight through this incredible gate. *Chazal* say that the gate of tears is never closed. If so, why does it even require a gate?

Rav Menachem Mendel Morgenstern *zt"l*, the **Kotzker Rebbe**, gives a beautiful answer. If you were to take a walk around an orphanage at night, you would notice that all is perfectly still; there is not a sound to be heard. In spite of the many young children there, no one cries. We only cry when we know someone will answer us. In an orphanage, no one is there to answer the tears.

During these holy Days of Awe, we should open our hearts and cry. We should do so because we know there is Someone there to answer us. That we have a Father who will deal with us with charity, kindness and love; a King who will grant us a year of hope, prosperity, and a good life with health and happiness, if we throw ourselves on His mercy.

אָבִינוּ מַלְכֵּנוּ חַדֵּשׁ עָלֵינוּ שָׁנָה טוֹבָה:
אָבִינוּ מַלְכֵּנוּ בַּטֵּל מֵעָלֵינוּ כָּל גְּזֵרוֹת קָשׁוֹת:
אָבִינוּ מַלְכֵּנוּ בַּטֵּל מַחְשְׁבוֹת שׂוֹנְאֵינוּ:

There is another kind of tears, however. A cry of hopelessness. A cry which doesn't implore G-d's help. It is a crying which demonstrates that we don't believe Hashem can really help us, or worse, that there is no one there to see our tears. One should never allow himself to fall to such a state, for if so, he will find that this sad gateway of tears does have a door and it remains closed.

אבינו מלכנו בטל מעלינו כל גזרות קשות

Our father, our King, annul all harsh decrees concerning us.

DRUSH
דרוש

One Rosh Hashanah, when his congregation was waiting for him to join them for the blowing of the shofar, the **Chozeh of Lublin, Rav Yaakov Yitzchak Hurvitz** ***zt"l***, remained in his study for a very long time. The Chozeh had seen that a dire verdict was threatening Klal Yisrael in the Heavenly Court and he was trying to intercede. Suddenly, he emerged and walked right over to a young boy, an orphan, who was reverently waiting for him.

The Chozeh turned to the child and asked him what he was learning in *cheder*. The boy answered that he was studying the passage in *Maseches Makkos* that discusses testimony. "And what questions seem to bother you about this?" asked the Chozeh.

With some hesitation, the boy finally answered, "I don't understand why the testimony of a relative is considered inadmissible in *beis din*, when it comes to bolster the case of the prosecution. In the case of the defense, it is understandable that the court would not allow it, for fear that a witness may lie in order to clear his relative when he is really guilty. Such testimony is therefore outlawed to begin with. But why should the testimony of a relative be inadmissible in the case of the prosecution if it is going to prove that he is guilty?"

The Chozeh nodded and asked, "Have you come up with an answer?"

"Well, I was thinking," replied the boy, "that concerning testimony, the Torah states (*Devarim* 19:17), *The two people shall stand.* From this we see that witnesses must be considered 'people.' However, a person who can offer evidence that will convict his relative, his very own flesh and blood, does not fall under the category of a 'person,' and will therefore be considered invalid as a witness."

אָבִינוּ מַלְכֵּנוּ הָפֵר עֲצַת אוֹיְבֵינוּ:
אָבִינוּ מַלְכֵּנוּ כַּלֵּה כָּל צַר וּמַשְׂטִין מֵעָלֵינוּ:

When the Chozeh heard this, he sighed with relief and said, "With your words, my son, all the accusations that had threatened us in the Heavenly Court have now been nullified. We are the sons of the Al-mighty, and He is our Father. We are indeed close relatives, as close as a father is to his son. How will He be able to tolerate any incriminating evidence against His own sons?"

With that, the Chozeh joined his waiting congregation for the blowing of the shofar.

אבינו מלכנו הפר עצת אויבינו

Our Father, our King, thwart the plans of our enemies.

STORIES
מעשה

During the mid-thirteenth century, immediately following the Golden Age of Spain, a time when Jews enjoyed respect, wealth, political power and religious freedom, jealous Christian clergymen used their influence with the king and local authorities to begin a sustained series of decrees, edicts and persecutions against the Jews of Spain. This was a prelude to the sinister agenda of the evil Inquisition a century later, and ultimately the final expulsion of Spanish Jewry in 1492.

One such decree involved the holy **Ramban, Rabbeinu Moshe ben Nachman *zt"l.*** King James I of Aragon, a relatively benign king, was influenced by the local cardinal to ban Torah study. The cardinal seemed to bemoan the former lost greatness of the Jewish people. "Your Majesty," he said one day, in a sad and almost reverent tone, "in days gone by, the Jews had great men of wisdom and prophecy. Where are they now? There are no great Jews today."

The king agreed with him and the cardinal, happy to have gained the king's interest, began to defame the Talmud. "You see, Your Majesty, ever since the Jews have been studying the Talmud, a book filled with all kinds of foolishness and nonsense, they have become fools themselves! These books prevent them from accepting the true faith of Christianity."

The king consented to ban the Talmud. When the new law became known, the Jews were panic-stricken. The Ramban, the leader of Spanish Jewry, recognized the effect this edict was having on his brethren and quickly sent messengers to all the Jewish communities throughout Spain that his yeshivah in Catalonia would remain

אָבִינוּ מַלְכֵּנוּ

אָבִינוּ מַלְכֵּנוּ סְתֹם פִּיוֹת מַשְׂטִינֵינוּ וּמְקַטְרְגֵינוּ:
אָבִינוּ מַלְכֵּנוּ כַּלֵּה דֶּבֶר וְחֶרֶב וְרָעָב וּשְׁבִי וּמַשְׁחִית וְעָוֹן וּשְׁמַד מִבְּנֵי בְרִיתֶךָ:

open for anyone who wished to come. Hundreds of young scholars flocked to the Ramban's yeshivah.

Of course, this was precisely what the cardinal expected, knowing all about the reputation of the Ramban and hating him for it as well. It wasn't long before he sent in young priests in the guise of yeshivah students to bear witness to the fact that indeed Talmud study was continuing in the school of the Jewish scholar known as Nachmanides.

When the king heard the news, he was incensed. "What! My trusted advisor disobeyed my order!" he exclaimed in shock. But he could not bring himself to punish the renowned rabbi without first allowing him to defend himself.

He summoned the Ramban to the court. "Is it true that you disobeyed my law?" the king asked sharply.

The Ramban did not hesitate. "Yes, Your Majesty, I did. But with your permission, I will explain my reason by means of a story." King James was intrigued and indicated his assent.

"In a distant kingdom," Rabbeinu Moshe began, "a king's daughter fell gravely ill. All of the doctors gave up hope. The king proclaimed a three-day fast for the entire realm, during which everyone would pray for the princess. On the second day of the fast, a Jew was caught eating and was immediately arrested. He was brought before the king and questioned harshly. 'Why did you eat? There is a royal decree. Don't you desire the recovery of the princess?'

"'Why, Your Majesty,' said the Jew, 'I have not ceased praying for her, but in our Talmud we have a rule: Where there is a certainty against a doubt, the certainty takes priority. Now, I had a serious doubt in my mind whether my fasting for three days would save your daughter. I was sure, however, that fasting for three days would kill me, because I have a weak heart and my doctor forbids it. Therefore, I decided to follow the rule of the Talmud, and that is why I was eating.'"

The king was listening closely as the Ramban continued. "Your Majesty, the story I told you is merely a parable; however, we are dealing here with a similar situation. I found it hard to believe that the king would issue a law which would pain me so greatly. On the other hand, I was certain that if I ceased to study the Talmud, which is the very source of my life, my life would no longer be worth living. So, like the man in the story, I followed the path of certainty." Looking directly at the king, he said, "I

אָבִינוּ מַלְכֵּנוּ מְנַע מַגֵּפָה מִנַּחֲלָתֶךָ:
אָבִינוּ מַלְכֵּנוּ סְלַח וּמְחַל לְכָל עֲוֹנוֹתֵינוּ:
אָבִינוּ מַלְכֵּנוּ מְחֵה וְהַעֲבֵר פְּשָׁעֵינוּ וְחַטֹּאתֵינוּ מִנֶּגֶד עֵינֶיךָ:
אָבִינוּ מַלְכֵּנוּ מְחֹק בְּרַחֲמֶיךָ הָרַבִּים כָּל שִׁטְרֵי חוֹבוֹתֵינוּ:
אָבִינוּ מַלְכֵּנוּ הַחֲזִירֵנוּ בִּתְשׁוּבָה שְׁלֵמָה לְפָנֶיךָ:
אָבִינוּ מַלְכֵּנוּ שְׁלַח רְפוּאָה שְׁלֵמָה לְחוֹלֵי עַמֶּךָ:

---

do not believe that Your Majesty would ever have issued so cruel an order unless he was ill-advised."

The king smiled. "Rabbi, you are correct. To my regret, I acted on bad advice. The law is henceforth repealed." A great cry of joy went up for the Jews of Spain. The Ramban remained a favorite of the king, who not only appreciated his great wisdom, but his great courage as well.

אבינו מלכנו סלח ומחל לכל עונותינו

Our Father, our King, forgive and pardon all of our iniquities.

MASHAL
משל

משל: One year, the chief rabbi of Moscow, **Rav Chaim Berlin** ***zt"l***, walked into the synagogue on the morning of Yom Kippur and found it empty. Not one person showed up to *daven*. In the "Proletariat Utopia," missing work was a crime that earned the offender a hefty punishment, and no one was willing to take that chance.

R' Chaim *davened* alone all day, but as soon as darkness began to fall and the workday was done, the people came streaming into the shul in droves. In a very short time, there was not an empty seat in the building.

The *rav* watched in fascination. Then he quickly walked up to the front, opened the *aron kodesh* and began to speak.

"Two neighbors once got into an argument over a chicken. Each one claimed the chicken belonged to him. They went to the *rav*, who advised that they put the chicken on the ground, with the two of them standing on opposite sides, and observe to which side the chicken will go. That would be a sign it was his."

R' Chaim raised his voice, "Master of the world, Your people are worked to the bone and don't have a moment to rest all day. But the minute they are released from their work, in what direction do their feet carry them? Home? To the pubs? No! Directly to You! To Your home! Why? Because we are Your sheep and You are our Shepherd!"

אָבִינוּ מַלְכֵּנוּ קְרַע רֹעַ גְּזַר דִּינֵנוּ:
אָבִינוּ מַלְכֵּנוּ זָכְרֵנוּ בְּזִכָּרוֹן טוֹב לְפָנֶיךָ:
אָבִינוּ מַלְכֵּנוּ כָּתְבֵנוּ בְּסֵפֶר חַיִּים טוֹבִים:
אָבִינוּ מַלְכֵּנוּ כָּתְבֵנוּ בְּסֵפֶר גְּאֻלָּה וִישׁוּעָה:
אָבִינוּ מַלְכֵּנוּ כָּתְבֵנוּ בְּסֵפֶר זְכֻיּוֹת:
אָבִינוּ מַלְכֵּנוּ כָּתְבֵנוּ בְּסֵפֶר סְלִיחָה וּמְחִילָה:

נמשל: Klal Yisrael has a special ability to evoke mercy from the Al-mighty. Not due to our righteousness, but because we are His children and He is our Father. With this knowledge in mind, let us take advantage and beg for forgiveness even when we don't truly deserve it!

אבינו מלכנו כתבנו בספר חיים טובים

Our Father, our King, inscribe us in the book of good life.

Rav Matisyahu Salomon *shlit"a* says:

"We beg the Master of the world to grant us a good life, to remember us for life; however, what sort of life are we really asking for? Life has different connotations for different people. For most people, it means simply to live. However, to some people their house is their life, and to others, their car is their life. A person must avoid focusing on these trivialities, for otherwise they become that person's 'life-wish,' prompting Hashem to answer this foolish wish instead of granting him the most important gift of all—the gift of real, true life."

אבינו מלכנו כתבנו בספר פרנסה וכלכלה

Our Father, our King, inscribe us in the book of maintenance and sustenance.

STORIES
מעשה

One of the famous sages of Sephardic Jewry was the great *chacham*, **Rav Yehoshua Basis *zt"l***, widely recognized as from among the great scholars of Tunisia. One year as R' Yehoshua was leading the *tefillos* on Yom Kippur, he tearfully entreated the Al-mighty with the words, *Aneinu Avinu aneinu, aneinu Boreinu aneinu*—"Answer us, our Father, answer us; answer us, our Creator, answer us." The entire congregation was moved to tears by the force of the rabbi's prayers. R' Yehoshua,

אָבִינוּ מַלְכֵּנוּ הַצְמַח לָנוּ יְשׁוּעָה בְּקָרוֹב:
אָבִינוּ מַלְכֵּנוּ הָרֵם קֶרֶן יִשְׂרָאֵל עַמֶּךָ:
אָבִינוּ מַלְכֵּנוּ הָרֵם קֶרֶן מְשִׁיחֶךָ:
אָבִינוּ מַלְכֵּנוּ מַלֵּא יָדֵינוּ מִבִּרְכוֹתֶיךָ:
אָבִינוּ מַלְכֵּנוּ מַלֵּא אֲסָמֵינוּ שָׂבָע:
אָבִינוּ מַלְכֵּנוּ שְׁמַע קוֹלֵנוּ חוּס וְרַחֵם עָלֵינוּ:

---

however, did not let up as he realized that the gates of compassion were closed and his prayers were unable to penetrate the heavens.

"Answer us, G-d of Avraham, answer us!" he cried out bitterly, begging for Heavenly intervention. The congregation responded with a thunderous "Answer us, Fear of Yitzchak, answer us!"

It was now apparent that the rabbi was struggling with a serious crisis on behalf of his people; something was amiss and it was negatively affecting the Divine Judgment. Indeed, with his *ruach hakodesh* (holy spirit), R' Yehoshua was able to discern that an iron blockade had barred the path of their prayers. The prosecution had persevered; the Divine anger had been aroused in Heaven. G-d forbid, it was not going to be a good year for the Jewish people. The congregation intensified their prayers.

Amidst the tremendous clamor, R' Yehoshua suddenly detected an unusual sound, that of a simple Jew repeating incessantly a single word with longing and yearning, "*Aneinu! Aneinu! Aneinu!*"

This man was not a learned man by any means and the *tefillos* themselves were something of a stretch for him. Yet, here he was crying and screaming with the rest of the congregation, calling out one single word in hopeless desperation, over and over again: "*Aneinu! Aneinu! Aneinu!*" The congregation continued the prayer, evoking the "Strength of Yaakov" and "Savior of the tribes." Meanwhile, the simple Jew kept on repeating over and over "*Aneinu! Aneinu! Aneinu!*"

And then the rabbi eased a bit in the forcefulness of his prayers. It seemed that this simple Jew's cry had accomplished what the whole congregation could not: he had softened the barrier, broken through the wall and opened the gates of Heaven. The harsh decree was lifted, and salvation and mercy carried the day!

Immediately after *davening*, R' Yehoshua went over to this man and asked him, "Please tell me, what were your intentions when you repeated that single word, *Aneinu*, over and over?"

אָבִינוּ מַלְכֵּנוּ קַבֵּל בְּרַחֲמִים וּבְרָצוֹן אֶת תְּפִלָּתֵנוּ:
אָבִינוּ מַלְכֵּנוּ פְּתַח שַׁעֲרֵי שָׁמַיִם לִתְפִלָּתֵנוּ:
אָבִינוּ מַלְכֵּנוּ זָכוּר כִּי עָפָר אֲנָחְנוּ:
אָבִינוּ מַלְכֵּנוּ נָא אַל תְּשִׁיבֵנוּ רֵיקָם מִלְּפָנֶיךָ:
אָבִינוּ מַלְכֵּנוּ תְּהֵא הַשָּׁעָה הַזֹּאת שְׁעַת רַחֲמִים וְעֵת רָצוֹן מִלְּפָנֶיךָ:
אָבִינוּ מַלְכֵּנוּ חֲמֹל עָלֵינוּ וְעַל עוֹלָלֵינוּ וְטַפֵּנוּ:

The man didn't understand the question. "Is our revered rabbi not familiar with the meaning of the words?"

R' Yehoshua persisted. Finally the man said, "Rabbi, this is not a single word. I have no doubt that the revered rabbi knows that it is really two separate words: *ani nu*. The word *ani* means a poor person and the word *nu* is loosely derived from the French word that means no." The man shrugged. "I was simply asking the Al-mighty that there should not be a single poor person during this entire year."

R' Yehoshua was silent in contemplative admiration. Then he said, "Indeed, with your prayer, your simple and basic understanding, you have brought us a year of abundance and prosperity."

אבינו מלכנו פתח שערי שמים לתפלתנו

Our Father, our King, open the gates of Heaven to our prayer.

MASHAL
משל

משל: A man once came to the *chacham*, **Rabbeinu Yitzchak Abuchatzeira** ***zt"l***, the **Baba Haki**, speaking terribly harsh and hurtful words. He insulted the *gaon* in front of all those present, and did not stop until he had lifted his hand and slapped the rabbi across his face.

R' Yitzchak was silent. Then he began to soothe the man and even invited him to his table, urging him to sit for a meal. He stood by him and served him like a waiter. After the meal, he gave him a substantial gift, found him a way home, and accompanied him on the way. Those present couldn't believe what they saw, and when he returned, they expressed their wonder and amazement.

The *gaon* answered, "There is a house nearby with a sign that reads, 'All who approach are welcome, except for those who do not say thank you.' But my version is that all who approach are welcome, even those who do not say thank you! I have done

אָבִינוּ מַלְכֵּנוּ עֲשֵׂה לְמַעַן הֲרוּגִים עַל שֵׁם קָדְשֶׁךָ:
אָבִינוּ מַלְכֵּנוּ עֲשֵׂה לְמַעַן טְבוּחִים עַל יִחוּדֶךָ:
אָבִינוּ מַלְכֵּנוּ עֲשֵׂה לְמַעַן בָּאֵי בָאֵשׁ וּבַמַּיִם עַל קִדּוּשׁ שְׁמֶךָ:

---

many acts of kindness for this man. However, that is precisely the point: If he does not recognize good, and can behave ungratefully, we must have pity on him. We must treat him like a sick person and heal him!"

נמשל: On Yom Kippur, what will we do if a sign greets us: "Only those who say thank you are welcome"? Every sin is an act of ungratefulness! Who amongst us is secure??

We receive life, health and sustenance, food, clothing and shelter—and how do we respond? With sin! With ingratitude! The only way we can persuade the Al-mighty to open up the Gates of Heaven for us, is if we show a bit of appreciation! Repentance, doing *mitzvos*, Torah study—that is how we'll do it!

אבינו מלכנו עשה למען הרוגים על שם קדשך

Our Father, our King, do it for the sake of those who were slain for Your holy Name.

משל: The German army invaded Soviet-occupied Poland on June 22, 1941, in Operation Barbarossa. Taking the Soviets by surprise, by the end of August they had pushed far into Russian territory, just outside of Leningrad.

MASHAL
משל

In Lvov, the local Ukrainian population welcomed the German troops, and played a major role in stirring up hatred of the Jews and murdering them. An incited mob attacked the Jews for three days. Thousands of Jews were incarcerated, where they were subsequently tortured and murdered.

On "Black Friday," July 25, 1941, Aktion Petliura was unleashed in the city of Lvov. The holy **Bobover Rebbe, Rav Benzion Halberstam *zt"l Hy"d***, and his family, were among the two thousand Jews who were arrested on that day. He was urged to escape from prison. "One does not run away from the sound of Mashiach's footsteps," he explained.

Four days later, on the fourth of Av, the rebbe, dressed in his Shabbos *kapote* and tall *shtreimel* (fur hat), marched with a dignified stride in the direction of Janov, where the open forest pits were waiting. He was murdered by the Nazis and their Ukrainian collaborators. *Yehi zichro baruch.*

נמשל: The spilled blood of millions of our Jewish brothers and sisters is all reflected in the words of the *pasuk* (*Vayikra* 22:32): *And I shall be sanctified among Bnei Yisrael—*

אָבִינוּ מַלְכֵּנוּ נְקֹם נִקְמַת דַּם עֲבָדֶיךָ הַשָּׁפוּךְ:
אָבִינוּ מַלְכֵּנוּ עֲשֵׂה לְמַעַנְךָ אִם לֹא לְמַעֲנֵנוּ:
אָבִינוּ מַלְכֵּנוּ עֲשֵׂה לְמַעַנְךָ וְהוֹשִׁיעֵנוּ:

Sacrifice yourselves in order to sanctify My Name...and when you sacrifice yourselves, do so on condition to die. A Jew who gives his life *al kiddush Hashem* is nothing less than a pure sacrifice on the Al-mighty's altar. His reward in the Next World is to bask in the Divine glow of the *Shechinah.*

אבינו מלכנו עשה למענך אם לא למעננו

Our Father, our King, do it for Your sake if not for ours.

STORIES
מעשה

When the **Kossoner Rebbe** of Forshay, **Rav Chaim Leibish Rottenburg *shlit"a***, was in Paris, France, a few years ago, he relayed a story about an affluent Parisian Jew, whom we'll call David. David lived in an exclusive and luxurious high-rise apartment building. Some of the wealthiest people in all of Paris lived in this building, and David and his family lived on the top floor, in the penthouse.

Although there were only two apartments on the top floor, David did not know his neighbor very well, for the latter was reserved and secretive. One day, when the two neighbors met in the hall, he discovered why.

In the midst of a passing conversation, the neighbor confided that he is currently married to the previous queen of Morocco, and that the present king, Mohammed VI, is his stepson! In fact, the man said, the king comes on occasion to Paris and stops in to visit his mother. Of course, security is paramount and the entire visit is usually conducted with utmost discretion, so not many people even know that the king was there.

David found this quite astounding and wondered if it would be possible to meet the king if and when he came the next time. The neighbor thought about this for a moment and then said he'd see what he could do.

Some time later, David received a phone call. It was his neighbor informing him that his stepson, the king, was in his house at that very moment and that David was welcome to meet the king. David was intrigued and brought his thirteen-year-old son along to meet the monarch.

After undergoing routine security measures, they were allowed inside. The king was very cordial and friendly. He shook David's hand and even engaged the boy in conversation.

אָבִינוּ מַלְכֵּנוּ עֲשֵׂה לְמַעַן רַחֲמֶיךָ הָרַבִּים:
אָבִינוּ מַלְכֵּנוּ עֲשֵׂה לְמַעַן שִׁמְךָ הַגָּדוֹל הַגִּבּוֹר וְהַנּוֹרָא שֶׁנִּקְרָא עָלֵינוּ:
אָבִינוּ מַלְכֵּנוּ חָנֵּנוּ וַעֲנֵנוּ כִּי אֵין בָּנוּ מַעֲשִׂים עֲשֵׂה עִמָּנוּ צְדָקָה וָחֶסֶד וְהוֹשִׁיעֵנוּ:

"How old are you?" he asked the boy. The boy replied that he had just turned thirteen a few days ago.

"That is a milestone in the Jewish faith, is it not?" asked the king.

The boy explained that when a boy turns thirteen, he is called a bar mitzvah. The king was impressed.

"Tell me, what does it mean to be a bar mitzvah?" he asked. "What must you do to celebrate this milestone?"

The boy explained that a bar mitzvah meant that by Jewish law he was now responsible for his actions and that he is required to fulfill the commandments as outlined in the Torah. It is usually celebrated with a party, said the boy, amidst festive music, food, guests, and presents from his family, friends, and well-wishers.

The king of Morocco was visibly impressed with the young boy and his mature words. They conversed on the topic a bit longer. Then the audience concluded and David and his son were led out of the apartment.

The next day, David received another phone call from his neighbor down the hall, informing him that the king requested that he return with his son. When the two arrived, the king took out an envelope with the royal seal of Morocco emblazoned on it, and handed it to the boy.

"Congratulations on your bar mitzvah," said the king. "Here is a little gift for you to celebrate your achievement. Go ahead, open it."

The boy hesitantly opened the envelope handed to him by the actual king of Morocco, his hand quivering slightly. His surprise turned to disbelief when he looked inside to find a check made out to his name in the amount of $50,000! He showed it to his father, who registered a look of absolute shock.

"Your Highness," David stammered. "You are too kind! A check of this amount is... is...far beyond what is normally presented as a gift! My son surely does not require a gift of this magnitude—it is far too extravagant for such a young boy. Perhaps a lesser amount would be more appropriate for a thirteen-year-old?"

The king of Morocco smiled. "Sir, I understand your concerns completely and in truth, a boy of thirteen does not need such a large amount. However," the king looked at David with an authoritarian look, "the reason I gave your son such a check

is because the king of Morocco cannot possibly give less! As befits the honor of my station, I am unable to present a gift of a lesser amount. Doing so is beneath the honor of my office and the stature of my position as a king!"

R' Rottenburg relates that David visited Eretz Yisrael not long after and recounted this story to none other than **Rav Chaim Kanievsky *shlit"a***. Characteristically, R' Chaim used this incident to clarify the words we say on Rosh Hashanah and during the Aseres Yemei Teshuvah, in *Avinu Malkeinu*: *Our Father, our King, do for Your own sake, and not for our sake.* He explained that when we beseech the Al-mighty to have pity on us during this serious time of year, we cannot rely upon our own merits for mercy. We are so unworthy that we do not even know what we need. Rather, we beg Hashem to have mercy for His sake, to take care of us in His own way. As befitting the King of all kings, we require that He deal with us in a royal manner with an overabundance of mercy, kindness and goodness, so we can serve Him properly in the coming year with true *malchus*.

אבינו מלכנו חננו ועננו כי אין בנו מעשים עשה עמנו צדקה וחסד והושיענו וגו'

Our Father, our King, favor us and answer us, for we have no accomplishments; deal with us charitably and kindly and deliver us.

MUSSAR/ HASHKAFAH
מוסר/השקפה

After reciting aloud forty-three verses of *Avinu Malkeinu*, the *minhag* is to say the last verse silently: *Our Father, our King, be gracious and respond to us, though we have no merits. Be charitable and kind with us and help us.* Why is this so?

The **Dubno Maggid, Rav Yaakov Kranz *zt"l***, explains this with a parable of a merchant who ordered goods from his supplier. He loudly specified how much of each item he wanted delivered. After the entire order was taken and the salesperson asked for payment, however, the merchant requested to speak with the proprietor. Taking him aside, he whispered, "I have fallen on hard times, and I cannot pay for the merchandise now. If you will extend me some credit, though, I will surely be able to sell the merchandise at a profit and pay you." Obviously, he said this quietly, as this is hardly a statement that any enterprising merchant would allow others to hear.

Similarly, when aroused to ponder Hashem's eternal beneficence, we boldly ask for many favors as though we have earned them. When we finish the list and come to our senses, however, we must silently entreat, "Hashem, we know we do not deserve what we have asked for because we have no merits, but please extend us credit. If You grant us life, health, livelihood, and peace, we will certainly be able to do Your bidding and be deserving of Your gifts." Pleading for an extension of credit because we are

סליחות

אֵל מֶלֶךְ יוֹשֵׁב עַל כִּסֵּא רַחֲמִים. מִתְנַהֵג בַּחֲסִידוּת מוֹחֵל עֲוֹנוֹת עַמּוֹ. מַעֲבִיר רִאשׁוֹן רִאשׁוֹן. מַרְבֶּה מְחִילָה לַחַטָּאִים וּסְלִיחָה

devoid of merits is something we only whisper. Yet we can be sure that Hashem, in His great mercy, responds to whispers as He does to loud and resonant prayers, with love and graciousness for His children.

סליחות

מתנהג בחסידות מוחל עונות עמו

He governs with kindness, forgives the iniquities of His people…

STORIES / מעשה

Once, a dispute broke out between two business partners. They wisely decided to present the case before a *posek* and hear the ruling according to the halachah. In the meantime, it was decided that the money in question would be kept in the hands of a reliable, neutral third party.

The two partners knew of a certain young yeshivah student who was studying for his *shechitah* license, whose mind was far from the world of commerce. Since he was honest and straightforward, they agreed to leave the disputed money with him while they presented their *din Torah* before the *posek hador*, **Rav Moshe Feinstein zt"l**.

The two partners went to the home of the young *shechitah* student and brought the money to him. They then made their way to the home of R' Moshe, who greeted them warmly, heard their claims, researched the relevant sources, and issued his ruling in favor of one of the partners. The two accepted this verdict and returned to the student's home. "Give my partner the money," said one, "he is right."

"What, this was R' Moshe's ruling? I also researched the halachah, and as it turns out, you are right! I am terribly sorry, but R' Moshe made a mistake." He then added arrogantly, "His logic does not make sense. Even a great *posek* can make an error!"

The two partners were infuriated. They had never seen such outright brazenness and arrogance. The great sage, when he heard, was also upset, as here was an outright infringement upon the honor of the Torah. Yet, he kept silent and sent a list of sources to the student. "Review these as soon as possible, and be sure to return the money to the first partner."

לַפּוֹשְׁעִים. עוֹשֶׂה צְדָקוֹת עִם כָּל בָּשָׂר וָרוּחַ. לֹא כְרָעָתָם תִּגְמֹל. אֵל הוֹרֵיתָ לָּנוּ לוֹמַר שְׁלֹשׁ עֶשְׂרֵה. וּזְכָר לָנוּ הַיּוֹם בְּרִית שְׁלֹשׁ עֶשְׂרֵה. כְּמוֹ

Some time later, the young student came to the home of R' Moshe. He was welcomed warmly and asked to sit. He told the rabbi that he passed his required exams in the laws of *shechitah* and requested a recommendation.

"I will give you a recommendation gladly," said the sage. He first quizzed the student briefly, and when it was evident that he was proficient in the relevant *halachos*, R' Moshe wrote him a flattering recommendation.

Those who remembered the young man's remarks about R' Moshe approached him and protested, "But this man insulted you terribly!"

R' Moshe looked at them uncomprehendingly and said, "Have you forgotten that Yom Kippur has passed in the interim and we forgave everyone who may have insulted us?"

מרבה מחילה לחטאים וסליחה לפושעים. עושה צדקות עם כל בשר ורוח. לא כרעתם תגמל

He increases forgiveness to sinners and pardon to transgressors, acting righteously with all who are of flesh and spirit; not according to their wickedness does He repay them...

The midrash tells us that Hashem fulfills all the *mitzvos* in the Torah. He even

MUSSAR/ HASHKAFAH מוסר/השקפה

fulfills the mitzvah of *teshuvah.* How so? For when He decides not to punish Klal Yisrael, to take back the evil that He was prepared to do to them, this is a form of regret, like the *pasuk* states: *And Hashem reconsidered the evil He was to do to His people* (*Shemos* 32:14).

However, **Rav Klonymous Kalman Shapira of Piaczeczna *zt"l* (*Aish Kodesh*)**, explains that the Jews are still in danger, for the respite is only temporary. Were we to sin again, Hashem may go forward and carry out the action that was supposed to have been done. Thus, we continue to pray: *Hashem, return—how long? And reconsider concerning Your servants* (*Tehillim* 90:13). We feel that we are not safe yet and we continue to beseech the Al-mighty to reconsider and find us in a favorable light. The *pasuk* then continues and says that when we do this, we will have made it through "the night"; we will have survived. Thus: *Satisfy us by morning with Your kindness; we shall sing and rejoice all our days* (ibid. 90:14). At last the danger will have passed!

שֶׁהוֹדַעְתָּ לֶעָנָו מִקֶּדֶם. כְּמוֹ שֶׁכָּתוּב וַיֵּרֶד יְיָ בֶּעָנָן וַיִּתְיַצֵּב עִמּוֹ שָׁם וַיִּקְרָא בְשֵׁם יְיָ: וַיַּעֲבֹר יְיָ עַל פָּנָיו וַיִּקְרָא:

וזכור לנו היום ברית שלש עשרה כמו שהודעת לענו מקדם

And remember unto us this day the covenant of the Thirteen Divine Attributes, as You made them known to the humble one (Moshe) *of old...*

MASHAL
משל

משל: During the Six Day War, many areas of Jerusalem were being shelled on a daily basis, including Meah Shearim and Beis Yisrael, where the famous Mirrer Yeshivah was situated. When the air-raid siren would go off, everyone would run down to the nearest bomb shelter to wait out the attack. There, they prayed and learned with great concentration, surrounded by the constant sounds of explosions.

The shelter next to the Mirrer Yeshivah contained a number of people other than members of the yeshivah. During one attack, a woman suddenly cried out, "L-rd of the universe! I have been married and divorced, and during my marriage, my husband treated me terribly for many years, humiliating me in public. But now I'm prepared to forgive him. Therefore, I pray that You, Hashem, will likewise forgive the Jewish people for the sins that are causing this present suffering!"

When the Mirrer Rosh Yeshivah, **Rav Chaim Shmulevitz *zt"l***, heard the woman's impassioned plea, he exclaimed, "If we get out of this alive, it will be due to this woman's merit!"

נמשל: When the anger of Hashem flared against the Jews and He intended to wipe them out, precisely at this moment, Moshe Rabbeinu stood up and beseeched the Al-mighty to have mercy on His people. Remember the merits of their forefathers, Moshe begged, the righteous *Avos* who served You under any and all conditions, and whom You promised to make a great nation. Moshe's words pierced the heavens, and Hashem's anger receded.

וירד ה' בענן ויתיצב עמו שם ויקרא בשם ה'. ויעבר ה' על פניו ויקרא וכו'

And Hashem descended in the cloud and stood with him there, and proclaimed the Name Hashem. And Hashem passed before Him (Moshe) *and proclaimed...*

STORIES
מעשה

The Gemara (*Rosh Hashanah* 17b) teaches: *From here we learn that* Hakadosh Baruch Hu *wrapped Himself in a* tallis *like a* shaliach tzibbur *(public emissary), and showed Moshe the proper order of the* tefillos. *He said, "Any time that Yisrael sins, let them (*daven*) before Me in this way and I will forgive them."* The power of prayer is great; the power of forgiveness is even greater.

One year, before Yom Kippur, a delegation came to the *rav* of Prague, **Rav Yechezkel Landau** ***zt"l***, author of ***Noda B'Yehudah***, and requested on behalf of the entire community that he lead the *kehillah* in the *tefillah* of *Ne'ilah* before the *amud*. If the holy *rav* would beseech the Heavens, they said, and employ his tremendous spiritual powers to effect a good judgment for the entire *kehillah* by interceding on their behalf before the *Ribono Shel Olam*, the community would be most gratified.

Now, R' Yechezkel was not a *baal tefillah*, nor had he ever attempted to be one. He was not blessed with the best of musical abilities and he understood that his talent as a *chazzan* would be decidedly uninspiring and lacking. He demurred, but they refused to take no for an answer. They begged and pleaded with him to accept this responsibility and each time that he excused himself, they persisted with the argument that who better than the *rav* should represent the *kehillah* at this most auspicious time.

Eventually, they wore him down and he agreed to *daven*. But as he was lacking in the basics of *nusach* and musical ability, he found it difficult to prepare himself for the task. There was one song that he was familiar with and he decided to incorporate this song into the *tefillos* in an attempt to bypass some of the *nusach* and allow the congregation to sing along and assist him.

When the time for *Ne'ilah* came, the Noda B'Yehudah made his way to the *amud* and began to *daven*. All through the first half of the prayer, he did his best to stick to the *nusach* as much as he was capable, and when he reached the words *mechalkel chaim b'chessed*, he began to sing his prepared tune. However, his lack of musical talent was sorely exposed and instead of the inspired congregation singing along with him as he'd intended, his performance took on an unfortunately comical twist, and the congregants did their best to stifle their reactions in order to preserve the honor of the *rav*.

The next day, one of the local beggars in Prague, a character with a lively sense of humor and a sharp tongue, was at the home of a wealthy individual. In the course of the regular give and take that collectors exhibit the world over, he suddenly burst into a mimicking tone and belted out the tune to *mechalkel chaim b'chessed* that the *rav* had sung the evening before. It was a perfect rendition, down to the terribly off-key intonation, and the host roared with laughter. On the spot, he doubled his donation. After similar performances in a number of other houses, where the hosts had appreciated and enjoyed his renditions so much that they, too, increased their donations, the poor man realized that this was his ticket to making a living.

However, word got around and eventually reached the caretakers and *gabba'im* of R' Yechezkel, who were incensed that this beggar was denigrating the honor of the *rav*—and making money off it, to boot!

יְיָ יְיָ אֵל רַחוּם וְחַנּוּן אֶרֶךְ אַפַּיִם וְרַב חֶסֶד וֶאֱמֶת: נֹצֵר חֶסֶד לָאֲלָפִים נֹשֵׂא עָוֹן וָפֶשַׁע וְחַטָּאָה וְנַקֵּה: וְסָלַחְתָּ לַעֲוֹנֵנוּ וּלְחַטָּאתֵנוּ וּנְחַלְתָּנוּ:

Immediately, they went into the private room of the Noda B'Yehudah and explained to him what the man was doing and how they believed he should issue an order to cease and desist his unflattering imitation of the *rav*.

R' Yechezkel picked his head up from the *sefer* he was learning and looked directly at the men. "If only," he declared cheerfully, "my (song of) *mechalkel chaim* should be this man's *mechalkel chaim* (provider of sustenance and livelihood)!"

ה' ה' ק-ל רחום וחנון ארך אפים ורב חסד ואמת... ונקה וגו' (לד-ו)

Hashem, Hashem, Al-mighty, Merciful, Gracious, Slow to Anger, and Abundant in Kindness, and Truth...and Acquitter of those who repent...

MIDDOS/ DERECH ERETZ מידות/דרך ארץ

According to **Rav Shimshon Pincus *zt"l***, the Thirteen Attributes of Mercy are a *tefillah*, a supplication to Hashem. He explains that just as a poor person approaches a rich man filled with hopeful anticipation and says, "You are a rich man with a big heart, and your hands are always open to the needy," without actually asking for anything, since the rich man understands what he wants; so too, when one recites the Thirteen Attributes beginning with, *Hashem, Hashem... All-powerful G-d, merciful, kind...*, his request is understood and he need not say anymore.

Rav Dovid Feinstein *shlit"a* (*Kol Dodi*) writes that a Jew should not just shout the Thirteen Attributes and think that it is sufficient for his prayers to be answered. One must attach himself to these beautiful characteristics of Hashem and follow in His ways, as *Chazal* tell us: *Just as He (Hashem) is merciful, you shall also be merciful; just as He performs kindness, you shall also perform kindness.* This is the manner in which we are truly able to arouse the mercy of Hashem.

However, more than anything else, our Father in Heaven wants us to be close to Him. And how does one come close to Hashem? If Hashem has no actual physical properties, how is it possible for a human being to be "close" or "far" or anywhere in between? The answer is that we are not talking about physical proximity. We are talking about IMITATING HIS *MIDDOS*! The more a person strives to perfect himself, the more he draws close to Hashem. Crying out during the Thirteen Attributes is powerful, but emulating His ways will establish an even stronger bond with Hashem, one that will always remain unbreakable.

סְלַח לָנוּ אָבִינוּ כִּי חָטָאנוּ מְחַל לָנוּ מַלְכֵּנוּ כִּי פָשָׁעְנוּ: כִּי אַתָּה אֲדֹנָי טוֹב וְסַלָּח וְרַב חֶסֶד לְכָל קוֹרְאֶיךָ:

סלח לנו אבינו כי חטאנו מחל לנו מלכנו כי פשענו, כי אתה ה' טוב וסלח ורב חסד לכל קוראיך

Pardon us, our Father, for we have sinned; forgive us, our King, for we have transgressed, for You, my Master, are good and forgiving, and abounding in kindness to all who call upon You.

DVAR TORAH
דבר תורה

The Thirteen Attributes of Mercy are a fundamental component of the Al-mighty's authority over His earthly subjects. And yet, the Torah explicitly details that Hashem will only invoke these attributes of kindness when He so desires: *I will be gracious to whom I will be gracious, and I will be compassionate to whom I will be compassionate* (*Shemos* 33:19). The **Maharal M'Prague, Rav Yehudah Loewy** *zt"l*, explains that Hashem clearly delineates that there is no guarantee of a favorable response to the invocation of the Thirteen Attributes. On the contrary, He will use them to show favor to Bnei Yisrael only when He desires to.

However, **Rabbeinu Moshe Cordovero** *zt"l* (***Tomer Devorah***) views the words of this *pasuk* from an entirely opposite angle. The midrash states: *Hashem showed Moshe all the treasures in which the rewards of the righteous are stored. Later, Moshe saw a huge treasure and inquired: "To whom is this great treasure?" Hashem responded, "Unto him who does not have (good deeds to his credit), I supply freely and I help him from this pile."*

There are people who are unworthy and evil, and yet *Hakadosh Baruch Hu* has mercy upon them. Their lives are filled with success, sustenance and happiness. How can this be so? There is a storehouse of grace from which Hashem graciously dispenses gifts to them, for He remembers the merits of their fathers and the oath He made to them, that even when their children will be unworthy, they will be shown grace.

This is what *Chazal* derive from this *pasuk*: *And I will be gracious to whom I will be gracious—Even when he may not deserve it.* (*Brachos* 7a) Even a wicked individual,

Rav Yechezkel Levenstein ***zt"l*** (***Ohr Yechezkel***) would say:

"Feel joy this day for Hashem's forgiveness. The greater our awareness of our atonement, the more joy we will have."

כְּרַחֵם אָב עַל בָּנִים כֵּן תְּרַחֵם יְיָ עָלֵינוּ: לַייָ הַיְשׁוּעָה עַל עַמְּךָ בִרְכָתֶךָ
סֶּלָה: יְיָ צְבָאוֹת עִמָּנוּ מִשְׂגָּב לָנוּ אֱלֹהֵי יַעֲקֹב סֶלָה: יְיָ צְבָאוֹת
אַשְׁרֵי אָדָם בֹּטֵחַ בָּךְ: יְיָ הוֹשִׁיעָה הַמֶּלֶךְ יַעֲנֵנוּ בְיוֹם קָרְאֵנוּ: סְלַח נָא
לַעֲוֹן הָעָם הַזֶּה כְּגֹדֶל חַסְדֶּךָ וְכַאֲשֶׁר נָשָׂאתָה לָעָם הַזֶּה מִמִּצְרַיִם וְעַד
הֵנָּה וְשָׁם נֶאֱמַר: וַיֹּאמֶר יְיָ סָלַחְתִּי כִּדְבָרֶךָ:

הַטֵּה אֱלֹהַי אָזְנְךָ וּשְׁמָע פְּקַח עֵינֶיךָ וּרְאֵה שֹׁמְמֹתֵינוּ וְהָעִיר אֲשֶׁר
נִקְרָא שִׁמְךָ עָלֶיהָ. כִּי לֹא עַל צִדְקֹתֵינוּ אֲנַחְנוּ מַפִּילִים תַּחֲנוּנֵינוּ
לְפָנֶיךָ כִּי עַל רַחֲמֶיךָ הָרַבִּים: אֲדֹנָי שְׁמָעָה אֲדֹנָי סְלָחָה אֲדֹנָי הַקְשִׁיבָה
וַעֲשֵׂה אַל תְּאַחַר לְמַעַנְךָ אֱלֹהַי כִּי שִׁמְךָ נִקְרָא עַל עִירְךָ וְעַל עַמֶּךָ:

---

who surely deserves no grace, is shown mercy, for he is, after all, a child of Avraham, Yitzchak, and Yaakov. We, too, should emulate His ways and not display cruelty, but rather conceal their shame and have mercy upon them.

סלח נא לעון העם הזה כגדל חסדך וכאשר נשאתה לעם הזה
ממצרים ועד הנה ושם נאמר: ויאמר ה' סלחתי כדבריך

Please pardon the sins of this nation, in accordance with the greatness of Your loving-kindness, and as you forgave this people from when it left Egypt until now. And there it is said: And Hashem said, "I have pardoned [them] as you have asked."

TEFILLAH
תפילה

On the night of *Kol Nidrei*, before reciting the words, *And Hashem said, "I have forgiven according to your words,"* the **Kozhnitzer Maggid, Rav Yisrael Hopstein** ***zt"l***, once announced the following: "*Ribono Shel Olam*! You know that in spite of my weakened state, I led the *davening* the entire month of Elul, praying for mercy. You know that I did not pray for my own sake, but for the sake of Klal Yisrael.

Rav Avraham Yehoshua Heschel ***zt"l*** **(Apter Rav)** would say:

"If I could, I would abolish all fast days except for two: Tishah B'Av and Yom Kippur. On Tishah B'Av, when the Beis Hamikdash was destroyed, how is it possible to eat? And on Yom Kippur, when every person is judged for the entire year, who wants to eat?"

But now, my fragile body cannot carry the heavy burden anymore. For the sake of Your cherished children, it is surely not too hard for You, Al-mighty G-d, to utter two words, סלחתי כדבריך, and forgive the sins of Your people who are doing *teshuvah* today."

R' Yisrael paused before raising his voice. "Perhaps You don't want to say *salachti k'dvarecha* because there are no *tzaddikim* in the world? Well, there are! There is the holy **Rav Mendel of Riminov** ***zt"l***, who is as great a *tzaddik* as all of our generation! And if You are reluctant to say it because there is no *Urim V'tumim* today, we have the saintly **Chozeh of Lublin** ***zt"l***, whose eyes shine with wisdom like the stones in the breastplate of the *kohen gadol*! And should You refuse to say it because You cannot find true *baalei teshuvah*, I, with my frail and broken body, am ready to do *teshuvah* on behalf of the entire Jewish people. So I beg You, *Ribono Shel Olam*, please declare already, *salachti k'dvarecha*!" the *maggid* sobbed.

Suddenly, he stopped and motioned to begin chanting the familiar solemn tune. With a thunderous roar that jolted the congregation, he cried out, "*Vayomer Hashem salachti k'dvarecha*!"

The saintly **Rav Yisrael Ruzhiner** ***zt"l*** commented, "I am convinced that the holy Kozhnitzer Maggid actually heard Hashem uttering the words *salachti k'dvarecha* just as Moshe heard it when Hashem said it to him."

כי לא על צדקתינו אנחנו מפילים תחנונינו לפניך כי על רחמיך הרבים

For it is not due to our righteousness that we cast down our supplications before You, but rather because of Your great compassion.

Rav Chaim Yosef Dovid Azulai ***zt"l*** **(Chidah)** would say:

MUSSAR/ HASHKAFAH
מוסר/השקפה

"There are so many people who perform kindness in this world; selfless, merciful individuals who support the poor and downtrodden, who look after the widows and orphans, who are involved in every communal act of *chessed*. Why, then, don't they look after those who need their attention most, the ones to whom they have the greatest responsibility? Why don't they do *teshuvah* and take care of their own souls?"

זְכוֹר לָנוּ בְּרִית אָבוֹת כַּאֲשֶׁר אָמַרְתָּ. וְזָכַרְתִּי אֶת בְּרִיתִי יַעֲקוֹב וְאַף
אֶת בְּרִיתִי יִצְחָק וְאַף אֶת בְּרִיתִי אַבְרָהָם אֶזְכֹּר וְהָאָרֶץ אֶזְכֹּר:
זְכוֹר לָנוּ בְּרִית רִאשׁוֹנִים כַּאֲשֶׁר אָמַרְתָּ. וְזָכַרְתִּי לָהֶם בְּרִית רִאשׁוֹנִים
אֲשֶׁר הוֹצֵאתִי אֹתָם מֵאֶרֶץ מִצְרַיִם לְעֵינֵי הַגּוֹיִם לִהְיוֹת לָהֶם לֵאלֹהִים
אֲנִי ה': עֲשֵׂה עִמָּנוּ כְּמָה שֶׁהִבְטַחְתָּנוּ. וְאַף גַּם זֹאת בִּהְיוֹתָם בְּאֶרֶץ

שמע קולנו

עשה עמנו כמה שהבטחתנו ואף גם זאת בהיתם בארץ איביהם
לא מאסתים ולא געלתים לכלתם להפר בריתי אתם

Do with us as You promised us, "And despite all that, when they will be in the land of their enemies, I will not have despised them nor abhorred them, to destroy them, to annul My covenant with them."

DRUSH
דרוש

When the **Noda B'Yehudah, Rav Yechezkel Landau** *zt"l*, was the *rav* in Prague, a decree was issued to draft Jewish boys into the army. The Noda B'Yehudah attempted to console those boys that were forced to serve, and even accompanied them when they reported for duty. Before parting, he instructed them to continue praying daily, and to volunteer for extra duty on Sundays so that their fellow soldiers might relieve them of their duties on Shabbos.

When he returned to Prague, he related to his congregants the following insight. Toward the end of the *Tochachah*, it states: *And yet for all that, when they are in the land of their enemies, I will not reject them, and I will not abhor them, to destroy them* (*Vayikra* 26:44). Why does it say *yet for all that*? This *pasuk* introduces words of comfort; why must we mention that it comes despite all the pain?

The Noda B'Yehudah explained that the decree drafting Jews into the army appeared to be somewhat beneficial for the Jewish nation, in that they were now equal to all citizens of the empire. Jewish soldiers were able to rise through the ranks and gain honor. However, this rise in prominence brought with it great pitfalls that are relevant until today. When the *pasuk* says, *yet for all that*, it reminds us that one more curse will yet befall the Jews in exile. When we will be *in the land of their enemies*, there will come a time when we will not be despised by the nations. We will even be granted equal rights. However, we must beware that we are only treated this way by the gentiles in order to change us, to bring us to the point where our Jewish faith is

אוֹיְבֵיהֶם לֹא מְאַסְתִּים וְלֹא גְעַלְתִּים לְכַלּוֹתָם לְהָפֵר בְּרִיתִי אִתָּם כִּי אֲנִי יְיָ אֱלֹהֵיהֶם: הָשֵׁב שְׁבוּתֵנוּ וְרַחֲמֵנוּ כְּמָה שֶׁכָּתוּב. וְשָׁב יְיָ אֱלֹהֶיךָ אֶת שְׁבוּתְךָ וְרִחֲמֶךָ וְשָׁב וְקִבֶּצְךָ מִכָּל הָעַמִּים אֲשֶׁר הֱפִיצְךָ יְיָ אֱלֹהֶיךָ שָׁמָּה: קַבֵּץ נִדָּחֵינוּ כְּמָה שֶׁכָּתוּב. אִם יִהְיֶה נִדַּחֲךָ בִּקְצֵה הַשָּׁמָיִם מִשָּׁם יְקַבֶּצְךָ יְיָ אֱלֹהֶיךָ וּמִשָּׁם יִקָּחֶךָ: מְחֵה פְשָׁעֵינוּ כָּעָב וְכֶעָנָן כְּמָה שֶׁכָּתוּב.

---

endangered. The nations want us to act like them, so that we will be unrecognizable as Jews, and our relationship with Hashem will be severed. Thus, Hashem will not forsake us, even as the nations will try to *annul My covenant.*

השב שבותנו ורחמנו כמה שכתוב ושב ה' אלקיך את שבותך ורחמך ושב וקבצך מכל העמים אשר הפיצך ה' אלקיך שמה

Bring back our captivity and have mercy on us, as it is written, "And Hashem your G-d will bring back your captivity and have mercy on you, and He will gather you in again from all the nations to where Hashem your G-d has scattered you."

DVAR TORAH
דבר תורה

As we stand before the Holy One Blessed be He, we implore Him to accept our repentance and *gather us in from all the peoples where Hashem our G-d has scattered us.* Our exile is long and arduous; we just want to come home! Year after year, we beg for the ultimate Redemption and we are still waiting...and still begging. How much longer will our exile last?

The **Kedushas Zion** of **Bobov, Rav Benzion Halberstam** *zt"l H"yd*, provides a remarkable insight into the ways of the Creator, based on the words of the *piyut* that we say on the night of *Kol Nidrei*: כי הנה כיריעה ביד הרוקם ברצותו מישר וברצותו מעקם כן אנחנו בידך ק-ל קנא ונוקם לברית הבט ואל תפן ליצר—*Like the curtain in the hand of the embroiderer; if he wants he can make it straight, if he wants he can make it uneven. So are we in Your hand, G-d who is jealous and vengeful. Look to the covenant and ignore the accuser.* A number of questions arise from the words of this *piyut*. First, what is the connection between an embroiderer with a length of cloth in his hand, to *G-d who is jealous and vengeful*? Second, why is it necessary to mention about this embroiderer that *if he wants he can make it straight, if he wants he can make it uneven*? And third, on the holy day of Yom Kippur, when we turn to the Al-mighty and throw ourselves upon His mercy and kindness, does it make sense to refer to Him as a *G-d who is jealous and vengeful*? Don't we want just the opposite from Him?

מָחִיתִי כָעָב פְּשָׁעֶיךָ וְכֶעָנָן חַטֹּאתֶיךָ שׁוּבָה אֵלַי כִּי גְאַלְתִּיךָ: מְחֵה פְשָׁעֵינוּ לְמַעַנְךָ כַּאֲשֶׁר אָמַרְתָּ אָנֹכִי אָנֹכִי הוּא מוֹחֶה פְשָׁעֶיךָ לְמַעֲנִי וְחַטֹּאתֶיךָ לֹא אֶזְכּוֹר: הַלְבֵּן חֲטָאֵינוּ כַּשֶּׁלֶג וְכַצֶּמֶר כְּמָה שֶׁכָּתוּב. לְכוּ נָא וְנִוָּכְחָה יֹאמַר יְיָ אִם יִהְיוּ חֲטָאֵיכֶם כַּשָּׁנִים כַּשֶּׁלֶג יַלְבִּינוּ אִם יַאְדִּימוּ

The **Kedushas Zion** elucidates these words as follows: Any respectable artisan undergoes a thorough planning stage before he is ready to begin his actual creation. This includes drawing up the plans, fixing and perfecting his first few drafts until they are just right, and then working up a prototype. To the untrained eye, looking at the artist's initial outlines would lead one to believe that the man is just drawing lines in all different directions with no apparent scheme or purpose. A person with understanding, however, knows that in fact, these lines are the foundation for his ultimate masterpiece.

Hakadosh Baruch Hu is the Master Artist and the world at large is His canvas. What He spends His valuable time on is "painting" the beauty and glory of His chosen nation—the Jewish people, as He ultimately leads them towards the future Redemption from exile. However, now, as we suffer through *galus* after *galus*, pain after pain, in countries all around the world, Hashem is simply "drawing the outline" for what will soon be. We are now in the "planning stage" of Mashiach. Thus, just as the embroiderer draws lines—some even, some uneven—as he prepares his cloth, so too, Hashem puts us through uncertain times and even appears to be "vengeful" as we suffer through the preparations for the *Geulah Sheleimah*!

מחיתי כעב פשעיך וכענן חטאתיך שובה אלי כי גאלתיך

I have wiped away your willful sins like a cloud and your errors like a mist; return to Me for I have redeemed you.

MIDDOS/ DERECH ERETZ
מידות/דרך ארץ

There are two circumstances in which a *beis din* may impose the penalty of *makkos* (lashes): If a person violates negative commandments, and if a person refuses to perform positive commandments, i.e. to wear *tefillin*. What is the difference between these two types of *makkos*? One who transgresses a negative commandment always receives thirty-nine lashes, while a person who refuses to perform a mitzvah is whipped until he gives up his obstinacy. Similarly, when the thirty-nine lashes are administered to a sinner, each lash brings him closer to atonement, whereas one who is whipped for refusing to do a mitzvah invokes Hashem's fury more with each lash, for he remains obstinate in the face of punishment.

כַּתּוֹלָע כַּצֶּמֶר יִהְיוּ: זְרוֹק עָלֵינוּ מַיִם טְהוֹרִים וְטַהֲרֵנוּ כְּמָה שֶׁכָּתוּב. וְזָרַקְתִּי עֲלֵיכֶם מַיִם טְהוֹרִים וּטְהַרְתֶּם מִכֹּל טֻמְאוֹתֵיכֶם וּמִכָּל גִּלּוּלֵיכֶם אֲטַהֵר אֶתְכֶם: כַּפֵּר חֲטָאֵינוּ בַּיּוֹם הַזֶּה וְטַהֲרֵנוּ כְּמָה שֶׁכָּתוּב. כִּי בַיּוֹם הַזֶּה יְכַפֵּר עֲלֵיכֶם לְטַהֵר אֶתְכֶם מִכֹּל חַטֹּאתֵיכֶם לִפְנֵי יְיָ

Rav Moshe Avigdor Amiel ***zt"l*** explained that the first Beis Hamikdash was destroyed because the Jews transgressed three commandments: idolatry, adultery, and murder. But that punishment was finite. Just as each *makkah* brings a sinner closer to atonement, each curse brought the generation of the first exile closer to forgiveness until, after seventy years, they returned to the Land.

The second Beis Hamikdash was destroyed because of *sinas chinam*, unwarranted hatred. In essence, the Jewish people refused to perform the commandment of *You shall love your fellow as yourself.* For such a refusal, the lashing persists until the obstinate person(s) repents or until he expires. This is why the *Tochachah* says: *All these curses will come upon you and pursue you and overtake you until you are destroyed.* We, in our exile, must learn to love our fellow Jew in order to stop the incessant lashes—the *galus*!

כי ביום הזה יכפר עליכם לטהר אתכם מכל חטאתיכם לפני ה' תטהרו

For on this day He will atone for you to cleanse you, of all your sins before Hashem you will be cleansed.

MUSSAR/ HASHKAFAH מוסר/השקפה

Why must the Torah add the words *to purify you*? If one has already reached the level where Hashem has seen fit to atone and forgive his sins, is this not purification enough?

According to **Rav Gedalya Schorr** ***zt"l***, we gain a tremendous insight from this *pasuk*—that after a person has been forgiven he is still in need of purification. Even if a person has worked hard and shown Hashem that he is indeed worthy of forgiveness and atonement, the process of purification is still necessary. This is because when a person sins, aside from the fact that he becomes liable for punishment, he also blemishes his soul. A pure, untainted soul is presented to each and every person at birth and it is our responsibility to maintain this unique purity throughout our lifetime. Thus, the process of atonement relates to a person's liability for punishment; purification, on the other hand, corrects the blemish on one's soul.

תִּטְהָרוּ: רַחֵם עָלֵינוּ וְאַל תַּשְׁחִיתֵנוּ כְּמָה שֶׁכָּתוּב. כִּי אֵל רַחוּם יְיָ אֱלֹהֶיךָ לֹא יַרְפְּךָ וְלֹא יַשְׁחִיתֶךָ וְלֹא יִשְׁכַּח אֶת בְּרִית אֲבֹתֶיךָ אֲשֶׁר נִשְׁבַּע לָהֶם: מוֹל אֶת לְבָבֵנוּ לְאַהֲבָה אֶת שְׁמֶךָ כְּמָה שֶׁכָּתוּב. וּמָל יְיָ אֱלֹהֶיךָ אֶת לְבָבְךָ וְאֶת לְבַב זַרְעֶךָ לְאַהֲבָה אֶת יְיָ אֱלֹהֶיךָ בְּכָל לְבָבְךָ וּבְכָל נַפְשְׁךָ לְמַעַן חַיֶּיךָ: הִמָּצֵא לָנוּ בְּבַקָּשָׁתֵנוּ כְּמָה שֶׁכָּתוּב. וּבִקַּשְׁתֶּם מִשָּׁם אֶת יְיָ אֱלֹהֶיךָ וּמָצָאתָ כִּי תִדְרְשֶׁנּוּ בְּכָל לְבָבְךָ וּבְכָל נַפְשֶׁךָ:

With this, we can understand *Chazal's* teaching, *(One) sin leads to another sin.* When a person sins, his soul becomes damaged. In turn, the soul is less attuned to holiness and more attached to sin. This cycle continues endlessly until one repents, and only then does he break the pattern. R' Yehudah Hanasi states (*Yuma* 85b): *Yom Kippur automatically atones for every sin.* Why then must we work so hard at repentance? Because Yom Kippur atones, but it does not purify! For that, only true repentance will suffice.

ובקשתם משם את ה' אלקיך ומצאת כי תדרשנו בכל לבבך ובכל נפשך

From there you will seek Hashem your G-d and you will find, when you will seek Him with all your heart and with all your soul.

MIDDOS/
DERECH ERETZ
מידות/דרך ארץ

According to **Rabbeinu Yonah** (*Shaarei Teshuvah* 1:47) and **Rabbeinu Bacheye**, one can rectify a *chillul Hashem* by performing an act of *kiddush Hashem.* The Gemara (*Yuma* 86a) describes an exemplary Torah life as a means to sanctify Hashem's Name by learning Torah, serving *talmidei chachamim*, and being pleasant, courteous and honest with people. When one sees such a person, he will exclaim, "Fortunate is his father, his *rebbi* who taught him Torah! Woe unto those who do not learn Torah. See how pleasant are his ways, how refined are his deeds! About him Hashem says, 'You are My servant, Yisrael, in whom I take pride.'"

Rav Avraham Pam *zt"l* notes that while this aspect of *kiddush Hashem* is applicable to every Jew in every generation, it has taken on special significance in our time due to the burgeoning *baal teshuvah* movement. Hundreds of thousands of Jews who had been deprived of a proper Torah upbringing have "returned" to Torah and *mitzvos.* It is quite common that their new life of mitzvah observance puts them at odds with their parents, who are unwilling to accept the great change that has taken place. Often their relationship is crippled by friction, and even estrangement.

תְּבִיאֵנוּ אֶל הַר קָדְשֶׁךָ וְשַׂמְּחֵנוּ בְּבֵית תְּפִלָּתֶךָ כְּמָה שֶׁכָּתוּב. וַהֲבִיאוֹתִים אֶל הַר קָדְשִׁי וְשִׂמַּחְתִּים בְּבֵית תְּפִלָּתִי עוֹלֹתֵיהֶם וְזִבְחֵיהֶם לְרָצוֹן עַל מִזְבְּחִי כִּי בֵיתִי בֵּית תְּפִלָּה יִקָּרֵא לְכָל הָעַמִּים:

שְׁמַע קוֹלֵנוּ יְיָ אֱלֹהֵינוּ חוּס וְרַחֵם עָלֵינוּ וְקַבֵּל בְּרַחֲמִים וּבְרָצוֹן אֶת תְּפִלָּתֵנוּ:

הֲשִׁיבֵנוּ יְיָ אֵלֶיךָ וְנָשׁוּבָה חַדֵּשׁ יָמֵינוּ כְּקֶדֶם:

This issue becomes more critical when two *baalei teshuvah* get married. The *kallah's* irreligious parents may be unhappy with the religious intensity of their new son-in-law. Yet, if the *chassan* will do everything possible to show that his new way of life is an expression of the pleasant ways of the Torah, and he has the utmost respect, care, and concern for his in-laws, they will soon realize that their daughter is fortunate to have such a husband. This will help them come to grips with their daughter's choice of a life partner and will often bring them closer to *Yiddishkeit* as well. What can be a greater expression of *kiddush Hashem* than that?

עולותיהם וזבחיהם לרצון על מזבחי

Their burnt offerings and their festive offerings will find favor on My altar.

DVAR TORAH
דבר תורה

Why does a Jew bring a *korban* (sacrifice)? The ***Sefer Hachinuch*** (Mitzvah 95) writes that the main tendency of the human heart is determined by a person's actions: *When a man sins, his heart will not be properly purified through words alone...through saying, "I sinned, and will never do it again." It is only by undertaking a significant action on account of his sin, by taking animals from his pen, and going through the trouble of bringing them to the* kohen *in the sacred House, and performing all the rituals outlined regarding the* korbanos *of sinners; as a result of all this immense activity the evil of the sin will be established in his heart, and he will avoid it on later occasions.*

Rav Moshe Avigdor Amiel *zt"l* would say:

"Yonah Hanavi attempted to flee from Hashem. Since this event was recorded for future generations, it must have been remarkable. How so? Because Yonah fled from Hashem only once. We flee from Hashem on a regular basis!"

אֲמָרֵינוּ הַאֲזִינָה יְיָ בִּינָה הֲגִיגֵנוּ:
יִהְיוּ לְרָצוֹן אִמְרֵי פִינוּ וְהֶגְיוֹן לִבֵּנוּ לְפָנֶיךָ יְיָ צוּרֵנוּ וְגוֹאֲלֵנוּ:

אַל תַּשְׁלִיכֵנוּ מִלְּפָנֶיךָ וְרוּחַ קָדְשְׁךָ אַל תִּקַּח מִמֶּנּוּ:

אַל תַּשְׁלִיכֵנוּ לְעֵת זִקְנָה כִּכְלוֹת כֹּחֵנוּ אַל תַּעַזְבֵנוּ:

אַל תַּעַזְבֵנוּ יְיָ אֱלֹהֵינוּ. אַל תִּרְחַק מִמֶּנּוּ:

עֲשֵׂה עִמָּנוּ אוֹת לְטוֹבָה וְיִרְאוּ שׂוֹנְאֵינוּ וְיֵבֹשׁוּ כִּי אַתָּה יְיָ עֲזַרְתָּנוּ וְנִחַמְתָּנוּ:

כִּי לְךָ יְיָ הוֹחָלְנוּ אַתָּה תַעֲנֶה אֲדֹנָי אֱלֹהֵינוּ:

The holy **Mezritcher Maggid, Rav Dov Ber *zt"l***, further explains that we find in the Torah, regarding the sacrifice of a *Korban Olah* (burnt-offering), that an individual must bring his offering לרצונו לפני ה'—*of his own (voluntary) will before Hashem.* The word עולה denotes height or elevation, teaching us that if a person truly desires to lift himself to greater heights and draw closer to *Hakadosh Baruch Hu,* he must sacrifice his own voluntary will before the will of Hashem. This, then, is how we can understand the words of *Chazal*: בטל רצונך בפני רצונו כדי שיבטל רצון אחרים מפני רצונך—*Nullify your will before His will in order that He will nullify the will of others before your will.*

עשה עמנו אות לטובה ויראו שונאינו ויבשו כי אתה ה' עזרתנו ונחמתנו

Make for us a sign for good so that our enemies may see it and be ashamed, for You are Hashem, our Helper and our Consoler.

STORIES
מעשה

The holy *tzaddik,* **Rav Naftali Tzvi Hurvitz of Ropshitz *zt"l***, was well known for his keen insight and sharp statements. He was once quoted as saying: "It would be better for me to be associated with a smart man in Gehinnom than to be stuck with a foolish person in Gan Eden!"

R' Naftali was once delivering his renowned Shabbos Shuvah *drashah* in the *beis medrash.* He was silent for awhile and then turned to his chassidim and said, "It is obviously the custom of most people to beg the *Ribono Shel Olam* for a favorable and merciful judgment. I have, therefore, a simple plan that just might work if it is implemented properly. You see, the Mishnah tells us that one's enemy may not

אַתָּה נוֹתֵן יָד לַפּוֹשְׁעִים. וִימִינְךָ פְּשׁוּטָה לְקַבֵּל שָׁבִים. וַתְּלַמְּדֵנוּ יְיָ אֱלֹהֵינוּ לְהִתְוַדּוֹת לְפָנֶיךָ עַל כָּל עֲוֹנוֹתֵינוּ. לְמַעַן נֶחְדַּל מֵעֹשֶׁק יָדֵינוּ. וּתְקַבְּלֵנוּ בִּתְשׁוּבָה שְׁלֵמָה לְפָנֶיךָ כְּאִשִּׁים וּכְנִיחוֹחִים. לְמַעַן

---

sit on a *beis din* to judge him (*Sanhedrin* 3-5). Now, what constitutes an enemy? The Mishnah explains that one who hasn't spoken to another out of animosity for three days is considered an enemy.

"Now the plan is like this: Each person should accept upon himself not to commit any sins for at least three full days before Yom Kippur! The reason is that the Gemara (*Brachos* 61b) tells us: *For sinners, the* yetzer hara *himself judges them.* Meaning to say, the same *Satan* that caused the man to sin will be the one to sit in judgment over him!

"However," continued R' Naftali with a warm smile, "it would be safe to say that if a person will avoid his *yetzer hara* completely for three full days before Yom Kippur, his *yetzer hara* will then have a *din* (status) of an actual enemy who is not allowed to judge him! And if there will be no one on the panel to antagonize and prosecute him, he will surely be granted a life of health and happiness."

לעי"נ
ר' צבי הירש
בן ר' משה
דוד בלונדר
נפ' י"ד שבט

נעילה

אתה נותן יד לפושעים וימינך פשוטה לקבל שבים...למען נחדל מעשק ידינו

You reach out Your hand to transgressors, and Your right hand is extended to receive those who [truly] repent...so that we may refrain from the injustice of our hands.

TEFILLAH
תפילה

The holy day of Yom Kippur culminates in the awesome *tefillah* of *Ne'ilah.* The gates of Heaven are thrown open wide and our prayers mingled with our tears are guaranteed not to go unanswered. At this auspicious moment, one would think that our prayers would deal solely with our needs and the needs of Klal Yisrael. Yet, specifically at this point in the *Ne'ilah* service, when we plead for forgiveness for all of our sins, we recite the words, *You taught us, Hashem our G-d, to confess all our sins before You, so that we may cease to engage in robbery.* How does the concept of robbery fit in to all of this?

The Gemara (*Sanhedrin* 108a) states*: Come and see how great is the power of robbery, for though the generation of the Flood transgressed all laws, their decree of punishment was sealed only because they stretched out their hands to steal.* The **Sfas Emes, Rav**

דְּבָרֶיךָ אֲשֶׁר אָמַרְתָּ. אֵין קֵץ לְאִשֵּׁי חוֹבוֹתֵינוּ וְאֵין מִסְפָּר לְנִיחוֹחֵי
אַשְׁמָתֵנוּ. וְאַתָּה יוֹדֵעַ שֶׁאַחֲרִיתֵנוּ רִמָּה וְתוֹלֵעָה לְפִיכָךְ הִרְבֵּיתָ
סְלִיחָתֵנוּ. מָה אָנוּ מֶה חַיֵּינוּ מֶה חַסְדֵּנוּ מַה צִּדְקֵנוּ מַה יְּשׁוּעָתֵנוּ מַה
כֹּחֵנוּ מַה גְּבוּרָתֵנוּ. מַה נֹּאמַר לְפָנֶיךָ יְיָ אֱלֹהֵינוּ וֵאלֹהֵי אֲבוֹתֵינוּ הֲלֹא

Yehudah Leib Alter ***zt"l***, suggests that in fact all sinning involves thievery. When we indulge in the forbidden, we are, in effect, taking that which is not ours. The *pasuk* tells us (*Bereishis* 6:11): *And the earth was filled with thievery.* All transgressions are essentially an aspect of thievery, since everything belongs to the Al-mighty.

The dreadful fate of the generation of the Flood was sealed because their sin of robbery tipped the scales. Thus, at *Ne'ilah*, when our individual lots for the coming year are signed and sealed, we pour out our hearts before the Al-mighty that we should not come to indulge in thievery or stealing of any kind, so as not to encounter a negative judgment, *chas v'shalom*.

ותלמדנו ה' אלקינו להתודות לפניך על כל עונותינו. למען נחדל מעשק ידינו

You have taught us, Hashem, our G-d, to confess before You all our iniquities so that we may refrain from the injustice of our hands…

DVAR TORAH
דבר תורה

Why is it that at the height of the *Ne'ilah* service, when we plead for forgiveness for all of our sins, we conclude with the words, למען נחדל מעושק ידינו—*In order that we may refrain from the injustice of our hands (engaging in robbery)*?

Rabbi Joseph Ber Soloveitchik ***zt"l*** explains this idea and says that in the *Selichos* prayers we acknowledge that *the soul is Yours and the body is Your work.* Although we may think that we control our actions and all of our bodily functions, in fact, all that we presumptuously call ours is really His—the Master of the world's. Thankfully, He allows us to use His gifts conditionally—in accordance with His stipulations. When we sin, these privileges are forfeited and nullified. Thus, we have become thieves, since our continued utilization of His gifts is nothing less than theft.

ואתה יודע שאחריתנו רמה ותולעה לפיכך הרבית סליחתנו

And You know that our ultimate end is the worm, and therefore You have increased the means of our pardon.

כָּל הַגִּבּוֹרִים כְּאַיִן לְפָנֶיךָ וְאַנְשֵׁי הַשֵּׁם כְּלֹא הָיוּ וַחֲכָמִים כִּבְלִי מַדָּע
וּנְבוֹנִים כִּבְלִי הַשְׂכֵּל כִּי רֹב מַעֲשֵׂיהֶם תֹּהוּ וִימֵי חַיֵּיהֶם הֶבֶל לְפָנֶיךָ.
וּמוֹתַר הָאָדָם מִן הַבְּהֵמָה אָיִן כִּי הַכֹּל הָבֶל:

MUSSAR/ HASHKAFAH
מוסר/השקפה

Akaviah ben Mahalalel begins the third *perek* of *Pirkei Avos* with a profound and dual message: *Observe three things (in your life) and you will not come to perform a sin* (3:1). He gives us a secret formula to prevent us from sin. Every human being is comprised of two opposing parts. We all possess a body and a soul. Of course, each of these human components pulls a person in completely different directions. The body wants *gashmiyus* and the soul wants *ruchniyus.* In order to address the importance of good over evil and have a positive effect on the entire make-up of a person, the body and the soul must be addressed in separate statements.

Thus, Akaviah ben Mahalalel first implores the *neshamah.* With minimal elaboration (after all, it is the *neshamah*!), he says, *Know where you came from*—from the loftiest and highest place; *and where you are going*—you, the holy and pure *neshamah,* will return to your Maker to receive your ultimate reward; *and before Whom you will give an accounting for all your deeds*—to the great and mighty Creator of the world, Who has sent you, His most precious treasure, on a sacred mission in this world.

Then he addresses the body. The materialistic aspect of the body requires more explanation and analysis. He says, *Know where you came from*—from a putrid drop, so do not become arrogant in this world; *and where you are going*—to a place of dust and worms, where you will have no form or influence. But after all is said and done, *and before Whom you will give an accounting for all your deeds*—you will have to answer for all your actions, before the King of kings, Master of the universe, Who rewards the righteous and punishes the wicked! Would you want to sin after all that?!

כי רב מעשיהם תהו וימי חייהם הבל לפניך ומותר האדם מן הבהמה אין כי הכל הבל

For most of their actions are a waste, and the days of their life are trivial in Your presence. The superiority of man over the beast is nil, for all is futile.

MASHAL
משל

משל: Two paupers were wandering from place to place looking for a bite to eat. They arrived at an inn belonging to a wealthy man and were told to sit down. One pauper said to the other, "Should we ask the man to give us some food?" The second pauper told him to wait.

After a while, the first pauper repeated his request, but the second pauper told him to remain still.

אַתָּה הִבְדַּלְתָּ אֱנוֹשׁ מֵרֹאשׁ וַתַּכִּירֵהוּ לַעֲמֹד לְפָנֶיךָ. כִּי מִי יֹאמַר לְךָ מַה תִּפְעָל. וְאִם יִצְדַּק מַה יִּתֵּן לָךְ: וַתִּתֶּן לָנוּ יְיָ אֱלֹהֵינוּ בְּאַהֲבָה אֶת יוֹם (לשבת הַשַּׁבָּת הַזֶּה וְאֶת יוֹם) **(צוֹם)** הַכִּפֻּרִים הַזֶּה קֵץ וּמְחִילָה וּסְלִיחָה עַל כָּל עֲוֹנוֹתֵינוּ לְמַעַן נֶחְדַּל מֵעֹשֶׁק יָדֵינוּ וְנָשׁוּב אֵלֶיךָ לַעֲשׂוֹת חֻקֵּי רְצוֹנְךָ בְּלֵבָב שָׁלֵם: וְאַתָּה בְּרַחֲמֶיךָ הָרַבִּים רַחֵם עָלֵינוּ כִּי לֹא תַחְפֹּץ בְּהַשְׁחָתַת עוֹלָם. שֶׁנֶּאֱמַר דִּרְשׁוּ יְיָ בְּהִמָּצְאוֹ קְרָאֻהוּ בִּהְיוֹתוֹ קָרוֹב:

Just then, a group of merchants arrived at the inn and demanded a meal. The innkeeper served a sumptuous feast, replete with aromatic dishes and wine aplenty. The men ate and drank to their hearts' content.

Now the first pauper became insistent. "We must also ask to be served a meal. Why are we just sitting here?"

"You will see the difference between us and the merchants very shortly," replied the second, more experienced pauper.

When the merchants finished eating, the innkeeper presented them with a bill, which they paid in full. At this point, the wealthy innkeeper now turned to the paupers and graciously invited them to join him at the table for a complete meal.

נמשל: The **Dubno Maggid** ***zt"l*** explains that there are some people whose sole desire is to pursue the delights of this world. They seek pleasure and luxuries, but fail to realize that Hashem is marking it all down and eventually He will present them with an exact bill for all their indulgences. The righteous individuals, however, detest the trivialities of this world and are oblivious to the pleasures that surround them; in time, Hashem presents everything to them as a gift.

ותתן לנו ה' אלקינו באהבה את יום צום הכפרים הזה קץ ומחילה וסליחה על כל עונותינו

And You, Hashem, our G-d, gave us with love, this Day of Atonement to be the end [of sin] and forgiveness, and pardon for all of our iniquities...

MIDDOS/ DERECH ERETZ
מידות/דרך ארץ

The day of Yom Kippur conjures up feelings of awe, fear and tension. However, in truth, Yom Kippur is a day of great joy. All of the workings of the *Satan* halt as our minds and hearts focus on atoning for our past sins, cleansing our souls and perfecting our character. All of the distortions, excuses, and justifications for sinning are completely removed from our consciousness as we elevate ourselves to the level of angels! For this reason, we begin this great day with the *brachah* of

וְנֶאֱמַר יַעֲזֹב רָשָׁע דַּרְכּוֹ וְאִישׁ אָוֶן מַחְשְׁבֹתָיו וְיָשֹׁב אֶל יְיָ וִירַחֲמֵהוּ וְאֶל אֱלֹהֵינוּ כִּי יַרְבֶּה לִסְלוֹחַ:

וְאַתָּה אֱלוֹהַּ סְלִיחוֹת חַנּוּן וְרַחוּם אֶרֶךְ אַפַּיִם וְרַב חֶסֶד וֶאֱמֶת וּמַרְבֶּה לְהֵיטִיב וְרוֹצֶה אַתָּה בִּתְשׁוּבַת רְשָׁעִים וְאֵין אַתָּה חָפֵץ בְּמִיתָתָם שֶׁנֶּאֱמַר אֱמֹר אֲלֵיהֶם חַי אָנִי נְאֻם אֲדֹנָי אֱלֹהִים אִם אֶחְפֹּץ בְּמוֹת הָרָשָׁע כִּי אִם בְּשׁוּב רָשָׁע מִדַּרְכּוֹ וְחָיָה: וְנֶאֱמַר שׁוּבוּ שׁוּבוּ

Shehecheyanu—thanking Hashem for giving us this extraordinary opportunity to become pure.

The ***Shaarei Teshuvah*** tells us that the mitzvah to eat a festive meal before Yom Kippur is to celebrate the great joy of this day! Since we cannot do this on Yom Kippur itself, we celebrate this great holiday before it even begins.

Rabbeinu Menachem ben Shlomo *zt"l* (Meiri) also explains that since the purpose of the fast is to raise ourselves spiritually, Hashem commands us to eat so that we will not be hungry and thus distracted from the purpose of the fast itself. Yom Kippur is a day to feel Hashem's love and when we actually feel it, we experience tremendous joy!

Rabbi Zev Leff *shlit"a* says: "If Yom Kippur represents *Olam Haba*, then Erev Yom Kippur represents *Olam Hazeh*. Our urgent eating on Erev Yom Kippur demonstrates that we must consume as much Torah and *mitzvos* as we can in this world because in *Olam Haba* they are unavailable!" Indeed, this is our ultimate goal—to be *zocheh* to experience the other-worldly bliss of this holy day so that our spiritual joy will spill over and fill the entire year with true *simchah*!

קץ ומחילה וסליחה על כל עונותינו למען נחדל מעשק ידינו
ונשוב אליך לעשות חקי רצונך בלבב שלם

...the end of [sin] and forgiveness, and pardon for all of our iniquities, so that we may refrain from the injustice of our hands and return to You, to fulfill the statutes of Your will, with a perfect heart...

STORIES
מעשה

Rav Yisrael Salanter *zt"l* once visited a wealthy merchant regarding a matter of communal importance. For whatever reason, there was a considerable sum of money on the living-room table. Suddenly the

מִדַּרְכֵיכֶם הָרָעִים וְלָמָּה תָמוּתוּ בֵּית יִשְׂרָאֵל: וְנֶאֱמַר הֶחָפֹץ אֶחְפֹּץ
מוֹת רָשָׁע נְאֻם אֲדֹנָי אֱלוֹהִים הֲלוֹא בְּשׁוּבוֹ מִדְּרָכָיו וְחָיָה: וְנֶאֱמַר כִּי
לֹא אֶחְפֹּץ בְּמוֹת הַמֵּת נְאֻם אֲדֹנָי אֱלוֹהִים וְהָשִׁיבוּ וִחְיוּ:

כִּי אַתָּה סָלְחָן לְיִשְׂרָאֵל וּמָחֳלָן לְשִׁבְטֵי יְשֻׁרוּן בְּכָל דּוֹר וָדוֹר
וּמִבַּלְעָדֶיךָ אֵין לָנוּ מֶלֶךְ מוֹחֵל וְסוֹלֵחַ אֶלָּא אָתָּה:

---

merchant was called out of the room on an urgent matter, and he was gone for a few minutes. When he returned, R' Yisrael was nowhere to be found.

The merchant searched the house, thinking that perhaps the *tzaddik* had wandered down the myriad hallways of his mansion and had gotten lost. But after checking hallway after hallway, it was apparent that R' Yisrael was not in the house.

Finally, the wealthy merchant walked outside, and lo and behold, there was the renowned rabbi standing in front of the door. The merchant hurried over and asked R' Yisrael for an explanation.

R' Yisrael Salanter, the founder of the *mussar* movement, innocently explained that in the Torah there is a prohibition of *yichud*—forbidding a man and a woman to be secluded alone in a room, for it may lead to *arayos* (illicit relations). Our Sages have taught us that a minority of people violate these prohibitions. However, R' Yisrael said, if that is the case regarding *arayos*, then it stands to reason that in the case of *gezel* (robbery), where many more people are guilty of this prohibition, there is an *issur yichud* (prohibition of being alone) with unguarded money.

"When I saw the pile of money laying on your table, I felt that I must comply with the prohibition of *yichud*. I was therefore compelled to leave the house."

אין לנו מלך מוחל וסולח אלא אתה

We have no king who forgives and pardons—only You.

DVAR TORAH
דבר תורה

Why do we say that Hashem pardons and forgives us? How can we be so sure that we will merit forgiveness from Him, that our repentance will be sincere enough to warrant a pardon from on High?

Rav Yisrael Friedman *zt"l* (Ruzhiner Rebbe) provided a unique response. "When I was a child," the Ruzhiner related, "I once had a great desire to eat an apple; however, my father **(Rav Shalom Shachna of Prohobisht *zt"l*)** wanted to teach me a lesson in austerity and wouldn't give me the apple. What did I do? I made the blessing over the apple anyway

and left him no choice but to give me the apple so that my blessing would not be in vain. It may have been brash, but I ended up with the apple!"

Similarly, when we call Hashem, *King Who pardons and forgives*—He must forgive us. Otherwise we would be saying His Name and describing Him in vain!

ברוך שם כבוד מלכותו לעולם ועד

Blessed [is His] Name, Whose glorious kingdom is forever and ever.

MUSSAR/ HASHKAFAH
מוסר/השקפה

Throughout the year, we recite *Krias Shema* and we then say the second *pasuk* quietly. Why is this so? Because when Moshe Rabbeinu ascended to heaven to receive the Torah, he heard the angels saying this *pasuk* and out of respect for their holiness, he did not say it aloud.

On Yom Kippur, however, we say these very special words loudly, in order to signify that on this day we are like the angels. Why, then, do we recite them on the first night, when our stomachs are full and our bodies are still grounded in *gashmiyus*, as opposed to the next night, the night of Motza'ei Yom Kippur, after a full day of emulating the angels?

Chacham Rabbeinu Elazar Abuchatzeira *zt"l* (*Divrei Elazar*), answers that we derive a very important lesson from this practice: A Jew must always look forward—and not backward! On *Kol Nidrei* night, every Jew WANTS to be an angel; that is his ultimate goal. Thus, he says the very words that the angels say. The next night, however, he is looking ahead to being himself, an earthly being again, so he does not say them. The focal point is not so much where you were but where you are *going*!

STORIES
מעשה

The following is an excerpt from the memoir of Rabbi Moshe Segal, a Lubavitcher chassid who was active in the struggle to free the Holy Land from British rule. In those years, the area in front of the Western Wall did not appear as it does today. Only a narrow alley separated the Kosel and the Arab houses on its other side. The British government forbade Jews to place an *aron kodesh*, tables or benches in the alley; even a small stool could not be brought to the Kosel. The British also instituted

Rav Levi Yitzchak of Berditchev *zt"l* would say:

"When I see a man of many sins, I think, 'How I envy him! When he will do *teshuvah* and rectify his sins, he will have many more merits than I do!'"

the following ordinances, designed to humble the Jews at the holiest place of their faith: it was forbidden to pray aloud lest one upset the Arab residents; it was forbidden to read from the Torah (those praying at the Wall had to go to one of the synagogues in the Jewish quarter to conduct the Torah reading); and it was forbidden to sound the shofar on Rosh Hashanah and Yom Kippur. Policemen were stationed at the Kosel to enforce these rules.

Rabbi Segal writes: "On Yom Kippur of the year 5690 (1930), I was praying at the Kosel Hamaaravi. During the brief intermission between the *Mussaf* and Minchah prayers, I overheard people whispering to each other, 'Where will we go to hear the shofar? It'll be impossible to blow here. There are as many policemen as people praying.' The British police commander himself was there, to ensure that the Jews would not, G-d forbid, sound the single blast that culminated the fast.

"I listened to these whisperings, and thought to myself: Can we possibly forgo the sounding of the shofar that accompanies our proclamation of the sovereignty of Hashem? Can we possibly forgo the sounding of the shofar, which symbolizes the redemption of Eretz Yisrael? True, the sounding of the shofar at the close of Yom Kippur is only a custom, but as we know, *A Jewish custom is* din *(law).* I approached Rabbi Yitzchak Horenstein, who served as the rabbi of our *minyan*, and said to him, 'Rabbi, give me a shofar—I will blow!' The rabbi abruptly turned away from me, but not before he cast a glance at the prayer stand at the left end of the alley. I understood that the shofar was in the stand.

"When the hour of the blowing approached, I walked over to the stand and leaned against it. I opened the drawer and slipped the shofar into my shirt. I had the shofar, but what if they saw me before I had a chance to blow it? I was still unmarried at the time, and following the Ashkenazic custom, did not wear a *tallis*. I turned to the person praying at my side, and asked him if I could borrow his *tallis*. My request must have seemed strange to him, but the Jews are a kind people, especially at the holiest moments of the holiest day, and he handed me his *tallis* without a word.

"I quickly wrapped myself in the *tallis*. All around me, a foreign government prevails, ruling over the people of Israel even on their holiest day at their holiest place, and we are not free to serve our G-d; but under this *tallis* is another domain. Here I am under no dominion save that of my Father in Heaven; here I do as He commands me, and no force on earth will stop me.

"When the closing words of the *Ne'ilah* prayer, *Shema Yisrael... Baruch Shem... Hashem Hu HaElokim...* were proclaimed, I took out the shofar and blew a long, resounding blast. Everything happened very quickly. Many hands grabbed me. The *tallis* was thrown off my head, and before me stood the police commander, who ordered my arrest. I was taken to the *kishlah*, the prison in the Old City, and a guard was posted. Many hours passed; I was given no food or water to break my fast. Finally

at midnight, the police received an order to release me, and I was freed without a word.

"I then learned that when the chief rabbi of the Holy Land, **Rav Avraham Yitzchak Kook *zt"l***, heard of my arrest, he immediately contacted the secretary of the High Commissioner of Palestine, and asked that I be released. When his request was refused, he stated that he would not break his fast until I was freed. The High Commissioner resisted for many hours, but finally, out of respect for the rabbi, he had no choice but to set me free.

"From then on, the shofar was sounded at the Kosel every Yom Kippur. The British well understood the significance of this blast; they knew that it would ultimately demolish their reign over our land as the walls of Yericho crumbled before the shofar of Yehoshua, and they did everything in their power to prevent it. But every Yom Kippur, the shofar was sounded by men who knew they would be arrested for their part in staking our claim on the holiest of our possessions."

Rav Nachman of Breslov *zt"l* (*Sichos Haran*) would say:

"The lesson of *teshuvah* is that nothing is beyond Hashem's power. Even sins can be transformed into virtues!"

Rav Menachem Breslover *zt"l* would say:

"As soon as Yom Kippur ends, I place my ear against the wall to listen for the *shamash* banging on doors and calling the Jews for *Selichos* in preparation of the next Rosh Hashanah and Yom Kippur."

Rav Yitzchak Zev Halevi Soloveitchik *zt"l* (Brisker Rav) would say:

"The reason many otherwise non-observant Jews observe Yom Kippur is not because Yom Kippur is so important to them, but rather because it is treated with such sanctity by us."

A Wise Man would say:

"In this season of forgiveness, remember: Always forgive your enemies—nothing else annoys them so much."

חג הסוכות

סדר אושפיזין

תפילה כשנכנסין לסוכה

נטילת לולב

הושענא רבה/חבטת הערבה

דברי קהלת

תפילה כשיוצאים מן הסוכה

Dedicated by

Mr. and Mrs. Heshy Schlosser

לעי״נ ר׳ **אליעזר** בן ר׳ **אברהם משה** ז״ל

נפ׳ י״ד תשרי תשס״ד

חג הסוכות

וַתִּתֶּן לָנוּ יְיָ אֱלֹהֵינוּ בְּאַהֲבָה מוֹעֲדִים לְשִׂמְחָה, חַגִּים וּזְמַנִּים לְשָׂשׂוֹן, אֶת יוֹם חַג הַסֻּכּוֹת הַזֶּה זְמַן שִׂמְחָתֵנוּ מִקְרָא קֹדֶשׁ, זֵכֶר לִיצִיאַת מִצְרָיִם.

Sukkos is the holiday when we utilize this world—with all its physicality—for the service of Hashem. Sukkos is a time when we realize that everything physical and worldly has great meaning and power, if utilized properly. The flimsy sukkah with its wooden boards or canvas walls becomes our holy temple, in which we experience a taste of the World to Come. Without doing anything, one is rewarded for simply being in the sukkah.

Each day of Sukkos we have a special mitzvah to take the *arbaah minim* and hold them together. **Rabbi Zev Leff *shlit"a*** quotes the midrash (*Bereishis Rabbah* 15:8) that the *eitz hadaas* (Tree of Knowledge) was actually an *esrog* tree. Adam was created on Rosh Hashanah and was commanded not to eat from the *eitz hadaas*, because he needed to undergo ten days of preparation, the Aseres Yemei Teshuvah, culminating with the purity of Yom Kippur, in order to be able to eat from the *eitz hadaas.* This would have taken place on the first day of Sukkos, the special time designated for uplifting the physical world to the spiritual. But Adam failed in this lofty endeavor and therefore Hashem gave us the special *mitzvos* of the *arbaah minim*, taking four different species of plants and utilizing them for the service of Hashem.

The *esrog* represents the heart of a man, the center of all feeling and emotion; the organ that pumps life throughout the body. The *lulav* represents the spine, which symbolizes intellect, since it is connected to the brain that has the power to think and understand.

The *hadassim* and *aravos* are bound to the *lulav*, representing the eyes and the lips which help a human being see, understand, and express his intelligence. The goal of every Jew is to concretize all his knowledge and understanding of Hashem. He must make it a part of his heart so that he serves Hashem with emotion and feeling in a true bond of love. We say each day in the *tefillah* of *Aleinu*, *And you will know today, and you will return to your heart.* The longest journey of a Yid is the million miles from his head to his heart. It takes incredible effort to transform our knowledge into a vibrant feeling and loving relationship. When we bring the *lulav* and *esrog* together, we are expressing our ability to traverse the millions of miles and serve Hashem with all our heart and soul, uplifting every physical aspect of our body to a source of holiness.

In the sukkah, our eating becomes holy, our sleeping becomes holy, our plants become holy and the mere existence in the confines of the sukkah becomes a

spiritual endeavor. Let us use our own free will to elevate all our thoughts, words, actions, and feelings during this time so that we can experience true closeness to Hashem—which is in essence what *Zman Simchaseinu* is really all about.

REMEZ
רמז

On Sukkos, we are commanded to leave our permanent dwelling and enter a temporary dwelling. This is to help us continue our upward climb in spirituality that began on the first day of Elul, through Rosh Hashanah and Yom Kippur, and escalates with the beautiful Yom Tov of Sukkos. There is so much meaning and deep understanding in everything we do on Sukkos, from the *lulav, esrog, hadassim* and *aravos* to the *Ushpizin* who come to visit us each night. But the significance of the sukkah itself is surely of paramount importance and has much to teach us.

According to **Rav Avraham Pam** ***zt"l***, the "permanent dwelling" of a person is his own mind! Human nature is to be self-centered. One's thoughts largely revolve around his own needs. This is what is most "permanent" in a human being. Of course, one also thinks about others—about *chessed*—but that is the "temporary dwelling" of the mind!

The fundamental mitzvah on Sukkos is ושמחתם—to be happy! For this reason, Sukkos is called *Zman Simchaseinu*, the time of our rejoicing. R' Pam explains that thinking of others' needs is the formula for a life of *simchah*! Thus on Sukkos we leave our "permanent dwellings," our self-centered thoughts, and enter our "temporary dwelling," focusing on the needs of others. As R' Pam often quoted, "The city of happiness that we're all looking for can only be found in the state of mind!"

The sukkah also represents humility and the need for a person to be yielding and relinquishing in the way he deals with others. From the halachic requirements of the sukkah, we can derive the meaning of the sukkah. *L'chatchilah*, one's sukkah should have four walls. However, if he can't manage that, three walls are sufficient. And if he is unable to build three walls, that too, is not a problem! Even a sukkah comprised

Rav Shloime Kluger ***zt"l*** **(*Yerios Shlomo*)** would say:

"When one approaches a mitzvah, he must feel the greatest joy at the opportunity that he is offered with this mitzvah. When completing the mitzvah, he should feel happiness at having achieved his goal. But while he is actually doing the mitzvah, he must feel the awe that is to be experienced by a mortal while he is standing before a King. He must recognize that any wrong word or move could result in a tragedy indeed!"

of two walls and a *tefach* (handbreadth) is still kosher. It's all about flexibility and compromise.

The **Vilna Gaon** ***zt"l*** famously writes that the ס of the word סכה represents all four walls. The כ comes second, for this alludes to three walls. And the ה symbolizes the two walls with an additional piece!

May we take the lessons of compromise and reconciliation to heart, and may the joy of this beautiful Yom Tov permeate our entire lives.

את יום חג הסכות הזה זמן שמחתנו מקרא קודש

...this day of the Festival of Sukkos, the season of our rejoicing, a day of holy assembly...

DVAR TORAH
דבר תורה

Every Yom Tov is a time of happiness and elation. However, only Sukkos is called *Zman Simchaseinu* (season of our gladness). Why, indeed, is *simchah* associated with Sukkos more than with Pesach and Shavuos?

The **Manchester Rosh Yeshivah, Rav Yehudah Zev Segal** ***zt"l***, explains the meaning of this joy: The season of soul-searching and introspection which commences with Rosh Chodesh Elul becomes more intense with the advent of Rosh Hashanah, and reaches its climax with Yom Kippur, when we enumerate our sins in confession upon confession and beg forgiveness. Those who approach this season with the seriousness that it demands might well become dispirited after having spent so much time pondering their spiritual failings. **Rav Yisrael Salanter** ***zt"l*** writes that in past generations, "every man was seized with dread by the voice which proclaimed the blessing of the month of Elul." Forty days and countless tears later, such a man might find it hard to mend his broken heart.

Sukkos is a time of special closeness between Hashem and His people; this closeness is the source of the joy that permeates the Yom Tov experience. The

Rav Yoel Teitelbaum ***zt"l*** **(Satmar Rebbe)** would say:

"When *Chazal* tell us that rain is a bad sign on Sukkos, because it is like a master who is not pleased with his servant's performance, that only applies to Eretz Yisrael where the rainy season begins after Sukkos. Therefore, if it rains on Sukkos, this is unusual and we take it as a bad sign. But here, in *chutz la'aretz*, where it's normal to have rain in the summer, it's not a bad sign at all if it rains on Sukkos. However, if it doesn't rain, that is definitely a good sign."

mitzvah of sukkah symbolizes this closeness in a most unique way. *Chazal* tell us that the sukkah represents the Clouds of Glory, through which Hashem's Presence was manifest during Bnei Yisrael's sojourn in the wilderness and which sheltered them from harm. Thus, Sukkos is the season of our gladness because its arrival revives our broken spirit and infuses us with joy, both because it is a holy day, a Yom Tov, and also because its primary mitzvah—sukkah—represents the special bond that exists between *Hakadosh Baruch Hu* and Klal Yisrael.

The First Night(s) of Sukkos

HALACHAH
הלכה

Apart from the general seven-day (eight outside Eretz Yisrael) mitzvah of *basukkos teishvu*—"You shall live in a sukkah," there is a special mitzvah on the first night of Yom Tov to eat bread in the sukkah, which is derived from the mitzvah of eating matzah on the first night of Pesach. We learn this[1] from a similar wording in the *mitzvos* of Pesach and Sukkos (חמשה עשר). We therefore apply the following *halachos*, exactly or similarly, to the *mitzvos* on the night(s) of Sukkos, several according to all opinions and several according to some opinions. These *halachos* apply outside of Eretz Yisrael on the second night of Yom Tov unless stated otherwise.

Erev Sukkos

One should eat bread or challah at his *seudah* with a good appetite. Thus, just like on Erev Pesach there are eating restrictions in order to eat the matzah with an appetite, similarly on Erev Sukkos, men should not eat bread or *mezonos* in the last quarter of the day so as not to become too satiated[2].

Earliest Time

Even if one accepted Yom Tov early, he cannot perform the mitzvah of sitting in a sukkah until *tzeis hakochavim*[3] (nightfall), just like regarding matzah, where the Torah says *on that night*.

Latest Time

One should make sure to perform the mitzvah before halachic midnight[4] (midpoint between sunset and sunrise).

1. סוכה כז
2. משנה ברורה תרלט:כז
3. שם:כה
4. שם:כו

How Much to Eat

The basic halachah is that one must eat bread to the equivalent of the volume of half an egg in a four-minute time span. Preferably, one should eat a bit more than the volume of an egg in an eight-minute time span[5], which is the volume one cannot eat outside the sukkah throughout the entire Yom Tov.

When Raining

On the first night of Sukkos, some opinions obligate one to eat bread in the sukkah even if it is raining outside, just like one has to eat the minimal amount of matzah on Pesach night even if it is difficult to swallow. Since others argue on this point, if it is raining on the first night of Sukkos, one should wait an hour or two and if it does not stop, he should then make Kiddush in the sukkah without the *brachah* of לישב בסוכה. He should then wash, eat bread in the sukkah and finish the meal in the house. If one has family members who can't wait or guests who might be hungry, he should do this procedure without waiting. On the second night, however, one waits just a short period of time and if it is still raining, he makes Kiddush in the house, eats the meal inside as well, and at the end of the meal, he eats some bread in the sukkah without the *brachah* of לישב בסוכה. The reason for this difference is explained in the ***Mishnah Berurah***[6].

During the rest of Sukkos, one doesn't have to eat in the sukkah when it rains or similar distressing circumstances.

The special intentions of the mitzvah of sukkah that one should have before eating the bread on the first night(s) are:

1. To fulfill the mitzvah of בסוכות תשבו—sitting in the sukkah the entire Yom Tov.
2. The special first-night obligation to eat bread as derived from the mitzvah of matzah. (These two items might be branches of one big mitzvah.)
3. To fulfill the mitzvah of rejoicing on Yom Tov, which is accomplished by eating bread[7].
4. To remember our exodus from Mitzrayim and the protective clouds in the desert.

Intentions 1 and 4 apply every time a person goes into the sukkah the entire *chag*[8]. Intention 3 applies every time one eats bread on the Yom Tov days and possibly on the Chol Hamoed days as well.

5. שם:כב
6. שם:לו
7. שו"ת רע"א סי' א'
8. משנה ברורה תרכה:א

סדר אושפיזין

עוּלוּ אוּשְׁפִּיזִין עִלָּאִין קַדִּישִׁין, עוּלוּ אֲבָהָן עִלָּאִין קַדִּישִׁין, לְמֵיתַב בְּצִלָּא דִמְהֵימְנוּתָא עִלָּאָה, בְּצִלָּא דְקֻדְשָׁא בְּרִיךְ הוּא. לֵיעוּל אַבְרָהָם רְחִימָא, וְעִמֵּיהּ יִצְחָק עֲקֵידְתָא, וְעִמֵּיהּ יַעֲקֹב שְׁלֵמְתָא, וְעִמֵּיהּ

סדר אושפיזין

Dedicated as a *zechus* for our parents and children, by **Susan and Meir Yoel Laub**

עולו אושפיזין עלאין קדישין עולו אבהן עלאין קדישין

Enter, esteemed holy guests, come in, esteemed holy Patriarchs…

MIDDOS/ DERECH ERETZ מידות/דרך ארץ

The concept of the *Ushpizin*, exalted guests, is one shrouded in mystery. **Rav Eliyahu Kitov *zt"l*** ventures the following explanation: The seven רועים, shepherds, wandered from *galus* to *galus*, and only attained rest after much toil and travail. Avraham Avinu left Ur Kasdim for Charan, came to Canaan, and then went down to Mitzrayim. Yitzchak sojourned in the land of the Plishtim. Yaakov fled to Aram Naharayim, and he and his sons made their way down to Goshen in Mitzrayim. Yosef was sold into slavery in a foreign land. Moshe fled to Midyan and together with his brother Aharon, led the people in the desert for forty years, although neither merited entering Eretz Yisrael. Dovid Hamelech also fled to the wilderness and he knew no rest from war.

Hashem bestows life and kindness upon all of the world's inhabitants. Why then, does He make those who dearly love Him wander from place to place without rest? The reason is so that they may shed light, goodness, and blessing all around the world.

Now the children of these great and righteous ones rejoice on the Yom Tov of Sukkos and leave their homes, as if to say to Hashem, "We desire neither grand homes nor overflowing fields—all we desire is You!" Through this statement of joy and submission, Bnei Yisrael, like their forefathers, become a source of blessing for themselves and the entire world, and through their merit, the whole world is blessed with bounty for the entire year.

Rav Menachem Mendel of Kotzk *zt"l* (Kotzker Rebbe) would say:

"Some people say they've seen the *Ushpizin*. I don't see them, but I believe they are in my sukkah. And believing is greater than seeing!"

מֹשֶׁה רַעֲיָא מְהֵימְנָא, וְעִמֵּיהּ אַהֲרֹן כַּהֲנָא קַדִּישָׁא, וְעִמֵּיהּ יוֹסֵף צַדִּיקָא, וְעִמֵּיהּ דָּוִד מַלְכָּא מְשִׁיחָא. בְּסֻכֹּת תֵּשְׁבוּ, תִּיבוּ אוּשְׁפִּיזִין עִלָּאִין תִּיבוּ, תִּיבוּ אוּשְׁפִּיזֵי מְהֵימְנוּתָא תִּיבוּ.

Only then does Hashem respond and say, "It is fitting for the loyal shepherds of old to come back down and dwell in the צילא דמהימנותא—*shadow of faith*, together with My faithful children."

למיתב בצלא דמהימנותא עלאה בצלא דקדשא בריך הוא

...to sit in the shade of sublime faithfulness, in the shade of the Holy One, Blessed is He.

MUSSAR/HASHKAFAH
מוסר/השקפה

The Gemara (*Sukkah* 26a) derives from the *pasuk* בסוכות תשבו שבעת ימים, that a person should dwell in his sukkah for the seven days of Yom Tov just as one dwells in his house all year—תשבו כעין תדורו. But it goes both ways, writes the **Satmar Rebbe, Rav Yoel Teitelbaum *zt"l.*** A person must always remember to dwell in his house with the same *kedushah* and respectful attitude that he has while living in his sukkah. Just as he dwells in the *shelter of faith* for seven days, he must incorporate faith and *emunah* in his home throughout the year.

לעול אברהם

Enter, Avraham...

STORIES
מעשה

Due to the tremendous distraction of scores of people knocking on his door day and night, seeking all sorts of spiritual guidance and important needs, the great **Rav Pinchas of Koritz *zt"l*** finally prayed to Hashem that he should become unpopular. In his mind that would be the solution; people would no longer disturb him and he would be free to serve Hashem with all his energy and undivided attention. Indeed, it would seem that his wish had come true, for after that time, R' Pinchas was never seen in the company of another individual, save for *davening* in shul. He lived in the most austere fashion and secluded himself for lone communion with Hashem.

When the Yom Tov of Sukkos approached, he could not find another Jew to help him build his sukkah and had no choice but to ask a gentile to do the chore. Likewise,

הֲרֵינִי מוּכָן וּמְזֻמָּן לְקַיֵּם מִצְוַת סֻכָּה כַּאֲשֶׁר צִוַּנִי הַבּוֹרֵא יִתְבָּרַךְ שְׁמוֹ: בַּסֻּכֹּת תֵּשְׁבוּ שִׁבְעַת
יָמִים, כָּל הָאֶזְרָח בְּיִשְׂרָאֵל יֵשְׁבוּ בַּסֻּכֹּת. לְמַעַן יֵדְעוּ דֹרֹתֵיכֶם, כִּי בַסֻּכּוֹת הוֹשַׁבְתִּי אֶת
בְּנֵי יִשְׂרָאֵל, בְּהוֹצִיאִי אוֹתָם מֵאֶרֶץ מִצְרָיִם. תִּיבוּ תִּיבוּ אוּשְׁפִּיזִין עִלָּאִין, תִּיבוּ תִּיבוּ
אוּשְׁפִּיזִין קַדִּישִׁין. תִּיבוּ תִּיבוּ אוּשְׁפִּיזִין דִּמְהֵימְנוּתָא, תִּיבוּ בְּצִלָּא דְקֻדְשָׁא בְּרִיךְ הוּא.

---

after *davening* the first night of Yom Tov, R' Pinchas asked various people to be his guests in honor of Yom Tov, but not a single one would accept his invitation—he was just too disliked!

R' Pinchas walked home alone. As he arrived, he began to recite the *tefillah* upon entering the sukkah, followed by the traditional invitation to the first of the *Ushpizin*. Just then, he looked up and saw an old man standing just outside the door of the sukkah. The old man, however, who R' Pinchas instantly recognized to be Avraham Avinu, would not step foot into the sukkah. R' Pinchas tried to convince him to enter, but to no avail.

Distressed, R' Pinchas turned to him and asked in anguish, "Why do you not enter my sukkah? What is my sin?"

The old man stroked his white beard and looked hard at R' Pinchas. "It is not my custom to enter a place where there is no *hachnasas orchim*," said Avraham Avinu.

R' Pinchas Koritzer now understood his mistake and from that day forward, sincerely prayed to the Al-mighty that he be restored in the eyes of his townspeople to his former situation. And indeed, he was once again able to find favor in the eyes of men.

בסכת תשבו שבעת ימים כל האזרח בישראל ישבו בסכות

In booths you shall dwell seven days; every born Israelite shall dwell in booths...

MIDDOS/ DERECH ERETZ
מידות/דרך ארץ

All seven days of Sukkos, one is required to make the sukkah his permanent abode and his house his temporary abode. Whence do we know this? From what *Chazal* have taught: *You shall dwell*—in the same manner as you ordinarily live (*Sukkah* 26a).

Rav Shamshon Raphael Hirsch *zt"l* notes that just as we must adhere to the principle of תשבו כעין תדורו—*Your sitting (in a sukkah) should be as your dwelling (at home)*, so conversely we should adhere to the principle of תדורו כעין תשובו—*A Jew's dwelling at home should be as his sitting in a sukkah.*

Rosh Hashanah is only comprised of two days for introspection, and Yom Kippur is only one day for fasting and repentance, while Sukkos consists of seven

זַכָּאָה חוּלְקָנָא, וְזַכָּאָה חוּלְקֵיהוֹן דְּיִשְׂרָאֵל, דִּכְתִיב: כִּי חֵלֶק יְיָ עַמּוֹ, יַעֲקֹב חֶבֶל נַחֲלָתוֹ. לְשֵׁם יִחוּד קֻדְשָׁא בְּרִיךְ הוּא וּשְׁכִינְתֵּהּ, לְיַחֲדָא שֵׁם י״ה בְּו״ה בְּיִחוּדָא שְׁלִים, עַל יְדֵי הַהוּא טָמִיר וְנֶעְלָם, בְּשֵׁם כָּל יִשְׂרָאֵל. וִיהִי נֹעַם יְיָ אֱלֹהֵינוּ עָלֵינוּ, וּמַעֲשֵׂה יָדֵינוּ כּוֹנְנָה עָלֵינוּ, וּמַעֲשֵׂה יָדֵינוּ כּוֹנְנֵהוּ.

בלילה ראשון כשנכנס לסוכה קודם שישב לאכול ובכל יום קודם סעודתו יאמר זה:

אֲזַמִּין לִסְעוּדָתִי אוּשְׁפִּיזִין עִילָּאִין אַבְרָהָם יִצְחָק יַעֲקֹב מֹשֶׁה אַהֲרֹן יוֹסֵף וְדָוִד:

---

days, an entire cycle of days for the joyful dwelling in our huts, and for enjoying our possessions before Hashem. This is what is most characteristic of what a Jew is all about; the normal mood of one's life is not the broken feeling of despair, but the perfect joy of life which runs equally through the year of a life of a Jew faithfully devoted to duty. Hence, תדורו כעין תשובו—one should endeavor to live throughout the year in the spirit of true *simchah* as generated during the joyous festival of Sukkos.

למען ידעו דורותיכם כי בסכות הושבתי את בני ישראל בהוציאי אתם מארץ מצרים

...in order that your generations may know that in booths I caused Bnei Yisrael to dwell when I took them out of the land of Egypt.

DVAR TORAH
דבר תורה

Our requirement to sit in the sukkah stems from the fact that Hashem *sat Bnei Yisrael in* sukkos *when they came out of Egypt.* Rashi says that the *sukkos* referred to here are really the Heavenly Clouds of Glory that protected the Jewish people as they traveled in the desert. If so, asks the **Tur** in his famous treatise, why don't we celebrate the holiday of Sukkos in the month of Nissan, when Bnei Yisrael were actually protected from the blazing sun with those special clouds of protection, and not in Tishrei, which is seemingly not connected to this reason?

Rav Yehudah Aryeh Alter *zt"l* (Sfas Emes) would say:

"Only regarding the Yom Tov of Sukkos does the *pasuk* state, *You shall observe it for seven days in the year,* implying that these seven days of joy constitute a vessel of *simchah* radiating joy throughout the year. Similarly, in our Kiddush on Yom Tov, we refer to our festivals as מועדים לשמחה (appointed times for rejoicing), rather than מועדים בשמחה (appointed times of rejoicing) to teach us that our festivals are not only days of rejoicing, but storehouses of joy and gladness for the remainder of the year."

The Tur answers that were we to sit in booths in the month of Nissan, the month when the weather is pleasant, it would not be recognized that we are doing so for a mitzvah, but rather it would appear that we are sitting outside for our own pleasure. Thus, in Tishrei, when the autumn season is gearing up and the weather is changing to a harsher climate, we make a point of dwelling outside in our sukkah, since now it is apparent that we are doing so for the mitzvah—and not for our pleasure.

The **Chiddushei Harim, Rav Yitzchak Meir Alter** ***zt"l***, adds another explanation based on the words in *Parshas Emor, In order that future generations will know that I had situated them in booths.* The *pasuk* implies that "knowledge" is one of the requirements for properly observing the mitzvah of sukkah.

During the course of the year, writes the Gerrer Rebbe, a Jew struggles with his *yetzer hara*, his evil inclination and the desires that tempt him, and he often finds himself falling time after time into transgression. However, as we know from the Gemara (*Sotah* 3a), a person does not commit a sin unless a *ruach shtus* (a spirit of folly) overtakes him; therefore, all year long a person acts with "folly"—which is the opposite of knowledge. And as we know, a Jew without knowledge is not able to properly fulfill the mitzvah of sukkah. Thus, only in the month of Tishrei, after the atonement of Rosh Hashanah and Yom Kippur, when a person is cleansed of his transgressions, and resolved to be righteous from then on, does he have the necessary "knowledge" to properly fulfill the mitzvah of sukkah.

Rav Michel Barenbaum ***zt"l*** provides a different answer to the Tur's question, based on the words of the **Rambam** (*Hilchos lulav* 8:15) who says that the joy of Sukkos is when *a person experiences joy in the performance of* mitzvos *and in the love of Hashem Who commanded them.* This is a recognition of what a privilege it is to observe *mitzvos*, for this is the primary purpose of creation. We recall the Clouds of Glory in which we, Bnei Yisrael, basked in the desert, when all of our daily needs were met through the direct intervention of Hashem.

Thus, specifically in Tishrei, during the harvest season, Hashem commanded us to leave our secure, comfortable homes and move into flimsy, temporary dwellings where we are exposed to the forces of nature and dependent on the grace of Hashem to protect us from them. This is to remind us, in the midst of harvesting the bounty of the year's crops, that we are indeed dependent upon Hashem for our daily sustenance, no less than in the days of the manna.

תיבו...בצלא דקדשא בריך הוא. זכאה חולקנא, וזכאה חולקיהון דישראל

Be seated...in the shade of the Holy One, Blessed is He. Worthy is our portion, and worthy is the portion of Yisrael...

MUSSAR/ HASHKAFAH מוסר/השקפה

Dovid Hamelech in *Tehillim* (27:4) makes a famous request: *I shall sit in the House of Hashem all my days...and visit His sanctuary.* The *sefarim* explain that *visit His sanctuary* refers to sitting in the sukkah, the private and intimate chamber of *Hakadosh Baruch Hu*, where a person is fully embraced in the Heavenly shade (צלא דהימנותא). The **Arizal** compares the halachah that a sukkah must have two walls plus a little bit, to an embracing arm. From the shoulder to the elbow is one wall, the elbow to the wrist is a second wall, and the hand is the extra little bit. When a Jew sits in the sukkah, it is as if he is literally being "hugged" by the *Yad Hashem*!

How much must a Jew appreciate this privileged and intimate relationship—being allowed to visit the King in His sanctuary? For this very reason, the halachah states that one who experiences pain and/or suffering is not required to be in the sukkah. Why? Because if a Jew feels pain or discomfort when entering Hashem's private chamber, he doesn't deserve to be there altogether! Imagine being allowed into a room where one hundred dollar bills are being given out to everyone in the room every minute. You come inside, but right away you feel hot and stuffy. If being uncomfortable is enough to drive you away from this great opportunity, then you are a fool and indeed, you don't belong there!

The sukkah is a place where we receive much more than one hundred dollar bills. We soak in infinite amounts of spirituality and holiness from the *Ribono Shel Olam*. It is our solemn duty to visit our King for the next seven days and really get to know Him!

אזמין לסעודתי אושפיזין עילאין אברהם יצחק יעקב משה אהרן יוסף ודוד

I invite to my meal the exalted guests: Avraham, Yitzchak, Yaakov, Moshe, Aharon, Yosef, and Dovid...

MUSSAR/ HASHKAFAH מוסר/השקפה

When Avraham Avinu was sitting outside his tent looking to invite guests, three angels appeared. Avraham ran to them and bade them to sit down under a tree where he served them a meal. He told them: *Rest yourselves under the tree* (*Bereishis* 18:4). Avraham Avinu had a very special thought in mind. Although he certainly wanted his guests to be comfortable in a shady spot, protected from the scorching sun, it was much deeper than just that.

After the guests had enjoyed a hearty meal, Avraham told them, "Bless Hashem! For everything is from Him." Avraham wanted to bestow physical nourishment upon his benefactors, but his goal was to bring them to the realization that there is a G-d from Whom all sustenance flows. The **Ksav Sofer, Rav Avraham Shmuel Binyamin Sofer *zt"l***, explains that Avraham specifically placed his guests under a tree, to hint

יְהִי רָצוֹן מִלְּפָנֶיךָ, יְיָ אֱלֹהַי וֵאלֹהֵי אֲבוֹתַי, שֶׁתַּשְׁרֶה שְׁכִינָתְךָ בֵּינֵינוּ,
וְתִפְרוֹשׂ עָלֵינוּ סֻכַּת שְׁלוֹמֶךָ, בִּזְכוּת מִצְוַת סֻכָּה שֶׁאָנוּ מְקַיְּמִין,

to them that even though this tree was planted and tended by man, it was only due to the rain that Hashem showered upon it that it grew.

So it is with all activities with which man is involved. All his business affairs, all his comings and goings, all his give and take. A person should never say, *Kochi v'otzem yadi asah li es hachayil hazeh*—"Look what I have accomplished! It is all from the work of my hand!" Rather, he should adopt the mentality of his Zaidy Avraham and say, "Let me bless Hashem because everything is from Him!"

This concept is truly the essence of the mitzvah of sitting in a sukkah. We leave our homes and sit under the *s'chach*, through which we can see the open sky and remember our Father in Heaven. This holy mitzvah was given to us as a gift and we owe a debt of gratitude to our dear forefather, Avraham Avinu, for his kindly actions and elevated intentions. The Ksav Sofer further explains that it was in the merit of these words—*rest yourselves under the tree*—that Hashem gave his children and all future generations this beautiful present called Sukkos.

So, when we sit in our sukkah and serve our guests (and remember Avraham Avinu is one of the *Ushpizin* guests!), we should fulfill the original intention—*Let us bless Hashem—**everything** is from Him!*

תפילה כשנכנסין לסוכה

ותפרוש עלינו סכת שלומך

And spread over us the shelter of Your peace...

משל: A simple villager was once walking in the big city and came across a store with an interesting display.

MASHAL
משל

"What are those colorful sticks you have in the window?" asked the villager. The storekeeper replied, "Those are umbrellas. They protect a person from the rain."

תפילה כשנכנסין לסוכה

לְיַחֲדָא שְׁמָא דְקֻדְשָׁא בְּרִיךְ הוּא וּשְׁכִינְתֵּהּ, בִּדְחִילוּ וּרְחִימוּ, לְיַחֲדָא שֵׁם י"ה בְּו"ה בְּיִחוּדָא שְׁלִים, בְּשֵׁם כָּל יִשְׂרָאֵל, וּלְהַקִּיף וְלַהֲגֵנּוּ מִזִּיו

The villager was enthralled and immediately purchased one which he brought back to his village. There he became the center of attention as he showed off his new umbrella.

Suddenly, someone called out, "Hey! It's starting to rain. Let's see how your new umbrella works."

The simpleton grabbed his colorful stick and dangled it over his arm like he'd seen the city folk do. But to his shock and embarrassment, he was soon soaked to the bone from the drenching rain. His umbrella was worthless.

He ran back to the store in the big city and complained that his umbrella did not protect him during the heavy rain.

"An umbrella is useless when closed," he was told. "You must open it and stand under it so the rain doesn't hit you."

נמשל: Throughout the year, we hide within the confines of our homes. We feel safe and secure, without the need for extra protection. But now, after we've done *teshuvah*, we say: ופרוש עלינו סכת שלומך—We must "open the umbrella" and truly recognize that it is Hashem Who is protecting us in our homes and even out in the street!

ותפרוש עלינו סכת שלומך בזכות מצות סכה שאנחנו מקימין

And spread over us the shelter of Your peace in the merit of the mitzvah of sukkah that we are performing…

MIDDOS/ DERECH ERETZ
מידות/דרך ארץ

The mitzvah that characterizes the holiday of Sukkos is *simchah*—pure joy and happiness. On top of that, it's also a very enjoyable Yom Tov, in that we build a temporary hut, covered in branches or bamboo, and we camp out in it for a week. But just as everything a Jew

---

Rav Yonasan Eibschutz *zt"l* (*Yaaros Devash*) would say:

"Praiseworthy is the person who learns Torah in the sukkah. He who sits in the sukkah for the sake of the mitzvah alone and rejoices in the Yom Tov will be surrounded by a Heavenly cloud. He may not see it—but it surely exists!"

כְּבוֹדְךָ הַקָּדוֹשׁ וְהַטָּהוֹר, נָטוּי עַל רָאשֵׁינוּ מִלְמַעְלָה כְּנֶשֶׁר יָעִיר קִנּוֹ. וּמִשָּׁם יַשְׁפִּיעַ שֶׁפַע הַחַיִּים לְעַבְדְּךָ (פלוני) בֶּן (פלונית) אֲמָתֶךָ. וּבִזְכוּת צֵאתִי מִבֵּיתִי הַחוּצָה וְדֶרֶךְ מִצְוֹתֶיךָ אָרוּצָה, יֵחָשֵׁב לִי בְּזֹאת כְּאִלּוּ הִרְחַקְתִּי נְדוֹד. וְהֶרֶב כַּבְּסֵנִי מֵעֲוֹנִי, וּמֵחַטָּאתִי טַהֲרֵנִי. וּמֵאוּשְׁפִּיזִין עִלָּאִין, אוּשְׁפִּיזִין דִּמְהֵימְנוּתָא, תִּהְיֶינָה אָזְנֶיךָ קַשֻּׁבוֹת רַב בְּרָכוֹת. (וְלָרְעֵבִים גַּם צְמֵאִים תֵּן לַחְמָם וּמֵימָם הַנֶּאֱמָנִים.) וְתִתֶּן לִי זְכוּת לָשֶׁבֶת וְלַחֲסוֹת בְּסֵתֶר צֵל כְּנָפֶיךָ בְּעֵת פְּטִירָתִי מִן הָעוֹלָם, וְלַחֲסוֹת

---

does has a purpose, there must be a purpose to our "pleasure" as well! Otherwise, Hashem would not have commanded us to do it this way!

Rav Raphael Leban ***shlit"a*** (*Torah Today*) shares the following observation: "Having built many *sukkos* in my life, I can tell you that it nearly impossible for one person to do it alone. You have to put up walls, attach them, support them and cover them with a layer of *s'chach*. How do you hold it up and hammer it at the same time by yourself? It's a big project, and it takes more than one person. Invariably, what ends up happening is that neighbors, friends and relatives help each other out. Whether it's holding up the walls while they're being attached, lending a drill bit or downright building a sukkah for someone who doesn't know their regular from their Philips screwdriver, we neighbors build our *sukkos*.

"Then, once they're up, we're all out in our backyards together, on opposite sides of the picket fence. You could practically smell what the neighbors are having for their *seudah* over there. I'll never forget the sound of Sukkos in Yerushalayim, where a dozen different festive songs wafted from the neighbors' temporary homes into the thin wooden walls of our own.

"In fact, the differences between your own sukkah and "the Jones'" are almost negligible. We may be on distant ends of the economic spectrum throughout the years, but for this week, out in the sukkah, we're all pretty much equal. A sanctified tent with firewood or a rough mat for the roof is hardly something to be proud of. Outside and away from the comfort of our homes, some of the distinctions that separate us fall away."

So in truth, the "fun" of Sukkos is in fact an essential characteristic of Sukkos—it brings us together. Part of the joy of the celebration is that it is shared with our community of neighbors. When we go out from the home into the sukkah, we become a part of the *Beis Yisrael*, the house of the Jewish people.

When we daven Maariv each night, we recite: ופרוש עלינו סכת שלומך—*And spread out over us Your sukkah of peace.* On the Yom Tov of Sukkos, we reconnect with the

מִזֶּרֶם וּמִמָּטָר, כִּי תַמְטִיר עַל רְשָׁעִים פַּחִים. וּתְהֵא חֲשׁוּבָה מִצְוַת סֻכָּה זוֹ שֶׁאֲנִי מְקַיֵּם, כְּאִלּוּ קִיַּמְתִּיהָ בְּכָל פְּרָטֶיהָ וְדִקְדּוּקֶיהָ וּתְנָאֶיהָ, וְכָל מִצְוֹת הַתְּלוּיִם בָּהּ. וְתֵיטִיב לָנוּ הַחֲתִימָה. וּתְזַכֵּנוּ לֵישֵׁב יָמִים רַבִּים עַל הָאֲדָמָה, אַדְמַת קֹדֶשׁ, בַּעֲבוֹדָתְךָ וּבְיִרְאָתֶךָ. בָּרוּךְ יְיָ לְעוֹלָם, אָמֵן וְאָמֵן.

רִבּוֹן כָּל הָעוֹלָמִים, יְהִי רָצוֹן מִלְּפָנֶיךָ, שֶׁיְּהֵא חָשׁוּב לְפָנֶיךָ מִצְוַת יְשִׁיבַת סֻכָּה זוֹ, כְּאִלּוּ קִיַּמְתִּיהָ בְּכָל פְּרָטֶיהָ וְדִקְדּוּקֶיהָ וְתַרְיַ"ג מִצְוֹת הַתְּלוּיִם בָּהּ, וּכְאִלּוּ כִּוַּנְתִּי בְּכָל הַכַּוָּנוֹת שֶׁכִּוְּנוּ בָהּ אַנְשֵׁי כְנֶסֶת הַגְּדוֹלָה.

בקידוש

בָּרוּךְ אַתָּה יְיָ אֱלֹהֵינוּ מֶלֶךְ הָעוֹלָם, אֲשֶׁר קִדְּשָׁנוּ בְּמִצְוֹתָיו, וְצִוָּנוּ לֵישֵׁב בַּסּוּכָּה:

Jewish people. And every carefully crafted, thought-out and drawn-up temporary edifice out in the yard or on the porch is another link in the chain to bring about the ultimate peace. May Hashem grant us this year, soon, that renewed bond with all of Klal Yisrael and peace for ourselves and the entire world.

ליחדא שמא דקדשא בריך הוא ושכינתה בדחילו ורחימו
ליחדא שם י"ה בו"ה ביחודא שלים בשם כל ישראל

To unify the Name of the Holy One, Blessed is He and His Presence, with reverence and love, to unify the Name Yud-Kei with Vav-Kei in complete unity, in the name of all Yisrael…

DVAR TORAH
דבר תורה

The temporary booths we sit in during the holiday of Sukkos, known by the same name, commemorate the special Clouds of Glory which encircled the Jewish people as they traveled through the wilderness. There were seven such clouds: one which traveled ahead of the camp, four on each side surrounding the people, one above them and the seventh cloud beneath them for comfort (*Bamidbar* 10:34, Rashi). This is evidenced by the *pasuk*: *And your feet did not wear out these forty years* (*Devarim* 8:4).

Many *mefarshim* ask the universal question: why are we commanded to build a sukkah to commemorate the Clouds of Glory which encircled us in the desert, but

we were given no *mitzvos* to commemorate any of the other miracles which Hashem performed for us in the desert, like the *mann*, quail, and the well?

The Sephardic *chacham*, **Rabbeinu Chaim Kefusi Baal Haness *zt"l***, answers with a beautiful insight. We do not commemorate miracles so that we remind ourselves of Hashem's unlimited power. We know that quite well already! Rather, we commemorate miracles because through them Hashem manifests His infinite love for us. In order for Bnei Yisrael to survive in the desert, the Al-mighty had to provide us with *mann*, quail, and the well, so that we wouldn't die of hunger or thirst. Therefore, His extraordinary love for us was not manifest through these phenomena. The Clouds of Glory, by contrast, signified His special affection for His people, as they served as extra protection—and even unexpected luxury—from the uncomfortable conditions of the desert. We therefore commemorate this manifestation of our unique relationship with Hashem, in order to reciprocate and show Him a measure of our love and affection for Him!

ולהקיף אותם מזיו כבודך הקדוש והטהור נטוי על ראשיהם מלמעלה

...and to surround us with the splendor of Your honor, holy and pure, spread over their [our] heads from above...

STORIES
מעשה

At the turn of the century, Jewish life in the United States was a tough proposition. Many immigrants who escaped their homeland dreaming of a new beginning on these "golden" shores found earning a decent living and maintaining a semblance of religious observance almost impossible. The American standard was to work seven days a week, and a person who wished to keep both Shabbos and his wage-earning job was often forced to choose between the two. Sadly, many observant Jews were unable to withstand the test and the holy Shabbos became an unfortunate casualty.

Rav Menachem Mendel Schneerson *zt"l* (Tzemach Tzedek) would say:

"There is a halachah that מצטער פטור מן הסוכה—*One who feels pain (or discomfort) is exempt from sitting in the sukkah.* Aside from the normal interpretation, perhaps *Chazal* are teaching us something deeper: מצטער—A person who finds himself in distress, פטור—is able to free himself, both mentally and physically. How? מן הסוכה—by correctly performing the mitzvah of sukkah!"

One man, however, would not give in. He was a skilled worker and his talents were in demand, yet no employer was willing to tolerate his absurd request to take off on Saturday. As a result, more often than not, when Friday would roll around, he was told that if he didn't show up the next day, he should not bother coming in on Sunday. This pious individual would nod his head but then would ask for one small favor: could his employer write him a "pink slip," so he could have his termination in print? The employer, seeing no reason not to, would usually oblige and fulfill this unusual request.

It was not until many months later that the man's reason for requesting the papers came to light. A few days before the Yom Tov of Sukkos, as his children were building and decorating their sukkah, he informed them that he had his own special decorations that he would like to put up.

What decorations could Papa have come up with? they thought. It was then that their father pulled out his stack of "pink slips" and began attaching them to the walls.

"My children," he said with an inner joy born of spiritual greatness, "this is the most glorious 'decoration' that we can put in our sukkah. For with these, we are declaring that we work for no one other than the 'Boss of all bosses'—*Hakadosh Baruch Hu*, and we do so wholeheartedly!" Incidentally, every one of his children and grandchildren remained true to *Yiddishkeit*, and many great *talmidei chachamim* emanated from his family.

ובזכות צאתי מביתי החוצה ודרך מצותיך ארוצה יחשב לי זאת כאלו הרחקתי נדוד

And in the merit of my leaving my house to go out [into the sukkah], and the path of Your commandments I will eagerly follow, may this be considered for me as though I have wandered far off [in exile].

STORIES
מעשה

In his later years, the health of the **Kapischnitzer Rebbe, Rav Avraham Yehoshua Heschel *zt"l***, deteriorated and he suffered a heart attack. The rebbe, however, ignored all his family's pleading that he give up his work for the *klal*. On one occasion, when the rebbe announced his intention to go to a certain fundraising event, the family called the Lakewood Rosh Yeshivah, **Rav Aharon Kotler *zt"l***, in desperation and asked him to try to make the rebbe change his mind. R' Aharon immediately canceled his *shiur* and traveled to New York to speak to the rebbe.

The rebbe, realizing that his family had been responsible for R' Aharon's visit, told them bitterly, "Tell me, my children, don't you all need air to breathe? Why can't you understand that a mitzvah is to me like air to breathe? Why am I alive if not to perform *mitzvos* and to help others? If I cannot continue to do *mitzvos*, why do I need

to live? If you are all truly interested in my health, then you must make sure that I can carry on doing *chessed* and *tzedakah*!"

The rebbe's selfless *mesirus nefesh* in the performance of all *mitzvos* knew no bounds. One year, a few days before Sukkos, the rebbe fell ill with pneumonia. His family knew that he would want to eat and sleep in the sukkah regardless of his condition. The family phoned the **Satmar Rebbe, Rav Yoel Teitelbaum** ***zt"l***, who was a close friend and admirer of the rebbe, and begged him to talk the rebbe out of it.

On Erev Sukkos, the Satmar Rebbe arrived at the home of the Kapischnitzer Rebbe and informed the rebbe in no uncertain terms that it was strictly forbidden for him to eat and sleep in the sukkah. A person has an obligation to look after his health, especially a leader of Klal Yisrael who has to set an example for others. For twenty minutes, the Satmar Rebbe elaborated on the severity of guarding one's health, and he ended off saying that if the rebbe would eat and sleep in the sukkah, it would not be a mitzvah but in fact an *aveirah*.

After the Satmar Rebbe had ended his long discourse, he turned to R' Avraham Yehoshua and asked, "*Nu*, Kapischnitzer Rebbe, are you going to sleep in the sukkah this year?"

The rebbe looked the Satmar Rebbe squarely in the face and replied, "Tell me, Satmar Rav. What would you do if the positions were reversed, *chas v'shalom*, if it was you who was lying in bed with pneumonia and I had just given you this *drashah*. Would you really not sleep in the sukkah, or would you stay in the sukkah despite the illness?"

The Satmar Rebbe stood up with a smile on his face. Then he said, "Kapischnitzer Rebbe, I give you my *brachah* (blessing) that you should be able to sleep in the sukkah and that no harm shall befall you!"

The rebbe slept in the sukkah the entire Yom Tov and not only did he not get sicker—he got better!

Rav Shamshon Raphael Hirsch ***zt"l*** **(*Chorev*)** would say:

"The sukkah is a symbol of universal peace and brotherhood, as we recite in the evening service on Shabbos and festivals: *Spread over us, Your sukkah of peace*. The term sukkah in this prayer is not used to describe the outdoor huts that we sit in but rather to symbolize peace and brotherhood, which shall be based not on economic and political interests, but on a joint belief in the one true G-d."

ותתן לי זכות לשבת ולחסות בסתר צל כנפיך בעת פטירתי מן העולם

Grant me the privilege to dwell and take refuge in the sheltering shadow of Your wings—at the time I leave this world…

STORIES
מעשה

Rav Shneur Kotler ***zt"l*** was known for his extraordinary kindness and love for his fellow Jews throughout his life. Close friends recall that as a young man he built a sukkah using old, broken boards, which were all he had. When R' Shneur's neighbor, a non-observant Jew, saw the shabby-looking sukkah, he promised to build R' Shneur what he called a "proper" sukkah the next year. And he did.

The sukkah stood for twenty years, built and rebuilt each year before Yom Tov, and each year R' Shneur thanked the man for his generous gift. Then the man died, and at the same time, the boards, which were exposed for two decades to rough autumn weather, began to warp so badly that they could no longer be used. The Kotler family wanted to discard the sukkah boards, and while R' Shneur did build a new sukkah, he refused to throw away the old boards. Instead, he used them for counter covers during Pesach.

Finally, however, the boards deteriorated so badly that the family again wished to replace them. Again, R' Shneur refused. "No," he said softly, "we can never replace these boards. The man who built us a sukkah from these boards did not have much in spiritual wealth, but he did have a very special *zechus* every year with the construction of this sukkah. I want his *zechus* to be remembered forever."

ותתן לי זכות לשבת ולחסות בסתר צל כנפיך

Grant me the privilege to dwell and take refuge in the sheltering shadow of Your wings…

MASHAL
משל

משל: There was once a Jewish innkeeper who provided food and lodgings for weary travelers. Though he was friendly and personable, his jealous competitors decided to slander him. Before long, he was ordered to appear in court to defend himself against the baseless charges.

The simple innkeeper was terrified about his fate, for he was told that if convicted, he could face a long jail sentence or possibly even execution.

One friend advised him to schedule an appearance before the emperor, who was a benevolent monarch and would no doubt exonerate the innkeeper if he were told the truth. But the poor man argued and said that he had no connections to the palace and no way to even arrange an appointment.

The emperor had a habit from time to time to dress up as a peasant and mingle with his subjects to get to know them. One night, he even came to the inn, where the kind innkeeper served him food and drink and made him comfortable. The inkeeper had no idea he was actually serving the emperor.

Later, when the inkeeper realized that his guest had been the emperor himself, he was truly distraught over the missed opportunity to plead his case and free himself.

נמשל: When we sit in our sukkah, the *Shechinah* rests among us and this gives us the opportunity to draw close to Hashem and plead for the things we need in life. The **Chafetz Chaim *zt"l*** advises us to seize the moment and not waste our precious time, for when else will we have this incredible opportunity to sit with the King of all kings in a personal setting, in our very own sukkah?

ולחסות מזרם וממטר כי תמטיר על רשעים פחים

...to take refuge from the stream [of fire] and from the rain [of fiery coals] when You rain snare-traps upon the wicked...

REMEZ
רמז

In this *Yehi Ratzon* we pray that Hashem protect us מזרם וממטר—*from storm and from (harsh) rain.* The *gematria* of the word זרם is 247, while that of the word מטר is 249. With this, explains the **Trisker Maggid, Rav Avraham Twerski *zt"l*,** we can understand the *pasuk* in the Torah, *Lo sosifu al hadavar...v'lo sigri'u*—"Do not add to the words (of the Torah) and do not subtract from it" (*Devarim* 4:2). Since there are 248 positive commandments, we find that זרם is one less (247), and מטר is one more (249). Thus, we pray that the sukkah, which represents the manifestation of the *Shechinah* (Divine Spirit), should protect Bnei Yisrael from זרם ומטר—any addition or subtraction of the *mitzvos*, which may cause a withdrawal of Hashem's presence from amongst His people, resulting in a lack of unity and a destructive force of separation.

Rav Eliyahu of Vilna *zt"l* (Vilna Gaon) would say:

"There are only two *mitzvos* which totally envelop a Jew when he performs them: living in Eretz Yisrael and living in a sukkah. In fact, both have something very unique in common as well, and that is that just as a sukkah is not deemed kosher unless it is built anew (תעשה ולא מן העשוי—*You shall make it, not that which is already made*), so too, Eretz Yisrael must be built up by each and every Jew."

ותהא חשובה לפניך מצות סוכה זו שאני מקיים כאלו
קימתיה בכל פרטיה ודקדוקיה ותנאיה

May it be considered—this mitzvah of sukkah that I perform—as though I had fulfilled it in all its particulars, exactness, and specifications…

STORIES
מעשה

The great love with which the saintly **Vilna Gaon *zt"l*** observed *mitzvos* is well known, as is the story of how he was prepared to sell his *Olam Haba*—his place in the World to Come, in order to observe a single mitzvah. In fact, in the last minutes of his life, on the fifth day of Sukkos in the year 5558 (1797), at the age of seventy-eight, the Gaon asked for a *lulav* and *esrog* in order to perform this great mitzvah one last time. R' Eliyahu managed to recite the *brachah* and he breathed his last breath on this world while clutching tightly to the *arbaah minim*, as if he was trying to take these precious *mitzvos* with him to his Eternal reward.

Many scholars and students would come from all over to visit with the Gaon and ask him their unresolved Torah questions. Others came just to see him and bask in his "four *amos* of halachah." It is told that one bright young student once came on Yom Tov morning, just before the prayer service, to wish the Vilna Gaon, "*A Gut Yom Tov.*" The Gaon, who was always absorbed in his learning, did not notice that he had a visitor. The young man thought that the Gaon was deliberately ignoring him due to something he might have said or done. He related this episode to his father-in-law, one of Vilna's leading laymen and a close acquaintance of the Vilna Gaon.

After the festive Yom Tov *seudah*, the father-in-law accompanied his son-in-law to the Vilna Gaon's home. The Gaon greeted the layman cordially and wished him a good Yom Tov. The man asked the Gaon whether he had any complaint or grievance against his son-in-law, mentioning what had happened that morning. R' Eliyahu replied, "*Chas v'shalom*! What are you saying? Me, angry? For what?" The father and son-in-law were satisfied and got up leave. In parting, the Gaon turned to the young man and added, "May you live to be a hundred."

Decades passed, and the young man reached a ripe old age, well into his nineties. At the age of ninety-eight, he fell sick. His family wanted to call a doctor, but the man said it wasn't necessary, because he was going to live for two more years, just as the Vilna Gaon had blessed him many years before. And so it was. The man recovered and went on to live the full hundred years with which the Gaon had blessed him.

ותזכנו לישב ימים רבים על האדמה אדמת קדש בעבודתך וביראתך

And may we be privileged to dwell many days upon the land, the Holy Land, in Your service and in Your reverence.

DRUSH
דרוש

Our early ancestors experienced the mitzvah of *aliyah l'regel* (going up to the Beis Hamikdash three times a year for the *Shalosh Regalim*) to its fullest. During the week of Sukkos, the gathering in Jerusalem and the immense celebration were exceptional. People traveled in camel caravans from Egypt. They came by boat from distant cities in the Mediterranean. They arrived on donkeys and in chariots. But those who traveled on foot received the greatest reward. It is said that Rabbi Hillel walked all the way from Babylonia!

Once in Jerusalem, the pilgrims were dazzled! There were wooden booths in every courtyard and on every roof. Thousands of men paraded in the streets, each one carrying his own *lulav*. At dawn, silver trumpets blew and *kohanim* with golden pitchers poured water on the Altar.

At night, the flames from enormous golden *menorahs*—150 feet tall—lit up the entire Temple area. All of Jerusalem glowed! Learned scholars juggled flaming torches. Others somersaulted and sang to the accompaniment of harps and cymbals. Nobody could sleep during the entire week of Sukkos! It is hardly any wonder, then, that *Chazal* said: *Whoever has not witnessed this celebration has not seen true rejoicing.*

It is said that the **Koloshitzer Rav, Rav Chuna Halberstam *zt"l***, once visited **Rav Meir Arik *zt"l*** and the two great scholars began a discussion in Torah. R' Meir asked, "Please explain to me the words of the great masters (**Baal Shem Tov, Shinover Rav**) who have said that the mitzvah of sitting in a sukkah is the most unique mitzvah in the Torah, for it is the only one which involves one's entire body. Every other mitzvah is performed with a single limb, whereas one must sit with his entire body in the sukkah." He paused for a moment. "But what about the mitzvah of *oleh regel*? When

Rav Menachem Mendel Schneerson *zt"l* (Lubavitcher Rebbe) would say:

"Although a sukkah is only a temporary dwelling, in certain respects we treat it as if it were our regular home—eating, drinking, and studying Torah in it. This, too, is the way we should treat the world at large. We should not regard the world as an end unto itself, but rather as a means of furthering our spiritual development and refinement. By properly utilizing the physical world, and making the most of it in a spiritual manner, we bring G-dliness into our surroundings, transforming the temporary into something lasting and eternal."

a Jew would go up to the Temple, his entire body would be immersed in the mitzvah since he would be standing inside the holy Sanctuary!"

R' Chuna shook his head vehemently. "How can you compare the two?" he asked. "When a person would go up to the holy Temple to be *oleh regel*, he was required to take off his shoes upon entering the holy site. However, the mitzvah of sukkah must be greater, since a Jew goes into his sukkah even מיט די שטיוול—*with his boot-straps*!"

The *Brachah* of לישב בסוכה

HALACHAH
הלכה

Proper *Kavanah*: During the entire Yom Tov of Sukkos, whenever a person sits down in the sukkah to eat and says the *brachah* of לישב בסוכה, he should have in mind:

- To fulfill the *mitzvah d'Oraisa* of sukkah[1].
- To remember the miraculous clouds of protection that sheltered Bnei Yisrael when we left Mitzrayim[2].

When to Make the *Brachah*: We make this *brachah* when:

- Eating a *kezayis* (half-egg volume) of bread on the first night within a four-minute span of time[3].
- Eating a bit more than an egg's worth of bread, within an eight-minute span, the rest of Yom Tov[4].
- Eating a *kezayis* of *Mezonos* (baked grain goods) to fulfill קידוש במקום סעודה—the obligation to have a meal or *Mezonos* snack after Kiddush[5].
- Eating more than an egg's worth of *Mezonos* within an eight-minute span during the rest of Yom Tov. In this specific case, since there is a bit of doubt as to requiring a *brachah*, one should sit in the sukkah for a while after he finishes his snack, to justify making the *brachah*[6].

When NOT to Make a *Brachah*: The *brachah* is not made:

- If one eats a non-*Mezonos* snack in the sukkah.

1. או"ח תרכ"ה
2. משנה ברורה תרכה:א
3. שם תרלט:יג
4. שם
5. שם:טז
6. שם

- If one eats an entire meal without washing or *Mezonos.* In this case, since there is a slight doubt regarding the *brachah,* one should try to exempt himself with someone else's *brachah*[7].
- For sleeping and other activities in the sukkah[8].

Order of the *Brachos*:

When eating bread, one should first make the *brachah* of *Hamotzi,* followed by the *brachah* of לישב בסוכה. When eating *Mezonos,* most people follow this custom as well. Some, however, have a different custom—to recite לישב בסוכה before *Mezonos*[9].

Forgetting the *Brachah*: If a person washed for bread and made a *Hamotzi* but forgot to recite a לישב בסוכה, he can still make it as soon as he remembers. If he finished his meal and already *bentched,* he can only say לישב בסוכה if he remains sitting in the sukkah for a while[10].

Making the *Brachah* After a Break: If a person stays in the sukkah, or just walked out for a short period of time, he does not say לישב בסוכה even if he begins a new meal[11]. If he left the sukkah to go *daven* or for any other prolonged activity, he should recite a new לישב בסוכה by his next meal[12]. If one goes from sukkah to sukkah without a prolonged break, he should not make a new *brachah*[13].

Women: In the circumstances mentioned above, when a man recites a לישב בסוכה, the Ashkenazic custom is for women to make the *brachah* as well. Sephardic women, however, do not have this custom to say the *brachah*[14].

אשר קדשנו במצותיו וצונו לישב בסוכה

...Who sanctified us with His commandments and commanded us to dwell in the sukkah.

DRUSH
דרוש

The blessing recited in the sukkah, *Leisheiv basukkah,* does not mean "to *sit* in the sukkah." If the mitzvah was really about "sitting," the *brachah* would be לשבת בסוכה, for in Hebrew, לשבת means to sit. The mitzvah on Sukkos, however, goes far beyond sitting. We are

7. שם: יג
8. שם:מו
9. שמירת שבת כהלכתה מח:מה
10. משנה ברורה שם:מח
11. שם:מז
12. שם
13. שער הציון תרלט:ד
14. מ"ב תרמ:כ

commanded to "live" (לישב) in the sukkah. As *Chazal* taught (*Sukkah* 28b): תשבו כעין תדורו—*You shall reside in the sukkah the way you (ordinarily) live.* The word תשבו teaches us that one lives in the sukkah in the same manner as one ordinarily lives; eating all meals in the sukkah, studying Torah in the sukkah, and sleeping in the sukkah.

Fulfilling the *mitzvos* of Sukkos in Auschwitz was unthinkable, for an attempt at religious observance carried the death sentence. Yet there were those who did their utmost to perform the *mitzvos* in spite of the mortal danger, displaying an extraordinary degree of self-sacrifice. When a new shipment of barracks came in, **Rav Tzvi Hirsch Meisels** ***zt"l***, the Veitzener Rav, spirited one bed out of the storage room and used an axe to break it into pieces. Several boards were used as sukkah walls; other sections were broken into splinters, to be used as *s'chach.* Miraculously, no one noticed or heard the banging of the axe during the day. Of course, under such conditions, there were no decorations in this sukkah!

The location of the sukkah, where the outer walls of two barracks nearly met, was kept a closely guarded secret. To the uninitiated observer, it appeared to be merely a pile of boards. Only a person who knew the secret would be able to traverse the maze that led into the sukkah itself. Each person would make his way inside, quickly eat a *kezayis* of bread, and then quickly run out.

During the course of the preparations, a unique question arose: is one allowed to make a *brachah* of לישב בסוכה in this situation? The *Shulchan Aruch* (*Orech Chaim*) rules that if one is afraid of thieves or bandits while sitting in the sukkah, he has not fulfilled his obligation. Some argued that since in Auschwitz, they were in mortal danger as they sat in the sukkah, was this a fulfillment of the mitzvah?

After much debate, the Veitzener Rav ruled that the *brachah* should be recited. He based his decision on the Gemara, *You shall reside in the sukkah the way you (ordinarily) live.* R' Tzvi Hirsch explained, "We ordinarily live under dangerous conditions—living in the barracks in Auschwitz is no less dangerous than sitting in a sukkah in Auschwitz. The Germans could come at any minute and take us to the gas chambers, no matter where we are! Our lives are endangered in exactly the same way—whether we are in the sukkah, or in our 'house'—our barracks. Therefore, this sukkah is quite identical to the way we ordinarily live, and it is kosher!"

נטילת לולב

יְהִי רָצוֹן מִלְּפָנֶיךָ, יְיָ אֱלֹהַי וֵאלֹהֵי אֲבוֹתַי, בִּפְרִי עֵץ הָדָר, וְכַפּוֹת
תְּמָרִים, וַעֲנַף עֵץ עָבוֹת, וְעַרְבֵי נָחַל, אוֹתִיּוֹת שִׁמְךָ הַמְיֻחָד
תְּקָרֵב אֶחָד אֶל אֶחָד, וְהָיוּ לַאֲחָדִים בְּיָדִי, וְלֵידַע אֵיךְ שִׁמְךָ נִקְרָא

נטילת לולב

Dedicated by
Mr. and Mrs.
Shmuel and Esther (nee Soroka) Perel
in memory of
לעי"נ שרה צביה
בת ר' יהונתן
פערל ז"ל,
נפ' י"ז תשרי
תנצב"ה

STORIES
מעשה

An individual once came to the *tish* of **Rav Menachem Mendel of Kotzk *zt"l***, hoping that the rebbe could bail him out of his difficult financial situation. When the fish course was served, the Kotzker called him to the head of the table, saying, "*Kum, ess roig, ess roig*" (Come, eat calmly, eat calmly). The chassidim present all wondered what the rebbe meant with these words and why this particular visitor should be told to "eat calmly."

Later that year, the man tried his hand at selling *esrogim* for Sukkos. He managed to obtain some of the most beautiful *esrogim* in the area, and as a result, he earned a handsome profit in the business, which sustained him for most of the next year. It was then that people understood the Kotzker's cryptic comment "*ess roig*" (אתרוג) as a hint to the source of the man's financial turnaround.

Arbaah Minim

HALACHAH
הלכה

The Yom Tov of Sukkos is the time of the year when we are judged on water (amount of rain that will fall)[1]. The Gemara in *Taanis*[2] says that rain and *parnassah* are equated as one. This was certainly true when we were a farming society, and even now it has much to do with *parnassah* and the price of commodities. The Gemara there adds that we perform the mitzvah of *arbaah minim* which grow on water to appease Hashem to continue giving us water. Many of the *Hoshanos* that we say during Sukkos, and especially on Hoshana Rabbah, are direct requests for rain and for the crops to grow well.

1. משנה ראש השנה טז
2. תענית ב

עָלַי, וְיִירְאוּ מִגֶּשֶׁת אֵלָי. וּבְנַעֲנוּעִי אוֹתָם תַּשְׁפִּיעַ שֶׁפַע בְּרָכוֹת מִדַּעַת עֶלְיוֹן לִנְוֵה אַפִּרְיוֹן, לִמְכוֹן בֵּית אֱלֹהֵינוּ. וּתְהֵא חֲשׁוּבָה לְפָנֶיךָ מִצְוַת אַרְבָּעָה מִינִים אֵלוּ, כְּאִלּוּ קִיַּמְתִּיהָ בְּכָל פְּרָטוֹתֶיהָ וְשָׁרָשֶׁיהָ וְתַרְיַ״ג

The midrash[3] says that through fulfilling the mitzvah of *arbaah minim,* one can merit a good *parnassah.* This is derived from the following: משכר לקיחה אתה לומד שכר לקיחה—*From the reward given for the mitzvah of* ***taking*** *(the* אזוב *plant in Mitzrayim), you can learn the reward for* ***taking*** *(the four* minim*).* If for taking the humble אזוב plant and performing one mitzvah with it (putting the blood of the *Korban Pesach* on their doorposts), Bnei Yisrael merited the wealth of the spoils of the Yam Suf, the spoils from the war with Sichon, as well as the spoils of the conquest of the thirty-one kings, certainly the many *mitzvos* we perform through the *arbaah minim*—which are not cheap commodities—can bring wealth. The ***Eitz Yosef***[4] writes that the midrash explains the *pasuk,* ולקחתם לכם, regarding the *arbaah minim,* to mean *You should take*—לכם—*for your own benefit,* which refers to the wealth that can come along with it.

בפרי עץ הדר כפת תמרים וענף עץ עבת וערבי נחל

With the fruit of the beautiful tree (esrog), a branch of palm trees (lulav), boughs of thick-leaved trees (hadassim), and willows of the brook (aravos)…

STORIES
מעשה

One year, the *esrogim* dealers of the town decided to band together to raise the price of *esrogim. Esrogim* had always been expensive; so much so, that it was customary for the wealthy leaders of the town to purchase one *esrog* to fulfill the mitzvah for the entire community. This year, however, the price was so exorbitant that even that one *esrog* was beyond their reach. How would the community manage to celebrate Yom Tov without even one set of the Four Species to share amongst themselves?

Finally, the *rabbanim* called a meeting at which they hoped to raise the money needed. Only the richest members of the town had been invited, as they had always supplied the *esrogim* for their fellow Jews.

After the formal request was issued, one wealthy businessman addressed the gathering. “I believe that it is an outrage to spend so much money on an *esrog.* Who do those dealers think they are to hold us hostage like this? There are other *mitzvos*

---

3. פרשת אמור ל:א
4. שם

מִצְוֹת הַתְּלוּיִם בָּהּ, כִּי כִוַּנְתִּי לְיַחֲדָא שְׁמָא דְקֻדְשָׁא בְּרִיךְ הוּא וּשְׁכִינְתֵּהּ, בִּדְחִילוּ וּרְחִימוּ, לְיַחֵד שֵׁם י"ה בְּו"ה בְּיִחוּדָא שְׁלִים, בְּשֵׁם כָּל יִשְׂרָאֵל. אָמֵן. בָּרוּךְ יְיָ לְעוֹלָם, אָמֵן וְאָמֵן.

---

which urgently need attention in our community. Why, what about marrying off poor brides? There is an orphaned girl in our very own town who is not getting any younger. Wouldn't that be a more fitting way to spend the community's money?"

One rabbi listened quietly until the rich man concluded his plea, and then he began to speak. "It is certainly true that the girl you speak of needs a match. And it is true, as well, that it is a great mitzvah to endow a poor bride and to help an orphan. But, I can't help thinking: Why, in all these years, did our speaker never think of helping this girl? Why, only now, when the question of acquiring an *esrog* arose did he remember her? I will tell you the reason. My friends, what we are witnessing here is the work of the *yetzer hara*, the evil inclination. The evil inclination is wily and crafty. He will use any argument to discourage a Jew from doing the mitzvah at hand, even if it means that he must convince him to do a different mitzvah in its stead!

"This," the rabbi explained, "is typical of human nature. Often, when a person is about to fulfill a certain mitzvah, the evil inclination steps in to cloud his mind with doubts. 'Why are you choosing to do this mitzvah instead of that one? That one is surely more important.' Then the person becomes confused and his will to perform the mitzvah is weakened. No, my friends, we must confront and expose the evil inclination for what it is and do battle with it. When we emerge successful, we will be able to perform the original mitzvah, thus fulfilling the will of G-d."

אותיות שמך המיחד תקרב אחד אל אחד והיו לאחדים בידי

The letters of Your Unified Name, You shall bring close, one to another, and they shall become as one in my hand.

MASHAL
משל

משל: A father once engaged his sons in a conversation regarding what they thought was the most important thing in life. The eldest son said money was the most important thing. It can provide and sustain one for life, and help him achieve great heights. Money provides a person with security and social status, and money can even make one appear smart!

The father did not respond. He asked his second son for his opinion. The son replied emphatically, "Education! Education brings many good things. It created civilization. If not for education, we'd still be living a backward life."

בָּרוּךְ אַתָּה יְיָ אֱלֹהֵינוּ מֶלֶךְ הָעוֹלָם, אֲשֶׁר קִדְּשָׁנוּ בְּמִצְוֹתָיו, וְצִוָּנוּ עַל נְטִילַת לוּלָב.

בפעם הראשונה מוסיף:

בָּרוּךְ אַתָּה יְיָ אֱלֹהֵינוּ מֶלֶךְ הָעוֹלָם, שֶׁהֶחֱיָנוּ וְקִיְּמָנוּ וְהִגִּיעָנוּ לַזְּמַן הַזֶּה.

Again the father did not respond. Now the third son spoke up. "Raising a fine family, in my opinion, is most important. Look, Father," he said in support of his two brothers, "we have money and we are educated, and consequently we are able to conduct a fine family life."

The father took out a bundle of sticks held together with a well-knotted cord. He handed it to his children and asked them to try to break the bundle. All of his children, grown and strong men, tried in vain to break the bundle. Removing the cord, the father then handed each child some individual twigs and told them to break them, which they did easily. The children looked at their father quizzically.

The father sensed that he had gained their undivided attention and told his children the purpose of his experiment. "You have seen that when the sticks were all bound together, you were unable to break them. But when they were taken one by one, you broke them easily. What does this tell you? That unity is the most important thing of all."

Turning to his two eldest sons, the father conceded that money and education are very important in life. But the most important thing, he emphasized, is unity. Unity is the cement that holds a family together, holds a nation together, and even holds together a group of nations.

"A day will come, my beloved children, when each one of you will go out into the world to build a home of your own. You will each establish your own family and make your own living. But I bid you to remember, dear children, stick together and remain unified and at peace with one another. This will empower you and nobody will be able to break you. If you lack unity, however, you may be sure that the lightest breeze will blow you over."

נמשל: In order to properly fulfill the mitzvah of taking the *arbaah minim* (Four Species), they must be bound together as one unit. The *Midrash Yalkut Shimoni* (*Nitzavim*), commenting on the Torah's command to take the Four Species, explains that the Four Species represent four types of Jews. The *esrog* represents the Jew who is both learned in Torah and performs good deeds. The *lulav* represents one who is learned in Torah but is not rich in deeds. The *hadassim* represent one who is ignorant in Torah but rich in deeds. The *aravos* represent a Jew who lacks both Torah knowledge and good deeds.

The Torah mandates that unity is the means of survival and a prerequisite for redemption. Only the unity of all types of Jews will guarantee the integrity and survival of the Jewish people. The same midrash further states that proper performance of the Four Species requires that the four must be bound into one single unit. By the same token, the Final Redemption and the restoration of the Jewish people in Eretz Yisrael will transpire when all Jews are united, for there is no greater blessing for a nation than genuine unity.

ובנענועי אותם תשפיע שפע ברכות מדעת עליו

And through my waving of them (the Four Species), You should bring forth an abundance of blessing from the Highest Da'as...

STORIES
מעשה

It was the first day of Sukkos, and the spirit of the *chag* was pervasive. The chassidim and congregants in the shul of the revered rebbe, **Rav Elimelech of Lizhensk *zt"l***, were in a festive mood. As R' Elimelech stood at the *amud* and began reciting Hallel, all eyes turned upon him in anticipation. However, it was clear that there was something unusual in his manner this Sukkos. With *lulav* and *esrog* in hand, he began sniffing the air! It was evident that something was on his mind, something rather exciting by the look on his radiant countenance.

The minute the *davening* was over, R' Elimelech hurried to where his brother **Rav Zusha** (who had come to spend Yom Tov with him) was standing, and said to him eagerly, "Come and help me find the *esrog* which is permeating the whole shul with the fragrance of Gan Eden!"

And so together they went from person to person sniffing the air until they reached the far corner of the shul where a quiet individual was standing, obviously engrossed in his own thoughts. "Here he is," called out R' Elimelech delightedly. "Please, dear friend, tell me, who are you and where did you obtain this wonderful *esrog*?"

The man, looking somewhat startled and bashful, was hesitant to reply. "My name," he began in a soft voice, "is Uri, and I come from the town of Strelisk. The mitzvah of *esrog* is very dear to me and each year I do my utmost to procure a beautiful *esrog*. Although I am not wealthy and cannot afford to buy an *esrog* according to my desire, my wife helps me by hiring herself out as a cook. She is independent of any financial help from me, and thus I can use my own earnings for spiritual matters. I am employed as a *melamed* (teacher) in the village of Yanev, which is not far from my native town. Each year, before Sukkos, I use half of my earnings for our needs and with the remainder, I buy an *esrog* in Lemberg. In order to save as much money as I can on the journey, I usually go on foot.

"This year, during the Ten Days of Repentance, I was making my way on foot as usual, with the hefty sum of fifty gulden in my wallet with which to buy a perfect *esrog*, when on the road to Lemberg I passed through a forest and stopped at a wayside inn to have a rest. It was time for Minchah so I stood in a corner and began *davening*. Suddenly, I heard a terrible moaning and groaning, the sound of one in great anguish. I hurriedly finished my *davening* and turned to see a most unusual and rough-looking person, dressed in peasant garb with a whip in his hands, pouring out his troubles to the innkeeper at the counter. From between his sobs, I managed to gather that the man with the whip was a poor Jew who earned his living as a *baal agalah* (wagon driver). He had a wife and several children and he barely managed to earn enough to make ends meet. And now, a terrible calamity had befallen him; his horse, the sole means of his livelihood, had suddenly collapsed in the forest and was unable to get up.

"The man's anguish was so tangible that I tried to encourage him by telling him that he must not forget that there is a G-d above us who could help him in his trouble. But he was in the depths of despair. Finally, the innkeeper told him that he had another horse that he could sell him for the paltry sum of fifty gulden, although it was worth at least eighty. 'I don't have fifty cents, let alone fifty gulden!' the man cried bitterly.

"I realized that here was my chance to do something good for this man in such a desperate plight that his very life, and that of his family, depended upon obtaining a horse. I said to the innkeeper, 'I'll give you forty-five gulden. Will you sell him the horse?' The innkeeper thought for only a moment and took the deal. The *baal agalah* was watching with eyes wide with astonishment. He was just speechless with relief, and his joy was absolutely indescribable!

"After he thanked me and left, I traveled on to Lemberg with the remaining five gulden in my pocket, and had to content myself with buying a very ordinary looking—but kosher—*esrog*! My *esrog* is usually the best in Strelisk, and everyone comes to my home to *bentch* with it, but this year I was ashamed to return home with such a poor-looking specimen, so my wife agreed that I should come here to Lizhensk, where nobody knows me."

"But my dear Reb Uri," cried R' Elimelech, now that the former had finished his story, "your *esrog* is indeed exceptional; it has the fragrance of Gan Eden! Now, let me tell you the sequel to your story!

"When the *baal agalah* whom you saved thought about his unexpected good fortune, he decided that you must have been none other than Eliyahu Hanavi whom the Al-mighty had sent down to earth in order to help him in his desperation. Having come to this conclusion, the happy man looked for a way of expressing his gratitude

to the Al-mighty, but since he is illiterate and unable to recite any prayers, he racked his simple brain for the best way of giving proper thanks.

"Suddenly his face lit up. He took his whip and lashed it into the air with all his might, crying out, 'Dear Father in Heaven, I love You very much! What can I do to convince You of my love for You? Let me crack my whip for You as a sign that I love You!' And the *baal agalah* cracked his whip in the air three times."

R' Elimelech's face turned serious. "Now, on the eve of Yom Kippur, the Al-mighty above was listening to the prayers of the Day of Atonement. **Rav Levi Yitzchak of Berditchev *zt"l*,** who was acting as the counsel for defense on behalf of his fellow Jews, was pushing a wagon full of Jewish *mitzvos* to the Gates of Heaven, when the *Satan* appeared and obstructed his path with piles of Jewish sins. R' Levi Yitzchak was trapped. My brother R' Zusha and I added our strength to help him move his wagon forward, but all in vain; even our combined efforts proved fruitless.

"Suddenly, there came the sound of the cracking of a whip which rent the air, causing a blinding ray of light to appear, lighting up the whole universe, right up to the very heavens! There we saw the angels and all the righteous seated in a circle, singing praises to the Al-mighty. Upon hearing the *baal agalah's* words as he cracked his whip in ecstasy, they responded in unison: 'Happy is the King who is thus praised!'

"All at once, the angel Michael appeared, leading a horse, followed by the *baal agalah* with whip in hand. Michael harnessed this horse to the wagon of *mitzvos*, and the *baal agalah* cracked his whip. The wagon gave a lurch forward, flattened out the Jewish sins that had been obstructing the way, and drove smoothly and easily right up to the Throne of Honor. There, the King of kings received it most graciously and,

Rav Tzvi Elimelech Shapiro of Dinov *zt"l* (*Bnei Yissaschar*) would say:

"The *Midrash Rabbah* (*Vayikra Rabbah* 30) teaches that the entire world—Jews and gentiles alike—are judged on Rosh Hashanah. However, when Bnei Yisrael walk outside with their *arbaah minim* on the first day of Sukkos, it is then known that they have succeeded in their judgment. How do the *arbaah minim* prove that we have been meritorious in *din*? Because unlike every blade of grass that has its own guardian angel telling it to grow (*Bereishis Rabbah* 10), the Four Species are under the direct protection of *Hakadosh Baruch Hu* Himself. This is likened to the Jewish people, who are elevated above the other nations and enjoy unique Divine protection. Thus, when Jews carry the *arbaah minim*, it demonstrates the uniqueness of our relationship with the Al-mighty and it is then clear to all that He has judged us favorably."

rising from the seat of Judgment, went over and seated Himself on the seat of Mercy. A happy new year was assured!

"And now, dear R' Uri," concluded R' Elimelech, "you see that all this came about through your noble action! Go home, and be a leader in Klal Yisrael, for you have proved your worthiness! And you shall carry with you the approval of the Heavenly Court! But before you go, permit me to hold this wonderful *esrog* of yours, and praise Hashem with it."

ותהא חשובה לפניך מצות ארבעה מינים אלו כאלו קימתיה בכל פרטותיה

And this mitzvah of the Four Species should be considered by You as if I fulfilled it with all of its details...

MASHAL
משל

משל: During World War II, **Rav Benzion Halberstam** ***zt"l Hy"d***, the previous **Bobover Rebbe**, fled Bobov for the relative safety of Lemberg. En route, he stopped in Lutzk, where he spent the Yom Tov of Sukkos. Due to war conditions, it was impossible to obtain an *esrog*; the only one available was a dried one from the previous year. The Bobover Rebbe sat together with other *rabbanim* who had fled to Lutzk, all of them despondent at the thought that they could not fulfill the mitzvah of taking the *arbaah minim* that year. Seeking to allay their sorrow, the Bobover Rebbe proceeded to tell the following story which his grandfather, **Rav Chaim Sanzer** ***zt"l***, had related on Sukkos:

Once, *sheker* (falsehood) was walking down the street when he met the *yetzer hara* (evil inclination), who appeared very ill. "What is the matter?" *sheker* asked him.

The *yetzer hara* replied, "Don't you realize that it is now the month of Elul, and the Jewish people are all occupied with doing *teshuvah* wholeheartedly? No matter how hard I try to get them to sin or prevent them from repenting, I cannot succeed! They're putting me out of business!

"And then comes Sukkos," he continued to lament, "when they will rejoice in their sukkah and fulfill the mitzvah of taking the *lulav* and *esrog*—that will finish me off!"

After thinking for a moment, *sheker* told his friend that he had a wonderful idea which would solve the problem: "The *esrogim* are imported by boat from Greece. Why not sink the ship? That way there will be no *esrogim* available, and the Jews will not be able to fulfill the mitzvah!"

Delighted with this nefarious plan, the *yetzer hara* hurried off to implement it immediately.

Some time after Sukkos, *sheker* again encountered the *yetzer hara* on the street. This time he looked even worse than he had the last time! When they met, the *yetzer hara* shouted, "You're no friend of mine! The advice you gave me backfired—it had the opposite of the desired effect!"

"Calm down," soothed *sheker*. "Tell me what happened."

"Well, in previous years, when the Jews had their *esrogim* for Sukkos, they fulfilled the mitzvah, but I was still able to score the occasional victory. There were some people who only had in mind that everyone should notice what a beautiful, expensive *esrog* they had; others wanted those around them to notice with what great *kavanah* (intent) they were performing the mitzvah. However, this year, since there were no *esrogim,* they were all heartbroken at being unable to fulfill the mitzvah, and cried out to Hashem, repenting wholeheartedly, remorseful that they did not merit performing this important mitzvah.

"Under such circumstances, Hashem considered it as if they had fulfilled the mitzvah, as it says: *When a person is prevented from doing a mitzvah, Hashem considers it as if he had indeed fulfilled it.*"

נמשל: "This is very relevant to our situation today," concluded R' Benzion. "We are unable to properly fulfill the mitzvah because we are in the category of one who is prevented from fulfilling the commandment. Thus, Hashem will perform the mitzvah for us in Heaven, and it will be considered as if we had fulfilled it in the best possible way!"

The **Stutchiner Rebbe** later noted, "The Bobover Rebbe's story comforted us, for we were shattered that we could not fulfill the mitzvah of taking the *arbaah minim.* Thanks to him we were able, despite the terrible circumstances, to feel some *simchas Yom Tov*."

Rav Nosson Adler *zt"l* (Chasam Sofer's rebbe) would say:

"A person should strive to obtain the four species of *lulav, esrog, hadas* and *aravah* from Eretz Yisrael. This is derived from the *pasuk* in *Tehillim* (137:5): תדבק לשוני לחכי אם לא אזכרכי אם לא אעלה את ירושלים על ראש שמחתי—*My tongue should cleave to my palate if I do not remember; if I do not set (the thought of) Jerusalem at the height of my joy*. The word אעלה spells out the first letters of אתרוג, ערבה, לולב, הדס and שמחתי refers to Sukkos."

ברוך ה׳ לעולם אמן ואמן

Blessed is Hashem forever, amen and amen.

STORIES
מעשה

During the Yom Kippur War in 1973, when Israel was caught by surprise and attacked by Arab countries on all fronts, one of the critical points of battle was near the Suez Canal as the Egyptian army pushed northward, intending to strike Israel hard from the south. For days after Yom Kippur and throughout Sukkos, **Rav Shammai Parnas *shlit"a***, one of the foremost rabbis of the Israeli army and a Yerushalmi going back many generations, traveled throughout the Sinai desert and southward toward Suez, where he cautiously and caringly gathered the bodies of those who had fallen in battle. Wherever he went, R' Shammai took along with him his siddur, Tehillim, *tallis*, *lulav* and *esrog*. At every camp that he stopped, soldiers approached him, asking for permission to use his *lulav* and *esrog*. Infantrymen who were otherwise irreligious would pick up his siddur and say, "R' Shammai, let us pray from your siddur... R' Shammai, could we say some Tehillim." He would help as many as he could, and at times he was detained from his work for quite a while. Much to his regret, though, he eventually had to say to the young men, "I can't stay any longer. I've been summoned elsewhere."

On Hoshana Rabbah (the last day of Sukkos), R' Shammai and his assistants found themselves near the Suez Canal. It was late morning as he drove toward a newly constructed army base in the wide open desert, and shortly after R' Shammai's arrival at the base, a long line of soldiers began to form, waiting to use his *lulav* and *esrog*. As the crowd assembled, a young non-religious soldier, Arik Shuali, driving an ammunition truck, was making his way southward. Looking through his powerful binoculars, he noticed a large crowd of fellow servicemen gathered in one area. Curious, he got out of his truck and made his way on foot to where the soldiers had assembled. As he came closer, he asked someone, "What is all the commotion about?" They explained to him that R' Shammai had come, and people were waiting for an opportunity to use his *lulav* and *esrog*. Arik was not interested in lingering. However, when one of his friends mentioned that it was the last day to perform this mitzvah, he agreed to wait his turn.

Eventually Arik's turn arrived. Just as he received the *lulav* and *esrog*, a flying shell hit his truck. The vehicle exploded, setting off multiple explosions of the ammunition on board and chasing servicemen running for cover in all directions. The blast was so intense that a crater was formed in the ground where the truck had been parked. When they later examined the spot where the truck had been, the soldiers couldn't find even a shard of metal remaining from the shattered vehicle.

Three months later, R' Shammai read a short notice in the Israeli army newspaper stating that the wife of serviceman Arik Shuali had given birth to a little girl. The

announcement included a statement by the new father. "I believe with every fiber of my being that I am alive today and that I merited seeing my new daughter only because of the mitzvah that I was doing at the time my truck was bombed." To remember Hashem's goodness, he named his daughter Lulava.

דברי קהלת

וגדלתי והוספתי מכל שהיה לפני בירושלם אף חכמתי עמדה לי (ב-ט)

So I became great, and I increased more than all who were before me in Yerushalayim; also my wisdom remained with me.

DVAR TORAH
דבר תורה

In the introduction to his masterpiece, *Avi Ezri*, the great **Ponovezher Rosh Yeshivah, Rav Elazar Menachem Mann Shach** ***zt"l***, writes: "Someone who studies (this *sefer*) will see the value in this work, for it has cost me effort." On the margin of his own copy of the *sefer*, the *rosh yeshivah* recorded the following comment of the **Rashba** (in the name of **Rav Hai Gaon**) in this connection: "Take care with this interpretation, for it was revealed to me after great exertion."

The Torah's secrets are only revealed to those who toil in it. *Chazal* comment on the verse, אף חכמתי עמדה לי—*My wisdom also stood for me*: *The wisdom which I learned with hard breathing* (אף) *stood for me* (*Koheles Rabbah* 2:13). Similarly, on the *pasuk*, *A soul's work toils for it* (*Mishlei* 16:26), the Gemara (*Sanhedrin* 99b) states: *A person strives in Torah in one place, and the Torah he has acquired exerts itself on his behalf in another place*. Rashi explains that the Torah a person has learned asks its Owner—Hashem—to reveal to the person who has learned it the underlying logic of the Torah and its order.

The **Rambam**, likewise, explains the famous mishnah, *L'fum tza'ara agra*—"According to the exertion is the reward," (*Avos* 5:26) as follows: "According to the extent you exert yourself in Torah, that will be your reward. The Sages said that the only wisdom that remains with you is that which you learn with effort, exertion and fear of the teacher, whereas what you read for pleasure and relaxation does not last or bring any benefit."

לכל זמן ועת לכל־חפץ תחת השמים...עת לחשות ועת לדבר (ג-א, ז)

Everything has an appointed season, and there is a time for every matter under the heaven…a time to be silent and a time to speak.

A well-meaning *maggid* (preacher) once came to a village and delivered a lengthy discourse which, for all its emotional energy, was totally devoid of substance. On and on he spoke, but he said...nothing! When he finally finished, he eagerly approached the rabbi to hear his view on the effectiveness of his sermon. The rabbi looked at the preacher in amazement and then answered, "I must tell you, you have done me a great favor. You have shown me the answer to a question that has been perplexing me for some time." The *maggid* replied that he was happy to oblige and then inquired as to the nature of the difficulty.

DRUSH
דרוש

The rabbi chose his words carefully, hoping to achieve the maximum effect. "In *Megillas Koheles*, the author, Shlomo Hamelech, states that there are different periods of time for everything in the world. *A time to cry and a time to laugh...a time to destroy and a time to build.* For each pair of extremes there is also a point of neutrality—a time neither to laugh nor to cry. Neither to construct nor to demolish. The only exception to this rule is, *A time to remain silent and a time to speak.* Where is the neutral point? One is either silent or he is talking, but there is no place in between, correct?"

The *maggid* agreed that this was indeed a difficult question and attempted to pose an answer, but the rabbi quickly cut him off. The *maggid* then listened as the rabbi gave his explanation.

"I was bothered by this question for years; for the longest time I could not come up with any kind of answer," the rabbi smiled, as he took the *maggid's* hand in his own, and shook it. "But today, I want to thank you for providing me with the answer. You see, you spoke for two whole hours—yet you said absolutely nothing! That must be the middle point between *a time to speak* and *a time to remain silent*! Personally," said the rabbi with a knowing wink, "I would have opted for the realization of the first half of the *pasuk*!"

עת לאהב ועת לשנא עת מלחמה ועת שלום (ג-ח)

A time to love and a time to hate; a time for war and a time for peace.

The Torah, and all areas of Judaism, in fact, are not only timely—as in relevant—but also intertwined with time itself. Time as a commodity. Time as a boundary-setter. Time as a vehicle for holiness. Time, above all, as a precious resource that is not to be squandered. In *Yiddishkeit*, every moment counts. Consequently, punctuality, order, and self-discipline are encouraged in our tradition, while laziness, disarray and procrastination are, of course, frowned upon.

DRUSH
דרוש

The overriding message is this: So much to do, so little time. So many distractions. So many impediments to holy service, good deeds and Torah study. Procrastination is chief among them, which no doubt prompted Hillel to issue this famous warning: *Do not say, "When I am free I will study (Torah), for perhaps you will not become free."* (*Avos* 2:5)

As a young *bachur,* **Rav Elazar Menachem Mann Shach** ***zt"l*** was required to travel from place to place in Russia, due to the uncertainties of war and the instability in the region. He once found himself at the home of a Jewish man in the countryside. The future *rosh yeshivah* had no watch with him, and the man had no clock in his house. At one point, R' Shach asked the man if he knew the time. The man responded, "No, I don't. I have no clock, and in fact there is no clock in this entire village."

R' Shach asked him in amazement, "How is it possible to live without ever knowing the time?"

Equally amazed at his question, the fellow answered, "I don't understand why one needs a clock. When I want to eat, I eat; when I want to sleep, I sleep; when I want to pray, I pray!"

R' Shach was very dismayed with this attitude. This is not the way of the Torah, he would say later. A Jew believes that everything has its own proper time. There is a time for learning, a time for sleeping, a time for eating, and a time for prayer. One must be meticulous in following these set times for their particular specific functions. For instance, the time for prayer and the time for learning are separate and distinct (*Shabbos* 10a), and should not be made to conflict or intermingle with each other.

הכל הולך אל־מקום אחד הכל היה מן־העפר והכל שב אל־העפר (ג-כ)

All go to one place; all came from the dust and all return to the dust.

STORIES
מעשה

Rav Itzele Volozhiner ***zt"l,*** son of the famed **Rav Chaim Volozhiner** ***zt"l,*** was the successor to his father as *rosh yeshivah* of Volozhin, and also the rabbi of that town. Whenever anyone spoke of "the *rav*" in that generation, they meant R' Itzele, for he was the undisputed *gadol hador* of the time.

Once, Sir Moses Montefiore traveled to Russia to visit the czar in order to appeal to him to alleviate the miserable plight of the millions of Jews living in his country. At that time, the Orthodox leaders were vying with the *maskilim* for Montefiore's attention, each camp seeking to influence the powerful philanthropist with its own version of what the future of the Jewish nation in Russia should look like. Montefiore was known to be a devout and scrupulously observant

Jew, but his appearance and educational background were totally different from that of the old-time Orthodox Jews of Russia. For this reason, he did not fully understand the fierce struggle of the *gedolim* of the time against the dangerous threat posed by the *maskilim.* For instance, when a delegation sent by the *gedolim* of Poland came to request of him to appeal before the czar (who ruled over Poland at the time) to rescind a decree mandating modern dress for all citizens, he told them that he did not understand why they thought it was so important for them to wear hats made from bearskin.

When Montefiore arrived in Lithuania, the Orthodox lay leaders came to escort R' Itzele, who was the leader and spokesman of the Jewish community, to greet the magnate. R' Itzele went along with them, but with mixed feelings. On the one hand, it was important and proper to greet the benevolent Jewish baron, and to encourage him in his mission to the czar, hoping that he would meet with some degree of success in alleviating the plight of the Jews. As a religious Jew, he would be in an excellent position to request a repeal of some of the anti-religious legislation that had been passed. But on the other hand, there was the possibility that the *maskilim* would influence Montefiore to agree to their own insidious plans, which they had presented to him cloaked in a deceptively alluring mantle. In that event, the *maskilim* would falsely portray R' Itzele's greeting of the nobleman as an endorsement for their objectives.

In the end, R' Itzele did go with the Orthodox delegation, but his heart was not in it. On the way, R' Itzele happened to meet **Rav Yisrael Salanter** ***zt"l***, who asked him, "To where is the *rav* being accompanied?"

R' Itzele answered, "I am not sure! When a wicked man gets to the next world and is being led to Gehinnom, is he aware of where they are leading him?"

לב חכם לימינו ולב כסיל לשמאלו (י-ב)

The heart of the wise man is at his right, whereas the heart of the fool is at his left.

DRUSH
דרוש

One Shabbos, **Rav Chaim Volozhiner** ***zt"l*** was walking down a narrow alley when he overheard a few yeshivah students chatting about mundane matters. This bothered him and he made a point of going over to the students.

"I couldn't help but overhear that you were conversing about things that do not pertain to Shabbos. I am quite surprised. I think you would do better if you spend your time sleeping," R' Chaim commented. "After all, our Sages tell us that the word Shabbos is an acronym for שינה בשבת תענוג (sleeping on Shabbos is a pleasure). Why must you violate the words of the Sages when you can just as easily fulfill them?"

Most of the boys were embarrassed at "being caught" by the *rosh yeshivah* and lowered their eyes in shame. One boy, however, mustered up his nerve and attempting to lighten the situation, he joked, "Rebbi, we go according to a different acronym. That is: שיחה בשבת תענוג (conversing on Shabbos is a pleasure)."

The other boys were shocked and even R' Chaim was a bit taken aback at the brazenness of the young student. But R' Chaim allowed a moment to pass before responding. "In a way, you are right," he said to the surprise of all present, "but there is a difference. The word שינה (sleep) is written with a *shin*—which has a dot on its right side, whereas the word שיחה (conversing) is written with a *sin*—which has a dot on its left side."

R' Chaim focused his gaze on the brazen young yeshivah student and concluded, "To paraphrase Shlomo Hamelech, the wisest of all men: לב חכם לימינו ולב כסיל לשמאלו—*A wise man's heart (is disposed) to his right side, while a fool's heart (is disposed) to his left.* It appears that rather than follow the example of the wise man and lean toward the right (the *shin*), you have chosen to steer yourself to the left—to the side of the fool!"

סוף דבר הכל נשמע את־האלקים ירא ואת־מצותיו שמור כי־זה כל־האדם (יב-יג)

The end of the matter, everything having been heard, fear G-d and keep His commandments, for this is the entire man.

MIDDOS/ DERECH ERETZ
מידות/דרך ארץ

What is meant by the words of *Koheles*: *For that is the entire (essence of) man*? Rabi Eliezer said, "The entire world was created only for such a man" (*Shabbos* 30b).

Rav Elchanan Wasserman ***zt"l*** explains that a person might think that *yiras Shamayim* (fear of Heaven), is merely one of several human virtues, that one may be a good and complete man even though he does not fear G-d. *Koheles* teaches us that this is not so. Fear of Heaven is the totality of man. Without it, one is not a man at all—he is merely one more animal!

The human aspect of a man can be measured only by his fear of Heaven, whether more or less. Whoever possesses abundant fear of Heaven is a great man; one who possesses little is mediocre. If someone lacks every vestige of *yiras Shamayim* and does not fear Hashem, then he is not truly a human being, but an animal in the guise of a human.

יְהִי רָצוֹן מִלְּפָנֶיךָ יְיָ אֱלֹהֵינוּ וֵאלֹהֵי אֲבוֹתֵינוּ, הַבּוֹחֵר בִּנְבִיאִים טוֹבִים וּבְמִנְהֲגֵיהֶם הַטּוֹבִים, שֶׁתְּקַבֵּל בְּרַחֲמִים וּבְרָצוֹן אֶת תְּפִלָּתֵנוּ וְהַקָּפוֹתֵינוּ, וּזְכָר לָנוּ זְכוּת שִׁבְעַת תְּמִימֶיךָ, וְתָסִיר מְחִיצַת הַבַּרְזֶל הַמַּפְסֶקֶת בֵּינֵינוּ וּבֵינֶךָ, וְתַאֲזִין שַׁוְעָתֵנוּ, וְתֵיטִיב לָנוּ הַחֲתִימָה, תְּלֶה

חבטת הערבה

ותסיר מחיצת הברזל המפסקת בינינו ובינך ותאזין שועתנו ותיטיב לנו החתימה

And remove the iron barrier that separates us from You. Give ear to our pleas, and may it be for our good when our judgment is sealed…

MASHAL
משל

משל: A chassid once traveled to the **Chozeh of Lublin *zt"l*** to spend Yom Tov. When he came before the rebbe, he was shocked when the Chozeh told him, "Go home! You don't belong here!" When the chassid tried again the next day, the rebbe exclaimed, "Didn't I tell you to go home?"

Deeply dejected, the chassid set out on his journey home. On the way, he stopped at an inn to spend the night. There he met a group of chassidim traveling to the Chozeh. After a few rounds of *l'chaim*, the chassidim cheerfully started to dance, drawing the disheartened chassid into their circle.

Round and round they went, joyfully singing Hashem's praises. Gradually the Chassid's gloom turned into *simchah* as he danced mightily. At the height of their ecstasy, the chassidim said to him, "Come back with us to the rebbe!"

The chassid decided to give it another try. To his great surprise, the Chozeh was delighted to see him. Embracing him warmly, the Chozeh said, "When you came the first time, I saw that Heaven had decreed that you were to die shortly. I sent you home, because I didn't want you to die here on Yom Tov. But with your *simchah*, you caused the Heavenly decree to be annulled." And indeed, the chassid lived to a ripe old age.

נמשל: The **Skulener Rebbe, Rav Eliezer Zisha Portugal *zt"l***, would tell people, "After our intense prayers on the Yamim Nora'im, and after the decree was sealed, we rejoice on the Yom Tov of Sukkos all the way to Simchas Torah. For even if the decree is not favorable, it is still possible to reverse it and change it into goodness and blessing through the power of *simchah*!"

אֶרֶץ עַל בְּלִימָה. וְחָתְמֵנוּ בְּסֵפֶר חַיִּים טוֹבִים. וְהַיּוֹם הַזֶּה תִּתֵּן בִּשְׁכִינַת עֻזְּךָ חֲמִשָּׁה גְבוּרוֹת מְמֻתָּקוֹת עַל יְדֵי חֲבִיטַת עֲרָבָה מִנְהַג נְבִיאֶיךָ הַקְּדוֹשִׁים. וְתִתְעוֹרֵר הָאַהֲבָה בֵּינֵיהֶם, וּתְנַשְּׁקֵנוּ מִנְּשִׁיקוֹת פִּיךָ, מַמְתֶּקֶת כָּל הַגְּבוּרוֹת וְכָל הַדִּינִין, וְתָאִיר לִשְׁכִינַת עֻזְּךָ בְּשֵׁם יו"ד

והיום הזה תתן בשכינת עזך חמשה גבורות ממתקות על ידי חביטת ערבה מנהג נביאיך הקדושים

On this day, place in Your glorious Presence five strict powers that have been sweetened through the beating of the aravos, the custom instituted by Your holy prophets…

REMEZ
רמז

The midrash compares the Four Species to four different groups within Bnei Yisrael. The *esrog* has a distinctive flavor and fragrance; it is comparable to *tzaddikim* who are filled with Torah and good deeds. The *lulav* bears fruit with flavor but without fragrance; it is comparable to people who possess Torah knowledge but lack good deeds. *Hadassim* are fragrant but have no flavor; they are comparable to Jews who perform good deeds but lack Torah knowledge. *Aravos* lack both flavor and fragrance; they are comparable to Jews who have neither Torah knowledge nor good deeds. By giving us the mitzvah of taking the four *minim* together, Hashem advises us that it is beneficial for all these groups within Jewry to act in unison. The merits of each group will offset that which the other group is lacking.

On Hoshana Rabbah, we have the custom to take the *aravos* alone, without the other *minim*, and bang them on the ground. **Rav Moshe Sternbuch *shlit"a*** evokes the above midrash in providing the following symbolism for our custom: The group that is represented by the *aravos* can only attain its proper standing amongst the Jewish people if it is willing to join with the others and learn from the *tzaddikim*. But if the members of this group persist in dissociating themselves from the *tzaddikim* and hence from Klal Yisrael, they must be smashed so that their influence will not affect Bnei Yisrael.

This concept fits in beautifully with the symbolism of the four *minim* of Sukkos. It emphasizes that the unity of Klal Yisrael must always be employed in the service of Hashem.

הֵ"א וָאֹ"ו שֶׁהוּא טַל אוֹרֹת טַלֶּךָ, וּמִשָּׁם תַּשְׁפִּיעַ שֶׁפַע לְעַבְדְּךָ הַמִּתְנַפֵּל לְפָנֶיךָ, מְחִילָה, שֶׁתַּאֲרִיךְ יָמַי וְתִמְחֹל לִי חֲטָאַי וַעֲוֹנוֹתַי וּפְשָׁעַי, וְתִפְשׁוֹט יְמִינְךָ וְיָדְךָ לְקַבְּלֵנִי בִּתְשׁוּבָה שְׁלֵמָה לְפָנֶיךָ, וְאוֹצָרְךָ הַטּוֹב תִּפְתַּח לְהַשְׂבִּיעַ מַיִם נֶפֶשׁ שׁוֹקֵקָה, כְּמוֹ שֶׁכָּתוּב: יִפְתַּח יְיָ לְךָ אֶת

ומשם תשפיע שפע לעבדך המתנפל לפניך מחילה
שתאריך ימי ותמחל לי חטאי ועונותי ופשעי

And from there, bestow upon Your servant, who prostrates
himself before You, forgiveness, so that my days be lengthened.
Forgive my sins, my iniquities, and my transgressions…

MASHAL
משל

משל: A king once visited a small, secluded island that was surrounded by water on all sides. Those citizens who needed to travel into the mainland were able to cross the river by ferry boats, although there were a few old-timers who never even bothered to do so. The king wished to meet his subjects on this secluded island and sent word that he was coming.

As part of the greeting committee, one old man stepped forward and welcomed the king to his city, where he has lived all of his ninety years, never once leaving its confines. The king was amazed. "The fact that you've never left your island," said the king to the old man, "is admirable. I commend you on your loyalty and I hereby command you to never leave this city until the day you die!" The king said it in jest and all those around him applauded.

However, a strange thing happened. That very day, as the king was busy touring a different part of the island, the old man hopped on a boat and traveled, for the first time ever, to the neighboring shore. Everyone was stunned, not least of all the king himself. When the king heard what happened, instead of being amused, he became angry. He ordered the old man back and then he said to him, "You never leave the island your entire life—until the moment I command you to remain here forever?"

"I don't know what happened," said the old man when he was confronted. "As soon as I was told not to go, I had this incredible urge to pick up and leave!"

נמשל: The *Yerushalmi* (*Yuma* 6:4) writes: *The yetzer hara does not urge (a person) to sin unless something is forbidden.* **Rav Chaim Kanievsky *shlit"a*** was once asked to be *sandek* at a *bris* on Hoshana Rabbah in a different city. He was afraid to travel during the day since he had stayed up the night before to learn as is the custom by many, and he feared he might doze off in the car—which would be tantamount to sleeping

חבטת הערבה

אוֹצְרוֹ הַטּוֹב אֶת הַשָּׁמַיִם, לָתֵת מְטַר אַרְצְךָ בְּעִתּוֹ וּלְבָרֵךְ אֶת כָּל מַעֲשֵׂה יָדֶךָ. אָמֵן.

---

outside of the sukkah! He only accepted the offer after receiving a *psak* that he may travel, because as R' Chaim told someone, he knew at that point that he wouldn't fall asleep because once it was permitted, he knew he wouldn't feel the urge to sleep!

יפתח ה' לך את אוצרו הטוב את השמים לתת מטר ארצך בעתו ולברך את כל מעשה ידך

Hashem will open for you His bountiful treasure—the heavens—to provide rain for your land in its proper time, and bless all the work of your hand...

STORIES / מעשה

The famine in Russia was worse than ever before. The markets quickly emptied and soon there was only a meager selection of vegetables, with little bread and margarine for sale. Letters from all over Russia were sent to the **Shpola Zeide, Rav Aryeh Leib** *zt"l*, asking him to beseech G-d to take pity on His people, for his prayers had always helped before to provide for the poor and downtrodden. Even the gentiles looked to the Shpola Zeide. Still, Hashem wasn't answering prayers for food. The famine spread.

The Shpola Zeide decided on a bold course of action. He requested ten of the generation's most venerated *tzaddikim* to meet with him in Shpola. When they all arrived, he arose to address them. "I have decided to take the Al-mighty to court. While according to halachah, the plaintiff must take his case to where the defendant is located, nevertheless, Hashem is called מקום (place), and there is no place devoid of His presence. Therefore, the court case will be conducted right here in this chamber three days from now."

For the next three days, the *tzaddikim* fasted and prayed, allowing no one to interrupt them. On the fourth day, wrapped in his *tallis* and *tefillin*, the Shpola Zeide instructed his attendant to call the court to order. "In the name of all of the men, women and children in Russia, I come to claim that the defendant, G-d Al-mighty, is failing to live up to His obligation to His people. Instead of sustaining them as is it written, *He opens His hand and satisfies every living thing* (*Tehillim* 145), He is allowing them to perish from hunger. Does not the Torah state, *Hashem will open His good treasure, the heaven, to give the rains...and to bless the work of your hand.* How can the Al-mighty disregard His own Torah? And if you were to argue for the defense that these servants do not serve the Master properly as they should, where is it written that if the servant is lazy and unfaithful, his wife and children should suffer?" The

תפילה כשיוצאים מן הסוכה

יְהִי רָצוֹן מִלְּפָנֶיךָ יְיָ אֱלֹהֵינוּ וֵאלֹהֵי אֲבוֹתֵינוּ כְּשֵׁם שֶׁקִּיַּמְתִּי וְיָשַׁבְתִּי בְּסוּכָּה זוֹ כֵּן אֶזְכֶּה לְשָׁנָה הַבָּאָה לֵישֵׁב בְּסֻכַּת עוֹרוֹ שֶׁל לִוְיָתָן:

Shpola Zeide fell silent, exhausted from the ordeal of bringing a lawsuit against the Al-mighty.

The judges huddled, discussing the case amongst themselves in hushed, solemn tones. Finally, the verdict was announced. "The court finds that justice is with R' Aryeh Leib ben Rochel. The Al-mighty is obligated to find whatever means He deems appropriate to provide for His people. We pray that the Heavenly Court concurs with the decision of this court." Then all ten *tzaddikim* rose to their feet, and declared the verdict aloud three times in unison. The Shpola Zeide jumped to his feet with great joy.

It was only five days later that the Russian government announced that they would be bringing wheat and grains from Siberia through a previously inaccessible route. The price of available grain plunged, and within the month, new supplies were on the market. That year, even the family with the most humble of means found themselves with plenty to eat.

HALACHAH
הלכה

There is a *segulah* for good *parnassah* to take—after Sukkos—some of the leaves from the *hoshanos* (*aravos*) that were banged on Hoshana Rabbah, and carry them around in one's wallet or pocket. This is brought down in the famous דבר בעתו calendar from **Rav Chaim Kanievsky *shlit"a*** (בשם ספרים).

תפילה כשיוצאים מן הסוכה

כשם שקימתי וישבתי בסוכה זו, כן אזכה לשנה הבאה לישב בסכת עורו של לויתן

Just as I have fulfilled the mitzvah and sat in the sukkah, may I be worthy in the coming year to sit in the sukkah of the skin of the Levyasan.

DVAR TORAH
דבר תורה

There are different customs regarding eating in the sukkah on Shemini Atzeres. Some eat in the sukkah, omitting the *brachah* לישב בסוכה (*Sukkah* 47a). Others don't eat in the sukkah on the night of Shemini Atzeres. In Kiddush we say *Shehecheyanu* on the new Yom Tov of Shemini Atzeres, signifying that it is not Sukkos anymore, and thus the mitzvah of eating in the sukkah does not apply (*Beis Yosef*

בספר יסוד יוסף כתב להתפלל אז תפילה זו:

רִבּוֹנָא דְעָלְמָא. יְהֵא רַעֲוָא מִן קֳדָמָךְ. שֶׁאוֹתָן מַלְאָכִים הַקְּדוֹשִׁים הַשַּׁיָּכִים לְמִצְוַת סֻכָּה וּלְמִצְוַת ד' מִינִים לוּלָב וְאֶתְרוֹג הֲדַס

---

568). Yet, others do not eat in the sukkah at all because on Shemini Atzeres we pray for rain. Eating in the sukkah implies that we don't want rain, and the prayer for rain would then be insincere.

According to all opinions, though, the time when we "say goodbye" (געזעגענען) to the sukkah with a special *tefillah*, is on the afternoon of Shemini Atzeres. This universal custom would seem to be out of place for those who do not eat in the sukkah on this day. Wouldn't it seem more logical to take leave one day earlier—on Hoshana Rabbah—which is the last time the sukkah will be utilized this season?

The present **Bobover Rebbe, Rav Benzion Halberstam** ***shlit"a***, clarifies the purpose of this custom. We find that when Yaakov Avinu left his parents' home to go to Charan, the *pasuk* tells us a second time—*Vayeitzei Yaakov*—"And Yaakov went out," implying that even after he left, he later returned. He did this because he realized that he was leaving Eretz Yisrael and his parents' home, a source of holiness that could never be compensated for. He came back for one last "shot" of spiritual energy and sanctity which, he hoped, would tide him over in the long years he was to spend in *chutz la'aretz.*

In much the same way, we too, come back a second time—even after we've officially left the sukkah behind—to gather up a few more remnants of *kedushah*, a final burst of purity and holiness which only the sukkah can afford us. Only when we've done that, can we finally say "goodbye"!

Rav Levi Yitzchak of Berditchev ***zt"l*** **(Kedushas Levi)** would say:

"The Gemara tells us that when Mashiach comes, the *tzaddikim* of that generation and all previous generations will sit in his sukkah wearing crowns. Well, I will be eager to share in these festivities and will try to push my way into Mashiach's sukkah. Of course, the guard at the door will turn me back saying, 'A coarse and simple man like you has no business in Mashiach's sukkah.'

"I will tell him, 'Listen, I always had simple people in my sukkah and I endured their company; surely Mashiach can put up with me!'"

וַעֲרָבָה. הַנּוֹהֲגִים בְּחַג הַסֻּכּוֹת הֵם יִתְלַוּוּ עִמָּנוּ בְּצֵאתֵנוּ מִן הַסֻּכָּה. וְיִכָּנְסוּ עִמָּנוּ לְבָתֵּינוּ לְחַיִּים וּלְשָׁלוֹם. וְלִהְיוֹת תָּמִיד עָלֵינוּ שְׁמִירָה עֶלְיוֹנָה מִמְּעוֹן קָדְשֶׁךָ. וּלְהַצִּילֵנוּ מִכָּל חֵטְא וְעָוֹן וּמִכָּל פְּגָעִים רָעִים.

ולהיות תמיד עלינו שמירה עליונה ממעון קדשך

And there should always be upon us a Heavenly protection from Your holy abode...

MIDDOS/ DERECH ERETZ
מידות/דרך ארץ

The Gemara (*Bava Metzia* 85a) tells of a young calf being led to slaughter that ran away and hid under the hem of the coat of Rabbeinu Hakadosh. Rebbi promptly returned it to the *shochet*, saying, "Go, for this is the purpose of your creation!" However, as a result, Rebbi suffered greatly since he showed no mercy toward the frightened calf. When a creature—any creature, even an animal—turns to you for shelter and begs to be saved from harm, the *Middas Harachamim* (Attribute of Mercy) dictates and demands that you show it mercy and do your utmost to protect it and not turn it away.

Similarly, expounds **Rav Nosson Wachtfogel** ***zt"l***, this is the concept of the sukkah, which is known as צילא דמהימנותא (shelter of Divine faithfulness). When we sit in the sukkah, we are begging for Heavenly protection and mercy, even though we may not necessarily deserve it. Nevertheless, one who takes pains to leave his home and reside in a sukkah for seven days is assured of Hashem's ever-vigilant protection and will never be turned away, for the *Middas Harachamim* dictates that it is so!

ויכנסו עמנו לבתינו לחיים ולשלום

And they should enter with us into our homes, for life and for peace...

MUSSAR/ HASHKAFAH
מוסר/השקפה

The **Rambam** in *Moreh Nevuchim* (3:43) writes that sitting in the sukkah teaches man *to remember his evil days in his day of prosperity. He will thereby be induced to thank Hashem repeatedly and to lead a modest and humble life.* The sukkah is meant to induce both a feeling of gratitude and a feeling of humility.

Rabbeinu Yitzchak Aboav ***zt"l*** **(*Menoras Hamaor*)** provides a different perspective on the purpose of the sukkah, one which applies when we are in the sukkah and even when we are back in our own homes: *When* Chazal (*Sukkah* 2a) *instruct us: "Go out from your permanent dwellings and live in a temporary dwelling," they meant that the mitzvah to dwell in the sukkah teaches us that a man must not place his trust in the size or strength or conveniences of his house, even though it may be filled*

וּמִכָּל שָׁעוֹת רָעוֹת הַמִּתְרַגְּשׁוֹת לָבֹא לָעוֹלָם. וְתַעֲרֶה עָלֵינוּ רוּחַ
מִמָּרוֹם. וְחַדֵּשׁ כִּלְיוֹתֵינוּ לְעָבְדְךָ בֶּאֱמֶת בְּאַהֲבָה וּבְיִרְאָה. וְנַתְמִיד
מְאֹד בְּתַלְמוּד תּוֹרָתְךָ הַקְּדוֹשָׁה לִלְמוֹד וּלְלַמֵּד. וּזְכוּת אַרְבָּעָה מִינִים

---

with the best of everything; nor should he rely upon the help of any man, even though he may be the lord of the land. But let him put his trust in Him whose word called the universe into being, for He alone is mighty and faithful, and He does not retract what He promises.

What the *Menoras Hamaor* is telling us is that the main point of living in the sukkah for seven days is to increase our faith in *Hakadosh Baruch Hu* for the entire year. When we live in a sturdy house, we are protected from the elements; rain, cold, and heat do not harm us. As a result, we begin to place our faith in our homes, in our wealth—and not where it should rightfully be—in Hashem. Likewise, we tend to place our trust in men, especially influential rulers and leaders and ignore that these rulers are in power by Divine decree.

By living in a flimsy sukkah for seven days, exposed once again to the elements, we realize that ultimately we must place our trust in Hashem Who rules over our homes, the elements, and all human rulers. Then, once we've established this foremost in our consciousness, we can carry this thought back into our homes and let it permeate our being as we go forward into the long and dark winter.

ונתמיד מאד בתלמוד תורתך הקדושה ללמוד וללמד

And we should constantly delve into Your holy Torah, to learn and to teach...

STORIES
מעשה

A number of days before the start of the Yom Tov of Sukkos, an announcement was proclaimed throughout the entire city of Vilna, emanating from the holy lips of the great **Vilna Gaon, Rav Eliyahu** ***zt"l.*** He issued a directive to his students informing them that it was their duty—an absolute obligation on the part of each and every one them—to study well and thoroughly familiarize themselves with a specific *masechta* in *Shas*, and even memorize it by heart! By doing so, they would minimize any possible *bittul Torah* as well as constantly fulfill the mitzvah of *You shall ponder in it (learn Torah) day and night"* in any given situation, such as traveling.

One of the students, who would later become a leading light of his generation, heeded his *rebbi's* call and took upon himself to memorize the entire *masechta* of *Sukkos.* He studied and reviewed it countless times until he truly believed that he had mastered the entire folio. He even asked his fellow students to test him on the

וּמִצְוַת סֻכָּה יַעֲמוֹד שֶׁתַּאֲרִיךְ אַפְּךָ עַד שׁוּבֵינוּ אֵלֶיךָ בִּתְשׁוּבָה שְׁלֵימָה לְפָנֶיךָ. וּנְתַקֵּן כָּל אֲשֶׁר פָּגַמְנוּ. וְנִזְכֶּה לִשְׁנֵי שֻׁלְחָנוֹת בְּלִי צַעַר וְיָגוֹן אֲנִי וּבְנֵי בֵיתִי וְיוֹצְאֵי חֲלָצַי. וְנִהְיֶה כֻּלָּנוּ שְׁקֵטִים וּשְׁלֵוִים דְּשֵׁנִים וְרַעֲנַנִּים. וְעוֹבְדֵי הַשֵּׁם בֶּאֱמֶת לַאֲמִתּוֹ כִּרְצוֹנְךָ הַטּוֹב בִּכְלַל כָּל בְּנֵי יִשְׂרָאֵל: יִהְיוּ לְרָצוֹן אִמְרֵי פִי וְהֶגְיוֹן לִבִּי לְפָנֶיךָ יְיָ צוּרִי וְגוֹאֲלִי:

masechta and all were duly impressed with his thorough grasp and knowledge of the Talmudic material.

On the first day of Chol Hamoed Sukkos, when many people would visit their *rabbanim* and *rabbeim*, the sukkah of the Vilna Gaon was overcrowded with students and well-wishers coming to greet and see the great Gaon. This young *talmid* was among them and when it was his turn to speak to his *rebbi*, he informed the Gaon that he had memorized the entire *Maseches Sukkos*. The Vilna Gaon looked at him intently and then asked with the hint of a twinkle in his eye, "Is that so? Would you like me to test you on it?" The *talmid* was confident of his knowledge and agreed.

R' Eliyahu then asked, "Tell me, please, how many arguments are there in this *masechta* between Rav Meir and Rav Yehudah? And how many between Rabbi Akiva and Rabbi Tarfon? Abaya and Rava? Rav Papa and Rav Huna brei D'Rav Yehoshua?" The Gaon could have gone on, but mercifully he stopped.

The young student tried as best as he could to answer the questions, but it simply was beyond his scope of knowledge. Indeed, he may have memorized every line in the Gemara and known the concepts well enough, but he still could not manage to count up all the Talmudic arguments that are found in the *masechta*.

The Gaon smiled and began to answer his own question. He started by listing every single *machlokes* between the various Tanna'im and Amora'im; the arguments and the counter-arguments. He pointed out every single halachic principle that was mentioned, as well as every Mishnaic, Aggadic and Talmudic dictum that was discussed by the Sages. Like a skilled surgeon, he neatly dissected the entire *masechta*, page by page and line by line, until he had clearly presented the entire contents of *Maseches Sukkah* before the awestruck wonderment of all in attendance.

By the time he had finished, the Gaon had enumerated eighty-five examples of a non-kosher sukkah, which amounted to the exact numerical value of סכה (without the *vav*). He also counted out ninety-one examples of kosher *sukkos*, which is the exact numerical value of (סוכה מלאה). In this way, the Gaon proved what he meant by "knowing a *masechta*"!

וזכות ארבעה מינים ומצות סכה יעמוד שתאריך אפך
עד שובינו אליך בתשובה שלימה לפניך

And may the merit of the Four Species and the mitzvah of sukkah assist, that You may withhold Your anger until we return to You in complete repentance…

MIDDOS/ DERECH ERETZ
מידות/דרך ארץ

There are two types of joy in this world. There is "direct joy" and "indirect joy." When a person experiences happiness without any form of exertion or suffering beforehand, this is referred to as "direct joy." On the other hand, "indirect joy" is that which one attains after prolonged preparation and even agony. According to **Rav Shlomo Yosef Zevin *zt"l***, most of the joy that is found in this world is of the latter type. One must work to achieve happiness. A classic example is the birth of a baby which follows difficult labor pains. Furthermore, there are times when one experiences suffering, but the likelihood of a joyous outcome is by no means obvious, and that may make the suffering even greater than that of childbirth.

In reality, we accept on pure faith, that all that transpires will ultimately work out for the best. For this reason, *Chazal* have enjoined us that *One is obligated to bless Hashem for the bad as well as for the good.* Likewise, we believe that all of Hashem's deeds will become clear to us at some future time, and we will then experience true joy. When we have been purified from the state which nearly forces us to see all events in a short-sighted perspective, we will see clearly what Hashem has in store for us, and we'll understand the meaning of true joy.

As the holiday of Sukkos concludes and Shemini Atzeres, followed by Simchas Torah begins, we get a taste of that ultimate happiness, the "direct joy" which comes without any pain. The joy of Sukkos, culminating on the last days, is not the outgrowth of agony and suffering; it is a result of the purifying effects of Rosh Hashanah and Yom Kippur. Thus, as we depart our sukkah and embark on the final days of Yom Tov, the Torah enjoins us that these days of Shemini Atzeres and Simchas Torah should be אך שמח—filled with nothing but the purest and most direct joy possible.

ונתקן כל אשר פגמנו ונזכה לשני שלחנות בלי צער ויגון אני ובני ביתי ויוצאי חלצי

And may we rectify all that we have blemished, and may we merit "both tables" without pain and suffering, both myself and my household and my offspring…

STORIES
מעשה

The story is told over by many chassidim throughout the years, that in the days before the famous **Sabba Kaddisha, Rav Yissachar Dov of Radoschitz *zt"l***, became well known as a *tzaddik* and miracle worker, he was so impoverished that he was often forced to fast simply because he had not even a slice of bread to eat. The situation deteriorated to the point that one year he had eaten

nothing for a few days before Yom Kippur, and even after the fast was over, he had nothing better than meager rations of bread and water to break his fast. Not only that, he could not even afford to prepare anything at all for the oncoming Yom Tov of Sukkos.

After the evening *tefillos* on the first night of Sukkos, R' Yissachar Dov remained in the *beis medrash, davening* and learning, for he knew that there was nothing at home to eat. He was too depressed to come straight home, especially on this holiday of joy, and felt the need to wait until he could reconcile himself with the situation. Unbeknownst to him, while he was preparing himself for the upcoming holiday, his righteous wife went out to the marketplace and sold some of her jewelry in exchange for *challos*, candles and a few potatoes for the *seudah*. Happily, she prepared these few items for their meal as she waited for her husband to come home.

When R' Yissachar Dov had finally washed away his unhappy thoughts and decided that most people had by then finished eating in the sukkah and probably returned to their homes, he left the shul and walked home. As he entered his sukkah, however, he was overjoyed to see candles and *challos* on the table. His wife told him what she did and he thanked her warmly. Then, without another word, he immediately recited Kiddush, washed his hands, and sat down to eat. At this point, he was so hungry that he devoured with great appetite the potatoes which his wife served him.

While he was eating in such a hurried manner, though, a sudden thought flashed through his mind. "Berel," he exclaimed to himself, "what are you doing? You should be sitting in the sukkah, but instead you're sitting in your plate!"

And right then and there, he stopped eating.

שמיני עצרת/
שמחת תורה

תפילת גשם

אתה הראת לדעת

סדר הקפות

שישו ושמחו בשמחת
התורה

Dedicated by

Mr. and Mrs. Tzvi Turner

לז״נ ר׳ **ישראל** בן ר׳ **יעקב טורנער** ז״ל

נפטר שמיני עצרת תשל״ה

ת.נ.צ.ב.ה.

שמיני עצרת/שמחת תורה

בַּיּוֹם הַשְּׁמִינִי עֲצֶרֶת תִּהְיֶה לָכֶם כָּל־מְלֶאכֶת עֲבֹדָה לֹא תַעֲשׂוּ (במדבר כט-לה)

DRUSH
דרוש

At the Yom Tov *tish* of the holy **Sochatchover Rebbe, Rav Avraham Borenstein *zt"l* (Avnei Nezer)**, sat a chassid who was in a constant state of inner turmoil. He tried to learn Torah and follow his rebbe's path but his impulses and evil inclinations seemed to always get the better of him. No matter how noble his intentions, he found himself thinking and often acting in an impure fashion.

All was quiet at the *tish* as the rebbe sat in deep meditation. Suddenly, he opened his eyes and began to speak: "וביום השמיני עצרת תהיה לכם—On this holy day of Shemini Atzeres, the *Ribono Shel Olam* enables us with a special power, עצרת. He restrains the evil inclination (ועצר את השמים) and the strength of the *Satan* is weakened. This special restraint is only for us, Bnei Yisrael who attach ourselves to His Torah and *mitzvos*. Any person who immerses himself in Torah will be free of this evil." The rebbe lifted up his eyes and gazed directly at his young Chassid.

Suddenly, the chassid felt as if a weight of guilt and evil had rolled right off him and from that moment, he had no further problem restraining his *yetzer hara*.

Kiddush and the Shemini Atzeres/Simchas Torah Meals

HALACHAH
הלכה

The Afternoon Before. One should not eat a heavy Hoshana Rabbah meal or eat late in the day, lest it detract from his appetite for the Shemini Atzeres meal.

The First Meal of Shemini Atzeres. According to the **Maharshal**[1], one should not make Yom Tov early, thereby starting his meal and Kiddush early. This is because it is still technically Hoshana Rabbah by day and one needs to make the *brachah* of לישב בסוכה. On the other hand, he has ushered in Shemini Atzeres and that *brachah* is not appropriate. Therefore, one must wait until nightfall (*tzeis hakochavim*) and then say Kiddush, thereby not needing לישב. This applies even this year when Shemini Atzeres is on Shabbos. The ***Turei Zahav***[2] argues that once he ushers in Shemini Atzeres, Hoshana Rabbah is effectively over in

1. שו"ת סי' סח
2. תרסח:א

Torah law and one can say Kiddush without לישב. Most *poskim*[3] rule strictly like the Maharshal and that is our custom.

In the Sukkah. Unless one has a clear family custom not to, one should eat all his meals on Shemini Atzeres in the sukkah[4]. Since there are some well-known customs to eat some or all the meals in the house, if one has such a family custom, he has upon whom to rely to continue this custom[5]. A snack that is only a preference to eat in the sukkah during Sukkos, is eaten in the house on Shemini Atzeres[6].

Bentching. If one mistakenly said חג הסוכות הזה in *bentching* (and similarly in every *Shemoneh Esrei* of Shemini Atzeres) instead of mentioning Shemini Atzeres (this mistake can be quite common after saying חג הסוכות הזה over forty times), there is a big discussion if he has to repeat it. The ***Chayei Adam***[7] and others maintain that he doesn't have to because: 1) Outside Eretz Yisrael, we do sit in the sukkah. 2) It is called "Shemini (eighth day) Atzeres," indicating that for certain laws, it is considered an eighth day of Sukkos. 3) Once he already said the words מועדים לשמחה, he has already declared it to be a special Yom Tov day and nothing he may say after that can invalidate it. The **Chida**[8] holds that he must repeat it, because this day has its own name both in halachah and as a point in reference. The later *poskim* rule that because of the doubt (ספק) one should not repeat it.

Kiddush on Simchas Torah. Everyone agrees that on Simchas Torah night, Kiddush should only be made after nightfall[9].

Bentching* on Simchas Torah.** If a person erred on Simchas Torah in *bentching* or in *Shemoneh Esrei* and said the words חג הסוכות, many *poskim*[10] say that he definitely must repeat it. (This would seem to depend upon the three reasons mentioned above by Shemini Atzeres, and indeed it seems that ***Aruch Hashulchan[11] is lenient even on Simchas Torah.)

3. מ"ב שם:ז ועוד
4. או"ח תרסח:א
5. אשל אברהם מבוטשאטש תרלט
6. מ"ב תרסח:ו
7. כלל כח:טו
8. מובא בשע"ת תרסח:ב
9. כף החיים תרסח:י
10. "א תנינא ודע"ת תרסח
11. תרסח:א

תפילת גשם

אַף בְּרִי אֻתַּת שֵׁם שַׂר מָטָר, לְהַעֲבִיב וּלְהַעֲנִין לְהָרִיק וּלְהַמְטַר,
מַיִם אִבִּים בָּם גֵּיא לַעֲטַר, לְבַל יֵעָצְרוּ בְּנִשְׁיוֹן שְׁטָר,
אֱמוּנִים גְּנוֹן בָּם שׁוֹאֲלֵי מָטָר. בָּרוּךְ אַתָּה יְיָ, מָגֵן אַבְרָהָם.

יַטְרִיחַ לְפַלֵּג מִפֶּלֶג גֶּשֶׁם, לְמוֹגֵג פְּנֵי נֶשִׁי בְּצַחוֹת לֶשֶׁם,
מַיִם לְאַדְרָךְ כִּנִּיתָ בְּרֶשֶׁם, לְהַרְגִּיעַ בְּרַעֲפָם לְנִפּוּחֵי נֶשֶׁם,
לְהַחֲיוֹת מַזְכִּירִים גְּבוּרוֹת הַגָּשֶׁם.

תפילת גשם

Laws and Customs that Merit a Good *Parnassah*

HALACHAH
הלכה

Shemini Atzeres: Rain. On Shemini Atzeres, we "*bentch geshem*"—we recite the lengthy *tefillah* for rain, which is really an introduction for us as we now begin mentioning, in the second *brachah* of *Shemoneh Esrei* during the entire winter, about rain. As we previously discussed, the Sages teach us[1] that rain and *parnassah* are equated as one. Therefore, one can have in mind various aspects that stimulate *parnassah*, as symbolized by the rain: 1) Just as rain comes down from heaven to earth, so too, all *parnassah* "comes down" from Heaven to us. 2) Just as the falling rain depends upon our actions and merits (as we say in the second *parshah* of *Krias Shema*), so too, *parnassah* depends upon our actions and merits.

Private Requests on Shemini Atzeres. There are a number of remarkable quotes about the closeness to Hashem that a Jew experiences on Shemini Atzeres, and the ability to ask for special requests, including *parnassah*, on this unique "Day of Days." The ***Zohar***[2] writes: (here is a loose translation) *During this day of celebration (Shemini Atzeres), the only (nation) with the King is the Jewish nation. When one is with the King alone, he can ask whatever he wants with a greater chance of receiving it.* Similarly, the ***Yalkut Shimoni***[3] says that on Shemini Atzeres, a person should "ask for all that he needs." The renowned **Chacham Chaim Falagi *zt"l***[4] writes that one should be very careful to *daven* with great concentration and feeling on Shemini Atzeres

1. תענית ב
2. פרשת נח דף סג, פרשת צו דף לב
3. במדבר תשפב (פנחס כט)
4. מועד לכל חי כה:א

אֱלֹהֵינוּ וֵאלֹהֵי אֲבוֹתֵינוּ,

זְכוֹר אָב נִמְשַׁךְ אַחֲרֶיךָ כַּמַּיִם, בֵּרַכְתּוֹ כְּעֵץ שָׁתוּל עַל פַּלְגֵי מָיִם,

גְּנַנְתּוֹ הִצַּלְתּוֹ מֵאֵשׁ וּמִמַּיִם, דְּרַשְׁתּוֹ בְּזָרְעוֹ עַל כָּל מָיִם.

הקהל עונה: בַּעֲבוּרוֹ אַל תִּמְנַע מָיִם.

---

because: 1) the whole spiritual structure of the prayers of Tishrei, starting from Rosh Hashanah, is completed on this day, and 2) there is no other day like this to have prayers accepted and answered in all that one can ask for.

A Relevant Question. One can ask: How do the above-mentioned quotes from the *Zohar* and the *Yalkut*, which encourage a person to ask for his needs on Shemini Atzeres, fit with the well-known halachah[5] that one is not permitted to ask for his private needs on Shabbos or Yom Tov? In fact, this halachah is cited in the *poskim* in many places[6]. The answer is that the only time that one cannot ask for his own personal requests on Shabbos and Yom Tov is when the person can wait until the next day to make his request. However, if an opportune time comes along on Shabbos or Yom Tov and this special time (*eis ratzon*) will not be around at a later time, one is permitted to make his request right then. This is found in a number of *teshuvos*[7] and is based on the **Ran** (*Rosh Hashanah* 32b).

יטריח לפלג מפלג גשם למוגג פני נשי בצחות לשם

He will impose [upon the rain angel] to divert rain from streams of water,
to soften the surface of the earth with sparkling, gem-like drops.

MUSSAR/ HASHKAFAH
מוסר/השקפה

The rain cycle is quite miraculous, designed by the Creator of the world in His infinite wisdom to sustain the world. The oceans of the world contain ninety-seven percent of the world's water. Two percent is frozen in the polar ice caps. The constant recycling of the remaining one percent provides us with all the water we use! It is amazing that all the water in the entire world's atmosphere only equals about ten days of normal rainfall! If water were a resource that became depleted like gas or oil, we would run out of water very quickly. But because water gets re-used constantly, we do not have this problem.

---

5. ירושלמי שבת פרק טו, מדרש רבה ויקרא פרשה לד

6. עיין מגן אברהם קכח:ע ומשנה ברורה קפח:ט

7.

זְכוֹר הַנּוֹלָד בִּבְשׂוֹרַת יֻקַּח נָא מְעַט מַיִם, וְשַׂחְתָּ לְהוֹרוֹ לְשָׁחֲטוֹ לִשְׁפֹּךְ דָּמוֹ כַּמַּיִם, זִהֵר גַּם הוּא לִשְׁפֹּךְ לֵב כַּמַּיִם, חָפַר וּמָצָא בְּאֵרוֹת מָיִם.

הקהל עונה: **בַּעֲבוּרוֹ אַל תִּמְנַע מָיִם.**

Water is an incredible liquid. It is a combination of two atoms of hydrogen and one atom of oxygen. Each of these two gases alone cannot feed us, yet when they combine, they form the wonder liquid from which we live. Would this not be so, the water vapor in the air would never condense and form clouds! Snow wouldn't fall in the winter, and if it snowed, it would never melt. Although the oceans are full of salty, undrinkable water, it vaporizes into the atmosphere and becomes a blessing for us. We use this pure, colorless, and odorless fluid to cook and bathe; it also serves to regulate our body temperature, aid digestion, lubricate our joints, and provides healthy recreation—swimming!

A rainy day is often called "nasty weather"; a "rotten summer" means it rained a lot. "The weather was just awful" implies that we do not like to be inconvenienced, and thus we spurn this most wonderful blessing—the blessing of rain.

Let us appreciate the magnificent gift of rain from our beloved Father and, even if it is inconvenient and even if you get wet, please don't ever call rain nasty again! **(*Dargah Yeseirah*, Rav Zalman Guttman *shlit"a*)**

זכור הנולד בבשורת יקח נא מעט מים

Remember the one whose birth was foretold [when Avraham said,] "Let a little water be brought."

MIDDOS/ DERECH ERETZ מידות/דרך ארץ

Avraham Avinu brought three non-Jewish guests into his abode and attended to them in a princely manner. However, before granting them entry he said, *"Let a small amount of water be brought so that you can wash your feet."* Rashi explains that this was because he thought that they were idol worshippers who bow down to the dust of their feet. So that this dust not be brought into his abode, he requested them to wash their feet before entering. Avraham Avinu did not feel he was asking too much of his guests in asking them not to bring something which would disturb him into his house. All the more so, a person is entitled to demand of others—family and friends—not to walk around his house in a distinctly immodest manner or unbecoming attire.

When **Rav Yaakov Yosef Herman *zt"l*** married off one of his children in New York in 1922, he sent out invitations to many people in the community. As per

זְכוֹר טָעַן מַקְלוֹ וְעָבַר יַרְדֵּן מַיִם, יִחַד לֵב וְגָל אֶבֶן מִפִּי בְאֵר מַיִם,
כְּנֶאֱבַק לוֹ שַׂר בָּלוּל מֵאֵשׁ וּמִמַּיִם, לָכֵן הִבְטַחְתּוֹ הֱיוֹת עִמּוֹ בָּאֵשׁ וּבַמָּיִם.

הקהל עונה: בַּעֲבוּרוֹ אַל תִּמְנַע מָיִם.

זְכוֹר מָשׁוּי בְּתֵבַת גֹּמֶא מִן הַמַּיִם, נָמוּ דָּלֹה דָלָה וְהִשְׁקָה צֹאן מַיִם,
סְגוּלֶיךָ עֵת צָמְאוּ לַמַּיִם, עַל הַסֶּלַע הָךְ וַיֵּצְאוּ מָיִם.

הקהל עונה: בְּצִדְקוֹ חֹן חַשְׁרַת מָיִם.

---

his insistence, the invitations included the following words: "Ladies, please come dressed according to the Jewish law." Although feelings for *tznius* were much weaker at that time, and these people were his guests, R' Yaakov Yosef nevertheless felt it was his right to request of those who wished to attend his *simchah* that they come in respectable and modest clothes, even if they might feel insulted at the notification.

This idea is one that manifests itself in many facets of society and everyday life. Just as guests can be requested to dress in a certain manner before attending a function, so too, an employed woman can be told to come to work in a basically modest manner of dress and can be requested not to sing even softly to herself if this will disturb members of the household/office (*Oz V'hadar L'vushah*).

יחד לב וגל אבן מפי באר מים

He unified his heart and rolled the stone off the mouth of the well of water.

MASHAL
משל

משל: Rav Zalman of Vilna ***zt"l*** (brother of **Rav Chaim Volozhiner** ***zt"l***) was once learning in a *beis medrash* when he realized that he needed a certain *sefer*. When he looked toward the bookcases, he noticed that a massive wooden box filled with heavy objects was placed directly in front of the bookcase, blocking any access.

R' Zalman thought for a moment. Then he stood up and began pacing up and down the aisle. As he did so, he was heard saying, "*Chazal* tell us that Torah is *not in the Heavens*—for if it were, one would be required to ascend and bring it down! Likewise, Torah is *not overseas*—for if it were, one would have to cross the oceans to get it!" He continued in this vein, working himself up into a righteous fervor, filled with love of Torah and the strength of a lion to fulfill Hashem's commands.

זְכוֹר פְּקִיד שָׁתוֹת טוֹבֵל חָמֵשׁ טְבִילוֹת בַּמַּיִם, צוֹעֶה וּמַרְחִיץ כַּפָּיו בְּקִדּוּשׁ מַיִם, קוֹרֵא וּמַזֶּה טָהֳרַת מַיִם, רָחַק מֵעַם פַּחַז כַּמָּיִם.

הקהל עונה: בַּעֲבוּרוֹ אַל תִּמְנַע מָיִם.

זְכוֹר שְׁנֵים עָשָׂר שְׁבָטִים שֶׁהֶעֱבַרְתָּ בְּגִזְרַת מַיִם, שֶׁהִמְתַּקְתָּ לָמוֹ מְרִירוּת מַיִם, תּוֹלְדוֹתָם נִשְׁפַּךְ דָּמָם עָלֶיךָ כַּמַּיִם, תֵּפֶן כִּי נַפְשֵׁנוּ אֲפָפוּ מָיִם.

הקהל עונה: בְּצִדְקָם חֹן חַשְׁרַת מָיִם.

שָׁאַתָּה הוּא יְיָ אֱלֹהֵינוּ, מַשִּׁיב הָרוּחַ וּמוֹרִיד הַגָּשֶׁם,
לִבְרָכָה וְלֹא לִקְלָלָה (אָמֵן).
לְחַיִּים וְלֹא לְמָוֶת (אָמֵן).
לְשֹׂבַע וְלֹא לְרָזוֹן (אָמֵן).

Suddenly, he stopped and ran right over to the massive box and with one quick motion, he lifted it and moved it away from the bookcase. Then, he reached out and pulled out the *sefer* he desired and sat down once more to learn!

נמשל: When Yaakov Avinu arrived in Charan to find a suitable wife, he encountered the shepherds milling about the well. Only he was able to lift the stone off the well when all the strong and burly shepherds were unable to do so. The midrash comments: *To inform us that he (Yaakov) was very strong.* Strong indeed, but *Chazal* were not simply referring to physical strength; Yaakov retained a strength of character that allowed him to channel his purity and righteousness into actual power. Before he was able to roll the stone off the well, he prepared himself by dedicating his heart to the Al-mighty, and with a pure faith, carried out the feat of strength. Bnei Yisrael, the descendants of our father Yaakov, also have this same ability to build up our inner fortitude to be able to accomplish great things—both spiritually and physically.

כנאבק לו שר בלול מאש וממים, לכן הבטחתו היות עמו באש ובמים

When he was attacked by an angel comprised of fire and water, You promised to be with him through fire and through water.

MUSSAR/HASHKAFAH
מוסר/השקפה

Who is this mysterious angel composed of fire and water that wrestled with Yaakov Avinu all throughout the night? It was Samael (*Satan*), Eisav's heavenly protective angel. *Chazal* tell us (*Brachos* 61a) that the *yetzer hara* resembles a fly, which locates every wound and is attracted to every bit of dirt. Similarly, when Yaakov wrestled with Samael, Eisav's heavenly angel, the *Satan* tried to find Yaakov's

Achilles' heel, his weakest point, in order to defeat him. The angel tried, to no avail; Yaakov was too powerful.

Rav Shamshon Raphael Hirsch ***zt"l*** writes that Yaakov's successful fight with the angel assures us that the spirit of Eisav will never be able to conquer the children of Yaakov throughout the long ages of *galus* and darkness on earth. Nevertheless, the fact that Eisav does manage to hamper us from time to time is inevitable, symbolized by the angel dislodging Yaakov's hip, to prevent him from standing firmly on both feet. It is true that we are few and often find ourselves in an inferior position against the physical powers in the world. It is important that we realize that our strength lies in other, higher factors which cannot be weakened by the nations of Eisav.

The midrash clues us in to another little trick that is a trademark of the *yetzer hara*: *At first he is like a guest and then like the master of the house.* At first, the *Satan* has little authority over man and is likened to a guest who visits his friend's home. Once he succeeds in causing man to yield to temptation, however, he becomes more authoritative, much like the master of the house.

The **Gaon of Vilna** ***zt"l*** adds that the way the evil inclination ensnares a man is by having him study Torah while enticing him to fulfill his desires. For if he were to persuade him to neglect studying Torah completely, the man would never listen. Once, though, the man has accustomed himself to physical pleasure and enjoyment, he instantly ceases to study Torah, for he is constantly occupied with the fulfillment of his desires.

על הסלע הך ויצאו מים

He struck the rock and water gushed out.

DVAR TORAH
דבר תורה

In *Tefillas Geshem*, the prayer for rain, we ask the Al-mighty to provide us with an abundance of water, i.e. *parnassah* (sustenance), in the merit of Moshe Rabbeinu, who was drawn from the water. The second line is a reference to the *pasuk* in *Parshas Chukas* that states that Moshe was commanded to speak to the rock, so that it will give forth its water. Instead of speaking to the rock, though, Moshe raised his hand and struck it. A huge amount of water gushed forth and the community was able to drink. However, for disobeying Hashem's command, Moshe was not permitted to enter Eretz Yisrael. The question arises: Since Moshe was punished for striking the rock, why is he praised in *Tefillas Geshem* for this act of disobedience?

Rav Moshe Yitzchak Gewirtzman ***zt"l*** **of Pshevorsk** explains that speech is a spiritual act of the highest level, and Moshe realized that if he just spoke to the

rock, the water that would emerge would benefit only scholars and other individuals of high repute, while the ordinary people would not share in it at all. He decided therefore to strike the rock, so that the water that poured forth could be enjoyed by all the people. Now it becomes clear that the prayer praises Moshe, because by striking the rock he sacrificed himself for the benefit of all the Jewish people.

A man suffering from kidney stones was told by his doctor that his condition was life-threatening and that he required immediate surgery. The patient called R' Itzikel, who told him, "Repeat after me the *pasuk, Who turns the rock into a pool of water, the flinty rock into a flowing fountain* (*Tehillim* 114:8). The man followed suit, and almost instantly, the pain subsided. Doctors confirmed that the stone had melted and passed, and the surgery was canceled.

צועה ומרחיץ כפיו בקידוש מים

He cleansed and washed his hands to sanctify them with water.

MASHAL
משל

משל: A young boy lived in the *shtetl* with his grandfather, an old *talmid chacham* who enjoyed nothing more than sitting with his Gemara and learning. Each morning, the *zeide* was up early sitting at the kitchen table with a Gemara in his hand. His grandson wanted to be just like him and tried to imitate him in every way he could.

But the young boy had a hard time comprehending the Gemara. One day, he just became so frustrated that he asked his grandfather, "Zeide! I try to learn every day just like you but I don't understand it, and what I do understand I forget as soon as I close the Gemara. What good does reading the Gemara do?"

The wise old *zeide* quietly turned from putting coal in the stove and picked up a basket. "Please do me a favor," he said to the boy. "Take this coal basket down to the river and bring me back a basket of water."

The boy did as he was told, but all the water leaked out before he got back to the house. The *zeide* laughed and said, "You'll have to move a little faster next time," and sent him back to the river with the basket to try again.

This time the boy ran faster, but again the basket was empty before he returned home. Breathless, he told his grandfather that it was impossible to carry water in a basket full of holes, and he went to get a bucket instead.

The old man said, "I don't want a bucket of water, I want a basket of water. You're just not trying hard enough," and he walked the boy out the door to watch him try again. At this point, the boy knew it was impossible, but he wanted to show his grandfather that even if he ran as fast as he could, the water would leak out before he got back to the house.

The boy again dipped the basket into the river and ran swiftly, but when he reached his grandfather, the basket was again empty. Frustrated, he said, "See Zeide, it's useless!"

"So you think it is useless?" the old man asked. "Look at the basket." The boy looked and for the first time realized that the basket was different. It had been transformed from a dirty, blackened, old coal basket to a thoroughly clean one.

"Son, that's what happens when you learn Torah and read the words of *Chazal*. You might not understand or remember everything, but when you read it, you will be changed, inside and out. That is the power that the Torah has on our lives!"

נמשל: Just as an atmosphere of Torah can change a person, likewise the atmosphere of Rosh Hashanah, Yom Kippur and Sukkos can transform a once dirtied individual into a pristine and spiritual person. But it is finally now on Shemini Atzeres, says the holy **Sfas Emes *zt"l* (Gerrer Rebbe)**, when we arrive at the culmination of all these twenty-one holy days—the numerical equivalent of אך שמח—that we can reflect and realize that in fact we have changed, for we are cleaner and purer than we were before. It is our job to move forward and maintain our pristine nature throughout the coming year.

בצדקם חן חשרת מים

In [the merit of] their righteousness, grant us abundant water.

משל: The people of Slonim were preparing a grand reception for their newly hired *rav*, **Rav Eizel Charif *zt"l***, and to their great fortune, the day of honor turned out to be bright and sunny—a perfect day for a reception.

MASHAL
משל

As the new *rav* was being led around town, one of the distinguished members jokingly remarked to R' Eizel, "Tradition has it that rainy weather on the day a new *rav* arrives in town is a good omen for both the *rav* and the community. Today, though, the sky is clear and blue without a cloud in sight. Can this be a bad omen?"

R' Eizel replied with characteristic wit, "It's true what you're saying, but the rainfall is only in accordance with the stature of the *rav*. If he is mediocre, only a moderate amount of rain will fall. If he is of medium stature, then a fair amount of rain will come down.

"But if," he paused with a twinkle in his eye, "the *rav* is truly great, then a veritable flood would fall. However, since Hashem swore that He would never again bring a *Mabul* to the world, He gave us beautiful weather instead!"

נמשל: We value *gishmei brachah* (blessed rains), which will allow our crops—and ultimately our entire *parnassah*—to prosper and grow. But in the same figurative sense, do we appreciate the message of the clear blue sky, the warm and luminous

sun? Hashem, in His mercy, is telling us: You are My children and I will never again do anything to hurt you!

שאתה הוא ה' אלקינו משיב הרוח ומוריד הגשם: לברכה ולא לקללה

For You, Hashem, our G-d, are Causer of the wind to blow and of the rain to fall—for blessing and not for curse…

DRUSH
דרוש

On the day of Shemini Atzeres, Jews recite the special prayer known as *Tefillas Geshem*—the prayer for rain. Since rain signifies the success of our crops, and due to the falling rain, we will, *b'ezras Hashem*, be sustained with plentiful bounty throughout the entire year, it is undoubtedly one of the most significant and awe-inspiring prayers to be recited throughout the Jewish calendar year, and is treated appropriately with extreme reverence and serious contemplation. It also inaugurates the "winter" cycle during which we recite משיב הרוח ומוריד הגשם (to be followed in several weeks by ותן טל ומטר לברכה), which extends from Shemini Atzeres until the first day of Pesach.

The special prayer for rain is recited all over the world, in every community where Jews reside. It wasn't always this way, however. Back in the 1800's, as the population of Australia increased, Jews found their way to this "land down under" on the other side of the world. Small communities were established at first, but they soon grew into cities like Melbourne and Sydney, until today thousands of Torah-true and G-d-fearing Jews live there.

Australia is unique in that the summer and winter seasons are reversed from those in the Northern Hemisphere. The months from June until September are the cold, rainy winter months, whereas the months of December through March are hot and dry. This poses a problem with regard to the *Tefillas Geshem* and reciting *morid hageshem*. Thus, when the first Jews came to Australia, they sent a halachic query to the chief rabbi of London, **Rav Nosson Adler** ***zt"l***, inquiring when to say the prayer for rain, since the rest of the Jewish world says this prayer between Sukkos and Pesach, as it is their rainy season. In Australia, however, rain at this time is detrimental to the crop and would appear to be anything but a blessing.

R' Adler ruled that they should not say it at all—not between Sukkos and Pesach, the Australian summer, because rain was detrimental at that time, and not between Pesach and Sukkos because *Chazal* never instituted this prayer to be said at that time. The matter remained as such for quite some time until a certain Rav Hershkovitz came to Australia and was perturbed by the ruling. How could it be that Jews should never recite this special prayer? So he wrote to **Rav Yitzchak Elchanan Spector** ***zt"l*** of Kovno, the leading *posek* of the generation, asking what should be done.

אַתָּה הָרְאֵתָ לָדַעַת, כִּי יְיָ הוּא הָאֱלֹהִים, אֵין עוֹד מִלְּבַדּוֹ. לְעֹשֵׂה נִפְלָאוֹת גְּדֹלוֹת לְבַדּוֹ, כִּי לְעוֹלָם חַסְדּוֹ. אֵין כָּמוֹךָ בָאֱלֹהִים, אֲדֹנָי, וְאֵין כְּמַעֲשֶׂיךָ. יְהִי כְבוֹד יְיָ לְעוֹלָם, יִשְׂמַח יְיָ בְּמַעֲשָׂיו. יְהִי שֵׁם

Rav Yitzchak Elchanan mulled over this question, taking into consideration the Gemara (*Taanis* 14b) which asserts that if a certain community needs rain at a time when the regular prayer for rain is not recited, it may be inserted into the blessing of שומע תפילה in *Shemoneh Esrei.* In the end, though, he overruled the previous ruling and instructed that the prayer should be said in Australia, although only between Sukkos and Pesach, so as not to be different from the rest of the world.

Naturally, this didn't sit well with long-standing members of the community who were used to the previous *psak* (ruling), and they wrote a *she'eilah* to the great *rav* of Jerusalem, **Rav Shmuel Salant *zt"l***, explaining that rain was harmful in their summer and to pray for rain at this time seemed to be inappropriate.

R' Shmuel ruled that R' Nosson Adler had been right all along and it should not be said at all. However, Rav Hershkovitz then wrote to R' Shmuel Salant and told him what R' Yitzchak Elchanan had said. He also brought proofs to his claim that, unlike Brazil (also in the Southern Hemisphere) where certain *gedolim* had ruled that this *tefillah* shouldn't be said after Sukkos, rain in Australia, although not necessary, was definitely not detrimental.

Upon hearing this, R' Shmuel changed his mind and ruled that the Australians should say the prayer for rain at the same time as the rest of the world.

Today the custom in both Australia and Brazil is to say the prayer from Sukkos to Pesach.

אתה הראת

STORIES
מעשה

Once, **Rav Simchah Zissel Broide *zt"l***, the *rosh yeshivah* of Knesses Yisrael-Chevron, was present in the *beis medrash* on Simchas Torah during the auction at which the privileges of reading *Atah Hareisa* and leading the *hakafos* were "sold" to the highest bidder—the one who publicly took upon himself to learn the most *blatt Gemara* during the new year. R' Simchah Zissel inquired about those who had competed in the bidding but hadn't won—what were they going to do?

יְיָ מְבֹרָךְ, מֵעַתָּה וְעַד עוֹלָם. יְהִי יְיָ אֱלֹהֵינוּ עִמָּנוּ, כַּאֲשֶׁר הָיָה עִם אֲבֹתֵינוּ, אַל יַעַזְבֵנוּ וְאַל יִטְּשֵׁנוּ. וְאִמְרוּ, הוֹשִׁיעֵנוּ, אֱלֹהֵי יִשְׁעֵנוּ, וְקַבְּצֵנוּ וְהַצִּילֵנוּ מִן הַגּוֹיִם, לְהֹדוֹת לְשֵׁם קָדְשֶׁךָ, לְהִשְׁתַּבֵּחַ בִּתְהִלָּתֶךָ.

R' Simchah Zissel was surprised to hear the answer. He was told that only those who had won the privileges were obligated to fulfill their bid and study the number of Gemara pages that they had pledged, whereas the others were exempt from fulfilling the offers they had made during the auction. He related that when the yeshivah was located in the actual city of Chevron (before they were forced to evacuate the city after the infamous Arab riots in 1929), the custom was to obligate each bidder to fulfill his pledge by studying the number of Gemara pages he had bid, even if he had failed to win the honor of saying *Atah Hareisa* or dancing with the Torah scroll during the *hakafos.*

"*Dos is a gresera kuntz!* (This is an even greater accomplishment!)" said the *rosh yeshivah* with a smile.

אתה הראת לדעת כי ה' הוא האלקים אין עוד מלבדו

Unto you it was made perceptible so that you might know that Hashem is G-d; there is nothing else aside from Him.

DRUSH
דרוש

The Gemara (*Chullin* 7b) quotes the words of Rav Chanina ben Dosa, that the words *ein od milvado*—"there is none other besides Him," include even the powers of sorcery. Once, a sorceress tried to take some earth from under Rav Chanina's feet, in order to cast a spell over him. "Go ahead," he said. "It will do you no good, for it is written, *ein od milvado*!"

Rav Chaim Volozhiner *zt"l* in ***Nefesh HaChaim*** explains that Rav Chanina was not relying on a miracle to save him. Rather, he had firmly established in his heart the *emunah* (belief) that there is no other force in the universe other than Hashem. He was so connected in his mind to the Al-mighty, that it was clear to him that nothing else has any control or existence at all. When Rav Chanina declared, "*Ein od milvado,*" he was emphasizing the clarity of his perfect faith.

True *emunah* is within our reach. The more we allow this awareness to permeate our daily deeds and thoughts, the closer we come to perfection.

When a shiny new car driven by an Arab pulled up at the Erez checkpoint on its way into Gaza, the soldiers on duty made their routine inspection to determine that it was not a stolen vehicle. The driver produced the proper documents and

יְיָ מֶלֶךְ, יְיָ מָלָךְ, יְיָ יִמְלֹךְ לְעוֹלָם וָעֶד. יְיָ עֹז לְעַמּוֹ יִתֵּן, יְיָ יְבָרֵךְ אֶת
עַמּוֹ בַשָּׁלוֹם. וְיִהְיוּ נָא אֲמָרֵינוּ לְרָצוֹן, לִפְנֵי אֲדוֹן כֹּל.

פותחים הארון

וַיְהִי בִּנְסֹעַ הָאָרֹן, וַיֹּאמֶר מֹשֶׁה, קוּמָה יְיָ, וְיָפֻצוּ אֹיְבֶיךָ, וְיָנֻסוּ מְשַׂנְאֶיךָ
מִפָּנֶיךָ. קוּמָה יְיָ לִמְנוּחָתֶךָ, אַתָּה וַאֲרוֹן עֻזֶּךָ. כֹּהֲנֶיךָ יִלְבְּשׁוּ
צֶדֶק, וַחֲסִידֶיךָ יְרַנֵּנוּ. בַּעֲבוּר דָּוִד עַבְדֶּךָ, אַל תָּשֵׁב פְּנֵי מְשִׁיחֶךָ.

---

the soldiers were about to let him drive into Gaza when they suddenly heard the commander order them to wait.

Coming from behind the car the commander approached the Arab and demanded to know whether the vehicle was his. The Arab insisted that it was, but he was warned by the commander that if he did not admit to theft his punishment would be more severe. His confidence shattered, the Arab confessed that he had stolen the car in Maale Adumim.

All the other soldiers were all amazed. "How did you know it wasn't his? What are you, some kind of prophet?"

"I'm no prophet," the commander replied. "Just look at the bumper sticker." On the back of the car were written three Hebrew words that explained everything: *ein od milvado.*

יהי ה' אלקינו עמנו כאשר היה עם אבתינו אל יעזבנו ואל יטשנו

May Hashem, our G-d, be with us as He was with our fathers;
may He not forsake us, and may He not abandon us.

STORIES
מעשה

The seven days of Sukkos were terribly difficult for the saintly **Klausenberger Rebbe, Rav Yekusiel Yehudah Halberstam *zt"l*,** during the years that he spent under inhumane conditions at the Muldorf labor camp. Aside from the rigors of daily life as a slave laborer for the Nazi war machine, the rebbe had no sukkah, no *arbaah minim*, and no *Ushpizin*. This lack of holiday *mitzvos* caused him added pain and distress, for the rebbe lived his entire life for the performance of *mitzvos*.

When Shemini Atzeres was but a day away, the Klausenberger Rebbe decided that no matter the fact that he was a prisoner, no one—not even the ruthless Germans—would take away his special Yom Tov, this special day when Hashem communes

וְאָמַר בַּיּוֹם הַהוּא, הִנֵּה אֱלֹהֵינוּ זֶה, קִוִּינוּ לוֹ וְיוֹשִׁיעֵנוּ, זֶה יְיָ קִוִּינוּ לוֹ נָגִילָה וְנִשְׂמְחָה בִּישׁוּעָתוֹ. מַלְכוּתְךָ מַלְכוּת כָּל עֹלָמִים, וּמֶמְשַׁלְתְּךָ בְּכָל דּוֹר וָדֹר. כִּי מִצִּיּוֹן תֵּצֵא תוֹרָה, וּדְבַר יְיָ מִירוּשָׁלָיִם.

אַב הָרַחֲמִים, הֵיטִיבָה בִרְצוֹנְךָ אֶת צִיּוֹן, תִּבְנֶה חוֹמוֹת יְרוּשָׁלָיִם. כִּי בְךָ לְבַד בָּטָחְנוּ, מֶלֶךְ אֵל רָם וְנִשָּׂא, אֲדוֹן עוֹלָמִים.

---

exclusively with the Jewish people. There was no way, he reckoned emphatically, that he was willing to forgo his celebration.

The camp doctor, Dr. Greenbaum, a Jew by birth, had agreed to issue the rebbe an exemption from work because he required extra rest, and the rebbe was fortunate to be able to spend the whole Yom Tov of Sukkos in the infirmary. He planned to do the same for Shemini Atzeres as well.

On Hoshana Rabbah, a young man and acquaintance of the rebbe, Moshe Eliezer Einhorn, who had obtained the rebbe's medical exemption for him, was informed privately that on the following day the Oberfuehrer, the senior commander of the camp, was coming to conduct a special inspection and selection. Together with him would be a certain Dr. Plukan, a thoroughly evil woman who was known for her practice of weeding out the weak and sick inmates and sending them to the crematoria in Dachau. It was imperative for anyone who wanted to remain alive to show up for work and prove that he was strong and capable of working. Woe to anyone who was missing at roll call!

Moshe Eliezer hurried to Dr. Greenbaum and asked him to add the rebbe to the list of those assigned to work for the next day. The doctor was surprised by the sudden request, since he was prepared to do the opposite, but Moshe Eliezer insisted. Although he could not explain why, the rebbe could not be excused from work the following day.

The rebbe, however, was understandably upset. Since he did not know why he had been reassigned to a work detail, he could not imagine forfeiting his Yom Tov solitude and decided not to report to work on Shemini Atzeres. He remained in the

Rav Yisrael Baal Shem Tov *zt"l* would say:

"The dancing on Simchas Torah is so exalted and so elevated that even the angel Michael comes down to this earth and collects all the fallen, torn straps of the shoes of the Jews as they dance. He then uses these to create a crown to exhibit the splendor of Klal Yisrael."

barracks and experienced the Yom Tov as only he was capable. He *davened* with tremendous emotion and his heartfelt prayers truly captured the spirit of the day.

When the prisoners were inspected and counted, it became clear that a prisoner was missing. Immediately, guards were sent to look for the missing prisoner. They found the rebbe standing in his barracks, deep in prayer, and dragged him to the prisoner lineup. There, they proceeded to beat him mercilessly in front of all the rest of the prisoners. When they finished, the rebbe was so badly hurt that he was barely breathing. He was taken to the infirmary for immediate medical attention.

The poor Jews who witnessed this scene went to work, certain that the rebbe had not survived the beating. They had witnessed with their own eyes the horrific beating and they helplessly cringed with every blow. It was as if each blow that connected to the Klausenberger Rebbe's body was felt by the many onlookers who considered him their mentor and leader.

When the work was finished for the day and the inmates returned to their barracks at night, they were astonished to find the rebbe not only alive, but back in his own barracks. He was limping around a small stool, holding a few pages from a small torn mishnayos in his hand. This was the Klausenberger Rebbe's *hakafos* in honor of Simchas Torah!

In his later years, R' Yekusiel Yehudah would often mention his experiences on that Shemini Atzeres. With satisfaction evident in his voice, he would say, "True, I was terribly beaten and barely survived, but in the end I defeated the *resha'im* because I did not work on Shemini Atzeres." **(*Heroes of Spirit*)**

ויהי בנסוע הארון ויאמר משה קומה ה׳ ויפצו איביך וינסו משנאיך מפניך

And whenever the Ark traveled, Moshe would say, "Rise, Hashem, and let Your enemies be scattered, and those who hate You, flee before You."

REMEZ

רמז

The holy *Aron* (Ark) is a *remez* (allusion) to the *talmid chacham*, who is called "*Aron.*" Just as the *Aron* is filled with the *Luchos*, the tablets of the law, so too, a *talmid chacham* is filled with knowledge of the law.

The *sefarim* tell us that Hashem wishes to bring a Torah scholar close to Him. The way to do this is by sending him many trials to see it he will overcome them. If the *tzaddik* strengthens himself and overcomes them, he will rise to a very high and wondrous level. When he is "on trial" by Hashem, a Torah scholar is considered like one who is "going down in order to rise (*yeridah l'tzorech aliyah*)."

The **Kozhnitzer Maggid, Rav Yisrael Hopstein *zt"l* (*Avodas Yisrael*),** writes that this concept is similar to a person going up a ladder. As he is set to rise up to the next

step, he must remove his foot from the ladder. He is then standing with one foot on the ladder and one foot in the air. At that time, he needs to be very careful not to fall. The same thing applies to a *tzaddik* in the middle of a *nisayon*. Even though he will rise to greater heights afterwards, at the time of the trial he needs a lot of protection. However, Hashem always protects those who wait for Him.

This is the meaning of the *pasuk*: *When the Ark would journey*—when the *talmid chacham* (Ark) is journeying from one level to another and in danger of possibly falling, *Moshe said, "Arise Hashem"*—one should pray for the welfare of the *tzaddik* that Hashem will indeed make him rise and protect him so that he will not fall. He should be strengthened so that he can rise ever higher. When that happens, the *tzaddik* and the people will realize the truth of: *let Your foes be scattered, and Your enemies from before You.* There should not be any power of opposition, until the people of Hashem will go up to the higher level.

כהניך ילבשו צדק וחסידיך ירננו

Let Your priests be clothed in righteousness, and let Your devoted ones sing for joy.

משל: In the times of **Rav Akiva Eiger *zt"l***, the fashion among the irreligious *maskilim* was to wear spectacles on a clean-shaven face and carry a walking stick. Every young *maskil* made sure to procure for himself these "identifying objects" so that everyone would know what he stood for.

MASHAL
משל

A group of young *maskilim* once pestered R' Akiva Eiger endlessly, trying to draw him into an argument about matters of religion and faith. R' Akiva Eiger looked at them with amusement and said, "I see that the modern-day *yetzer hara* has grown wiser than ever before and polished up his methods. It used to be that when a Jew grew old and needed spectacles to see and a walking stick to help him walk, he would realize that his days were numbered and he would try to repent and mend his ways before it was too late."

R' Akiva Eiger shook his head at the troublemakers and shrugged. "Today's *yetzer hara* has found a way to combat that tendency. He created this 'fashion' in order to ensure that clean-shaven Jews would begin using spectacles and walking sticks while still in their prime."

נמשל: The Torah tells us that the priestly clothing worn by the *kohanim* in the Beis Hamikdash were for one purpose: *l'kavod ul'tiferes*—to enjoin honor and splendor to its wearer. Soiled and dirty clothing reflects the wearer's character. However, **Rav Nachman of Breslov *zt"l*** explains that fashionably loud and ostentatious garments

mark their wearer as an adherent to the ways of the *Satan*! One who dons such clothing indicates that his clothing is more important to him than his G-d! A *kohen*—and every Jew for that matter—must "be clothed in righteousness." In other words, the clothes a Jew wears is a reflection of his righteousness. Let us strive to be like the *kohanim* who wore their clothing in an immaculate and respectable manner—not for their own sake—but in order to glorify the holy Name of the Al-mighty.

יהי כבוד ה' לעולם ישמח ה' במעשיו

The glory of Hashem will endure forever; Hashem will rejoice in His work.

Simchas Torah is a *simchah* for every Jew, provided that the Torah is as happy with us as we are with it, and we rightfully identify with it.

MIDDOS/ DERECH ERETZ
מידות/דרך ארץ

Rabbi Dr. Abraham J. Twerski *shlit"a* relates that one time at the Simchas Torah celebration, with people singing and dancing joyously with the Torah, a person who had virtually no contact with Torah study was particularly lively. Someone couldn't resist and asked him, "Do you have any idea what is contained in that Torah with which you are dancing? In what way does the celebration of the Torah concern you?"

The man's answer was enlightening. "Suppose my brother was marrying off his child. Would I not rejoice in my brother's *simchah*, even though it's not my actual child who is getting married?

"I know nothing of the Torah," continued the man emotionally, "but the Torah scholars are my brothers, and their *simchah* is my *simchah*!"

R' Twerski explains that this man is absolutely right. The *simchah* of one Jew with the Torah should be a *simchah* for all Jews. In this respect, most especially, we are all one family.

ואמר ביום ההוא הנה אלקינו זה קוינו לו ויושיענו זה ה' קוינו לו נגילה ונשמחה בישועתו

And it will be said on that day, "Behold, this is our G-d; we have hoped for Him and He delivered us! This is Hashem, for Him we have hoped; we will exalt and rejoice in His deliverance."

Chazal tell us that the secret behind the custom to dance *hakafos* on Simchas Torah is based on the fact that: *In the future (time of Mashiach), the Holy One, Blessed be He will make a circle for the righteous and He will sit in the middle, in Paradise. And each and every one will point with his finger, as it says, "And he will say on that day, behold this is*

MUSSAR/ HASHKAFAH
מוסר/השקפה

our L-rd, we trust in Him and He will give us salvation" (*Taanis* 31a). Thus, we dance in a circle just as the *tzaddikim* will dance in a circle around Hashem.

What is clear is that the focal point of the circle is what is in the middle. All seven days of Sukkos, we circle the *bimah* as we hold our *arbaah minim*, and on Hoshana Rabbah, our *avodah* is to go around seven times, clutching our *lulav* and *esrog* tightly, reciting *piyutim*, as the *sefer Torah* is held in the middle. We are establishing our connection between performing the *mitzvos* and our total allegiance to the Torah, and thus, we circle the Torah as we hold the *mitzvos* in our hands. However, on Simchas Torah, when we no longer hold the *arbaah minim*, we now go in a circle, clutching the *sifrei Torah* as we dance around...the *bimah*! When did the *bimah*—a glorified table—become the focal point of our service? Why, on this wonderful day, when we celebrate the primacy of Torah in our lives, do we make the *bimah* the centerpiece?

Rav Aizik Sher *zt"l* explains that without the *bimah*, where would we put the *sefer Torah* down? Where would we open it and read from it? Where would we learn all the timeless teachings that it has to offer? The *bimah*—and to the *yeshivah bachur*, his beloved *shtender*—represents the study of Torah that is so essential to living and promulgating a life of Torah and *mitzvos*, that will endure for ourselves, our children and all generations to come! It is not enough to just hold the Torah, dance with the Torah, and honor the Torah—we must learn the Torah! We must open it, study it and

Rav Moshe Sofer *zt"l* (Chasam Sofer) would say:

"On the first day of Sukkos, the Torah commands us to fulfill many *mitzvos:* sukkah, *lulav, esrog, simchah,* etc. On the rest of the days of Yom Tov, there are just two *mitzvos*: sukkah and *simchah*. But on Shemini Atzeres the Torah is very clear. There is only one mitzvah that we must perform with every fiber of our being: והיית אך שמח—*And you shall be only joyous."*

Rav Yisrael Salanter *zt"l* would say:

"Simchas Torah is a bittersweet holiday for me. On the one hand, I rejoice greatly in our precious Torah. On the other hand, I am saddened over the many Jews who violate the Torah daily. Thus, the more joy I feel on Simchas Torah, the more keenly I feel pain over the level to which our people have sunk!"

הקפה ראשונה

אָנָּא ה׳, הוֹשִׁיעָה נָּא. אָנָּא ה׳, הַצְלִיחָה נָא. אָנָּא ה׳, עֲנֵנוּ בְיוֹם קָרְאֵנוּ.

אֱלֹהֵי הָרוּחוֹת, הוֹשִׁיעָה נָּא. בּוֹחֵן לְבָבוֹת, הַצְלִיחָה נָא. גּוֹאֵל חָזָק, עֲנֵנוּ בְיוֹם קָרְאֵנוּ.

תּוֹרַת יְיָ תְּמִימָה, מְשִׁיבַת נָפֶשׁ.

מִזְמוֹר לְדָוִד, הָבוּ לַייָ בְּנֵי אֵלִים, הָבוּ לַייָ כָּבוֹד וָעֹז. הָבוּ לַייָ כְּבוֹד שְׁמוֹ, הִשְׁתַּחֲווּ לַייָ בְּהַדְרַת קֹדֶשׁ קוֹל יְיָ עַל הַמָּיִם, אֵל הַכָּבוֹד הִרְעִים, יְיָ עַל מַיִם רַבִּים.

לַמְנַצֵּחַ בִּנְגִינוֹת מִזְמוֹר שִׁיר. אֱלֹהִים יְחָנֵּנוּ וִיבָרְכֵנוּ, יָאֵר פָּנָיו אִתָּנוּ סֶלָה.

אָנָּא, בְּכֹחַ גְּדֻלַּת יְמִינְךָ, תַּתִּיר צְרוּרָה. כִּי אָמַרְתִּי, עוֹלָם חֶסֶד יִבָּנֶה.

---

allow it to permeate our very being! To be a "Torah Jew," one must become one with the Torah, and not just look at it from afar!

סדר הקפות

STORIES
מעשה

During *hakafos* on Simchas Torah, when we carry the *sefer Torah* in our arms and dance lovingly in a circle, the holy **Vilna Gaon *zt"l*** would be very stringent regarding people standing by the *bimah*. Since we dance in a circle to represent the future circle that will surround Hashem, how can we dare stand in the middle of the dancing as if we are taking the Al-mighty's place!

Rav Chaim Soloveitchik (Brisker) *zt"l* was honored with the first *hakafah* each year, as befitting the *rav* of the city of Brisk. One year, however, the *rav* held onto the *sefer Torah* for all seven *hakafos*, singing and dancing for many consecutive hours! When someone later asked him why he had taken all seven *hakafos*, he shrugged and replied, "The Gemara in *Brachos* writes that three things can shorten the lifespan of an individual. One of them is if someone gives a person a *sefer Torah* to read from and he does not read it. I believe that the same applies if someone gives another a Torah to hold by *hakafos* and he gives it away to another. Thus, I will not give over a *sefer Torah* that I am holding to another person unless they ask to take it from me."

R' Chaim shrugged. "Since no one offered to take it from me, I held it the entire time!"

אנא ה' הושיעה נא אנא ה' הצליחה נא אנא ה' עננו ביום קראנו

We implore You, Hashem, deliver us! We implore You, Hashem, grant us success! We implore You, Hashem, answer us on the day we call!

MUSSAR/ HASHKAFAH מוסר/השקפה

If one were to peruse all the writings of the holy **Arizal**, not surprisingly, one could find comments, explanations and hidden secrets for just about every mitzvah—both *d'Oraisa and d'Rabbanan* (Bibilical and Rabbinical), every prayer ever instituted by the Anshei Knesses Hagedolah, and even *minhagim* or distant customs that are not well known and not all kept by varying groups in Klal Yisrael. All this notwithstanding, with regard to the mitzvah of *hakafos* on Simchas Torah, the writings of the Arizal contain....nothing! No penetrating illumination of the mitzvah through Kabbalistic sources, not even the most minor of allusions. This is obviously an unusual circumstance.

To attain a bit of understanding, one must first discern the nature of the mitzvah. **Rav Shimshon Pincus *zt"l*** explains that when a person comes before Hashem with an urgent request, he may use the phrase הושע נא—*save, please.* When one feels the need to thank Hashem, he employs the word, הללו-יה—*praise G-d.* But when a person has no words with which to express his innermost thoughts and feelings of awe, gratitude, love and holiness towards the *Ribono Shel Olam*, there is only one way for him to truly make his feelings felt; it is then that he bursts forth with song and dance.

On Simchas Torah, when a person grasps the holy Torah in his loving embrace, there are no words to be spoken. Whether subconsciously or through a deep-rooted feeling of spirituality, his only recourse is to sing and dance. This is the mitzvah of *hakafos*. It is possible, concludes Rav Shimshon, that when the Arizal sat down to write the esoteric meanings of the *hakafos*, he realized that there truly are no words to be spoken. It can only be expressed with joyous singing and dancing.

תורת ה' תמימה משיבת נפש

The Torah of Hashem is perfect, restoring the soul.

MASHAL משל

משל: Before World War II, a renowned artist by the name of Van Meergeren claimed to have found a very valuable picture, *The Supper at Ammaus*, by the great Dutch painter Vermeer. Experts had even authenticated his find. However, after the war, he was accused of selling great art treasures to the Nazis for his own benefit. In order to clear his name, he admitted that the so-called "treasures" were really fakes

הקפה שניה

דּוֹבֵר צְדָקוֹת, הוֹשִׁיעָה נָּא. הָדוּר בִּלְבוּשׁוֹ, הַצְלִיחָה נָא. וָתִיק וְחָסִיד, עֲנֵנוּ בְיוֹם קָרְאֵנוּ.

עֵדוּת יְיָ נֶאֱמָנָה, מַחְכִּימַת פֶּתִי. קוֹל יְיָ בַּכֹּחַ. לָדַעַת בָּאָרֶץ דַּרְכֶּךָ, בְּכָל גּוֹיִם יְשׁוּעָתֶךָ. קַבֵּל רִנַּת עַמְּךָ, שַׂגְּבֵנוּ, טַהֲרֵנוּ, נוֹרָא. לְךָ זְרוֹעַ עִם גְּבוּרָה, תָּעֹז יָדְךָ, תָּרוּם יְמִינֶךָ.

---

that he painted himself, a defense that had far-reaching consequences for him and the art world. But with his subsequent admission that he had faked many old masters during the war, art experts revised their view and condemned the Vermeer as a fake, and accused Van Meergeren of being the imposter.

Van Meergeren was arrested and taken to trial. At the trial, he asked a question as part of his defense. "I don't understand. Yesterday, this picture was worth millions of guilders and experts and art lovers would come from all over the world and pay money to see it. Today, it is worth nothing, and nobody would cross the street to see it for free. But the picture has not changed. So what's the difference?"

One of the expert witnesses at the trial answered the question this way: "The 'magic' has gone out of this picture. Like the first edition of a book, an original painting is part of history, a history that contains all of our dreams, our fears and our loves. A fake is...a fake! No more, no less!" In the end, Van Meergeren was tried, found guilty, and sentenced to prison. He died soon after.

נמשל: There are those who find it difficult to believe that the Torah came directly from Hashem through our teacher, Moshe Rabbeinu. They would rather accept the Torah as a great historical work—albeit written by the hand of man—due to its own intrinsic qualities, rather than because of its Divine origins. They would prefer to value the Torah as though it were an authentic painting, even when they believe deep down that it is a "fake," that it was painted by another. However, although the great refinement of the Torah's ethical code, its highly advanced legal system, and the genius of its wisdom may attract the praise and even study by these so-called "connoisseurs," for them to deny its Divine origins, to actually think that it could have been written by anyone other than *Hakadosh Baruch Hu* Himself, is to take the "treasure" out of it. Torah cannot be divorced from its origins, or rather, from the One who gave it and how it was given to the Jewish people. Given by Hashem through the hands of His servant Moshe is the history and heritage of Bnei Yisrael. No more, no less!

הקפה שלישית

זַךְ וְיָשָׁר, הוֹשִׁיעָה נָּא. חוֹמֵל דַּלִּים, הַצְלִיחָה נָא. טוֹב וּמֵטִיב, עֲנֵנוּ בְיוֹם קָרְאֵנוּ.

פִּקּוּדֵי יְיָ יְשָׁרִים, מְשַׂמְּחֵי לֵב. קוֹל יְיָ בֶּהָדָר. יוֹדוּךָ עַמִּים, אֱלֹהִים, יוֹדוּךָ עַמִּים כֻּלָּם. נָא גִבּוֹר, דּוֹרְשֵׁי יִחוּדֶךָ, כְּבָבַת שָׁמְרֵם. תִּתֵּן אֱמֶת לְיַעֲקֹב, חֶסֶד לְאַבְרָהָם.

חומל דלים הצליחה נא טוב ומטיב עננו ביום קראנו

Merciful to the poor, grant us success! Benevolent One and Bestower of goodness, answer us on the day we call!

STORIES
מעשה

On one of the days of Chol Hamoed Sukkos, in the midst of World War II, a whispered message flitted around the Hassag labor camp: the shoemaker had been delayed in his return from the ghetto. The shoemaker was one of the "fortunate Jews" in the camp who had special status. As "skilled," valuable Jews, these individuals possessed special talents and consequently enjoyed certain privileges, such as assignment to unguarded factories or performing various personal services for high-ranking German officers. This shoemaker was truly an expert, whom the Germans actually honored with the title *Schuster Meister* (Master Shoemaker). Very little was known about him personally, but it was clear that he was unsurpassed in the craft of boot-making and as a result, his talents were much in demand by the German elite. It was this unassuming man, whose life was so assured (comparatively), who risked his life two weeks earlier to smuggle in a shofar for Rosh Hashanah.

Some members of the *Aufraumungs Kommand* (the clean-up squad) guessed that he used his special status with the S.S. command to be allowed to search for special materials for his craft among the stores of ghetto plunder, which were kept under particularly heavy guard. Once inside, it was quite simple to slip the shofar under his loose clothing. This was simple but risky, for had he been apprehended by the guard, few questions would have been asked, and little heed given to the answers. The sentence would have been swift—a rifle bullet on the spot or perhaps a prolonged torture followed by a public hanging. But *baruch Hashem* the cobbler was not caught and the shofar was delivered.

Now, during the holiday of Sukkos, he was looking to fulfill the dictum of the Sages: *One mitzvah brings on the fulfillment of another.* Fortified by the success of his first venture, the shoemaker was prepared to further the Yom Tov celebration. He had gone off to work in the morning like any other day. When he finally returned, he did not head for the kitchen for his especially generous portion, but instead hurried

הקפה רביעית

יוֹדֵעַ מַחֲשָׁבוֹת, הוֹשִׁיעָה נָא. כַּבִּיר וְנָאוֹר, הַצְלִיחָה נָא. לוֹבֵשׁ צְדָקוֹת, עֲנֵנוּ בְיוֹם קָרְאֵנוּ.

מִצְוַת יְיָ בָּרָה, מְאִירַת עֵינָיִם. קוֹל יְיָ שֹׁבֵר אֲרָזִים, וַיְשַׁבֵּר יְיָ אֶת אַרְזֵי הַלְּבָנוֹן. וַיַּרְקִידֵם כְּמוֹ עֵגֶל, לְבָנוֹן וְשִׂרְיֹן כְּמוֹ בֶן רְאֵמִים. יִשְׂמְחוּ וִירַנְּנוּ לְאֻמִּים, כִּי תִשְׁפֹּט עַמִּים מִישֹׁר, וּלְאֻמִּים בָּאָרֶץ תַּנְחֵם סֶלָה. בָּרְכֵם, טַהֲרֵם, רַחֲמֵם, צִדְקָתְךָ תָּמִיד גָּמְלֵם. נְעִמוֹת בִּימִינְךָ נֶצַח.

into his hut. What had happened? The incredible had come to pass for the second time in a month! He had successfully spirited a *sefer Torah* out of the clutches of the dreaded Gestapo and smuggled it into the camp. He simply rolled it around and around his body, draped his loose tunic over it, and then walked into the camp. Where he had gotten it from, he adamantly refused to reveal.

It was later learned that he had literally saved the *sefer Torah* from desecration because a short while later the Gestapo burned all the *sifrei Torah*, *sefarim*, and various sacramental cloths and articles in one gigantic bonfire. This one *sefer Torah* was the sole surviving remnant of the sacred articles of the Czestochowa ghetto. The intrepid cobbler decided to bribe one of the guards and offered the Nazi something that he could never have purchased for any sum: a pair of officer's boots! (The Germans seemed to have regarded handcrafted boots as a singular luxury and thus reserved for high-ranking officers. Hence, too, the shoemaker's privileged status.) The shoemaker was allowed to select one item from the pile and he took this Torah scroll because of its small size, which made it feasible for him to wrap it around his stomach without causing a telltale bulge, and later, in camp, its size permitted easy concealment.

A regular *minyan* on Shabbos had already been instituted in one of the barracks, and it was there, on Shabbos Chol Hamoed Sukkos, that the heroic shoemaker demanded, "Who wants to hide the *sefer Torah*?"

Two brave Jews decided to assume the responsibility. They immediately removed a board from the head of one of the wooden cots that was used for sleeping, and in the hollow underneath it, they concealed the scroll.

The news of the *sefer Torah's* arrival had naturally electrified the entire camp. All Sukkos, the Torah was used, and on Simchas Torah night, crowded *hakafos* in the cramped run-down shack were held. These *hakafos* would have been outlandish in any other situation. Carrying the *sefer Torah* in their arms as in conventional *hakafos* was impossible, as they would have been running quite a risk. Being caught carrying the Torah would have meant certain death, but what value did their lives have,

הקפה חמישית

מֶלֶךְ עוֹלָמִים, הוֹשִׁיעָה נָּא. נָאוֹר וְאַדִּיר, הַצְלִיחָה נָא. סוֹמֵךְ נוֹפְלִים, עֲנֵנוּ בְיוֹם קָרְאֵנוּ.

יִרְאַת יְיָ טְהוֹרָה, עוֹמֶדֶת לָעַד. קוֹל יְיָ חֹצֵב לַהֲבוֹת אֵשׁ. יוֹדוּךָ עַמִּים, אֱלֹהִים, יוֹדוּךָ עַמִּים כֻּלָּם. חֲסִין קָדוֹשׁ, בְּרֹב טוּבְךָ, נַהֵל עֲדָתֶךָ. יְיָ אֲדֹנֵינוּ, מָה אַדִּיר שִׁמְךָ בְּכָל הָאָרֶץ, אֲשֶׁר תְּנָה הוֹדְךָ עַל הַשָּׁמָיִם.

---

anyway? It would have been worth it! But the scroll would have also been destroyed, G-d forbid, and this was a loss they would not risk. The *sefer Torah* remained safely ensconced in its hollow behind the board. The inmates stealthily walked around the wooden cot that contained its sacred treasure. As they passed it, they leaned over and kissed the board that lay directly above the *sefer Torah.*

And so it went, far into the night. The silent "dancers" held themselves strenuously in check, as the joyous songs surged repeatedly to their lips. One song echoed softly in their ears. Because of its obvious relevance, they could not contain it inside. As they walked around the *sefer Torah*, they were almost deafened by the silent screaming that enveloped each and every one of them: *Rejoice on Simchas Torah, because it (the Torah) is our strength and our light!*

The *sefer Torah* miraculously survived the war, although the whereabouts of the heroic shoemaker are unknown. Today, the *sefer Torah* is safely ensconced in the *aron kodesh* of the Gerrer Beis Medrash in Bnei Brak.

סומך נופלים עננו ביום קראנו

Supporter of the fallen, answer us on the day we call!

STORIES
מעשה

As was the custom years ago by many of the Chassidic rebbes, and remains even until today, many chassidim would come from far away to the court of their rebbe for the High Holidays, and they would remain there, absorbing the *kedushah* of their rebbe, until after the final days of Simchas Torah.

Once, a chassid went to visit his rebbe, the holy **Rav Meir of Premishlan** ***zt"l***, and emerged with the following story. At that time, R' Meir's daughter was very sick. The doctors tried everything at their disposal to heal her, but after some time, even they despaired, and as Simchas Torah drew near, her condition worsened until she was close to death.

הקפה ששית

עוֹזֵר דַּלִּים, הוֹשִׁיעָה נָּא. פּוֹדֶה וּמַצִּיל, הַצְלִיחָה נָא. צוּר עוֹלָמִים, עֲנֵנוּ בְיוֹם קָרְאֵנוּ.

מִשְׁפְּטֵי יְיָ אֱמֶת, צָדְקוּ יַחְדָּו. קוֹל יְיָ יָחִיל מִדְבָּר, יָחִיל יְיָ מִדְבַּר קָדֵשׁ. אֶרֶץ נָתְנָה יְבוּלָהּ, יְבָרְכֵנוּ אֱלֹהִים אֱלֹהֵינוּ. יָחִיד גֵּאֶה, לְעַמְּךָ פְּנֵה, זוֹכְרֵי קְדֻשָּׁתֶךָ. צַדִּיק יְיָ בְּכָל דְּרָכָיו, וְחָסִיד בְּכָל מַעֲשָׂיו.

הקפה שביעית

קָדוֹשׁ וְנוֹרָא, הוֹשִׁיעָה נָּא. רַחוּם וְחַנּוּן, הַצְלִיחָה נָא. שׁוֹמֵר הַבְּרִית, עֲנֵנוּ בְיוֹם קָרְאֵנוּ. תּוֹמֵךְ תְּמִימִים, הוֹשִׁיעָה נָּא. תַּקִּיף לָעַד, הַצְלִיחָה נָא. תָּמִים בְּמַעֲשָׂיו, עֲנֵנוּ בְיוֹם קָרְאֵנוּ.

R' Meir'l was understandably distraught but he understood that he had a mitzvah to perform—and perform it he would! He carried on in his usual manner, and danced with the Torah with a heart bursting with joy. However, while her husband was rejoicing during the *hakafos* as usual, the *rebbetzin* urged a number of the close chassidim to interrupt R' Meir'l and beg him to do something to save their daughter. A small contingent approached R' Meir'l and passed along his *rebbetzin's* tearful request.

The *tzaddik* finally stopped dancing and walked into his daughter's room. The girl lay there, literally in the throes of death, and R' Meir'l, realizing how her fever was unnaturally high and just how critical her condition was, began praying, silently at first, but gradually his voice began to rise. "*Ribono Shel Olam*," he said, "You commanded us to blow the shofar on Rosh Hashanah and Meir complied. You commanded us to sit in the sukkah on Sukkos and Meir sat. You commanded us to be happy on Simchas Torah—and Meir is happy.

"But *Ribono Shel Olam*, now You have made Meir's daughter very ill and of course, Meir is required to accept your decree with happiness, as it states, *A man is required to make a blessing on evil just as he is required to make a blessing on good.* The Gemara teaches that a man must therefore accept the evil decree happily.

"I, Meir, accept Your decree happily. But *Ribono Shel Olam*, there is also the halachic ruling that one may not mix one joyous event with another joyous event. How, then, can I accept this decree with happiness on Simchas Torah, the day of pure happiness—and mix the celebrations together?"

With that, R' Meir'l gazed intently at his daughter's prone position, until suddenly, a change was noticeable in her breathing. A doctor quickly came to examine her and announced, "Her fever has broken!"

הַנֶּחֱמָדִים מִזָּהָב וּמִפָּז רָב, וּמְתוּקִים מִדְּבַשׁ וְנֹפֶת צוּפִים.

קוֹל יְיָ יְחוֹלֵל אַיָּלוֹת, וַיֶּחֱשֹׂף יְעָרוֹת, וּבְהֵיכָלוֹ, כֻּלּוֹ אֹמֵר כָּבוֹד. יְיָ לַמַּבּוּל יָשָׁב, וַיֵּשֶׁב יְיָ מֶלֶךְ לְעוֹלָם. יְיָ עֹז לְעַמּוֹ יִתֵּן, יְיָ יְבָרֵךְ אֶת עַמּוֹ בַשָּׁלוֹם.

יְבָרְכֵנוּ אֱלֹהִים, וְיִירְאוּ אוֹתוֹ כָּל אַפְסֵי אָרֶץ. שַׁוְעָתֵנוּ קַבֵּל, וּשְׁמַע צַעֲקָתֵנוּ, יוֹדֵעַ תַּעֲלוּמוֹת. לְךָ ה׳ הַגְּדֻלָּה וְהַגְּבוּרָה וְהַתִּפְאֶרֶת וְהַנֵּצַח וְהַהוֹד, כִּי כֹל בַּשָּׁמַיִם וּבָאָרֶץ, לְךָ יְיָ הַמַּמְלָכָה, וְהַמִּתְנַשֵּׂא לְכֹל לְרֹאשׁ. וְהָיָה יְיָ לְמֶלֶךְ עַל כָּל הָאָרֶץ, בַּיּוֹם הַהוּא יִהְיֶה יְיָ אֶחָד וּשְׁמוֹ אֶחָד. וּבְתוֹרָתְךָ כָּתוּב לֵאמֹר: שְׁמַע יִשְׂרָאֵל, יְיָ אֱלֹהֵינוּ, יְיָ אֶחָד. בָּרוּךְ שֵׁם כְּבוֹד מַלְכוּתוֹ לְעוֹלָם וָעֶד.

Immediately, the sick girl broke into a heavy sweat and within a few short days, she recovered fully from her illness.

שומר הברית עננו ביום קראנו

Preserver of the covenant, answer us on the day we call!

MUSSAR/ HASHKAFAH מוסר/השקפה

Rav Itzele Peterburger ***zt"l*** quotes an incredible statement from the **Rosh** (*Yom HaKippurim* 24) as follows: *The* Satan *advocates on behalf of Yisrael on Yom Kippur, for they resemble angelic beings.* This is truly amazing! The *Satan* actually advocates on our behalf? He wants us to merit a good judgment on the holy day? What comes over the *Satan* that he is suddenly so congenial toward the Jewish people?

The answer, says **Rav Michel Barenbaum** ***zt"l***, is that the *Satan* is no fool—he knows it is in his best interests to praise the exalted spiritual level of Bnei Yisrael on Yom Kippur, for then, when the awe of that day wears off and they resume their regular mundane—and often less than desirable—routine, he will point a finger at them and call to the Heavenly Court, "Look at the Jewish people now! This is the nation that resembled angels on Yom Kippur! See how far they've fallen!" His words of advocacy were nothing more than a ploy to antagonize the Jewish people later!

Rav Yonasan Eibschutz ***zt"l*** would say:

"An ignoramus who buys *Chassan Torah* on Simchas Torah is indeed extremely pious. Imagine, he is a *chassan*—but he hasn't seen his *kallah* for the entire past year!"

Thus, when we reach Simchas Torah, the holiday which marks the end of the spiritual renewal we call the Yamim Nora'im, all the cleansing and uplifting are behind us and the ripples of joy have reached their crescendo. Now, we reassume our daily routines with a heightened awareness and determination to fulfill our spiritual potential. Although we recognize that formidable obstacles have been placed in our way, nevertheless, we must ponder this idea following Simchas Torah and focus our energy on Torah study to take advantage of every moment, for otherwise all our achievements will be used against us in the Heavenly Court.

הנחמדים מזהב ומפז רב ומתוקים מדבש ונפת צופים

More desirable than gold [are His commandments], even more than much fine gold.

STORIES
מעשה

During the Battle of Britain in WWII, London fell victim to nightly bombing raids by the German Luftwaffe. Like all the city's residents, **Rav Yechezkel Abramsky *zt"l***, then head of the London Beis Din, was forced to take refuge in the nearest bomb shelter. This meant going to the bank one flight down from his apartment and entering a steel walk-in vault. The bank's gentile director was a close acquaintance of R' Abramsky and he had built a special staircase descending directly from the rabbi's apartment into the bank to facilitate his family's flight to safety.

When the bombings would begin, at all hours of the day or night, everyone would rush into the vault where they'd wait for the deadly raids to end. The bank workers who also found shelter in the huge vault noticed that each time R' Yechezkel entered the vault, he would begin whispering something to himself and he continued to do so for the length of time they remained in the vault. People just assumed that he was praying for the safety of the refugees huddled inside, until one finally mustered up the courage to ask the rabbi's son what prayer he was actually saying.

R' Yechezkel's son explained that his father was always praying for their safety, however, inside the vault, he would pray for something else.

"Throughout the course of my father's life, he has recited the verse, *I prefer the Torah of Your mouth than thousands of pieces of gold and silver*, countless times. But now, each time he enters this vault and is surrounded by millions of pounds sterling, my father is immediately filled with joy. Because now he truly perceives how he feels about the wisdom of Hashem. Indeed, he really feels deep down that he would not trade one drop of Torah for all the money in the world. It is this verse that you see my father whispering each time he walks into the vault!" (***Heroes of the Spirit***)

HALACHAH
הלכה

Learning *V'zos Habrachah*. On Simchas Torah, we finish the yearly cycle of reading the whole Torah in public. This is also the time for individuals to learn the *parshah* of *V'zos Habrachah*, each *pasuk* twice and *Targum Onkelos* once. This is also the end of the private cycle of learning the entire Torah each year (twice, plus *Targum*). The assumed deadline to finish is by Simchas Torah, when one's *minyan* finishes their reading of the Torah, or at least before the end of that day. It is, however, not clear how early one can fulfill his obligation on this last *parshah* of the year. Since this *parshah* is not read on a Shabbos, the regular time span of the whole week, Sunday through Shabbos, might not apply.

Regarding the ideal time, some *poskim* mention Hoshana Rabbah[1], others say Shemini Atzeres[2], while others say Simchas Torah itself[3]. Some contemporary *poskim*[4] write that these might indeed be the only appropriate days and one cannot fulfill his obligation earlier. Others[5] say that the above-mentioned times are just the preferred times but one can start the day after (or, according to some, the minute after) this *parshah* was read in shul. However, which Shabbos is itself debatable. Some say that right after the first time it is read (Shabbos of *Haazinu*, י"ב תשרי by Minchah) is already time to do the mitzvah. There might be another opinion that right after Shabbos is only good if it will be read the next Shabbos. Here, however, the next Shabbos—י"ט תשרי—has a different *kriah* for Chol Hamoed Sukkos, disqualifying the previous week from performing the mitzvah. If so, one can then do the mitzvah after Shabbos Chol Hamoed (י"ט תשרי). As mentioned earlier, the preferred time is either Hoshana Rabbah, Shemini Atzeres or Simchas Torah.

1. פרי מגדים (אשל אברהם) או"ח רפ"ה:י
2. מגן אברהם שם
3. משנה ברורה תרס"ט:ג
4. שו"ת קני בושם א:ט"ז
5. בירור הלכה ג:רפ"ה

Rav Shimon Shkop *zt"l* would say:

"When Hashem blesses a human being with wealth, He is in reality appointing that person as a trustee to apportion the funds to the needy. If one fulfills his duty faithfully, Hashem raises his rank and appoints him over an even greater treasure."

שישו ושמחו בשמחת תורה

לאחר קריאת התורה וההפטרה ביום שמחת תורה אומרים זה:

שִׂישׂוּ וְשִׂמְחוּ בְּשִׂמְחַת תּוֹרָה, וּתְנוּ כָבוֹד לַתּוֹרָה, כִּי טוֹב סַחְרָהּ מִכָּל סְחוֹרָה, מִפָּז וּמִפְּנִינִים יְקָרָה.

נָגִיל וְנָשִׂישׂ בְּזֹאת הַתּוֹרָה, כִּי הִיא לָנוּ עֹז וְאוֹרָה.

אֲהַלְלָה אֱלֹהַי וְאֶשְׂמְחָה בּוֹ, וְאָשִׂימָה תִקְוָתִי בּוֹ, אֲהוֹדֶנּוּ בְּסוֹד עַם קְרוֹבוֹ, אֱלֹהֵי צוּרִי אֶחֱסֶה בּוֹ.

נָגִיל וְנָשִׂישׂ בְּזֹאת הַתּוֹרָה, כִּי הִיא לָנוּ עֹז וְאוֹרָה.

שישו ושמחו בשמחת תורה

מסיני בא וזרח משעיר למו הופיע מהר פארן ואתא מרבבות קודש וכו' (קריאה לשמחת תורה, דברים לג-ב)

Hashem came forth from Sinai and He shone forth to them from Se'ir; He appeared from Mount Paran, and came with some of the myriads of holy angels.

DRUSH
דרוש

On the *pasuk*: *Hashem came forth from Sinai and He shone forth to them from Se'ir; He appeared from Mount Paran* (*Devarim* 33:2), Rashi comments that *He shone forth to them from Se'ir* is referring to when Hashem offered the Torah to *bnei Eisav*, who rejected it. The words *He appeared from Mount Paran* refer to how Hashem then offered it to the children of Yishmael, who gave a similar refusal.

Rav Akiva Eiger *zt"l* cites this midrash and explains that Hashem offered the Torah to all the nations and they all refused. However, within those nations, there were individuals who wished to accept it, but they remained silent out of fear. These were the souls of the converts who in the course of time eventually did join Klal Yisrael. On the other hand, within Yisrael there were individuals who didn't want to accept the Torah, but they were ashamed or fearful, so they joined in and said, *"We will do and we will listen."* Years later, however, these souls would depart from their faith and tragically convert or assimilate, *r"l*.

It is told that when **Rav Eizel of Slonim *zt"l*** (known as Reb Eizel Charif—"the sharp one"—because of his keen mind) published one of his scholarly works on the Talmud, he sent a copy to one of the wealthy citizens of his community in the hope that he could get him interested in perhaps underwriting the cost of this and/or

בְּכָל לֵב אֲרַנֵּן צִדְקוֹתֶיךָ, וַאֲסַפְּרָה תְּהִלָּתֶךָ, בְּעוֹדִי אַגִּיד נִפְלְאוֹתֶיךָ, עַל חַסְדְּךָ וְעַל אֲמִתֶּךָ.

נָגִיל וְנָשִׂישׂ בְּזֹאת הַתּוֹרָה, כִּי הִיא לָנוּ עֹז וְאוֹרָה.

גּוֹאֵל תָּחִישׁ מְבַשֵּׂר טוֹב, כִּי אַתָּה מִגְדַּל עֹז וְטוֹב, גְּאוּלִים יוֹדוּךָ בְּלֵב טוֹב, הוֹדוּ לַיְיָ כִּי טוֹב.

נָגִיל וְנָשִׂישׂ בְּזֹאת הַתּוֹרָה, כִּי הִיא לָנוּ עֹז וְאוֹרָה.

---

future *sefarim*. However, after receiving the *sefer*, the wealthy man brazenly rejected it and even sent it back.

Some time later, R' Eizel met the wealthy man at a community function and said to him, "I must thank you for what you've done. You have no idea how grateful I am to you."

The wealthy man looked at him suspiciously, clearly recalling the poor treatment and impudence that he had shown this respected Torah scholar earlier. "Why would you be grateful?" the man asked, not sensing that he was being set up. "After all, if I remember correctly, I sent your book back."

"Precisely," answered R' Eizel, as a big smile crossed over his face. "You see, when my *sefer* was published, I sent it out to many different cities, and various scholars perused it carefully. They seemed to like it and I was thrilled at the warm reception it received from all the Torah scholars. But then I began thinking: Is it possible, perhaps, that my Torah writings are really not *emes*—the truth? After all, the midrash relates that when Hashem offered the Torah to all the nations of the world, they rejected it, and only after that was it given to Klal Yisrael, who accepted it, no questions asked. It made me wonder if perhaps something that is so quickly and readily accepted by the masses is not truly Torah! This idea tormented me night and day."

The wealthy man recalled this famous midrash and responded with a nod of his head. Unbeknownst to him, his hook was now snagged firm and tight. "However," concluded R' Eizel, with a broad sweep of his hands, "when I sent you my *sefer* and you rejected it outright, I felt vindicated. Now I know that my writings, like the Torah itself, are indeed true, because just like the Torah, my book was rejected by those ignorant of its content and worth!"

דָּגוּל גֹּאֵל נָא הֲמוֹנַי, כִּי אֵין קָדוֹשׁ כַּיְיָ, דְּגוּלִים יוֹדוּךָ יְיָ, מִי יְמַלֵּל גְּבוּרוֹת יְיָ.

נָגִיל וְנָשִׂישׂ בְּזֹאת הַתּוֹרָה, כִּי הִיא לָנוּ עֹז וְאוֹרָה. הֲלֹא בְּאַהֲבָתוֹ בָּחַר בָּנוּ, בְּנֵי בְכוֹרֵי קְרָאָנוּ, הוֹד וְהָדָר הִנְחִילָנוּ, כִּי לְעוֹלָם חַסְדּוֹ עִמָּנוּ.

נָגִיל וְנָשִׂישׂ בְּזֹאת הַתּוֹרָה, כִּי הִיא לָנוּ עֹז וְאוֹרָה.

שישו ושמחו בשמחת תורה, ותנו כבוד לתורה

Be happy and rejoice with the simchah *of the Torah, and give honor to the Torah.*

MIDDOS/ DERECH ERETZ
מידות/דרך ארץ

If Rosh Hashanah is the climax of Elul, and Yom Kippur is the climax of the Aseres Yemei Teshuvah, then Sukkos, which is *Zman Simchaseinu* (a time of joy) is the climax of them all. The tremendous levels that we attain during these days are achieved through a continuous upward spiral of drawing ever closer to Hashem, which peaks on the final day of this lofty period. This most lofty and joyous day is called Simchas Torah.

Why is this day the highlight of all the exquisite Yamim Nora'im that precede it? The reason, explains **Rabbi Zev Leff *shlit"a***, is because the happiness of Simchas Torah bridges the gap between the great days before it and provides the practical avenue of implementing this lofty joy of true *avodas* Hashem into the long winter months ahead.

After we were elevated by the sound of the shofar, were embraced by Hashem in the sukkah, and inspired through the *arbaah minim*, we put all of those aside because they no longer have the power to help us achieve greatness. But when we put all of these objects of mitzvah away, what are we left with? The greatest of all treasures that we as a people can attain. It is the singular most precious gift that will enable us to retain and build upon the great level of *kirvas Elokim* that we have attained until now. We sing and dance with our most prized possession—the *sefer Torah*—because we know that only through learning and living a true Torah life can we achieve true *simchah* in this world, the kind of joy that is deep, real, lasting and satisfying.

Rav Shmuel Zvi of Alexander *zt"l* (*Tiferes Shmuel*) would say:

"Hashem tells Bnei Yisrael, קשה עלי פרידתכם—*Your separation is difficult for Me*. This separation refers to the parting of Jews from each other. Each Jew traveling to his own home after being so close to each other during the festival in Yerushalayim— this separation, says the Al-mighty, is difficult for Me!"

אַשְׁרֵיכֶם יִשְׂרָאֵל, אַשְׁרֵיכֶם יִשְׂרָאֵל, אַשְׁרֵיכֶם יִשְׂרָאֵל, אֲשֶׁר בָּחַר בָּכֶם אֵ-ל,
וְהִנְחִילְכֶם הַתּוֹרָה מִמִּדְבָּר מַתָּנָה.

This great and awesome day of Simchas Torah will pull us through the entire year until we can begin the upward spiral once again, next Elul, on a higher and more exalted level after a year of growth through serving Hashem with true Torah joy.

שישו ושמחו בשמחת התורה... ישיש עליך אלקיך כמשוש חתן על כלה

Be happy and rejoice with the simchah *of the Torah, and give honor to the Torah...May Hashem rejoice over you as a groom rejoices over his bride...*

STORIES
מעשה

On Simchas Torah, when the annual reading of the Torah is completed, it is customary to call a learned scholar, one who has delved into the intricacies and tasted the sweet pleasures of the Torah, to the reading of the final portion. This honor is referred to as *Chassan Torah*—literally, the bridegroom of the Torah, indicating a loving relationship between the person who is engaged in study and the Torah itself. Just as a groom and bride share a loving relationship, so too the Torah and its scholars achieve a lasting bond.

The story is told that in one community, a wealthy man who was completely unlearned wished to receive the distinct honor of *Chassan Torah*. He approached the *gabbai* and requested to be given this wonderful honor; however, the *gabbai* was extremely hesitant and reluctant to oblige. A man unaccustomed to having his wishes refused, the rich man offered a substantial sum of money to the *gabbai*, and the caretaker could not resist the temptation. When the rich man was actually called up and performed his obligation smugly, the *rav* of the shul, suspecting that this was done for financial gain, confronted the *gabbai*. "Is it true that you were paid to give this honor to him?" asked the *rav* in an accusatory tone. The *gabbai* held out for a time before admitting that he was indeed paid to extend this honor to someone absolutely ignorant of Torah.

Seeing that the man was truly sorry, the *rav* softened his tone in order to mollify the chastened *gabbai*. After all, it was a mistake and he was unable to resist the forceful manner in which the rich man approached him. The *rav* looked at his trusty *gabbai* and said, "In truth, I can understand this situation quite well. You see, the *Chassan Torah* is a bride-and-groom relationship. When a young man and a young woman are acquainted with one another and are mutually attracted, there is no need to have a matchmaker involved, and no payment is necessary. However, if the two are total strangers and are brought together by a matchmaker, the latter receives a fee for his services.

"The same is true in this case," quipped the *rav*. "When a Torah scholar receives the honor of *Chassan Torah*, it is a loving relationship, because he and the Torah have known each other for a long time and have developed a mutual fondness. In a situation, though, where the person receiving this special honor is a total stranger to the Torah, there obviously had to be a matchmaker, who had to be given his fee!"

נגיל ונשיש בזאת התורה כי היא לנו עז ואורה

We will rejoice and be happy with this Torah, for it is our strength and light.

MUSSAR/ HASHKAFAH
מוסר/השקפה

It is important to recognize that every day that one merits spending in a yeshivah learning Torah is a great accomplishment. This is especially important in our times when there is a tremendous need for people to devote their entire lives to Torah study.

Rav Avraham Yaakov Pam ***zt"l*** notes that on Simchas Torah, we rejoice at the completion of the yearly cycle of weekly Torah readings and immediately begin a new cycle with *Parshas Bereishis*. It is a time to contemplate the central role that Torah study plays in a Jew's life and the vital importance of supporting the growth of Torah scholarship. From where will the future Torah leaders—its scholars and *poskim*—arise, if not from the great *yeshivos* and *kollelim*? As we dance with the parchment-and-ink *sifrei Torah*, we must remember the self-sacrifice of the living *sifrei Torah*—the Torah scholars. They are the future leaders of our nation who will lead us toward the coming of Mashiach speedily and in our days.

גואל תחיש מבשר טוב כי אתה מגדל עז וטוב

Hurry the redeemer, bearer of good tidings, for You are a Tower of strength and goodness.

Rav Avraham Shalom of Stropkov ***zt"l*** would say:

"Hashem commands us to sing and dance on this holy day, but how can a Jew truly feel happiness while mired in this bitter *galus*? The answer is that Hashem is really testing us to see how we will respond. Will we be sad and bitter, proving that we have no faith in the coming Redemption, or will we fulfill His command joyously, because we believe that our Father, our King, will soon save us?"

בכל לב ארנן צדקותיך ואספרה תהלתך

Wholeheartedly I will sing of Your righteousness, and I will recount Your praises.

MASHAL
משל

משל: The students in the yeshivah of **Rav Yitzchak Blazer *zt"l*** would dance and sing with tremendous enthusiasm during the *simchas beis hasho'evah* celebrations and on Simchas Torah. Their energy was infectious and even R' Yitzchak, the famed *baal mussar* himself, who was always restrained and in control of his emotions, would get up and sing *grammen* to enliven the atmosphere.

At one point in the festivities, the boys lifted R' Yitzchak on a chair and began singing an exuberant tune to the words, *Tzaddik katamar yifrach*—"A righteous one shall flourish like a date palm," with great emotion.

Normally humble to a fault, R' Yitzchak clapped his hands and urged them on to sing these words of praise over and over again. Those in attendance were surprised at R' Yitzchak who seemed, to the untrained eye, to be enjoying the heaping praise and honor being accorded him—although it was clearly uncharacteristic. Later on, however, he explained to the astonished viewers, "When it comes to teaching my students to respect the Torah and their *rabbeim*, I have no right to stop them, even if it appears as if I am a *baal gaavah*!"

But one of the revelers who was in earshot of the *rav* was able to hear R' Yitzchak singing the same song, albeit with words of reproach and admonition—about himself!

נמשל: When we rejoice on Simchas Torah, we must constantly remind ourselves about what we are rejoicing. Is it for us to have fun, to laugh and sing with unrestrained outbursts, which can lead to a complete lack of decorum and respect? Or do we rejoice with Hashem and His Torah, in His *beis medrash*?

אשריכם ישראל אשריכם ישראל אשריכם ישראל אשר
בחר בכם א-ל והנחילכם התורה ממדבר מתנה

You are fortunate, Yisrael... that Hashem chose you and gave you the Torah as an inheritance, a gift in the desert.

MUSSAR/
HASHKAFAH
מוסר/השקפה

On Simchas Torah we honor the Torah by expressing an outpouring of love to the Torah and those who learn it. We have two *chassanim* (grooms) on this special day whom we honor. There is a *Chassan Torah* and a *Chassan Bereishis*. Why do we need two grooms? The reason, says **Rav Avraham Pam *zt"l***, is that at this special time, we celebrate our accomplishments in Torah—yet we do not rest on our laurels. We also celebrate our future goals and aspirations in Torah growth.

Bereishis literally means "in the beginning," and also symbolizes the beginning of a new cycle of the Torah. There is always a tremendous excitement and feeling of renewal at the start of something new. It is a time of great inspiration, and fortunate is the one who utilizes the opportunity to achieve great levels in spiritual growth!

How do we make inspiration into realization? R' Pam explains that renewal begins with *kabbalos* (resolutions). Just as we all made resolutions before Rosh Hashanah to solidify our *teshuvah* into real growth, so too, as the holiday of Sukkos comes to a close with the exuberance and joy of Simchas Torah, it is imperative not to lose that "high" feeling by accepting new *kabbalos* in Torah learning. Maybe start going to a *shiur*, learn *Chumash* with a new commentary, or get a new study partner! The goal of Simchas Torah is the literal meaning of the words—happiness of the Torah! As much as we rejoice with the Torah, the main goal is when the Torah rejoices with us! If we renew our dedication to Torah and strive to upgrade our learning and performance of *mitzvos*, we will dance with the Torah on the holiday itself, but the Torah will rejoice with us all year long.

Rav Eliyahu Lopian *zt"l* would say:

"The joy in life which dedicated Torah study brings with it, cannot be conveyed in mere words. It must be experienced!"

Rav Akiva Eiger *zt"l* would say:

"Every year on Simchas Torah, they give me *Chassan Torah*. What shall I do? It's been already fifty years, and I still don't even know the *kallah*!"

הערות והארות
בעניני
ימים נוראים

תוכן הענינים

■ **אלול - "אם תקום עלי מלחמה"**......294
מרן הגאון הרב חיים יעקב שטיין זצ"ל,
ראש הישיבה דישיבה הגדולה והקדושה דטעלז

■ **ראש השנה - "כתבנו בספר החיים"**......300
מרן הגאון הרב יצחק אייזיק אזבנד זצ"ל,
ראש הישיבה דישיבה הגדולה והקדושה דטעלז

■ **יום הכיפורים - יסוד התשובה והשבת בריה חדשה**......304
כמהר"ר החכם רבי אלעזר אבוחצירא זצוקללה"ה,
בעהמח"ס דברי אלעזר - באר שבע

■ **שמחת תורה - "קשה עלי פרידתכם"**......309
הרה"ג המקובל רב גמליאל הכהן רבינוביץ שליט"א,
ראש ישיבת שער השמים, ירושלים עיה"ק

■ **חודש תשרי הנקרא "ירח האיתנים"**......312
הרב שלום פערל שליט"א,
ר"ם בישיבת היכל התורה בירושלים ומגיד מישרים בק"ק בית שמש

■ **חג הסוכות - "ראשון לחשבון עונות"**......315
הרב דוד יואל בן אאמו"ר פנחס הופמן,
מחבר ספרי "תורה תבלין" "ליקוטי תורה תבלין" "זכרון יצחק"

מרן הגאון הצדיק רבי חיים יעקב שטיין זצ״ל
ראש הישיבה דישיבה הגדולה והקדושה דטעלז
בעמח״ס ברכת חיים - בענייני אלול

״אם תקום עלי מלחמה״

בעומדנו עתה בפתח חודש אלול, על מפתן ימי הדין והמשפט שהם גם ימי הרחמים והסליחות, עולה בזכרון המוחשי איך עמדנו בחודש אלול דאשתקד והרצינו כהיום הזה דברי התעוררות, ואיך בכל שנה בימים ההם בזמן הזה כך נעשה כאילו מאיליו. והדבר מחליש את הדעת. הנה שוב נתעוררה ונחפשה ונחקורה כבכל שנה, ונקבל קבלות, ונשיג השגות, והכל יחלוף כיום אתמול כי יעבור! ומה יצא מכל העסק הלזה? הלא כאשר נמשמש באמתחתנו יש אך מעט מזעיר מכל ההתעוררויות של כל השנים...

אולם מאידך גיסא, אל לנו להמעיט ערכו של החודש היקר הזה. כי באמת, התועלת הבאה לאדם מתשובה ודקדוק המעשים אינה דוקא אותה קבלה, אותו תיקון, אלא כל האדם מתעלה ומתקדש. אי אפשר בכלל לבשר ודם לנסות למדוד את ערך ההתעלות המצטברת, ההולכת ומצטברת בתוך פנימיותנו מכל ימי הדין של כל השנים, ביודעים ובלא יודעים. מי יודע איך היינו נראים אילו היו הימים והשנים חולפים בלי ימים קדושים אלה!

״אם יתקעו שופר בעיר ועם לא יחרדו״

החל ממחר ישמע קול השופר יום יום בכל תפוצות ישראל. השופר, הרבה טעמים נאמרו בו והרבה עניינים רבים ונשגבים, אך החשוב מכל הוא פשטותם של דברים. הרמב״ם, בדברו על עיקר מצות השופר שהוא תקיעת שופר בראש השנה, לא נותן לנו לשכוח את הפשטות, את הרושם הבסיסי שעלינו לקבל משמיעת קול השופר. כדאי לנו להתבונן היטב בדבריו ולהתפעל מכל מילה (הל׳ תשובה, פרק ג הל׳ ד):

״אף אל פי שתקיעת שופר בראש השנה גזירת הכתוב (ויש בה המון טעמים נשגבים), רמז יש בו (ר״ל שזה מה שבא לרמז לנו ע״פ פשטותם של דברים), כלומר עורו ישינים משנתכם ונרדמים הקיצו מתרדמתכם (ה׳תרדמה׳ עמוקה יותר מ׳שינה׳. כולנו, ואפילו הצדיקים בינינו, ׳ישינים׳ כל השנה, לפחות. שוכחים לפני מי אנו קמים בבוקר, לפני מי אנו עתידים ליתן דין וחשבון), וחפשו במעשיכם (כל אחד כפי דרגתו ושכלו) וחזרו בתשובה! וזכרו בוראכם אלו השוכחים את האמת בהבלי הזמן ושוגים כל שנתם בהבל וריק אשר לא יועיל ולא יציל (השכל מחייב חשבון נפש, כמה זמן אוזל לאיבוד על שטויות והבלים, כמה תורה היתה נלמדת אילו היינו ערים ועירנים לחשבונו של עולם כל השנה), ...הביטו לנפשותיכם (ולמען טובת עצמיכם עשו נא), והטיבו דרכיכם ומעלליכם, ויעזוב כל אחד מכם דרכו הרעה (אפילו בלא מעשים רעים יש ׳דרך רעה׳ דרך של עצלות וביטול זמן), ומחשבתו אשר לא טובה (גם אם פגום רק במחשבה יש להתעורר ולתקן).״

וכן בפרט התקיעות של כל חודש אלול. כבר הביא החיי אדם (כלל קלח, סעי׳ א) שאחד מן הטעמים הוא שכשעלה משה למרום באחד

באלול להביא את הלוחות השניות, נכנס פחד בלב העם שמא גם הפעם יתגבר היצר ויפתם בתחבולותיו לטעות, ולכן העבירו קול שופר במחנה להסיר כל מכשול, עד שירד משה לסוף ארבעים יום ביום הכיפורים עם בשורת "סלחתי כדבריך". ולכן, הגם שבתורה לא מוזכר סגולת ימי חודש אלול, נתהוו ימים אלה לימי רצון ורחמים, ימים שנקל בהם לעלות בהר ה'.

אבל כתב שם, שעיקר הטעם הוא "לעורר לב העם ולהחריד לבותם שיעוררו לבותם לתשובה כי כן טבע קול השופר להחריד כמש"כ 'אם יתקע שופר בעיר ועם לא יחרדו.'"

וכתב רבינו יונה (סוף ספר היראה) "משנכנס אלול עד מוצאי יום הכיפורים יהא חרד וירא מאימת הדין". בכל יום ויום מימי אלול על האדם לעורר עצמו. אין אלו ימים רגילים. אלו ימים שיש בהם הרבה מה לפחד ולירא! ולזה בא קול השופר, לבל נשכח זאת אפילו יום אחר.

כי תצא למלחמה - "התעתדו למלחמה הגדולה"!

עורו עורו ישינים משנתכם...

לא רק כדי להתכונן כראוי לימי הדין, אלא בכלל אסור לאדם להיות ישן על משמרתו בעולם הזה. וטמון בזה ענין חשוב עד מאד. הנה מלבד תקיעת השופר עומדים אנו להתחיל מחר לומר פרק "לדוד ה' אורי וישעי". ורגילים אנו להתפלא על כך שהלא בתהלים מצינו פרק אחר, פרק נכבד שנקרא "פרק התשובה" (תהלים נא), והוא מה שאמר דוד בעשותו תשובה על חטאו: "כי פשעי אני אדע וחטאתי נגדי תמיד", "תחטאני באזוב ואטהר ...לב טהור ברא לי אלקים ורוח נכון חדש בקרבי", ... "זבחי אלקים רוח נשברה". ...וכל הפרק נראה ראוי והגון ביותר לחודש אלול, ומה ראו בפרק כז "לדוד ה' אורי" שהוא כל כך נחוץ לחודש אלול?

והנה ידועים דברי האור החיים הק' בפרשתינו, על הפסוק "כי תצא למלחמה על אויבך וראית סוס ורכב עם רב ממך לא תירא מהם כי ה' אלקיך עמך המעלך מארץ מצרים" (דברים כ א), שמרמז הפסוק למלחמה הנצחית של האדם עם יצרו. על האדם לזכור שלמרות כל כחות היצר וחיילותיו יכול הוא לנצח, "כי ה' אלקיך עמך" - הרי בא הוא בכחו של ה' יתברך! כמו שאמרו חז"ל שאלמלא הקב"ה עוזרו אין יכול לו (קדושין ל ע"ב), עי"ש בכל דבריו.

אולם עלינו להדגיש דבר יסודי יותר. ראשית כל צריך שיהיה "כי תצא למלחמה על אויבך", צריך שיהיה "וראית סוס ורכב עם רב ממך". דמנו בנפשנו אם נשכח שבאנו לעולם זה למלחמה נגד אויב ושונא איום ונורא. האויב הכי גדול שיכול להיות שוכן הוא בתוכנו ושולט בנבכי נפשנו! וכל חיינו אינם שוים מאומה אם לא נלחם בו בכל מאדנו.

וכמו כן בריש פ' כי תצא: "כי תצא למלחמה על אויבך ונתנו ה' אלקיך בידך ושבית שביו", שאמרו חז"ל על זה" לא דברה תורה אלא כנגד יצר הרע" (קידושין כא ע"ב) שאם יידע האדם שהוא יוצא למלחמה על יצרו הרע, אזי מובטח הוא - "ונתנו ה' אלקיך בידך...".

ידועים דברי החובות הלבבות, בשער יחוד המעשה (פרק ה), שמאריך להתריע על חומר מלחמת היצר מכל מלחמה אחרת. כל תיבה של בעל חובות הלבבות יקרה מפנינים, באשר ידוע כי רב כחו לסקור את כל פרטי כל ענין וענין. [שמעתי ממורי האב"ד דטעלז, הגרא"י

בלוך הי"ד, שהרבה מכחו בניתוח סוגיות חמורות בהלכה קיבל מעיונו בדברי החובות הלבבות. ואמר, שאצל הרבה מגדולי המחברים גדול כחם לכלול פרטים רבים תוך כלל אחד, אבל כחו של החובות הלבבות הוא לפרוט ולחלק הכלל לפרטים ופרטי פרטים.] וזה לשונו שם: "בן אדם! ראוי לך לדעת כי השונא הגדול שיש לך בעולם הוא יצרך, הנמסך בכחות נפשך והמעורב במזג רוחך, והמשתתף עמך בהנהגת חושיך, הגופניים והרוחניים, המושל בסודות נפשך וצפון חייך, בעל עצתך בכל תנועותיך הנראות והנסתרות, שתהיינה ברצונך, האורב לפתות פסיעותיך, ואתה ישן לו והוא ער לך, ואתה מתעלם ממנו והוא אינו מתעלם ממך, לבש לך בגדי הידידות, ועדה עדי האהבה לך, ונכנס בכלל נאמניך ואנשי עצתך וסגולת אוהביך, רץ אל רצונך בנראה מרמיזותיו וקריצותיו והוא מורה אותך בחציו הממיתים לשרשך מארץ חיים...

"ואמרו על חסיד שפגע אנשים שבים ממלחמת אויבים, ושללו שלל אחרי מלחמה חזקה, אמר להם: שבתם מן המלחמה הקטנה שוללים שלל, התעתדו למלחמה הגדולה! אמרו לו: ומה היא המלחמה הגדולה? אמר להם: מלחמת היצר וחיליו.

"ומן התמה, אחי, כי כל אויב כשתנצח אותו פעם ושתים ירף ממך ולא יעלה על לבו להלחם בך, לדעתו יתרון כחך על כחו, והוא מתייאש מִלְנַצֵּחַ אותך וּמלהתגּבר עליך. אבל היצר אין מספיק לו ממך ניצוח פעם ומאה פעמים, בין שניצח אותך בין שניצחתו. כי אם ינצח אותך ימיתך, ואם תנצחהו פעם אחת יארב לך כל ימיך לנצח אותך. כמו שאמרו חז"ל וז"ל (אבות ב ד): אל תאמן בעצמך עד יום מותך. ואינו מקל בקטנה שבקטנות עניניך לנצח אותך בה כדי שתהיה לו מדרגה לנצח אותך במה שלמעלה ממנה. ועל כן ראוי לך שתהיה נזהר ממנו, ואל תמלא ממשאלותיו בך מאומה, רק יגדל בעיניך המעט שבמעט מניצוחו..."

אמירת "לדוד ה' אורי וישעי"...

ולכן תקנו לומר מזמור זה בחודש אלול, כי לפני שניגש לעשות תשובה חשוב יותר שנכיר במצב. אין כאן יצר אשר בא למענינו להנעים ולענג לנו ורק במקרה הוא רע לנו, אלא לפנינו אויב מסוכן שבא לכלותינו. בפרק "לדוד ה' אורי וישעי" מוצאים אנו תפילה של חיזוק בעת מלחמה ועל אויבים שבאים לרוצחנו נפש.

וראיתי להג"ר אברהם בן הגר"א ז"ל (בפירושו על התהלים באר אברהם, פרק כד) שמפרש כל המזמור באופן שמוכח מתוכו שמדבר דוד במלחמת היצר.

"בקרוב עלי מרעים לאכול את בשרי" - כשארגיש תאוות ורצונות שלוחיו של היצר, אדע כי - "צרי ואויבי לי" (דאם במלחמה רגילה קמיירי, מאי קמשמע לן? פשיטא שצרי ואויבי לי.)"!

"אם תקום עלי מלחמה בזאת אני בוטח, אחת שאלתי... וגו'". ועתה ירום ראשי על אויבי סביבותי - "באמת יודע האדם בפנים תוך נשמתו מה הם דרכי חיי נצח, לטוב לו בעולם הזה והבא. בקוראינו בתורה "ולא תתורו אחרי לבבכם ואחרי עיניכם" פשוט אצלנו שכך טוב לנו, אלא שבשעת מעשה בא היצר ומבלבל את האדם, ולכן מתפלל האדם "ועתה ירום ראשי על אויבי סביבותי" שיזכה להגביר כח דעתו ושכלו על פתויי היצר.

"אל תתנני בנפש צרי" - "מתחנן אני לפניך ה' "אל תשלט בנו יצר הרע" שלא ישלוט בנו ובכל אשר לנו להוליכנו אל מחנהו ח"ו. "כי קמו בי עידי שקר - "כמה נורא הוא האויב הזה, שנכנס אל חדרי שכלנו ומעמיד עידי שקר האומרים לרע טוב ולטוב רע"!

וגם רצו חז"ל שכשיתבונן ויראה כי נתון הוא במלחמה גדולה, שלא יתייאש ויאמר מה לי תקות רמה ותולעה ולמלחמה גדולה כזו, איך אוכל לנצח כל חיילות היצר מלאכי חבלה אשר באים עם מצודים וחרמים גדולים. כי ע"י תפילה וחיזוק בכחו של ה' ית' אכן בכחנו לנצח. נתחזק נא, ונקום בשאגת קודש על האויב הזה - "ה' אורי וישעי ממי אירא, ה' מעוז חיי ממי אפחד."

ולכן, הדבר הראשון שעלינו לעשות הוא "עורו ישינים משנתכם". אחד מתכססיי היצר הוא להרדים את האדם. חכמינו ז"ל המשילו את היצר הרע לכלב שרצה לגנוב מארמון, שכל עוד היה הכלב תוהה על פתח הארמון עמד בעל הבית על משמרתו. מה עשה הכלב? עושה עצמו כמתנמנם, והחל בעל הבית גם הוא מתנמנם, ואז הסתער הכלב לתוך הארמון וגנב ככל אות נפשו. וז"ל המדרש (בראשית רבה כב ו'): "לפתח חטאת רובץ, חטאת רובצת אין כתיב כאן, אלא חטאת רובץ, בתחלה הוא תש כנקבה אחר הוא מתגבר כזכר וכו'. א"ר תנחום בר מריון אית כלבין ברומי דידעין למשתדלא, אזיל ויתיב קמי פלטירא ועביד גרמיה מתנמנם ומרי פלטירא מתנמנם והוא שמוט עיגולא ארעא עד דהוויא מצמית לון הוא משתכר עיגולא ומהלך ביה".

כך הוא דרכו של הצר ואויב היצר הרע הזה! ב"ה שתקנו חז"ל את קול השופר בכל חודש אלול לעוררנו חודש אחד בשנה. ועתה, נתחיל את החודש הזה במלחמה בכל עוז, באומרנו מזמור "לדוד ה' אורי וישעי..." נתבונן נא בתפילתנו ותחינתנו שאנו מוציאים מפינו, שיש כאן מלחמה מסוכנת ורק בעורתו ית' נוכל לנצח. נתפלל אל ה' שיקוים בנו הכתוב "כי תצא למלחמה על אויבך וראית סוס ורכב...לא תירא מהם! כי ה' אלקיך עמך."

"ועתה ירום ראשי על אויבי" - הגברת הדעת

איך מנהלים מלחמה גורלית זו? גם זה כלול במזמור "לדוד ה' אורי", וכמו שהזכרנו לעיל: "ועתה ירום ראשי על אויבי סביבותי". אינך זקוק להשגות גבוהות ונעלות, כי אם להגביר את כח השכל, מה שכבר ידעת בודאות ברורה.

הנה כתב בעל 'מסילת ישרים' (פרק כד, בביאור יראת חטא): "מיני היראה הם שנים שהם שלשה. האחת קלה מאד להשיגה, אין דבר קל כמוהו, והשני קשה וכו'. יראת העונש כפשוטה שאדם יירא מעבור את פי ה' אלקיו מפני העונשים אשר לעבירות, אם לגוף ואם לנפש. והנה זאת קלה ודאי, כי כל אדם אוהב את עצמו ויירא לנפשו, ואין דבר שירחיק אותו מעשות דבר א' יותר מן היראה שלא תבואהו בו איזה רעה".

ובמבט ראשון יפלא, האם באמת כל כך קל הוא? ולמה א"כ רבו חללי היצר דרק מעטים זוכים לעולם הבא? אך כונתו לומר שההשגה לכשעצמה אכן קלה היא עד מאד, ומה שקשה הוא לחיות על פיה, לשומה על לב. כי זה כחו של היצר, שניתנו בידו בני האדם לעשות בתוכם מחיצת ברזל בין ידיעותיהם והשגותיהם ובין הנהגת החיים. ידוע מה שאמר רבי יוחנן בן זכאי לתלמידיו בעת פטירתו (ברכות כח ע"ב): "אמרו לו: רבינו ברכנו, אמר להם: יהי רצון

שתהא מורא שמים עליכם כמורא בשר ודם. אמרו לו תלמידיו: עד כאן? אמר להם: ולואי, תדעו כשאדם עובר עבירה אומר שלא יראני אדם".

ופירש רש"י שם שכשעובר עבירה "בסתר ממורא הבריות, ויודע שהכל הוא גלוי להקב"ה ואינו מניח בכך". מה שחסר אינו הידיעה כלל וכלל, אלא שלמרות הידיעה אינו ירא. ולכן לא בירכם שיזכו לידיעה ברורה, להשגה עליונה, אלא שיזכו להגביר כח השכל ולהכניס יראה בלבבם.

וכל עבודת המוסר, כמו שנראה ממכתבו של הגר"י מסלנט ז"ל, הוא לדרבן את האדם לא לקחת את ידיעותיו הפשוטות הברורות ולהשימם על לב, "וידעת היום, והשבת אל לבבך", לעשותם חלק מחושיו והרגשותיו. וזה אכן לא קל כלל.

אבל נקודת תקוה חשובה מאוד יש כאן. באמת אין ליצר שום כח של ממש. אם רק ינהל האדם את עצמו לשמוע בקול שכלו, ולא להתפעל משאר רוב בני האדם הנשמעים לו, יוכל להרגיל את עצמו בנצחונות גדולות, ויתבונן בחלקלקות לשונו ויראה שאין כלום בדבריו (ראה המשך דברי החובות הלבבות שם). הג"ר שמחה זיסל מקלם זצ"ל התפעל מאד, כדרכו בקודש, כשמצא דברי מדרש בענין זה. מדברי המדרש משתמע שכל כחו של אברהם אבינו נבע והתחיל מזה שהתבונן ביצר הרע ולא התפעל ממנו. וזה לשון המדרש (בראשית רבה כב ו): "א"ר אבא, היצר הזה דומה ללסטים שפוף שהיה יושב בפרשת דרכים, כל מאן דעבר הוה אמר הב מה דעלך, עבר פקח אחד וראה שאין בו תוחלת לגזול לו כלום, התחיל מכתתו. כך כמה דורות אבד יצר הרע דור אנוש ודור הפלגה ודור המבול, כיון שנגמר אברהם אבינו וראה שאין בו תוחלת התחיל מכתתו, הה"ד (תהלים פט כד) וכתותי מפניך צריו ומשנאיו אגוף."

וידעו שעתה הוא הזמן להכנס בעבודה זו. כמה קל בשנות הנעורים לשנות הרגלים ולקבוע דרך בחיים, ביחס לשנות הבגרות. מתפללים אנו: "אל תשליכנו לעת זקנה". ועיין פירוש רש"י שם (תהלים עא ט) וז"ל: "לעת זקנה, אם זקנתי בחטאים כלומר שחטאתי הרבה". שנותם בישיבה הם השנים הכי מובחרים, הכי יקרים והכי חשובים להצלחה בחיים, וביכולת לפצול גדולות ונצורות!

מלחמת היצר רק תוך התחזקות בלימוד התורה

בני תורה, הנכנסים עתה לחודש אלול, יידעו כי ההתחזקות בלימוד הוא הנשק למלחמת היצר - "שבתי בית ה' כל ימי חיי" ...והוא הוא הדרך לתשובה שלמה. "השיבנו אבינו לתורתך, וקרבנו מלכנו לעבודתך, והחזירנו בתשובה שלמה לפניך". וכמובן שההתחזקות צריכה להיות פרוסה על כל סוגי הלימוד כאחד, בין לימוד הגמ' - בעיון ובהתמדה - ובין לימוד המוסר כדבעי, ואל יסתפק בן תורה בלימודינו כאן 'מוסר ברבים' בחודש אלול. וע"י זה יהיה נחשב 'ביאת כולו' לחודש אדיר זה.

זכינו בבית מדרש זה להתעוררות מיוחדת, שנכנסים לחודש אלול בכובד ראש, עם הכנה ראויה. אכן, במקומות אחרים גם להם חיזוקים אחרים. אצלם יש מעלה שנמצאים הם בין כותלי הישיבה כל ימי בין המצרים. ימי האבלות הם הכנה נפלאה לימי הדין. כל מועדי ישראל בתקופת השנה תכלית אחד להם: להתקרב לקב"ה, אלא שבבין המצרים זה נעשה ע"י ההתבוננות במדת הדין שפגעה

קשות בעמנו במשך שנות גלותינו הארוכה, ובאלול זה נעשה ע״י לימוד מוסר לחקור איך נוכל להשתפר מכאן ואילך.

הנה מתחילה המלחמה! מחר ישמע קול השופר, ונתפלל ונבטח בה׳ שילחם לנו - ״ה׳ אורי וישעי״. ...יתבונן כל בן תורה באיזה מגרעת אשר בו עומד הוא להתרכז בשנה זו, אם ענין שמירת הלימודים, או שמירת פיו מדיבורים אסורים ודברים בטלים, וכל אחד יודע נפש בהמתו מה עליו לתקן. העיקר הוא להיות שליט ברוחו. אמרו לי על בחור שרוצה רוצה באמת, אך אינו יכול, וחבל שאינו מחליט שהוא הוא השליט בעצמו ויהי מה. אם נבין שיש כאן מלחמה על הנפש נוכל להשתלט על עצמנו. ואם כי כל אחד אחראי לעצמו, מ״מ ישים לב להבין שבהתנהגותו משפיע על שאר בני האדם, ויכול הוא בנקל להיות ממזכי הרבים או ממחטיאי הרבים, ח״ו.

ונזכה להגיע שיקויים בנו ״והחזירנו בתשובה שלמה לפניך.״

מרן הגאון הצדיק רבי יצחק אייזיק אזבנד זצ"ל

ראש הישיבה דישיבה הגדולה והקדושה דטעלז

בעמח"ס לקח דעת

"כתבנו בספר החיים"

צריכים אנו להבין, למה אומרים בראש השנה "לשנה טובה תכתבו" ולא סתם "לטובה תכתבו", ויכלול יותר משנה אחת? ובשלמא מה שאומרים בשבת "שבת שלום" או ביו"ט "חג שמח" וכן "חודש טוב" או בכל יום "א גוטען טאג", ל"ק שמדברין על מה שנגד עיניו, אבל ביום הדין למה לפרט "שנה" דנשמע מכלל הן אתה שומע לאו?

עוד קשה למה קוראים "מלכיות" לסדר התפילה, והול"ל "עבדות" שהרי העבודה היא שנכנע לפניו, והוא בל"ה מלך?

וכן יש להעיר למה נאמר "כתבנו בספר החיים", דבשלמא כשמחדשים מה, צריכים ספרים כדי לכתוב בהם, אבל באלו שנשארים כקדם ולא מחדשים בהם מאומה א"צ להכתב דממילא הוא כן. וכמו מלכות דלמטה, כשמתקנת תקנות חדשות כותבים רק החדשים ולא הישנים, ובשלמא "זכרנו" ניחא דצריכים להזכיר אלו לחיים, אבל לכתוב "בספר" לכאורה אינו צריך.

וגם, למה הוצרך לסיים "זכרנו לחיים וכו' מלך וכו' למענך אלוקים חיים" בתיבת "חיים", ולא סגי ב"למענך אלוקים", ומובן כבר דקאי על חיים שהזכיר תחילה? מיהו בזה י"מ דקאי על "אלוקים" כלומר, אלוקים שהוא חיים, לאפוקי מאלהי העמים אלילים. אבל קמייתא עדיין קשה.

והביאור לכל זה הוא, דכשנברא העולם נברא בלי מיתה ובלי חטא, ואז לא הי' צורך ליום הדין, כי העולם הי' פשוט וטוב, כמו לעתיד לבא בלי יצה"ר, וכמו שלא הי' צורך לשופטים למטה כי כל איש הישר בעיני ה' יעשה. אך מאחר שנתקלקל העולם ע"י החטא בו ביום ששי שנברא האדם, נשאר יום זה ליום דין לעולם ועד, ונתקיימה האזהרה "כי ביום אכלך ממנו מות תמות" (בראשית ב' י"ז), לא רק כפי הדרש דאלף שנים בעיניך כיום אתמול (ונתן אדה"ר ע' שנים לדוד המלך ע"ה), אלא גם לפי הפשט, בב' אופנים: א' דמצד החטא הי' ראוי שימות כפי שניתן בבריאה החוק, אך עשה תשובה והקב"ה חתר לו חתירה מתחת כסא הכבוד וקבלוהו, כי הבריאה הוא דבר ה', והיתה בריאה כזו של ביום אכלך ממנו מות תמות, אך התשובה שיוצאת מגדרי הבריאה פעלה. אמנם לפמש"נ בסמוך יתבאר זה באופן אחר.

בנוהג שבעולם כשממנים אדם למשרה חשובה עושים עמו חוזה בתחילה לשנה אחת ואח"כ כשרואים דאתמחי גברא מאריכים לו לכמה שנים כמו לז' או ח' ויותר, ואחר זמן רב כשרואים שמצליח הרבה ומצטיין בעבודתו נותנים לו חוזה לפעמים לכל ימי חייו. (ובאירופא כשהי' ממנים ובוחרים ברב הקהל הי' בכתב לו ולזרעו ולזרע זרעו עד עולם אם יהיו ראויים כי ידעו שהוא גדול בתורה ויר"ש ובעל מדריגה, ופה שמדריגת הנבחר והבוחרים

אינה קבועה ויציבה כל כך יראים מזה.) וכמו כן אם הבריאה היתה במדריגה גבוה של קודם החטא, היתה אפשריות לחתום "קונטרקט עולמי". אך מאחר שנתקלקל ע"י החטא, והלאה מתחלת הבריאה שיורדים הנבראים מטה מטה, שוב אינם במדריגה לבטוח עליהם, ולא נותנים קונטרקט יותר משנה, ובכל שנה צריכים לחדשו. והיינו ספר החיים, כי לכל נברא צריכים מחדש לכתוב לו קונטרקט זה, והוא ספר החיים.

וזהו מה שמברכים "לשנה טובה", כי ליותר מזה הרי הוא תפילת שוא, כי אין כותבים הקונטרקט ליותר.

וגם מתפרש לפי זה ענין "מלכיות" בסדר התפילה, כי אין מלך בלא עם, ומלך אינו כנשיא שנבחר רק לזמן, ומהות מלכות היינו לתמיד. ומבקשים בזה שיאריך ויתן חיים נצחיים לכולם כדי שתתקיים מלכותו בעולם התחתון, ובלא זה ליכא מלכות. והיינו "אמרו לפני מלכיות כדי שתמליכוני עליכם" (ראש השנה ט"ז ע"א), כדי שתעבדוני לא נאמר אלא כדי שתמליכוני, שעי"ז שתתפללו שאמליך עליכם, אשמע בקולכם ואתן חיות לכל העולם, בלי הגבלה לשנה, אלא לנצח כי יתבטל היצה"ר ולא נצטרך לא לדין ולא ליום הדין.

וגם "אמרו לפני זכרונות ושופרות" (שם), לפי הסדר, מלכיות זכרונות ושופר, היינו כמו ה' מֶלֶךְ מָלָךְ ימלוך, כלומר הוה הי' ויהי', כי המלכיות היא עתה להמשיך הבריאה, ואח"כ זכרונות מלפני החטא, ושופרות על העתיד שיהי' למלך על כל הארץ שתתבטל הרע וישאר רק הטוב.

וניחא עפ"ז מה דאמר "זכרנו לחיים... וכתבנו בספר החיים" - ד' פעמים חיים — כי תחילה מבקשים שלא יענש. מיהו עדיין אין זו הוכחה לחיות, כי יש מדירגה שניצל מעונש מיתה ובכל זאת לא ניתן לו חיים, והיינו הבינונים שתלויים ועומדים, כלומר שלא נגזר עליהם מיתה אבל גם לא נכתבו בספר החיים. וזהו מה שקרה לפעמים אדם ישן שלא קם בבוקר, שאין זה מגדר עונש מיתה, דהעונש הוא על ידי חלאים ויסורים, אבל זהו רק שלילת החיות שלא ניתן לו חיות. וממילא מתפרש הכי "זכרנו לחיים" כלומר, ולא למות, היינו רק שלילת העונש מיתה, "מלך חפץ בחיים", כלומר, יותר מזה מפרשים שאין כוונתינו רק בשלילת המות, אלא נתינת חיים כמו שאתה חפץ בחיים. "וכתבנו בספר החיים", היינו החיים בה"א הידיעה שידוע לנו בתורה "ראה נתתי לפניך את החיים ואת הטוב" (דברים ל' ט"ו) דהכוונה לחיים רוחניים. כי רשעים קרויים מתים על שם פעולתם שהן מתות שאין בהן נשמה וכח החיות, משא"כ צדיקים קרויים חיים גם במיתתם על שם הפעולות שעשו שהן המצות ומעשים טובים, שכח המצוה שבהן נותן בהם נשמה וחיות.

(והיינו גם מה שנשנה "ראה נתתי לפניך היום את החיים ואת הטוב", ואח"כ נשנית (ל' י"ט) "החיים והמות נתתי לפניך הברכה והקללה ובחרת בחיים", כמו בה"א הידיעה, החיים המפורסמים דהיינו החיים הרוחניים שהבאתי מלמעלה ושמתים לפניך, והוא קדמך. משא"כ בפעם ראשונה דבר על החיים הגשמים שאתה קדמת אותו, לכן תחילה אמר שם נתתי לפניך את החיים.)

והמדריגה הרביעית היא "למענך אלוקים חיים", כלומר, חיים שמתקיימים על פי מדת הדין כפי מחשבתו של הקב"ה בתחילת הבריאה, שלא יהא צורך לשיתוף רחמים כי

יעשו רק הטוב והישר, והיינו לשוב למדריגה של אדם קודם החטא.

ולפי"ז מתבאר "כי ביום אכלך ממנו מות תמות" כפשוטו, ביום של כ"ד שעות, מפני שקודם האכילה לא הי' ענין של דין ויום הדין של ר"ה, והחיים היו נצחיים בלי דין ומות, אבל אם תאכל, יקבע עליך דין, וגם יום הדין לדורות, וכל החיות יהי' רק מתחדשים בכל שנה ושנה ויגמור חיותך. ואם תחי' לשנה שני' היינו רק מכח החיים החדשים. אבל החיים הראשונים יגמרו, והיינו מיתה על חיים הראשונים שהיו נצחיים ונגמרו ויצטרכו להתחדש כמתנה חדשה בספר החיים.

"והעלהו שם לעולה"

כתוב בתורה"ק (במדבר כ"ח ד') "את הכבש אחד תעשה בבוקר ואת הכבש השני תעשה בין הערבים". ואיתא במדרש (ילקוט שמעוני רמז צ"ט): אותו היום שהעלה אברהם אבינו את יצחק בנו על גבי המזבח תיקן להם הקב"ה שני כבשים אחד בשחרית ואחד בין הערבים, שנאמר את הכבש אחד וגו'."

ומצאתי כתוב (בקול התורה חוברת ל"א עמ' ע"ב מר' ש. פאללאך) בשם בעל החשב סופר (להרב א.ש.ב. סופר זצ"ל רב בק"ק פרשבורג) שביאר את דברי הילקוט, שמעשה העקידה מתבלט האחדות ושיווי הדעות בין אב לבנו, "וילכו שניהם יחדיו" (בראשית כ"ב ו'), כאיש אחד ובלב אחד הלכו יחד לקיים את מצות ה'. הנה קרבן תמיד מרמז על אחדות ישראל, כי כל הצבור הם שותפים בתמיד וק"ז זי"ע ב"שערי שמחה", מפרש הקרא (במדבר כ"ח ו') "עלת תמיד העשיה בהר סיני", כי ע"י שישראל היו בלב אחד ובדעה אחת במעמד הר סיני, כדכתיב (שמות י"ט ב') "ויחן שם ישראל נגד ההר וכו' "זכו לקרבן תמיד המאחד את כל העם הישראלי בקרבן אחד, וזה "בהר סיני", שנעשה וניתקן התמיד ע"י האחדות שנתבלט בהר סיני, ומשו"ה כתיב את הכבש האחד "תעשה" בבקר בלשון יחיד, שכל הצבור מאוחד בדבר זה.

ועל פי זה פירש בכוונת המדרש, אותו היום שהעלה אברהם אבינו את יצחק בנו על גבי המזבח תיקן להם הקב"ה שני כבשים, יען שההתמסרות של אב ובן מתבלט באופן נעלה ונשגב כזה שבאחדות ובאהבה עשו את רצון אביהם שבשמים, ע"כ תיקן הקב"ה שני תמידים המיוסדים על אחדות ישראל כאמור עד כאן דבריו הקדושים.

והנה מה שראיתי שטרח לבאר ע"פ רמז, ולכאורה יש לפרש דפשוטו שזה נגד ב' העלאות שהעלה אברהם, את יצחק ואת האיל. ומהי המעלה הב' להעלות האיל, וכי נגד כל קרבנות האבות - ואברהם בכלל - נתקן קרבן קבוע לדורות, אפנע דבר גדול הי' בזה.

הנה לכאורה איך חזר ה' מדבריו שאמר "והעלהו שם לעולה" (בראשית כ"ב ב') ואע"פ שלא אמר שחטהו, הלא במוסף שבת ג"כ לא נאמר כי אם ב' כבשים לעולה והיינו קרבן עולה אף שלא נזכר עש' והקרבה כיון דשם עולה מורה על קרבן עולה, דאל"ה אין תועלת בהעלאה. והרי בנינוה מקשה הש"ס איך חזר,

הא "אני ה' לא שניתי", ומפרש הש"ס דנתקיימו שפיר דברי ה' כיון שלא אמר נינוה נחרבת, אלא נהפכת ונתהפכה מרע לטוב, אבל בעקדה איך נתקיימו דברי ה' ומה"ט נתעקש אברהם קצת בשמעו "אל תשלח ידך אל הנער" (כ"ב י"ב), עד שהוצרך המלאך להוסיף "ואל תעש לו מאומה". ובזה רמז לו לאברהם שמתוך דבקותו בה' וחביבתו לקיים דבריו, נזכר מיד ולא עמד להתבונן ולדקדק היטיב בלשון ה' שיש שם תיבה אחת מיוחדת במש"א לו ה' "לך לך אל ארץ המורי' והעלהו 'שם' לעולה אל אחד ההרים אשר אומר אליך", והנה תיבה "שם" אין שם מקומה ומיותרת לגמרי דהל"ל "והעלהו לעולה על אחד ההרים אשר אומר אליך".

אלא שבזה מונח הסוד ד"שם לעולה" מוכן משׁשת ימי בראשית - איל, ואינו מחובר ל"והעלהו" דקאי על יצחק, דליצחק סגי העלאה לקיים הנסיון, ושם מוכן משהו לעולה. וזה נרמז ג"כ בל' "אל תעש 'לו' מאומה" - כי אם לאיל תעשה עולה.

ובזה נתנסה אברהם שנית, דלכאורה אחר שנפטר מלשחוט את יצחק אהובו, הי' לו להזדרז לשוב לבשר את שרה שהרי מובן הי' לו על מזימת השטן שנתחזק לעכבו, ובטח הלך גם לשרה לזרזה שתלך לעכב את אברהם מלהקריב את יצחק בנה יחידה. וא"כ בטח מצטערת הרבה ומצוה רבה להחיות את נפשה בבשורה טובה שכל אדם מזדרז וכש"כ אברהם אבינו בעל החסד והרחמים, וזריזות זו כמו הראשונה, היתה לו למונעו מלהתעמק בדבר ה' ולחפש הסבר בכל תיבה ותיבה, שיוכל לעשותו אח"כ. אמנם לא כן אברהם, אלא עומד ומתבונן עד שעומד על כוונת ה' דיש "שם" - משהו אחר לעולה, והטעם "כי אני ה' לא שניתי". ולפיכך מיד "וישא אברהם את עיניו" ומחפש, ומוצא איל נאחז בסבך והולך ומפרידו, וזה נסיון שני. ולפיכך מקריבים שני כבשים נגד ב' העלאות, אחת העלאת יצחק וב' על העלאת האיל, דלולא מדריגת אברהם באהבת ה' לא הי' מגיע לידי זה.

ומובן לפי"ז מה שבקריאה ראשונה של המלאך לעכבו מלשחוט את יצחק, לא הובטח שום שכר ורק אחר הקרבת האיל קראו שנית והובטח לשכר גדול.

ומובן ג"כ מה שיש מקשים, איך לא חשש אברהם שמא יש לו בעלים לאיל, וגזל הוא, אלא שהבין הקב"ה להקריבו שמוכן לזה מקודם.

ומובן השתא מה שנתקן ב' תמידים א' נגד העאלת יצחק והשני נגד האיל שהי' זה דבר גדול מצד אברהם, שהי' בכח לעמוד ולהתבונן אם יש עוד איזה דבר לקיים כל תיבה ותיבה מציווי השם, ולא להעשות בהול להזדרז לשוב לבשר את שרה, על הבן יחידי יצחק. דביקת בה' נפלאה.

יה"ר שנזכה כולנו ל"עקדת יצחק לזרעו היום ברחמים תזכר".

כמהר"ר החכם רבי אלעזר אבוחצירא זצוקללה"ה
בעהמח"ס דברי אלעזר - באר שבע

יסוד התשובה והשבת בריה חדשה

יסוד התשובה הוא, שהאדם הופך להיות בריה חדשה כמאמר רבנו הרמב"ם בהלכות תשובה (פ"ב ה"ד), "מדרכי התשובה להיות השב וכו' ומתרחק הרבה מן הדבר שחטא בו ומשנה שמו, כלומר אני אחר ואיני אותו האיש שעשה אותן המעשים".

וכן מצינו בגמ' ברכות (דף י ע"א) במעשה דחזקיהו המלך שחלה ובא אליו ישעיהו הנביא ואמר לו נגזר עליך מיתה, משום שלא עסקת בפריה ורביה, וענה לו חזקיה המלך משום שראה ברוח הקודש שעתיד לצאת ממנו בן רשע והוא מנשה המלך וע"כ לא נשא אישה, א"ל ישעיהו אינך צריך להתעסק בסתרים של הקב"ה ומה שאתה מצווה אתה צריך לעשות. ויש להקשות והרי כמו שראה חזקיהו ברוח הקודש שעתיד לצאת ממנו בן רשע, היה לו לראות גם שיחזור בתשובה. אלא מוכח מכאן כמו שביארנו שבעל תשובה נהיה בריה חדשה, ולכן את זה לא יכל לראות שהרי זה אדם אחר.

ויש עוד להביא ראיה לזאת מהא דקי"ל בדין שבע ברכות דבעינן כל יום 'פנים חדשות', אולם התוס' בכתובות (ז ע"ב ד"ה והוא) כתבו בשם המדרש שבשבת לא בעינן פנים חדשות, כיון שהשבת עצמה היא פנים חדשות, ולכן היא גם עושה את האדם פנים חדשות.

וצריך להבין, איך השבת משפיעה על האדם להופכו לפנים חדשות?

ולפי דברינו ניחא, דהרי נודע דיסוד השבת הוא כענין התשובה (וכמאמר רז"ל שבת קיח ע"ב, כל השמור שבת כהלכתו וכו' מוחלין לו", וראה החיד"א בס' דבש לפי מערכת הש' אות ד) שאדם הופך להיות מציאות אחרת, והופך לאדם קדוש.

וכן מצינו ברז"ל (בראשית רבה כב יג) "בשעה שפגש אדם הראשון לקין ושאלו מה נעשה בדינו. ענה לו שעשה תשובה ונתכפר לו. מיד חזר אף הוא בתשובה ופתח ואמר מזמור שיר ליום השבת", ולכאורה מה שייך שבת לתשובה שפתח ואמר מזמור שיר ליום השבת, אלא מכאן אנו רואים את היסוד ששבת ותשובה ענין אחד הוא, הפיכת האדם לבריה חדשה שבשבת יש נשמה יתרה וכשאדם חוזר בתשובה זה בריה חדשה, ולכן אתי שפיר דברי המדרש דבחינת שבת הוא 'פנים חדשות באו לכאן'.

ובזה נסביר מה שקוראים לשבת זו 'שבת תשובה' (לבוש ס' תר"ג ס"א) שהתשובה היא כמו בחינת שבת, שבשניהם האדם נהיה בריה חדשה.

עיקר התשובה - וידוי

ומהות התשובה היא שהאדם מתחרט על העבר, ומקבל על העתיד, ומתוודה על חטאיו. (וכדברי הרמב"ם בהלכות תשובה פ"ב ה"ב), ומובא בשם הגר"א - על ענין התשובה ביום כיפור, דהמון העם נוטים להניח העיקר ונוהגים ביום כיפור כדוגמת 'ביעור חמץ' בערב פסח, שהרי מדאורייתא אדם מבטל את החמץ בליבו ובכך סגי (פסחים ד ע"ב). אולם רבנן תקנו עוד דרכים לבער את החמץ כגון: ע"י שריפה, מכירה לגוי. ואנשים מהדרים בשריפת חמץ ומוכרים את

החמץ, ואילו את הביטול בלב שהוא מדאורייתא לא עושים, וכמו"כ ביום כיפור מתעסקים בדברים הנלווים לתשובה, כגון מקבלים מלקות, עומדים כל התפילה, צמים, עושים תענית דיבור, ואילו את העיקר שהוא הוידוי שוכחים, ואפילו אם האדם יבכה כל היום ולא יתוודה כאילו לא עבר עליו כיפור. וע"כ צריך להיזהר בזה שאדם יתוודה על כל חטאיו, על כל חטא שזוכר יתוודה עליו, ויאמר כך וכך עשיתי ואני מתחרט על כך.

ויש להבין מהי מעלת יום הכיפורים על כל ימי השנה שהרי תשובה אפשר לעשות כל השנה, אלא שבכל השנה תשובה מועילה על חטאים שהתוודה עליהם, ומה ששכח אינו מועיל לו, אבל ביום הכיפורים אם עשה תשובה כראוי מועיל לו אף לעבירות ששכח מהם, וזאת רק בתנאי שעל כל מה שזוכר מתוודה.

מתנאי הכפרה עד שירצה את חברו

מביא הרב חידא זי"ע (בברכי יוסף או"ח סימן תר"ו בשם יש מי שכתב) דמה שאמרו חז"ל (יומא פה ע"ב) שאין יום הכיפורים מכפר על עבירות שבין אדם לחברו אא"כ ריצה את חברו - הכוונה היא שאם לא עשה כך אז גם על עבירות שבינו לבין קונו אינו מתכפר לו. וצריך כל אחד לילך אצל מי שפגע בו ולבקש ממנו סליחה, ויש ענין שילך בעצמו לנפגע, כמו שמצינו בגמרא ביומא (דף פז ע"א) בההוא עובדא דרב שפגע בו אותו קצב, ובערב יום הכיפורים הלך רב והסתובב בשוק אצל אותו קצב, וזאת כדי שיבוא בדעתו של הקצב לבקש מחילה מרב, ולא היה סגי בכך שרב היה ממקומו מוחל לו אלא הטריח את עצמו כדי שהקצב יבקש ממנו מחילה, כיון שהפוגע צריך לבקש מהנפגע מחילה.

וכן בימים אלו עלינו לבקש סליחה מהקב"ה שבימים אלו הוא מסתובב בינינו כמש"כ בישעיה (נה, ו) "דרשו ה' בהמצאו קראוהו בהיותו קרוב". ובזה יובן מדוע אין דין עליה לרגל בראש השנה וביום הכיפורים כמו בשלשת הרגלים, וזאת משום שבימים אלו הקב"ה מסתובב בינינו ולא צריך לעלות אליו, אלא הוא נמצא איתנו!

וצריך להיזהר בענין זה שאדם ירצה את חברו שפגע בו, והמון העם טועים בזה ומבקשים סליחה רק מאוהביהם וקרוביהם, אבל ממי שבאמת פגעו בו לא מבקשים סליחה. ואדם שגזל מכמה אנשים, ודיבר לשון הרע ולא זוכר ממי גזל ועל מי דיבר.

כתב בספר חובת הלבבות (שער תשובה פרק י) ע"ז שתקנתו היא שאם שב בתשובה אמיתית הקב"ה מגלגל בליבם של אלו שפגע בהם שימחלו לו בלב שלם.

בינוניים תלויין ועומדין - דרגת הכלל

מובא בגמ' בראש השנה (דף טז ע"ב) אמר רבי כרוספדאי אמר רבי יוחנן שלשה ספרים נפתחין בראש השנה אחד של רשעים גמורין ואחד של צדיקים גמורין ואחד של בינוניים, צדיקים גמורין נכתבין ונחתמין לאלתר לחיים, רשעים גמורין נכתבין ונחתמין לאלתר למיתה, בינוניים תלויין ועומדין מראש השנה ועד יום הכפורים, זכו נכתבין לחיים, לא זכו נכתבין למיתה.

ויש תמיהה גדולה על דברי הגמ', כיצד יתכן שאדם יעשה בדיוק חצי מצוות וחצי עבירות, וגם אם נאמר ששייך הרי זה מיעוטא דמיעוטא וא"כ נמצא שיום הכיפורים מיועד רק למיעוט זה.

אלא הביאור הוא, שצדיקים גמורים הם שעושים מצוות ומעשים טובים והכל לשם שמים באמת, ואין בנמצא כאלו שהרי 'אין צדיק בארץ אשר יעשה טוב ולא יחטא'. ורשעים גמורים גם אין בנמצא במעט, שהרי כולם יצרם תוקפם ולתיאבון הם עושים ולא להכעיס. וע"כ כולנו במדרגת 'בינוניים' והכוונה 'בינוניים' הם באיכות ולא בכמות המצוות והעבירות. ועל כן צריכים להיזהר בימים האלו של עשי"ת שכולם נמצאים בסכנת מוות חלילה שהרי כולנו בינוניים, וצריכים לנצל ימים אלו לבקש סליחה מהקב"ה.

וכן מצינו על חומרת הימים הללו, שכתוב בהלכה (ברכות נח ע"ב, ונפסק בשו"ע או"ח רכה סי' א) שמי שלא ראה את חברו י"ב חודש מברך עליו "ברוך מחיה המתים" וביאר המהרש"א (שם) שהטעם הוא מכיון שעבר עליו ראש השנה ויום הכיפורים ועדיין חי, אם כן ניצל ממוות. וכן אמרו חז"ל (ר"ה לב ע"ב) שלא אומרים הלל בראש השנה משום שספרי חיים ומתים נפתחים, ואדם שעומד לפני גזר דין על חייו אין זה נאה שיאמר הלל.

על כן צריך להיזהר בימים אלו לשוב בתשובה שלימה וקודם שמגיעים הצרות על האדם, ואמרו חז"ל בגמרא בשבת (דף לב ע"א) לעולם יבקש אדם רחמים שלא יחלה שאם חלה צריך הרבה זכויות על מנת להינצל.

מעלת תפילת נעילה - לרצות על חילול ה'

הרמב"ם בהלכות תשובה (פ"א ה"ד) מביא ענין ארבעה חילוקי כפרה והם מצוות עשה, מצוות לא תעשה, חייבי כריתות ומיתות בית דין, חילול השם.

והנה במצוות עשה אם שב בתשובה מתכפר לו מיד, ובמצוות לא תעשה תשובה תולה ויום הכיפורים מכפר, חייבי כריתות ומיתות בית דין תשובה ויום הכיפורים תולה ויסורין ממרקין, וחילול ה' אין לו כפרה עד המיתה.

וכתב בספר משך חכמה על התורה (פרשת וילך, ד"ה בהפטרה) כי באמת ענין חילול ה' שבא מן העבירה, קשה כפליים יותר מן העבירה עצמה והתקנה לזה היא דהנה מלכותא דרקיעא כעין מלכותא דארעא, ובדינו של מלך בשר ודם יושבים המלך והשופטים בדין וכל אחד מצדד זה לזכות וזה לחובה, אבל כשמדובר בעבירה שהיא פגיעה בכבוד המלך כולם מצדדים לחובה כי מי יוכל למחול על כבוד המלך. וכן בדינו של מלך מלכי המלכים הקב"ה בעבירה שהיא פגיעה בכבודו של הקב"ה, דהיינו חילול ה' כולם מחייבים, כי מי יוכל למחול על כבוד ה' וכל הפמליא של מעלה פוסקים דינו למיתה בלעדי המלך עצמו, וזה ע"י בכיות ותחנונים והוא בשעת הנעילה, שבחיתום הקב"ה יושב לבדו ורק בעת החתימה שהקב"ה דן יחיד אז היא שעת רצון שהקב"ה יסלח ברוב טובו אחרי גודל הבכי והחרטה כי אם הוא ימחל על כבודו מי יאמר אליו.

לכן בנעילה סידרו הפסוקים (יחזקאל יח, לא-לג) "למה תמותו וכו' כי לא אחפוץ במות המת ...והשיבו וחיו" וכיוצא בזה, כי הכל על עוון חלול השם יתברך. ורק בנעילה מוזכרים הפסוקים הללו משום שכל העניין בנעילה הוא על עוון חילול ה'.

אל דמעתי אל תחרש

ומצינו שמעלת הבכי והדמעות גדולה עד מאוד. כתוב אצל ישמעאל (בראשית כא, יז) "וישמע אלוקים את קול הנער" ולכאורה איזה תפילה התפלל ישמעאל והרי קטן היה, אלא הכוונה שה' שמע את בכיו, וכן מצינו במדרש

ששמע ה׳ לרחל בגלל בכייתה יותר מתפילתם של האבות הקדושים, שכתוב (ירמיהו לא, יד) ״רחל מבכה על בניה״. ועד כדי כך בכייתה היתה גדולה שהיתה ׳מבכה׳ דהיינו שהייתה גורמת לאחרים לבכות ולכן שמע תפילתה יותר.

ועוד מצינו בטעם למה תוקעים בר״ה מאה ואחת קולות אע״פ שמדאורייתא סגי בשלושים קולות, שכתב הערוך שהטעם הוא משום שהם כנגד מאה ואחת יבבות שיבבה אם סיסרא על שאחר לשוב מהמלחמה ובשביל בכיה של רשעה זו תיקנו להוסיף שבעים ואחת קולות לבטל קטרוג זה.

ועוד רואים במעלת הבכי שכתוב בזוהר הקדוש שכל הבוכה בשעת קריאת מיתת בני אהרון מובטח לו שלא ימותו בניו בחייו, וע״כ צריכים להתפלל ולהתוודות בבכיות גדולות והבכי צריך להיות אמיתי ומהלב, עם חרטה עמוקה ולא בכי שנובע מהתרגשות גרידא.

וזהו שכתוב במגילת איכה (פ״א ב) ״ודמעתה על לחיה״ - שהדמעות נשארו על לחיה, שזה לא היה דמעות אמיתיות, ולכן נשארו על לחיה ולא עלה לשמיים.

וכן מצינו בגמרא בכתובות (דף סב ע״ב) בההיא עובדא דרבי רחומי שכל השנה היה לומד ובערב יום הכיפורים היה מגיע לביתו, ושנה אחת שקע בלימודו ושכח מלבוא ואשתו היתה מצפה שיגיע והוזילה דמעה ונפל הגג מתחתיו ומת.

ודבר הלמד מענינו מכאן, שאסור לזלזל בכבוד האישה שגם נשים צדקניות חשוב להם כל העניינים האלו, וכמו שמצינו (ירושלמי שבת פו ה״א) על רחל אשת רבי עקיבא שקנה לה תכשיט ירושלים של זהב וראתה אותו אשת רבן גמליאל וביקשה גם כן מבעלה שיקנה לה, וא״כ רחל ענדה את התכשיט דאל״כ איך ראתה אותה אשת רבן גמליאל, ואם נשים צדקניות אלו היה חשוב להם החיצונית הזאת כ״ש שעלינו להיזהר בכבודה של האישה.

דרשו ה׳ בהמצאו - חסד ה׳ עלינו

בימים אלו צריכים להתבונן דהקב״ה מתהלך בינינו ונותן לנו הזדמנות לחזור בתשובה וזהו חסד שהקב״ה עשה איתנו.

והנה כתוב במדרש (בראשית רבה פרשה סה סי׳ י) דיצחק היה סומא בשתי עיניו וזאת משום שבשעת העקידה ירדו דמעותיהם של המלאכים לתוך עיניו ובזה נסמה. וצריך להבין מדוע גילגל הקב״ה כך? ועוד מובא בגמרא בשבת (דף פט ע״ב) שכשבא הקב״ה לאברהם אבינו ויעקב אבינו ואמר להם בניכם חטאו, אמרו לו ימחו על קדושת שמך, אולם שכשבא ליצחק אבינו אמר לו וכי בני הם ולא בניך וכו׳? וזו היא תמיהא גדולה שהרי יצחק מידתו היא פחד, ודוקא הוא לימד זכות על עם ישראל ואדרבה היה על אברהם לסנגר שמידתו היא חסד.

אלא חדא מיתרצא בחברתה דמה שהתגלגל שיצחק נהיה סומא בשתי עיניו הוא כדי שלא יראה ברעתו של עשו ויאמין לו לכל צדקותיו, ויכנס בו מידת הרחמים וכל זה בשביל שבסופו של דבר יבקש רחמים על עם ישראל. רואים בזה חסד ה׳ שגילגל הדברים כך.

הבא להיטהר - אפי׳ כחודה של מחט

מובא בחז״ל (שה״ש ה, ב) פיתחו לי פתח כחודה של מחט ואני אפתח לכם פתח כפתחו של אולם. ולהמחיש מהו חודו של מחט

שמוטל עלינו לפתוח, איתא בגמרא במס׳ קידושין (דף מט ע״ב) המקדש את האישה ע״מ שאני צדיק אפילו רשע גמור מקודשת שמא הרהר תשובה בדעתו. והקשה הלחם משנה (על הרמב״ם הלכות אישות פ״ח ה״ה) א״כ למה המקדש בפני עדים פסולין מחמת רשע אינה מקודשת נחוש לקידושין מהאי טעמא שמא הרהרו תשובה בליבם? ותירץ שיש הבדל ביניהם שבמקדש אישה כיון שגילה דעתו במה שאמר ׳ע״מ שאני צדיק׳, לכן תולין שהרהר תשובה בליבו משא״כ בעדים פסולים שלא שמענו מהם גילוי דעת לתשובה.

רואים מכאן שבמה שאמר ע״מ שאני צדיק גמור די לו בכך, וזהו הפיתחו לי פתח כחודו של מחט, ואז הקב״ה פותח לו כפיתחו של אולם, כמו שכתוב הבא להיטהר מסייעין בעדו, וכן כתוב בתהלים (פרק פא פסוק יא) ״הרחב פיך ואמלאהו״. דהיינו שהאדם יתחיל ואז הקב״ה אומר ואמלאהו. וכן בעניין התפילה שמתפללים כל יום לבקש על צרכינו, אע״פ שהקב״ה יודע כל אחד מה הוא צריך מ״מ הקב״ה רוצה שנתחיל לבקש ואז ואמלאהו.

וכן מצינו בעניין המן שבכל יום ירד מן מהשמים, ולא ירד פעם אחת לכל הזמן, מפני שהקב״ה רוצה שהאדם יבקש שזה ההשתדלות מצידו, ואז הקב״ה יעזור לו.

חדשים לבקרים

שלמה המלך אומר (משלי כח, ט) ״מסיר אוזנו משמוע תורה גם תפילתו תועבה״, והקשר בין הדברים הוא דכשאדם שומע דברי תורה לא יאמר הדברים ידועים לי, שמעתי דברים אלו מכבר, דא״כ הקב״ה מתנהג עימו באותה מידה, וגם על תפילתו יאמר, אתמול ושלשום התפללת אותה תפילה ומה חידוש יש בתפילה זו, ולכן צריך להתבונן ולהשכיל תמיד דגם בדברים המוכרים והידועים צריך לשמוע ולהוסיף לקח ודעת, ויהיו בעיניו כחדשים.

יהי רצון שנזכה לחזור בתשובה שלמה לפני הקב״ה, ונזכה לכתיבה וחתימה טובה.

הרה״ג המקובל רב גמליאל הכהן רבינוביץ שליט״א
ראש ישיבת שער השמים, ירושלים עיה״ק

שמחת תורה - ״קשה עלי פרידתכם״

הנה זה עכשיו זכינו שעברו עלינו הימים טובים לחיים ולשלום בשמחה ובששון, ובירכנו בכניסתו של חג הסוכות ׳שהחיינו וקיימנו והגיענו לזמן הזה׳, בראש ובראשונה—מודים להשי״ת על אשר זכינו לחיים, כי בוודאי עצם החיים הוא דבר נפלא. ועתה כאשר הגיענו ליום טוב, אנו מוסיפים להודות על קבלת היום טוב, בשמחה וטוב לבב.

והנה יום ׳שמחת תורה׳ הוא יום שכל בני ישראל שמחים בו באופן נפלא כִידוע בכל חצרות הקודש שבכל פזורות ישראל. ויש לנו להתבונן מהו גודל השמחה ביום זה, שהלא בכל חג הסוכות היינו כולנו אצל השי״ת, וכל אחד הרגיש את הקדושה, וכאשר יוצאים מהיום טוב הרי שלכאורה חוזרים לגלות, שכל אחד חוזר לכרמו ולזיתו, איש על מחנהו ואיש על דגלו, ומה השמחה.

וקצת יותר בעומק, הלא התמיהה היא עצומה, כי לשמחה זו מה היא עושה, הרי למחרת חוזרים למקום השבי, והיה מן הראוי לישב ולבכות ביום האחרון. משל למה הדבר דומה? לבן מלך שנתפס בשבי, ונתנו לו יום אחד להיות עם אביו, וכי ביום זה ירקוד וישמח? אדרבה, יש לו לבכות כל היום לפני אביו שירחם עליו ולא יזדקק לחזור אל מקום שביו.

וביותר יתמה על המנהג שנהגו שבמוצאי יום טוב שלהם, עושים ׳הקפות שניות׳ ורוקדים ריקודים של שמחה עד אשמורת הבוקר.

אלא אפשר לומר שביום טוב היתה לנו האפשרות להיות אצל אבינו שבשמים, וביום טוב סוכות היינו תחת כנפי השכינה בצל הסוכה—צילא דמהימנותא, לאחר הימים הנוראים שהיינו אצל המלך, וביום האחרון הקב״ה כביכול אומר: קשה עלי פרידתכם (ראה רש״י ויקרא כג, לו ;במדבר כט, לו).

וההסבר בזה נראה כך. דעצם השמחה הגדולה שישנה בעת הפרידה, זהו סימן מובהק שבאמת אין אנו נכנסים מכאן לבור השבי. והוא על פי מאמרי מרן הבעש״ט זי״ע המתייחסים למאמר התורה בתוכחה (דברים לא, יז-יח): ׳ועזבתים והסתרתי פני מהם וגו, ואנכי הסתר אסתיר פני ביום ההוא׳.

ונביא כאן דבריו בכמה אנפין (נתקבצו כולם מ׳בעל שם טוב׳ עה״ת, פרשת וילך): כשהאדם אינו יודע שיש הסתרה, בוודאי אינו טוב, שסובר שהוא צדיק גמור ואינו שב בתשובה. אבל כשיודע שיש הסתרה ומרגיש בנפשו, אז הוא נכנע מלפני השי״ת ומבקש מלפניו. וזהו—׳ואנכי הסתר׳ פירוש: ההסתרה עצמה אני אסתיר, ולא ייוודע שהוא הסתרה.

כלומר, שהתוכחה היא מה שהאדם אינו משיג שישנה הסתרה, כי כשיש הסתרה—הוא מכניע עצמו לפני השי״ת, וכאמור.

ובדרך דומה הסביר עוד, שזהו ׳ואנכי הסתר אסתיר׳ היינו שההסתרה גופו אצלו בהסתר, ואינו מאמין שוודאי טוב גנוז בה. כי כשהוא על כל פנים מאמין באמונה שוודאי טוב גנוז

בה, הגם שאינו מבין הטוב, מכל מקום נמתק הדין ממנו.

ומרגלא היה בפומיה דמרן הבעש"ט זי"ע: מאד אני מפחד ונרתת, מזו ההסתרה הנקראת 'הסתר אסתיר' יותר מההסתרה גופה!

ולביאור הענין בעומקו, ראוי להקדים את התמיהה שעמד ותמה מרן הבעש"ט זי"ע, בגוף ענין ההסתרה איך ייתכן שהקב"ה יסתיר פניו מישראל חלילה, הרי זה כל חיותם. אך המשיל זאת: למלך שעשה כמה מחיצות של חומות, אש ונהרות באחיזת עינים וכך הסתתר מפני בניו. והנה מי שהיה חכם, נתן לב לדבר, שלא ייתכן כי אב רחמן לא ירצה להראות פניו לבניו, א"כ בהכרח אין זה כי אם 'אחיזת עינים' שהאב רוצה לנסות אם ישתדל הבן לבא אליו, ובאמת אין שום הסתרה. אך הסכל והטיפש ירא להתחיל לעבור המחיצות, או שעובר המים אבל חוזר מפני החומות ומפני האש. והנמשל מובן.

ולא עוד–מוסיף הבעש"ט–אלא שמי שמוסר נפשו ועובר בכל המחיצות, ודוחק עצמו עד שבא אל המלך, אז יבא למעלה יותר גדולה מקודם, וזהו שנאמר בפרשת ויגש (בראשית מו, ד): 'אנכי ארד עמך מצרימה ואנכי אעלך גם עלה וגו' היינו כשתתן לב ותבין שאפילו בירידה יש גם כן 'אנכי' היינו שההסתרה היא גם כן לטובתך, אז–'ואנכי אעלך גם עלה' היינו שתזכה למעלה יתירה, וזהו 'גם עלה'.

וזהו שנאמר (דברים לא, ו): 'כי ה' אלקיך הוא ההולך עמך לא ירפך ולא יעזבך', היינו שתמיד הן בירידה והן בעלייה–'לא ירפך ולא יעזבך' ותרגומו: לא ישבקינך ולא ירחקינך, היינו אפילו כשנסתתר לפעמים, מכל מקום לא להרחיק ממך הוא. והוא שמרמז כאן 'ואנכי הסתר' היינו שתתן לב להבין ש'אנכי' מצוי תמיד אפילו בבחינת 'הסתר אסתיר' - בכמה הסתרות.

ולסיום, מענין לענין עוד מאמר ממרן הבעש"ט זי"ע, על הפסוק (תהלים צב, י): 'כי הנה אויביך ה', כי הנה אויביך יאבדו, יתפרדו כל פועלי און'. דאם אדם מאמין דאף בעת צרה חס ושלום, שהוא בחינת 'אויב' יש שם גנוז בחינת ה, היינו רחמים וחסדים, אז בזה עצמו יהיה ש'אויביך יאבדו ויתפרדו כל פועלי און' דעל ידי אמונה שאין דבר רע יורד משמים, בוודאי יתהפך הדבר לטוב, ומתגלים החסדים נסתרים, שבתוך הדינים הנגלים.

מעתה נבא לסוד הפרידה של שמחת תורה. כי כאמור בפסוק של הסתרה טמון סוד הגילוי, שאם השי"ת אומר שהוא מסתיר עצמו סימן הדבר שהוא נמצא עמנו. שאם לא היה עמנו, הרי שלא היה מן הצורך להסתיר עצמו. אלא שבאמת הרי הוא נמצא עמנו ומשגיח עלינו תמיד, ומזה יקח האדם חיזוק עצום.

וכמו כן יש לומר, לגבי הפרידה במוצאי שמחת תורה, שהריקודים והשמחה בשמחת תורה מוכיחים שעוצם נשמות ישראל נמצאים בקביעות אצל אבינו המלך ואין כאן כלל פרידה, וכל הפרידה הוא רק לפנים, שנדמה שאין נמצאים לפני השי"ת, אבל באמת הרי אנו נמצאים כסדר לפני השי"ת, והוא המוליכנו תמיד. וכיון שגילוי זה מתגלה לנו בשמחת תורה, הרי זה מביא אותנו לידי השמחה הגדולה.

וזהו הזמן האמיתי, לו נתכוונו הצדיקים הק' באמרם שכל יום הוא בחינת ראש השנה יום הכיפורים ושמחת תורה, שבכל יום מאיר

האורות הללו - ׳כי אני ה׳ לא שניתי׳ - וכל החילוק הוא אצל אותם הרחוקים ואינם מרגישים, הם רואים חילוק בין אור השבת לאור שאר הימים, אבל באמת שאור ההתגלות שוה בכל יום, שתמיד יש גילוי האלקות, וכאמור את הסוד הזה גילינו בשמחת תורה, ומזה בא כח הריקוד ב׳שמחת תורה.׳

מסופר על אחד מתלמידי הבעש״ט זי״ע, שפעם אחת נכנס בנו ובכה לפניו. לשאלת אביו למה הוא בוכה, סיפר הבן, ששיחק עם חבריו במשחק המחבואים, והחביא עצמו ולא באו חבריו לחפשו, ולכן הוא בוכה. תיכף התחיל גם הצדיק לבכות ואמר: הרי רבונו של עולם, טומן עצמו מאתנו שהרי הוא ׳א-ל מסתתר׳ ואין איש המחפש אחריו!

וזהו הגילוי של שמיני עצרת שהשי״ת הוא א-ל מסתתר והוא נמצא עמנו תמיד, וזהו ענין השמחה של שמחת תורה שמתגלה האור שהשי״ת נמצא עמנו תמיד, והוא מציץ מן החרכים.

ובבחינה זו דומה היום לזמן שבית המקדש היה קיים, שאין הסתר פנים, ובלבד שיהיה לאדם האמונה שהשי״ת שורה עמנו כסדר, או אז יהיה עליו גילוי האלקות כמו שהיה בזמן הבית. וזה גם הענין מה שאמרו צדיקים, שהם כבר זכו לחלק ביאת המשיח שלהם, דהיינו שזכו לבא לגילוי האלקות שה׳ נמצא עמהם כסדר, כמו בזמן הבית שאז היתה ההנהגה בגלוי, ולא כהיום שהוא בהסתרה.

ויהי רצון שנזכה לביאת משיח צדקינו אמן.

הרב שלום פערל שליט"א

ר"ם בישיבת היכל התורה בירושלים
ומגיד מישרים בק"ק בית שמש - מאוצרותיו של המגיד

חודש תשרי הנקרא "ירח האיתנים"

חודש תשרי נקרא "ירח האיתנים" (מלכים א', ח' ב'), וביאר המצודות דוד, שזאת משום ש"בחודש תשרי, יש את המועדים היותר חזקים - 'איתן מלשון חוזק' במובן הרוחני, המיישרים את האדם אל השלמות הרוחנית", (בין לגבי קיום רצון ה' כראוי, ובין לגבי התנהגות עם מידות טובות.)

וזה יתבאר, בהקדם דברי הגמרא (תענית כ"ג), "אמר רבי יוחנן, כל ימיו של אותו צדיק' היינו, חוני המעגל - 'היה מצטער על מקרא זה, 'שיר המעלות' - לשון עילוי (רש"י) [והיינו שמדובר אודות התעלות עם ישראל במובן הרוחני והגשמי], בשוב ה' את שיבת ציון, היינו כחולמים - כחלום נדמה גלות בבל שהיה שבעים שנה (רש"י), אמר, מי איכא דניים שבעין שנין בחלמא - דאין חלום בלא שינה (מהרש"א), וא"כ תמה, האם יש אדם שישן שבעים שנה בשינה אחת (רש"י), ואע"ג ד'חולמים' נאמר בלשון רבים, וא"כ היה מקום לומר שמדובר על כמה שינות, מ"מ 'חולמים' משמע בלי הפסק, וגם גלות בבל שנאמר עליה 'היינו כחולמים', היתה של שבעים שנים רצופות, וא"כ על כרחך דשינה אחת היא (מהרש"א), יומא חד הוה אזל באורחא, חזייה לההוא גברא דהוה נטע חרובא, אמר ליה, האי עד כמה שנין טעין, אמר ליה עד שבעין שנין וכו', יתיב קא כריך ריפתא, אתא ליה שינתא, נים, אהדרא ליה משוניתא, איכסי מעינא, ונים שבעין שנין, כי קם חזייה לההוא גברא דהוה קא מלקט מינייהו וכו', אמר, שמע מינה דניימי שבעין שנין וכו'."

ולפי פשוטו, התקשה חוני המעגל רק לגבי זה שדימה הפסוק את גלות בבל לאדם שישן וחלם שבעים שנים רצופות, שהוא דבר שאינו שייך במציאות, וכלשונו 'מי איכא דניים שבעין שנין בחלמא', והרדימו הקב"ה שבעים שנים רצופות בתור תשובה על שאלתו, והכיר שנרדם כך, כיון שנרדם בשעת נטיעת החרוב וקם בשעת לקיטת פירותיו, והזמן בין זה לזה הוא שבעים שנים.

אבל המהרש"א (שם, ד"ה היינו כחולמים) מוסיף, שהתקשה גם לגבי זה שדימה הפסוק את שבעים שנות חיי האדם, אל חלום האורך שבעים שנים רצופות, שהרי הבין, שכוונת הפסוק 'בשוב ה' את שיבת ציון, היינו כחולמים' היא, ש"יש לדמות את עם ישראל השב מגלות בבל אחר גמר שבעים שנה, לאדם שגמר לחיות את שבעים שנותיו הנמשלות לחלום האורך שבעים שנים רצופות', ותמה 'מי איכא דניים שבעין שנין בחלמא', והיינו, הכיצד יש לדמות שבעים שנות חיי האדם, אל חלום שאין בו ממש, והשיב לו הקב"ה תשובה גם על תמיהה זו, ע"י שהראה לו את החרוב המניב את פירותיו רק אחר גמר שבעים שנה, ובכך, במשך שבעים השנים יש להחשיבו כדבר שאין בו ממש ותועלת, וכן יש לומר גם לגבי שבעים שנות חיי האדם, שכיון שאוכל את פירות מעשיו ושכרו רק אחר שנגמרים שבעים

שנותיו, יש להחשיב את שבעים שנותיו כחלום שאין בו ממש ותועלת.

וכלשונו, "והענין, שמדמה שבעים שנות הגלות כאילו אינן רק כחלום, וכה"ג מדמי שנות האדם שהן שבעים שנים, לחלום, וכמו שנאמר באיוב (כ' ח') 'כחלום יעוף', והיינו, דמפרש לקרא ד'היינו כחולמים' ,כלומר, שהיינו בגלות בבל כחולמים, כשנות אדם ע' שנים שאינן אלא כחלום יעוף, וע"ז הוה מצטער, שיהיה נחשב עולמו של אדם רק כחלום שאין בו ממש, ואמר, הוה אזיל באורחא, חזייה לההוא גברא דנטע חרובא וכו, 'דהיינו, שהראו לו, שכמו שהחרוב הזה כל ע' שנין לא נחשב לכלום, אבל נוטעין אותו לעשות פירות לאחר ע' שנין, כן האדם נברא בערב שבת כדי שיהיה טורח במעשיו עד ע' שנין, ואכילת פירותיו ושכרו הוא רק לאחר ע' שנין בעוה"ב הנמשל לשבת", וא"כ יש להחשיב את שבעים שנותיו כחלום שאין בו ממש ותועלת, כיון שאינו אוכל בהן את פירות מעשיו ושכרו.

ויש להוסיף, שיש להמשיל את שבעים שנות חיי האדם אל חלום המדומה, משום שנמשך בהן אחר חיי השקר המדומים, שהרי "האדם לא נברא אלא להתענג על ה' וליהנות מזיו שכינתו, שזהו התענוג האמיתי והעידון הגדול מכל העידונים שיכולים להימצא, ומקום העידון הזה באמת הוא העולם הבא, כי הוא הנברא בהכנה המצטרכת לדבר הזה, אך הדרך כדי להגיע אל מחוז חפצו זה, הוא זה העולם, והוא מה שאמרו חכמינו זכרונם לברכה, 'העולם הזה דומה לפרוזדור בפני העולם הבא, התקן עצמך בפרוזדור כדי שתיכנס לטרקלין'.

והאמצעים המגיעים את האדם לתכלית הזה, הם המצוות אשר צוונו עליהן הקל יתברך שמו, ומקום עשיית המצוות הוא רק העולם הזה, על כן הושם האדם בזה העולם בתחילה, כדי שעל ידי האמצעים האלה המזדמנים לו כאן, יוכל להגיע אל המקום אשר הוכן לו, שהוא העולם הבא, לרוות שם בטוב אשר קנה לו על ידי האמצעים האלה, והוא מה שאמרו חכמינו זכרונם לברכה, 'היום'-בעוה"ז 'לעשותם', 'ומחר'-בעוה"ב 'לקבל שכרם'" (מס"י ריש פרק א.)

אבל במקום שישתדל האדם בקיום רצון ה' כראוי, ובכך ייהפך מחומרי לרוחני ויזכה לחיי העוה"ב הרוחניים ותענוגיו האמיתיים, הוא נמשך אחר התענוגים החומריים המדומים, ומהם אל החטא החומרי, שמגבירים בו ביותר את חומריותו, וזה מונע ממנו ליהנות מתענוגיו הרוחניים של חיי העוה"ב.

ולכן, חמל ה' עליו, וקבע לו יום בתחילת השנה, שבו ידון אותו על כל מעשיו, שבכך יפחד ויתעורר משנתו וחלומו החומרי, וישתדל לקיים את רצון ה' כראוי, וייהפך מחומרי לרוחני ויזכה לחיי העוה"ב הרוחניים ותענוגיו האמיתיים. (וגם ב'ספר החינוך' [מצוה שי"א, ד"ה ומשרשי] מבאר את הקביעות של יום הדין של ראש השנה, בתור חסד אלוקי, "ומשרשי מצות המועד הזה'-של ראש השנה, 'שהיה מחסדי הקל על ברואיו לפקוד אותם ולראות מעשיהם יום אחד בכל שנה ושנה, כדי שלא יתרבו העוונות ויהיה מקום לכפרה, והוא רב חסד מטה כלפי חסד, וכיון שהם מועטים מעביר עליהן, ואם אולי יש בהם עוונות שצריכים מירוק, נפרע מהם מעט מעט, וכעין מה שאמרו חכמינו זכרונם לברכה', אוהבו, נפרע ממנו מעט מעט, 'ואם לא יפקדם עד זמן רב, יתרבו כל כך עד שיתחייב העולם כמעט כלייה חלילה. נמצא שהיום הנכבד הזה הוא

קיומו של עולם, ולכן ראוי לעשות אותו יום טוב, ושיהיה במניין מועדי השנה היקרים.")

וכן כתב הרמב"ם (פ"ג מהלכות תשובה ה"ד), לגבי מצות תקיעת שופר בראש השנה, "אע"פ שתקיעת שופר בראש השנה גזירת הכתוב, רמז יש בו, כלומר, עורו ישנים משנתכם ונרדמים הקיצו מתרדמתכם, וחיפשו במעשיכם, וחיזרו בתשובה, וזיכרו בוראכם, אלו השוכחים את האמת בהבלי הזמן, ושוגים כל שנתם בהבל וריק אשר לא יועיל ולא יציל, הביטו לנפשותיכם, והטיבו דרכיכם ומעלליכם, ויעזוב כל אחד מכם דרכו הרעה, ומחשבתו אשר לא טובה וכו'.

ומפני ענין זה, נהגו כל בית ישראל להרבות בצדקה ובמעשים טובים ולעסוק במצוות, מראש השנה ועד יום הכפורים, יתר מכל השנה וכו'.

ואחר שפחד והתעורר משנתו וחלומו החומרי בראש השנה ושב אל ה' מיראה, והתחיל להשתדל ביותר לקיים את רצונו כראוי, אינו יכול לסבול את עוונותיו, והוא זוכה למחילה עליהם ביום הכיפורים.

וכאשר הוא מתבונן בחסדו הגדול של ה' שמחל לו על עוונותיו ביום הכיפורים, מתעוררת בלבו אהבה אליו ושב אליו מאהבה, ורוצה לקיים את רצונו כראוי כדי לגרום לו נחת רוח עצומה, וגם רוצה להידמות אליו במידותיו הטובות, והוא זוכה שיקרבנו ה' אליו ויכניסנו לביתו-לסוכה, 'שחל שם שמים עליה' (סוכה ט). ויחוש את התענוג האמיתי של קירבת ה', וכמו שאמר דוד המלך עליו השלום, "ואני, קירבת אלוקים לי טוב" (תהילים ע"ג כ"ח.)

וא"כ, חודש תשרי שנקרא ירח האיתנים - משום, שיש בו את המועדים היותר חזקים - 'איתן מלשון חוזק' במובן הרוחני, המיישרים את האדם אל השלמות הרוחנית, בין לגבי קיום רצון ה' כראוי, ובין לגבי התנהגות עם מידות טובות, וכנתבאר, 'תחילתו יסורין' -היינו, פחד הדין של ראש השנה, אשר מביא אל תשובה מיראה, ואל תשובה מאהבה, ולקירבת אלוקים, 'וסופו שלוה' - היינו, 'התענוג האמיתי של קירבת אלוקים', בישיבה בסוכה (סדר היום, סוף סדר שמיני עצרת, ד"ה הימים).

הרב דוד יואל בן אאמו"ר פנחס הופמן
מחבר ספרי "תורה תבלין" "ליקוטי תורה תבלין" ו"זכרון יצחק"

חג הסוכות - "ראשון לחשבון עונות"

איתא במדרש (תנחומא ל) וז"ל: ולקחתם לכם ביום הראשון, וכי ראשון הוא, הלא ט"ו יום הוא, ואת אמרת ביום הראשון. אלא ראשון הוא לחשבון עונות. ר' מני ור' יהושע דסכנין בשם ר' לוי אמר משל לה"ד למדינה שהיתה חייבת ליפס למלך ולא היו יכולין ליתן הלך אצלם ובאו לפניו גדולי המדינה והניח להם מחצה. באו לפניו בינוני המדינה והניח להם מחצה על מחצה. באו לפניו כל בני המדינה והניח להם את הכל, ומכאן ואילך ראש חשבון הוא. המלך זה הקב"ה, בני המדינה אלו ישראל, ערב ר"ה גדולי הדור מתענין והקב"ה מוותר להם שליש מעונותיהם. מר"ה עד יוה"כ יחידים מתענין והקבה מוותר להם שליש מעונותיהם. וביוה"כ כל ישראל מתענין ומבקשין רחמים אנשים נשים וטף והקב"ה מוותר להם את הכל. מה ישראל עושין נוטלין לולביהן ביו"ט ראשון של חג ומהללים ומקלסים לפני הקב"ה, והקב"ה מתרצה להם ומוחל להם ואומר להם הרי ויתרתי לכם את כל עונותיכם הראשונות אבל מעכשיו הוא ראש חשבון, שנא' ולקחתם לכם ביום הראשון, ראשון לחשבון עונות עכ"ל. (ועיין בויקרא רבה ובפסיקתא).

ולכאורה יש לנו להקשות על מה שמשמע מהמדרש דהזמן של "ראשון לחשבון עונות" הוא עת רציני מאד, דאז מתחיל הקב"ה לבדוק ולחקור אחר המעשים של כלל ישראל אם טובים הם אם לאו, ואז הוא זמן חשבון הנפש בשמים של כל אחד ואחד. והיה ראוי לפי זה שבזמן רציני כזה יהיה כל אחד מתדבק בקונו ויושב בתשובה ומפשפש במעשיו, ומסתבר היה שבזמן כזה כל אחד צריך לבקש מלפניו יתברך סליחה וכפרה על כל חטאיו כדי שלא יתחיל חשבונו של עונות. אבל למעשה הרי אינו כן, דזמן זה אינו נחשב כזמן של תשובה כלל אלא זמן של שמחה הוא, כמש"כ הרמב"ם בהל' לולב (פ"ח הלכה י"ח) וז"ל: אע"פ שכל המועדות מצוה לשמוח בהן, בחג הסוכות היתה במקדש יום שמחה יתירה, שנאמר 'ושמחתם לפני ה' אלקיכם שבעת ימים,' עכ"ל. ויש לעיין בזה, דאם זמן שמחה הוא, א"כ איך יכולים אנו לבוא על ידי זה למדרגת תשובה וכפרה, הראויה לזמן של ראשון לחשבון עונות, הלא היינו צריכים להיות במצב הפוך של פרישות ועינוי ולא של שמחה וחדוה? ומצאתי שכבר עמד על קושיא זו בספר בית אברהם וז"ל: ראשון לחשבון עונות אינו מובן, דא"כ שהוא ראשון לחשבון עונות מהו דכתיב בתריה "ושמחתם לפני ה' אלקיכם" שמחה זו למה?

והנה בילקוט מעם לועז בשם ספר החינוך כתב וז"ל: סוכות הוא זמן של שמחה גדולה וכו' ולכך א"א שלא יחטא מתוך הטובה המופלגת שהוא שרוי בה, שאין יצר הרע מצוי אלא במקום שיש בו שמחה יתירה עכ"ל. ולפי"ז הדר יקשה דאם הזמן של סוכות הוא ראשון לחשבון עונות, כשהאדם צריך להפריש את עצמו מכל עניני חטא ועון ויעסוק בתשובה וכפרה, תפלה ותנונים, א"כ איך שייך לו לקיים

מצות החג של שמחה יתירה כשהשמחה בעצמה מוכשרת להביא אותו לידי חטא?

ועוד יש לנו להבין בדברי האברבנאל שכתב וז"ל: וכבר ידעת שבחג הזה באו שתי מצות, שהם הסוכה והלולב, ושאינם שוים בטעמיהם כי מצות סוכה היא לזכרון העבר כמ"ש "כי בסכות הושבתי את בני ישראל בהוציאי אתם מארץ מצרים" (ויקרא כג-מג), והלולב הוא מפני ההווה בכל שנה, ר"ל, לתת שבח והודאה אליו על אסיפת התבואות, שבזמן ההוא היו נאספות מן השדה. ולפי שהיה ענין הסוכות בראשונה נקרא חג הסוכות ולא חג הלולב עכ"ל. והיינו, שהאברבנאל בא ליישב מדוע נקרא חג זה חג הסוכות ולא חג הלולב, הלא ישנן שני מצות בחג זה שאינם שוים בטעמיהם, וא"כ מדוע לא נחקק חג הלולב כשם החג, וע"ז יישב משום שענין הסוכות בא בראשונה, על זכרון העבר, שהרי זה היה כבר במדבר כשהשי"ת הושיב את בני ישראל בסוכות, אבל מצות לולב היא לתת שבח להשי"ת על ההווה, לכך נקרא חג הסוכות ולא חג הלולב, עיי"ש בדבריו. אלא שיש לדקדק בלשונו במש"כ שישנן ב' מצות בחג זה, דלכאורה המעיין בפסוקי התורה בענין זה יראה שישנן שבע מצות השייכות לימים אלו, הלא הן: אתרוג, לולב, הדס, ערבה, חגיגה, שמחה, וסוכה, וכולן מצוות דאורייתא ואין אחד יותר חמור מהשני, וא"כ מדוע נקט האברבנאל שישנן רק שני מצות - סוכה ולולב?

וכן בתירוצו של האברבנאל שהחג הזה נקרא חג הסוכות משום שענין זה היה בראשונה לפני ענין הלולב, דסוכות מורה על העבר ולולב מורה על ההווה, דלכאורה תירוץ זה אינו מספיק, דהרי מצינו בשאר המועדות שהם נקראים על שם המצות המתקיימות בהם, וכגון חג המצות, וחג הביכורים, וא"כ לאו דוקא תלוי באיזה מהן בא קודם, ה"ה שני מצות אלו של סוכה ולולב ניתנו באותו זמן בהר סיני ביחד עם כל התורה כולה, וא"כ מה נשתנה זה מפני זה? ועוד תמוה, הרי בסדר הכתובים מוזכר ענין הלולב אפילו קודם ענין הסוכות, דמקודם כתוב "ולקחתם לכם וגו' ענף עץ עבת וגו'", ואח"כ כתוב "בסכות תשבו שבעת ימים", הרי חזינן שהתורה לא הקפידה בזה על סדר הענינים, וא"כ תמוה מה שתירץ האברבנאל שמהאי טעמא נקרא החג בשם חג הסוכות משום שהוא אירע לראשונה, והדרא קושיא לדוכתה, מדוע באמת נקרא החג בשם חג הסוכות ולא חג הלולב?

ומבואר קושית הטור (או"ח סי' תרכ"ה) שהקשה וז"ל: ואע"פ שיצאנו ממצרים בחדש ניסן, לא צונו לעשות סוכה באותו זמן לפי שהוא ימות הקיץ ודרך כ"א לעשות סוכה לצל ולא היתה ניכרת עשייתנו בהם שהם מצות הבורא ית'. לכן צוה אותנו שנעשה בחדש השביעי שהוא זמן הגשמים ודרך כ"א לצאת מסוכתו ולישב בביתו. ואנחנו יוצאין מן הבית לישב בסוכה ובזה יראה לכל שמצות המלך היא עלינו לעשותה, עכ"ל הטור. הרי שהוקשה לטור מדוע נצטוינו לישב בסוכה בחדש תשרי, הלא הנס אירע כשיצאנו ממצרים בחדש ניסן. והוא מתרץ משום שבחודש ניסן לא היו סוכותינו ניכרים כמצות השם יתברך, כי כולם יושבים בסוכות בזמן ההוא, ורק בחדש תשרי יהיה ניכר לכל שעיקר ישיבתנו בסוכה הוא מחמת מצות הבורא.

ואשר נראה בביאור הענינים האלו, בהקדם מה דאיתא בבראשית רבה (טו-ז): מה היתה אותו אילן שאכל ממנו אדם וחוה? רבי אבא דעכו אמר אתרוג היה, הה"ד "ותרא האשה כי טוב העץ וגו'" (בראשית ג-ו), אמרת צא וראה

איזהו אילן שעצו נאכל כפריו ואין אתה מוצא אלא אתרוג, ע"כ במדרש.

והנה מבואר מזה דהחטא הראשון הנעשה בעולם, חטאם של אדם וחוה באכילת עץ הדעת כנגד ציווי ה', היה נעשה עם אתרוג, וזהו מה שאכלו. ועיין בספר פנים יפות לבעל ההפלאה ז"ל שכתב שנטילת האתרוג בחג הסוכות הוא ענין כפרה על חטא עץ הדעת שנעשה באתרוג, וז"ל: כי אחז"ל, כי עץ הדעת הוא אתרוג שעל ידו נטרד מגן עדן וכו' ויש רמז בכל ארבע מינים לתקן חטא עץ הדעת, והוא מספר ערבי נחל, כמספר עץ הדר עם הכולל, וכן מספר עץ עבות וכן כפות תמרים וכן שלשה מצות סוכה ושמחה וחגיגה, אלו הן רומזים בתיקון חטא עץ הדעת וכו' עכ"ל ההפלאה, ועיי"ש שמאריך במספר הרמזים. ומבואר מדבריו שבכל אחד ממצות החג יש רמז מיוחד לתיקון חטאו של אדם הראשון בעץ הדעת, וזהו הכל חלק מהמצוה בחג הסוכות.

ונראה לומר בביאור דבריו, כי מצינו שם במדרש עוד ענין וז"ל: בשעה שאכל אדם הראשון מאותו אילד טרדו הקב"ה והוציאו חוץ לגד עדד והיה מחזר על כל אילנות ולא היו מקבלין אותו ומה היו אומרים לו אמר רבי ברכיה הא גנב דגנב דעתיה דברייה, הה"ד אל תבואני רגל גאוה, רגל שנתגאה על בוראו עכ"ל. ומבואר מדברי המדרש, ששורש חטאו של אדם הראשון באכילת עץ הדעת נבע ממקור גאוה, שמכיון שהיה אדם מתגאה על בוראו ורצה לגנוב דעתיה דברייה מחמת גאותו, וסיבה זו הביאה אותו לידי חטא עד שבסופו של דבר גרם חטא זה להבאת מיתה לעולם ולהשפעת הרע בפנימיות האדם, כי קודם החטא היה האדם כולו רוחני בלי שום נטיות לחטא (עיין דברי הרמב"ם במורה נבוכים פ"ב, ובספר נפש החיים ש"א פ"ו), א"כ נמצא דהסיבה ראשונה לחטא היא הגאוה, והיא התחלת כל הרע שבעולם ושורש החורבן בעולם. ואולי דזהו הביאור בדברי חז"ל (אבות ד-כח): הכבוד מוציאין את האדם מן העולם, שרדיפת הכבוד בכוחה להוציא את האדם מך העולם, כי הרי ענין הגאוה הוא זה שגרם כל עניך המיתה בעולם, כמש"כ (בראשית ג-יט) "כי עפר אתה ואל עפר תשוב", דעל ידי שחטא אדם הראשון בעץ הדעת נגזר ענין המיתה עליו ועל כל העולם כולו, וא"כ הרי היא מוציאה את האדם מן עולמו ממש.

והנה הרשב"ם מביא טעם למצות סוכה כשכתב על הפסוק למעד ידעו דורותיכם כי בסכות הושבתי את בני ישראל וז"ל: למען תזכרו כי בסוכות הושבתי את בני ישראל במדבר ארבעים שנה בלא יישוב ובלא נחלה, ומתוך כך תתנו הודאה למי שנתן לכם נחלה ובתים מלאים כל טוב ואל תאמרו בלבבכם כחי ועוצם ידי עשה לי את החיל הזה וכו' ולכך יוצאים מבתים מלאים כל טוב בזמן אסיפה ויושבים בסוכה לזכרון שלא היה להם נחלה במדבר ולא בתים לשבת ומפני הטעם הזה קבע הקבה את חג הסוכרת בזמן אסיפת גורן ויקב לבלתי רום לבבו על בתים מלאים כל טוב, פן יאמרו ידינו עשו לנו את החיל הזה, עכ"ל הרשב"ם.

הנה דברי הרשב"ם מאירים לנו שהטעם שצונו השי"ת לעשות סוכות הוא בכדי להכניע בני ישראל לפני בוראם יתברך שיתנו שבח והודאה אליו על כל הטוב שזכו, שבתיהם מלאים כל טוב דגן תירוש ויצהר, והכל בא ממנו ממש. ממילא לא יחשוב האדם שהוא פעל את הכל לעצמו, וכחו ועוצם ידו עשה לו את החיל הזה, כי בודאי הכל בא מחסדי

השי"ת, ולכן בני ישראל יוצאים מבתיהם מלאים כל טוב לזכרון שלא היו להם אפילו בתים לשבת במדבר, אלא סוכות, ומחסדי השי"ת ניתן להם בתים וכל טוב, ועל ידי זה הם מכניעים את עצמם ומקבלים עליהם ההכרה שכל טוב בא מהשי"ת ולא מעצמם.

ואפשר דזה מה שכוון ההפלאה שצריכים אנו לתקן חטא עץ הדעת בסוכות, כי האילן שאכל אדם ממנו היה אתרוג, והסיבה שגרם והביא אותו לידי החטא היתה המידה מגונה של גאוה שהיה נתגאה על בוראו, א"כ התיקון לחטא זה הוא הנהגה של ענוה והכנעה לפני הקב"ה, ואיזה מן המצות שבחג זה מראה הכנעה והשפלה, אלא מצות סוכה, כמו שפירש הרשב"ם, שיוצאים אנו מבתינו מלאים כל טוב לתוך סוכה בעת הגשמים בתחילת החורף, להראות שאין לנו המידה מגונה של "כחי ועוצם ידי עשה לי את החיל הזה", דהיינו גאוה ממש, אלא נוהגים במדה נכונה של ענוה והכנעה לפני השי"ת. ממילא שפיר מתוקן החטא הראשון על ידי קיום מצות סוכה יותר משאר מצות החג, כי רק מצוה זו מראה ענין הענוה, שיכול לתקן החטא שקדם לכל החטאים שנעשה בגאוה.

ולפי"ז יתיישבו כל הקושיות היטב, דודאי מראש השנה עד יוה"כ עסוקים כל בני ישראל בתשובה ומעשים טובים, ובאימה וביראה יושבים ומצפים לראות איך יפול הדין ומה תהיה תקותם בזאת השנה, אבל מדריגה זו אינה אלא מדרגת תשובה מיראה, כי מורא הדין הוא שממריצם ודוחפם לשוב בתשובה שלימה. והנה רבינו יונה (שערי תשובה א-כג) כתב וז"ל: "זבחי אלקים רוח נשברה לב נשבר ונדכה אלקים לא תבזה" (תהלים נא-יט) רוח נשברה רוח נמוכה, למדנו מזה כי ההכנעה מעיקרי התשובה עכ"ל. ומבואר מדבריו שתשובה אמיתית שייכת שתבוא רק ע"י ההכנעה והענוה, ולכך מצות סוכה, המורה על שפלות האדם וכניעתו קמיה קודשא בריך הוא, היא באה תמיד אחר ר"ה ויוה"כ, כי אחרי שהאדם משפיל את עצמו לבוא לקיים תשובה מיראה בר"ה וביוה"כ, ימשיך בעניני השפלה והכנעה לפני השי"ת במצות סוכה כדי לבוא לידי תשובה מאהבה, כי זהו תפקיד חג הסוכות כמו שביארו המפרשים. וממילא לא קשה קושית הטור שמצות סוכה שייכת יותר לחודש ניסן כי בו יצאנו ממצרים, כי ודאי מקומה הראויה היא בתשרי שכל החודש אנשים עסוקים בענינים של הכנעה וענוה, וכך הוא הענין של מצות סוכה, לכך ציונו הקב"ה לעשות מצוה זו בחג זה בזמן אסיפת התבואה דוקא, ועל ידי זה האדם ממשיך בהנהגותיו כדי לבוא לידי תשובה גמורה מאהבה.

ולפי זה נראה לומר שמהאי טעמא נקרא שם החג על שם מצות סוכה יותר ממצות לולב או שאר מצות החג, דכפי שביארנו עיקר מהות החג הוא לכפר באופן ענוה והכנעה על חטא עץ הדעת שנבע מגאוה ומשרירות, שלכן יוצאים בני ישראל מבתיהם המלאים כל טוב לביתן ארעי וצנוע, בכדי להמחיש בנפשם שכל מה שיש להם, מהשי"ת הוא ולא מכחם ומעוצם ידם, א"כ מצות סוכה היא המצוה שמקיימת את העיקר תכלית של החג בעצמה ובמציאותה ולכך נקרא שם החג "חג הסוכות" - חג הענוה וההכנעה, חג ההכרה במציאות השי"ת ובכוחו.

ולאור זה יובנו דברי התנחומא הנ"ל באופן חדש, דאמנם ראשון לימי הסוכות הוא ראשון לחשבון עונות, ומה שהיה קשה לנו דא"כ היה יום זה צריך להיות יום כפרה וסליחה, ולא יום שמחה וריקוד. אמנם ע"ז י"ל לפי מה שביארנו

שחג הסוכות בא לכפר על חטא עץ הדעת, וכבר ביארנו שחטא עץ הדעת הוא היה הגורם לכל החטאים שבאו אחריו, כי הרי לפני החטא היה האדם כולו רוחני, וחטא זה הוא שזיהם אותו והכניס בקרבו את התאוה הגופנית והגשמית, וזה גם גרם לכל ענין מיתה בעולם כפי שנתבאר, וא״כ אפשר שזהו הכוונה בדברי חז״ל שחטא זו הוא החטא הראשון לכל העונות, והיינו שמהחטא הזה נבע ונשרש כל ענין חטא שבעולם, ולכך הקיום של המצוות בימי הסוכות, שכפי שביאר ההפלאה בא לכפר על אותו החטא, הוא הזמן שנקבע לכפר על הראשון לחשבון עונות, היינו על החטא הראשון שממנו נמשכו כל העונות וכל העונשים. וזהו מש״כ במדרש: מה ישראל עושין, נוטלין לולביהן ביו״ט ראשון של חג ומהללים ומקלסים לפני הקב״ה וכו, ׳לכך כתוב ״ולקחתם לכם ביום הראשון״ ראשון לחשבון עונות, כלומר, שע״י קיום מצות החג, בפרט מצות סוכה שמורה על ענוה והכנעה, וכך מה שנוטלין לולביהן וכו׳, בזה מתקנים בני ישראל ע״י מעשיהם והנהגותיהם את החטא הראשון, שהרי אדם הראשון אכל אתרוג, היינו שהתגאה על קונו, ועבודה זו של ישיבה בסוכה שמראה הכנעתינו ושפלותינו היא זו שמביאה את האדם לידי תשובה מאהבה, שהיא המדרגה יותר גבוהה במעלות התשובה, ועבודה זו באה לאדם ע״י מצב של שמחה והתעלות הנפש, כי תשובה מיראה נובעת דוקא ממורא העונש ומהפחד, אבל תשובה מאהבה בחג הסוכות היא ההיפך, היא באה כולה מתוך התעלות ועיון בנפלאות השי״ת שמביא את האדם לידי שמחה עילאית ולידי חדות הנפש, ולכך על ידי קיום מצות סוכה, היא היא תשובתו מאהבה, ולכך נקרא זמן של חג זה ״ראשון לחשבון עונות״, ר״ל בזמן ההוא בני ישראל מתקנים על ידי מצות החג את החטא הראשון לחשבון כל העונות וכל העונשים שבאו אחריו.